WELCOME TO

Just A Minute!

WELCOME TO

Just A Minute!

A CELEBRATION
OF BRITAIN'S BEST-LOVED
RADIO COMEDY

WRITTEN BY
NICHOLAS PARSONS

CANONGATE

Edinburgh · London

Published in Great Britain in 2014 by Canongate Books Ltd,
14 High Street, Edinburgh EH1 1TE

www.canongate.tv

1

British Library Cataloguing-in-Publication Data
A catalogue record for this book is available on
request from the British Library

ISBN 978 1 78211 247 1

Printed and bound in Great Britain by Clays Ltd, St Ives plc

To the late Sir David Hatch, without whose talent and commitment *Just a Minute* would never have been launched on to the airwaves.

Contents

Preface

I do not like surprise parties when I am the one to be surprised, especially when I have been warned in advance. It was October 2013. I had just celebrated my 90th birthday with a magnificent party organised by my wife, Annie, and myself at the Churchill Hyatt Hotel, Portman Square, in London's West End. We had invited over 200 guests, family, close friends and many show-business colleagues and acquaintances. It was a huge success and a memorable occasion, with wonderfully witty speeches from my friends Paul Merton and Gyles Brandreth, and a clever musical parody about me from Kit Hesketh-Harvey. My own speech was well received and it was an exceptionally enjoyable, even emotional, evening. Various newspapers and magazines covered the event, and my anxiety that advertising my advanced years would inhibit prospects of future work engagements proved wrong. In fact it turned out to have the reverse effect. I received many more requests and enquiries than usual.

I was overwhelmed with cards and gifts, and the last thing I then wanted was this surprise party that could only be an anti-climax. Annie, who was in on the secret, refused to give me a clue as to whom was organising the event. If you have warning of these occasions, as a performer you can prepare some thoughts on what you might say in your thank you speech to ensure you respond in appropriate style. I reluctantly went along with the subterfuge. My assumption was that the invitation was from one of the charities for which I actively work. Facetiously I suggested to Annie that if the party was to surprise me, I could surprise them by going in my pyjamas. She firmly pointed out that I should wear something smart and formal.

The hire car duly arrived. The driver had already been made

aware of what was happening, so we set off from our London flat in silence. All my preconceived ideas of where I might be going turned out to be incorrect as he took us to the outside of the main entrance of Broadcasting House in Portland Place. 'They don't run charity functions here,' I thought. Inside we were greeted by Trudi Stevens, the assistant to the producer of *Just a Minute*, who led us up to the Council Chamber, the central meeting place for BBC executives. Trudi ushered me into this spacious room, where there were a hundred people: actors, writers, producers and senior staff. They gave me a huge round of applause as I entered. I was overwhelmed. I stood there speechless. I recognised a lot of the faces, professional friends and others with whom I had worked. Someone had undertaken research and discovered that I had made my first professional broadcast 72 years ago performing impersonations of James Stewart and Charles Boyer on a radio variety show called *Carroll Levis Carries On* as one of what the Canadian showman called his 'discoveries' – new performers whom he tipped for success. At around the same time I was also playing small roles in productions at Glasgow BBC. This was the city in which I had been based during the War, serving an apprenticeship with a firm on Clydebank that made pumps for ships, important work for the war effort and a reserved occupation. I was endeavouring to become an engineer while dreaming of becoming a full-time entertainer.

In fact over the years since then I have rarely been off BBC radio. At different times either guesting in plays, performing in variety shows, undertaking a long spell in the BBC Drama Reparatory Company, appearing in a series of *Much-Binding-in-the-Marsh* playing comedy characters, partnering my long-term colleague Arthur Haynes in his radio series and presenting the satirical programme *Listen to this Space*, a show I devised and for which I received the Radio Personality of the Year award. Also, we were just about to celebrate the 46th anniversary of *Just a Minute*, a programme with which I have been associated since the pilot show in December 1967. I have not missed a single recording, which now amounts to almost 900 performances.

This party was to celebrate all this and more. It was a truly moving occasion and I was overwhelmed that the BBC had decided to honour me in this way. There were some brief speeches, including Paul Merton, who sent me up in his usual delightfully humorous way, and then Tilusha Ghelani, one of the producers of *Just a Minute*, played a tape that she had gone to a great deal of trouble to prepare. It consisted of some of the many humorous moments from the archives of *Just a Minute*, including an embarrassing one in which I had made an unintentional verbal slip known as a Spoonerism, referring to Tilusha as 'Gilusha Tilhani'. The guests loved it all and laughed affectionately at the fun that was being had at my expense.

Then I was asked to say a few words. It is always a challenge when speaking to your own profession, especially when you have nothing prepared. On this occasion it was easier than I could have imagined. It was such a warm and responsive audience, all of whom were there out of affection to pay a tribute to me. It was certainly the most emotional experience of my professional life. I was deeply touched that so many show-business friends and colleagues had found time in their busy lives to assemble secretly to drink my health and toast my career, including the Director General. We humble thespians do not expect such accolades!

I mingled and talked with the many guests, hoping the party would never end. There were some lovely moments and over-the-top compliments. I just wanted to thank everyone personally for surprising me in such a delightful way. There was one particularly touching incident when Emma Freud, a charming and talented broadcaster and writer, gave me a gift of her father's witty articles collected together in book form. I had known Emma since she was a little girl as I had been very friendly with Clement. I was not only at school with him, St Paul's, but he had employed me regularly to work in cabaret at his Royal Court Theatre Club in Sloane Square. I even socialised with him when he entertained my wife and I at his home in St John's Wood, where he cooked the most amazing dinners. He was, of course, a trained chef.

Emma's thoughtful gift touched me greatly. As she presented

the book, Emma sweetly said that she knew her dad had become grumpy with me as he grew older, but the feeling did not extend to the rest of the Freud family. I was delighted to hear such warmth and reassurance. In Clement's later years his attitude had changed from one of friendship to something approaching disdain. The reasons for this stemmed from the difference of opinion we each held over how *Just a Minute* should develop as the years passed.

In almost direct contrast to Clement, my belief had always been that if *Just a Minute* was to achieve any longevity, it would have to adjust and adapt to changing attitudes and taste. However popular a programme is, it cannot rest on its laurels. During the early days of the show there were two other panel games on radio, which were all male and very successful – *My Word!* and *My Music*. They were of their era, with a formula that never changed. As a result they slowly faded away. Success cannot be taken for granted in show business. You have to analyse what works, tweak the rules slightly, polish and improve. If you have a basic idea that is strong, and Ian Messiter had certainly created such a show with *Just a Minute*, continual refining can only improve it.

While Ian was still with us he made little changes in the early stages, together with our first producer, the very talented David Hatch, who contributed with all kinds of thoughts, ideas and, of course, creative casting. In more recent years, because of my love of the show and commitment to its success, I have in consultation with our producers, suggested small subtle adjustments that have helped to take the programme forward. These refinements, from whatever source they arose, you can read about in the following pages. I certainly do not seek any long-term credit for my input. As an experienced performer of many years, it is something that you do instinctively to improve the quality of a great product and they would not have worked if the core concept of the creator, Ian Messiter, had not been brilliant.

Putting this book together could not have been possible without some assistance from a man who is the most ardent fan of *Just a Minute*, Keith Matthews. Keith is a member of a London-based *Just a Minute* fan club and possesses an amazing knowledge of the show from the archive of recordings he has kept. If we wanted a fact from the past, he was usually able to supply it. I must also thank Dean Bedford, a dedicated follower of the programme, who lives in New Zealand. Dean compiled the fascinating Top 20 lists that appear at the end of this book and runs a website full of interesting information on the show plus an incredible number of transcripts of broadcasts (www.just-a-minute.info). This has proved to be a very useful source on occasions.

I am indebted to my literary agent, Gordon Wise of Curtis Brown, who had the foresight to see that a book about the history of *Just a Minute* could be popular and took the idea to Canongate, where Jamie Byng saw the potential and has backed the project with enthusiasm, along with his editorial colleague Jenny Lord and the rest of the Canongate team.

It has also been my good fortune to work with a large number of very talented BBC professionals, including at the helm of the show our excellent producers, our sound engineers and, of course, the delightful whistleblowers who have sat next to me through the years. I thank them all. The BBC have been very supportive throughout the writing of this book but for the sake of clarity I must make it clear that all the opinions expressed here are my own and do not represent the views of the corporation or of anyone currently working there.

My final thanks go to a man whose literary skills and love of the programme have helped to make this book possible, David Wilson. What I have not written by hand, he has transcribed from my dictation, managing to reproduce my words with great accuracy and an instinct for my style and phraseology.

It is time to present the story of *Just a Minute*, with its fascinating history, extensive cast of superb panellists and unique format. The programme has achieved an amazing level of popularity with the general public and inspires deep affection in its devoted followers. One of the reasons for this, I believe, lies at the very heart of the show: nothing is prepared in advance. Everything you hear is improvised spontaneously, resulting in countless moments of wonderful humour, many of which I relive in this book. The theatre audience at the recordings are aware that what they are seeing is instantaneous comedy. I think they feel they are part of a happening and respond accordingly. The laughter being generated is very natural, which in turn spurs us on. All of this is then conveyed across the airwaves to the listener. That to me is part of the secret of *Just a Minute*.

Writing this book has been a labour of love, recalling the pleasure I have gained from being associated with such an iconic programme over so many years. Reliving those outstanding, unusual, amazing and humorous moments has allowed me to express the genuine joy I experience every time we make a recording. It has also been a pleasure to think back on my years working with some of the most talented performers in show business. These are the people who, throughout 47 years and counting, have propelled *Just a Minute* forward with panache and style.

I hope you enjoy our story.

The Sixties

The decade through Just a Minute

Paying the bills at the end of the month

I was once sent one from a certain store, which I shall not name. Five hundred pints of milk and a mink coat! Well, obviously I don't walk around in a mink coat drinking 500 pints of milk!! And so I rang them up and I said, '*Here*, I've had this bill, 500 pints of milk and a mink coat!' And they said, 'What is the name please?' And I said, 'Kenneth C. Williams.' And they said, 'Oooh! It should have gone to Tennessee Williams!'

**KENNETH WILLIAMS
21 JANUARY 1969**

Equal pay for women

This is a ludicrous idea. Everyone knows that the men are the prime movers of this world!!!

**KENNETH WILLIAMS,
10 NOVEMBER 1969**

Bankers

Bankers are people who look after your money fairly carefully, keep it for a long time and charge you for the privilege. This is a revolting exercise and many bankers are rightfully very unpopular as a result.

**CLEMENT FREUD
23 FEBRUARY 1968**

Hackneyed phrases

A long time ago when Clement Freud was a young man, 'Do you come here often?' was a hackneyed phrase. Nowadays, however, the fashion has changed and hackneyed phrases tend to be much more obscure and multi-syllabic. Things like 'counterproductive' and 'participation of the people', 'democratisation of factories'.

**GERALDINE JONES
11 FEBRUARY 1969**

Manners

Terribly interesting the way that police sergeants, constables and even inspectors refer to their particular beat as their 'manor'. In fact within the central London district I believe there are nine manors belonging to different branches of the constabulary. This becomes terribly useful when they're fighting their endless wars with the hippie population, Hell's Angels and skinheads.

DEREK NIMMO
3 NOVEMBER 1969

Au pair girls

Au pair is French for 'to the pair', which is a very good description. Because invariably you don't just get one. She has a friend who phones up and to whom she phones, reversing the telephone charges.

CLEMENT FREUD
14 JANUARY 1969

Pantomimes

Pantomime principal boys are no longer played by girls with lovely legs but by young men with lovely voices, these days. Looking very like Derek Nimmo and sounding very like Clement Freud!

CHARMIAN INNES
15 MARCH 1968

Parking meters

The essential thing to remember about parking meters is that you must always treat them with respect and affection. There are some inanimate objects like can openers which you can successfully bully. But parking meters should always be treated rather as you treat donkeys. You should feed them little coins as you would feed donkeys sugar lumps. And in this way you establish a bond with the parking meter against the traffic warden.

GERALDINE JONES
21 OCTOBER 1968

'Nicholas, the word "naked" is forbidden.'

It is the early 1960s and I am talking to Bill Worsley, producer of *Henry Hall's Guest Night*, on which I am engaged to appear. We are going through my proposed act for the show. Within the BBC, everything of even a mildly risqué nature has to be cleared in advance with the producer. They are responsible if anything untoward slips through the net.

'But, Bill, the joke doesn't work without that. It has to finish on "and the girl let her mink coat slip to the ground leaving her standing absolutely naked".'

Bill thinks for a moment. 'No, I'm sorry, Nicholas. As producer I have responsibilities. There is a list of words you can't use, and "naked" is definitely on it. Can't you say "leaving her standing with absolutely nothing on"?'

'Come off it, Bill. That will kill it stone dead. How about "starkers"?'

Bill picks up the booklet in front of him, rather imposingly entitled *BBC Variety Programmes Policy Guide for Writers and Producers* and flicks through the pages. I know what he is looking at; it is commonly known as 'The Little Green Book', the bible of BBC decency. Not that I could say such a thing on air. Religious references are one of many no-nos.

Bill looks up from the book with a smile. 'All right, Nick, "starkers" it is. There's nothing in here to indicate that word is banned. Good luck.'

Such was the world that BBC entertainers were living in during the so-called Swinging Sixties. Public morals were protected by

The Little Green Book and there was nothing you could do about it. This selection of 'highlights' will, I hope, provide a sense of the broadcasting environment within which we were operating.

VULGARITY

Programmes must at all cost be kept free of crudities, coarseness and innuendo. Humour must be clean and untainted directly or by association with vulgarity and suggestiveness. Music hall, stage, and to a lesser degree, screen standards, are not suitable to broadcasting. Producers, artists and writers must recognise this fact and the strictest watch must be kept. There can be no compromise with doubtful material. It must be cut.

A. General. Well known vulgar jokes (e.g. the Brass Monkey) 'cleaned up', are not normally admissible since the humour in such cases is almost invariably evident only if the vulgar version is known.

There is an absolute ban upon the following:-

Jokes about:-
• Lavatories
• Effeminacy in men
• Immorality of any kind

Suggestive references to:-
• Honeymoon couples
• Chambermaids
• Fig leaves
• Prostitution

- Ladies' underwear, e.g. winter draws on
- Animal habits, e.g. rabbits
- Lodgers
- Commercial travellers

Extreme care should be taken in dealing with references to or jokes about:-
- Pre-natal influences (e.g. 'His mother was frightened by a donkey')
- Marital infidelity

Good taste and decency are the obvious governing considerations. The vulgar use of such words as 'basket' must also be avoided.

* * *

Jokes built around Bible stories, e.g. Adam and Eve, Cain and Abel, David and Goliath, must also be avoided or any sort of parody of them.

Religious References
Reference to and jokes about different religions or religious denominations are banned. The following are also inadmissible:-
- Jokes about A.D. or B.C. (e.g. 'before Crosby')
- Jokes or comic songs about spiritualism, christenings, religious ceremonies of any description (e.g. weddings, funerals)
- Parodies of Christmas carols
- All such words as God, Good God, My God, Blast, Hell, Damn, Bloody, Gorblimey, Ruddy, etc., etc., should be deleted from scripts and innocuous expressions substituted.

IMPERSONATIONS

All impersonations need the permission of the
people being impersonated and producers must
reassure themselves that this has been given
before allowing any to be broadcast.

Artists' repertories of impersonations are
usually restricted to:-
(a) leading public and political figures;
(b) fellow artists.

As to (a) the Corporation's policy is against
broadcasting impersonations of elder statesmen,
e.g. Winston Churchill, and leading political
figures. Any others in this category should
invariably be referred.
As to (b) there is no objection, but certain
artists have notified the Corporation that no
unauthorised impersonations may be broadcast.
The present list is given below but should
be checked from time to time with the Variety
Booking Manager. A double check by producers as
to permission is advisable in these cases:-
• Gracie Fields
• Vera Lynn
• Ethel Revnell (with or without Gracie West)
• Renee Houston
• Jeanne de Casalis (Mrs Feather)
• Nat Mills and Bobbie
• Harry Hemsley

POPULAR MUSIC

(a) British Music

It is the Corporation's policy actively to encourage British music so long as this does not lead to a lowering of accepted musical standards.

(b) Jazzing the Classics

The jazzing by dance bands of classical tunes or the borrowing and adaptation of them is normally unacceptable.

MISCELLANEOUS POINTS

Avoid derogatory references to:-
Professions, trades, and 'classes', e.g. solicitors, commercial travellers, miners, 'the working class'.

SPECIAL CONSIDERATION OF OVERSEAS BROADCASTS

Jokes like 'enough to make a Maltese Cross' are of doubtful value.

In addition to these strict guidelines ('jazzing the classics'! – who would dare?), advertising in any form was unacceptable, including references to newspapers. And as for jokes involving the Royal Family …

This Reithian edifice the BBC had first erected in the 1940s and '50s was, however, beginning to crumble in the era of the Beatles and the Rolling Stones. The enormously enjoyable satirical television show *That Was the Week That Was*, fronted by David Frost, had started to knock holes in it during its thirteen-month run through to late

1963. A year on from then and the time was ripe for a couple of 'rebels' to deliver a blow that would eventually knock the wall down and pave the way for *Just a Minute*.

Step forward Alistair Foot, a writer who had worked on the popular radio sketch *The Arthur Haynes Show*, and myself.

That Was the Week That Was worked wonderfully well, but I was aware there was nothing equivalent on the radio. By 1964 I had been working with the talented comedian Arthur Haynes on the television version of his show for ten years and was keen to try my hand at something different. I admired Alistair's writing – he had a distinctive style – and I approached him with an idea for a political satire programme for radio. Alistair was keen and we worked on the format for a show I called *Listen to This Space*, which would trample over many of The Little Green Book's strictures if it was to work. We were going to quote from named newspapers, send up the politicians of the day with impersonations and poke fun at the Establishment in general. Talk about taking risks …

I presented the idea to Roy Rich, then head of Radio Light Entertainment, a man I knew fairly well from his days as a theatre director. That is how the system worked in those days; performers with ideas had direct access to the key decision makers. It is a little more complicated now, with many more bureaucratic layers – otherwise known as commissioning editors – requiring navigation. Roy was a creative man, he loved our concept and immediately commissioned a pilot to be produced by the very experienced Bill Worsley and on which Alistair and I worked with another writer called Anthony Marriott. It seemed to go down well. Or so we thought anyway. The BBC executives at the time remained very nervous, worried that we had pushed the boundaries of what was acceptable too far. Even Bill thought the show was unlikely to receive the go-ahead. Indeed, a series was not commissioned until, somehow, and I think I can thank Roy Rich here, a tape of the pilot found its way on to Director General Hugh Carleton Greene's desk. He was enthusiastic, the series received the go-ahead and went on to run for a number of years.

As for The Little Green Book, it took a hit from which it never recovered and the broadcasting landscape changed forever.

It was 1967 and I am speaking to Ian Messiter, a producer and creator of radio entertainment shows. Following the success of *Listen to This Space* the Variety Club had presented me with the award for Radio Personality of the Year. I was deeply honoured, and I was hoping that this recognition would act as a springboard for me to embark on a new venture. Exactly what that was going to be, I was not sure. Ian and I had been good friends for many years, socialising together in each other's houses often, and professionally I was well aware of his talents. That's why I was here, to find out if he could help.

'Ian, *Listen to This Space* has been a great success and I've thoroughly enjoyed it, especially the opportunity to do my Edward Heath impersonations. But as the host I don't think I was really using my skills to the full. I want to return to my comedy roots for the next project and I was wondering, do you have any new programme ideas?'

'Funny you should ask, Nick. You remember *One Minute Please!*? Well, I've adapted it, made it better, I think. I tried it out when I was over in South Africa and it worked well. It's called *Just a Minute*. Would that be of interest?'

As he outlined the format of his new show I immediately saw the potential. It's hardly a surprise. It is not overstating it to say that when it comes to devising panel games, Ian is exceptional. You just have to look at his track record. As a BBC producer back in the late 1940s and early '50s he worked on the classic radio show *Twenty Questions*, chaired by Gilbert Harding, in which panellists asked 'yes' or 'no' questions in an attempt to deduce the identify of mystery objects. At the same time Ian was devising, producing and appearing in the panel game *One Minute Please!* which ran for three series before Ian left the BBC to try his luck at a commercial station in South Africa.

...on the subject of *One Minute Please!*

Ian Messiter's *One Minute Please!* (*OMP!*) was the progenitor to *Just a Minute*. There were key differences between the two formats – *OMP!* focused more on the individual panellists talking and being amusing, rather than the interaction and banter that drives *Just a Minute* – but the basic structure of the games was similar.

Ian always said that the seeds of *OMP!* (and therefore *Just a Minute*) were sown at Sherborne School, when his history master caught him daydreaming in class and offered him the option of facing the cane or talking about Henry VIII and his wives for two minutes without hesitation or repetition. From there the idea percolated slowly, was refined by a similar exercise given to him during his army training, and finally honed through trial runs with his wife Enid and their young family.

By 1951 the rules of *Off the Cuff*, as the game was then known, had been established, and he presented the idea to the BBC. A pilot was commissioned, with the new name *One Minute Please!*, and it proved to be an immediate hit.

OMP! was billed as a battle of the sexes in which teams of three men and three women were pitted against each other, with the winning team returning the following week. Each panellist was given a topic by chairman Roy Plomley (the creator of *Desert Island Discs*) on which they were required to talk for a minute without pausing, repeating themselves or drifting off track. Success won a point for the player's team. However, if the opposing panel considered the speaker had committed one of the specified sins they could interrupt with a buzzer and state their case. The challenge was then put before a jury of three for adjudication, the members of which changed each week. Juries comprised, for example:
- Three Charing Cross Hospital nurses
- Three police constables

- Three Windmill Theatre showgirls
- Three air hostesses
- Three Father Christmases
- Three Beverley Sisters

A correct challenge, as decided upon by the jury, scored two points; if incorrect, the speaker's team gained two points.

Ian also incorporated an additional element to the game – a 'secret word' known to the studio audience and listeners but not the panellists. This word would have some relevance to the given subject – for instance, for the topic 'Cricket' it might be 'grass'. If the speaker mentioned this word they were alerted to the fact, and awarded three points, but the specific identity of the word would not be made known until the end of the round. If during the time remaining the speaker inadvertently repeated the secret word, a point was deducted for each occurrence. All clear so far?

To add to the fun, gimmick rounds were introduced, with the speaker told, for instance, that a point would be deducted if they used the definite article.

Three series were broadcast between 1951 and 1952, comprising a total of 31 episodes, and making a radio star out of cartoonist Gerard Hoffnung. He made his debut in the third broadcast and went on to appear in all but six of the remaining shows. Following Ian's departure to South Africa in 1952, a fourth series was not commissioned. The public reaction to *OMP!* had been very favourable. Throughout the years of Ian's absence, the BBC received many hundreds of requests for copies of the rules from people who wanted to play at home and in clubs. However, it was not until Ian returned to Britain that the fourth series was broadcast, with Roy Plomley replaced by disc jockey Michael Jackson. Ian continued to push for a fifth series but that door was finally closed forever with Gerard Hoffnung's untimely death in September 1959 at the age of 34.

Why the BBC decided not to continue with *OMP!* at the

height of its success in 1952 is not clear. Although Ian had moved abroad he left extensive production notes to ensure the series continued, but nothing happened. One reason may be that Ian apparently found himself in a wrangle with the BBC over *OMP!* According to an interview with Ian published in the *Daily Sketch* at around this time, it seems the US television station DuMont had purchased the rights to produce the show for a sum said to be £285,000. If accurate, this is an astonishing figure from which, the article states, Ian was to receive a token amount. The issue was eventually settled, and many years later I read in the press that Ian had given the small fee he received to charity. Perhaps surprisingly, after this incident Ian continued to have a good relationship with the BBC, a very positive reflection on the quality of the man.

Ian returned to Britain in the mid 1950s, initially to a job in advertising, while his radio-show creativity continued to flourish. *One Minute Please!* returned for a fourth series, followed by *Many a Slip*, with Roy Plomley hosting, in which the players had to identify deliberate mistakes in written passages and musical segments, and also *Petticoat Line*, a show that invited listeners to submit questions to an all-female panel presided over by well-known broadcaster Anona Winn. He had also recently recorded a pilot for a card-based quiz show called *Fair Deal*.

'Ian, it's great,' I told him, once he had finished outlining his ideas for *Just a Minute*. 'Exactly what I was looking for. The BBC are going to love it, I'm sure.'

I was correct. Roy Rich was very positive about Ian's idea when I presented it to him, deciding it would be ideal for the soon-to-be-launched Radio 4 (born out of the old Home Service at the end of September 1967). He immediately commissioned a pilot, handing the reins over to a very talented young producer called David Hatch. David had recently joined the corporation after appearing as a panellist on the anarchic radio comedy game *I'm Sorry, I'll Read That*

Again, having gained experience as a performer with the Cambridge University Footlights drama club.

To chair the pilot David engaged comedian Jimmy Edwards, an excellent choice as he had proved very successful as host of the popular radio comedy panel game *Does the Team Think?* I was to be a panellist. Alongside me, David booked the multi-talented chef, restaurateur, writer and nightclub host Clement Freud, together with the hugely respected comic actress Beryl Reid, leaving one seat available for another woman.

David decided to hold a day of auditions in a studio in Broadcasting House and asked me to assist in the role of chairman, a request to which I readily agreed. David was an astute producer, with an eye and an ear for what combinations of characters and voices would gel over the airwaves, and by the end of the day's test-runs he was not convinced we had found our fourth player. He did, however, say something that proved prophetic as we sat chatting.

'I'll tell you what, Nick, we might have come up dry on a panellist, but if for any reason Jimmy Edwards can't make it for the pilot I know we've found someone else who can fit perfectly comfortably in that chair.'

I smiled at the compliment, but shook my head. 'No, no, no, David. I'm on the panel. I want to be actively involved. Not just sitting listening to others perform. And that's final.' My ambitions were fixed squarely on demonstrating my love of quick-fire, ad-lib, improvised comedy. The chairmanship held no interest for me.

'Don't worry, Nick. Jimmy's the man. I was merely passing comment on how well you did today.'

Our search for the final member of the team eventually led to an unlikely candidate – one of my neighbours, Wilma Ewart. My wife at the time, Denise, and I were friendly with Wilma and her husband who were both Americans. We'd enjoyed dinners together on a number of occasions and I had always found Wilma witty and entertaining. She had no experience of performing, as far as I knew, but when David met Wilma on my suggestion he could see the potential and offered her the job.

With the cast now in place, David's next task was to find a date to record the show, which proved harder than anticipated. At the BBC, pilots were recorded on a Sunday, and therein lay the problem. Despite repeated attempts by David to pin our chairman down, Jimmy was never available, claiming each time that he had an existing commitment to play polo. That is what David told me anyway. I always wondered if that was the real reason.

In our business, if you are offered something you think is good you go for it. You do not say no because of a polo match. I suspect that Jimmy was simply not very interested in becoming involved in this new *Just a Minute* show. His own programme, *Does the Team Think?* – featuring regular funny men such as Ted Ray, Tommy Trinder and Cyril Fletcher gagging to questions put to them by the audience, and presided over hilariously by Jimmy – was well established. Surely that was a better bet for continued success?

Whatever the reason, Jimmy Edwards' reluctance to commit left David in a difficult situation, from which he could see only one way out.

'Nick, I'm desperate to get this pilot going but Jimmy always seems to be tied up. I need a favour. Will you take the chair? I know you can handle it.'

'Absolutely not, David. I don't want the job. I'm not right for the job. I don't think I can do it. It's not me. I want to be on the panel.'

'I understand that, Nick, I do. But we're in a fix here. Tell you what, I'll do a deal with you. Be the chairman for the pilot, and if we get the series you go back on the panel. In the meantime I know Derek Nimmo is free so he can substitute for you.'

On that basis I agreed. As I said, in this profession you don't turn down work you believe will be good.

On 20 June 1967 the following memo was sent out to relevant BBC personnel.

<u>Just a Minute</u> programme identified as TLN 29/LB 212 H.

Home Service has commissioned a pilot programme of this panel game by Ian Messiter — freely adapted from his own game <u>One Minute Please!</u> which will be recorded as follows:

Date: Sunday 16th July 1967
Rehearsal: 16.00 — 18.00pm
Recording: 19.30 — 20.15pm
Studio: The Playhouse Theatre

Catering department was advised to cater for 12 people from 16.00 — 18.00pm.

The chairman will be Nicholas Parsons and the panel will be Clement Freud, Beryl Reid, Derek Nimmo and Wilma Ewart.

Announcer was requested to arrive at 19.00pm to rehearse and that it be John Dunn if he be available.

That date, Sunday 20 June 1967, marks the beginning of *Just a Minute*. It also nearly marked the end of the show.

The pilot, recorded in front of a studio audience, was not very good. I think we all knew it at the time. It just didn't take off in the way we had hoped. The reasons? Well, there were a number.

The main issue, I believe, is that the rules had not yet been properly defined. They were too loose, making it difficult for listeners to engage in what was going on, which is of course essential. The game became haphazard, not sharp enough, with the emphasis placed on individuals trying to be interesting and entertaining, while the banter between the panellists was secondary. On the surface, that may not appear to be a mistake, but in my opinion a show needs boundaries that people can recognise in order for them to appreciate how clever and witty the contestants are as they bounce off each other. Without identifiable and enforceable rules, the show becomes random and bitty, with inconsistent challenges and adjudications. How can the listening audience immerse themselves in a show when they do not really understand what is happening?

The interpretation of 'repetition' is a good example. For the pilot, and indeed during the first few series before Ian refined his rules, 'repetition' seems to have related to repeating an idea rather than a word. However, that interpretation was not applied consistently. Here, for example, is Clement Freud speaking on the subject of 'Knitting a Cable Stitch Jumper'.

Clement: You get the wool on to the knitting needle and you engage it and you then purl one, plain two, purl two, plain three, purl three, plain one, plain …

BUZZ

Derek: Repetition.

Nicholas: Did you say hesitation or repetition?

Derek: Repetition. He said 'purl one, purl two, purl one, purl two …'

Nicholas: Yes, though I don't know a great deal about knitting I thought they were all different stitches. They were all completing a jumper which would have an end product. It was building something, wasn't it? No, I think probably I would say that Clement Freud's still with it here, and you have an extra point, 15 seconds to go with your cable stitch jumper, going from now.

Then in the following round, Beryl Reid is talking on 'Keeping Fit'.

Beryl: Well, I don't hold with that at all. I think it's absolutely awful, keeping fit. It takes up all your life! I mean, first of all, to start with … keeping fit …

BUZZ

Nicholas: Derek Nimmo, your challenge?

Derek: A great deal of hesitation I thought.

Nicholas: Yes, I think that's true, yes. Derek Nimmo, you have an extra point and would you continue talking now for 47 and a half seconds on the subject of 'Keeping Fit'.

Derek: Cold baths. Cold baths are absolutely essential …

BUZZ

Nicholas: Clement Freud, on what are you challenging?

Clement: Repetition. [BIG LAUGH FROM DEREK AND AUDIENCE FOLLOWED BY APPLAUSE]

Nicholas: It's not your day at the moment, is it, Derek? Clement Freud, I award you a point. Would you continue talking about 'Keeping Fit', starting now.

Derek: He said, 'purl one, purl two, purl one, purl two' six times but that didn't count! I only said 'cold bath' twice! [AUDIENCE LAUGH]

Nicholas: You've made your point. Clement Freud, would you continue on 'Keeping Fit', starting now.

How could anyone make any sense of those rulings?

There were other problems. On the surface Beryl Reid was an obvious choice, but when it came to the recording it quickly became clear that improvisation was not her metier. Beryl was a talented variety performer, actress, and a funny and engaging comedienne, who would go on to appear in a range of comic and straight roles, including a lesbian actress in the controversial film *The Killing of Sister George* and the part of Connie Sachs in the BBC's adaptations of *Tinker Tailor Soldier Spy* and *Smiley's People*. What Beryl was used to was a script or a well-rehearsed routine. That takes great skill, no doubt about it, but it was not what was required for *Just a Minute*. Beryl did her upmost to contribute, and she made numerous interjections, but very few of them really came off.

Then there was myself. My manner can best be described as

laborious – verbose, even – which may have been the style then, but it comes across as rather pompous now. In addition, to add to the general sense of confusion I often awarded points haphazardly. In this example, Wilma Ewart is speaking on the very first subject – 'Excuses for Being Late'.

> **Wilma:** The important thing about excuses for being late is never, never tell the truth. If one is really in difficulty and caught by the traffic, one should never say so. Only that there was an accident and you had to stop to give the kiss of life! [AUDIENCE LAUGH]
>   BUZZ
> **Nicholas:** Beryl Reid, on what are you challenging?
> **Beryl:** Hesitation.
> **Nicholas:** Well, I don't think she hesitated and I award you a bonus point, Wilma. Continue talking, please, for another 40 seconds on 'Excuses for Being Late'.

Why did I award a 'bonus point' there? It should just have been a point for an incorrect challenge.

Wilma then continues.

> **Wilma:** Yes, we had a great American author called F. Scott Fitzgerald who was always late. Always late. And he had a million good excuses for that. He, for instance, came in to meet his publisher who was very important to him, you know and … er … directed his whole life …
>   BUZZ
> **Nicholas:** Clement Freud, you've challenged. On what basis?
> **Clement:** Well, I haven't said anything yet. I thought …
> [BIG AUDIENCE LAUGH AND APPLAUSE]
> **Nicholas:** You have received your round of applause and you've made your presence felt. Now, seriously, as regards the game, on what do you challenge Wilma Ewart?
> **Clement:** Ah, hesitation with just a *touch* of deviation!

[AUDIENCE LAUGH]

Nicholas: I can't give you any extra points for the *touches* but I will give you a point for the deviation, yes.

I am wrong there as well. There was no deviation, perhaps a slight hesitation and, yes, repetition of 'always late' which no one picked up on because the rules were still somewhat fluid in everyone's mind – but deviation?

This example highlights one of the more negative aspects of that pilot, but it also acts as an illustration of what could work well. Clement's first ever challenge on *Just a Minute*, 'Well, I haven't said anything yet,' is very witty and in keeping with the spirit and ethos of the show as it developed.

The fact that in this very first show I play with the concept of 'bonus points' (incorrectly as it happens, with Wilma Ewart, above) is another positive that can be taken from the pilot. Some clever and amusing interjections had generated big laughs (such as Clement's play on the pronunciation of 'pause', below) and although the awarding of bonus points faded away once the rules became more defined (I reintroduced the concept years later to add to the humour) such interjections were clearly to be encouraged as they contributed to the overall sense of fun.

Here Derek has taken up the subject of 'Keeping Fit', cleverly referring back to his 'cold baths' from earlier, much to the amusement of the audience.

Derek: Chilled liquid is terribly important for keeping fit. Every morning I would advise people who are listening to this programme to leap into cooled …
BUZZ
Nicholas: Beryl Reid, you challenged.
Beryl: Hesitation!
Nicholas: Beryl, you seemed to watch Derek's lips because you challenged on the same basis last time. What were you trying to say, Derek?

Derek: I was trying to say w-w-water. [AUDIENCE LAUGH]

Nicholas: No, you weren't stuttering, you were fishing for a word.

Derek: In the water!

Nicholas: Well, your word wasn't in the water. The point goes to Beryl Reid. Would you continue, you have just under 30 seconds to talk about 'Keeping Fit', Beryl Reid, starting now.

Beryl: Well, if you have a cold bath that closes your pores. If you have a hot bath that opens them. Eventually …

> BUZZ

Nicholas: Clement Freud, you're challenging?

Clement: Pores! [BIG LAUGH FROM PANEL AND AUDIENCE FOLLOWED BY APPLAUSE]

Neither Beryl Reid nor Wilma Ewart ever appeared on *Just a Minute* again, Beryl, I think, because her particular style of performance did not fit the show and Wilma because she and her husband moved back to the US. I cannot say whether David Hatch would have engaged Wilma again, but in the pilot I think she does well, contributing some offbeat and humorous lines, in particular this somewhat surreal take on 'Phrenology'. Derek eventually brings Wilma to a halt with a successful challenge, not for repetition (which would undoubtedly have been the case today) but for hesitation as Wilma struggles to complete her sentence. It is amazing to think that modern players *do* manage to produce moments such as this without any repetition.

Wilma: Phrenology is a science, as you all know. It began in Polynesia where it was the custom of the natives to bang their heads together. This was a greeting rather than rubbing noses or shaking hands. So the more people … the more bumps on a person's head indicated how friendly he was. [AUDIENCE LAUGH] How many friends he had. And the natives in Polynesia are splendid at reading one's head to discover if your friends are sincere, warm, or … if they're …

> BUZZ

Following the recording I found myself more in a state of hope rather than expectation that a series would be commissioned. David Hatch, however, was determined. He knew we had something special here, he saw the potential despite its initial flaws, and fought hard on our behalf in the less-than-enthusiastic corridors of power at the BBC.

David told me later that he had been willing to put his job on the line to secure a series for *Just a Minute*, and I suspect that part of the BBC's decision to give him the green light was that they did not wish to risk losing such a clearly talented producer. The process took some time to reach a conclusion, but eventually David came to me with the good news. Well, mostly good news.

'Nick, as you know they didn't like it, and they were reluctant to commission a series. I know we made some mistakes, we struggled a bit in certain areas, but all that can be put right. We've learned what works and what doesn't. There's huge potential, and it is on that basis I have fought hard to get us the series, and at last I've won, with one caveat. The one thing they did like about the pilot was your chairmanship. So I'm afraid if we are to go ahead you are stuck in the chair.'

Frankly, the fact that the executives upstairs liked 'Nicholas Parsons' as chairman surprised me; *I did not like Nicholas Parsons as chairman*! It had not been my best performance – too stilted, in my opinion. However, even if I was not particularly happy about this turn of events, I was not about to complain. I had been offered a whole series and that is not something you turn down. I thought, well, I can draw on my professional experience from many areas of the business to make this job work for me and for the show. That has been my approach ever since.

Trying to analyse the BBC reaction now, perhaps the truth is that my performance as chairman appealed to them because it was in the prevalent style of that era, quite stiff and correct. I was forcing it, projecting myself in the way I thought it should be done, rather than in the way I would do it naturally. Over time, a more natural approach evolved.

The first series of *Just a Minute* consisted of sixteen shows, broadcast from 22 December 1967 (the pilot) to 5 April 1968, with myself, Clement and Derek appearing in every episode, supported by a variety of female guests including, amongst others, actresses Andree Melly (seven shows), Betty Marsden (two), Charmian Innes (two) plus once-only visits from agony-aunt Marjorie Proops and Una Stubbs. Sheila Hancock also made her first appearance, in our second broadcast.

...on the subject of *Whistles, Hooters, Cuckoos and Bells*

Ian Messiter had two of the best ears in the business for what makes radio work, and in the 1950s and '60s he judged that a cacophony of noises to entertain the audience, disrupt proceedings and startle contestants was just the job.

In *One Minute Please!* he incorporated:

- a hammer and block to indicate the start of the player's minute
- a cymbal and brush to announce that the 60 seconds had elapsed
- an electric bell to alert the speaker to the fact that the secret word had been stumbled upon
- a klaxon horn to highlight every subsequent mention of that secret word

Just a Minute was no exception.

For the first couple of shows Ian employed a cuckoo noise to indicate the completion of the minute. From show seven he alternated between a whistle and a bicycle hooter and then stayed with the hooter for the remainder of that first series. In Series 2 Ian migrated to a doorbell-style buzzer to announce

{ the completion of the 60 seconds. It was not until our third
series that the now familiar whistle became established. }

Throughout the first series Ian Messiter acted as whistleblower, scorer and timekeeper (as he did almost consistently up to the show broadcast on 30 May 1989). To aid Ian the BBC supplied a traditional stopwatch, which ran forwards, showing the seconds that had elapsed. That may not sound particularly relevant, but in the heat of the game, with so much on which to concentrate (did he deviate? did she repeat a word there?), when Ian showed me the stopwatch it required swift mental arithmetic to calculate how many seconds remained. That wasn't a problem when, say, ten seconds had passed, but if it was seventeen, that could be tricky as this delightful snippet on the subject 'Spooks' from 4 November 1968 involving Kenneth Williams and newcomer Geraldine Jones illustrates.

Geraldine: Spooks's Christian name was Jim. He was a very tall, thin young man and he used to drink vast quantities of whisky and brandy. And because all the people he associated with were high-powered dynamic wits, they used to make lots of puns on his name and call him Spirits for short. Of course he used to also … live in a …
  BUZZ
Nicholas: Kenneth Williams.
Kenneth: Hesitation.
Nicholas: Hesitation. I agree, you have another point. Kenneth, you have 48 seconds for … no less than … no, 43 seconds for 'Spooks' starting now.
Kenneth: This is of course the plural form of 'to cock a snook', which means to act derisively with a form of gesture …
  BUZZ
Nicholas: Geraldine Jones.
Geraldine: Regrettably, deviation.
Nicholas: Yes, could you justify it just for the audience?

Geraldine: Well, 'snooks' instead of 'spooks' with a P.

Nicholas: Yes, and it's spooks.

Kenneth: Oooh! Your diction's dreadful! [HUGE AUDIENCE LAUGH AND LONG APPLAUSE]

Nicholas: However *bad* my diction may be, if you'd been listening to Geraldine Jones *at all* attentively, you'd realise that she was on about spirits and such like.

Kenneth: But I'm concentrating on whether she hesitates or not. How can I be expected to follow what she's saying?! [BIG LAUGH]

Ian and I accepted the stopwatch situation for a number of years – I doubt we thought there was any option – but fortunately now the watch counts down, making my job much easier.

That first series can be categorised as a 'slow burner'. Having finally been commissioned we knew improvements on the pilot were required and with 15 shows in which to hone and develop the game, myself, Ian, Clement and Derek were confident we would soon gain ground, even if we were not a huge instant success as demonstrated by the mixed Audience Research Report commissioned after the pilot was broadcast.

AN AUDIENCE RESEARCH REPORT

JUST A MINUTE
A Panel Game
Produced by David Hatch
Friday, 22nd December, 1967. 7.30-8.00 pm,
Radio 4

Size of audience (based on results of the
Survey of Listening and Viewing)

It is estimated that the audience for this

broadcast was 0.8% of the population of the United Kingdom.

Reaction of audience (based on questionnaire completed by a sample of the audience. This sample, 246 in number, is the 17% of the Listening Panel who heard all or most of the broadcast.)

The reaction of this sample of the audience were distributed as follows:-

A+	A	B	C	C-
%	%	%	%	%
12	27	40	18	3

giving a REACTION INDEX of 57. The average of Panel Games for the first nine months of the year was 68.

This new panel game in which each member of a team of four scores if able to talk for one minute on a given subject (unless interrupted for hesitation, going off the point, deviation, or repeating himself), met with a somewhat lukewarm response from a good many of those reporting. This type of panel game depended to a great extent on the skill and personality of those taking part and although Derek Nimmo and Clement Freud certainly managed to 'hold this first show together', the basic idea of the game, it was felt, was 'dangerously thin', and likely to pall after a few hearings. Moreover the organization of the game seemed 'amateurish' and 'uncertain'. Panellists had interrupted each other far too frequently without justification, and the constant stops

and starts had proved irritating, some said,
making the game appear 'bitty' and disjointed.
It was also suggested that the studio audience
('who should always be unobtrusive in radio')
had played too large a part in the proceedings
and that it would be preferable if the umpire
would make his own decisions without recourse
to them. Their laughter had often drowned the
speakers' words and, sitting at home, some felt
it was hard to share the audience's enjoyment:-

- 'There was too much team and audience,
  interruptions, claque applause and so-called
  "deviations", which together made a mish-
  mash of what appeared to be talking for
  talking's sake, instead of giving "just a
  minute" to the actual subject calling for
  discussion. None of it made sense. None
  of it was good nonsense. It was a rather
  mediocre bonanza for the boys and their
  women panellists.'(Invalid)
- 'Silly, pointless interruptions. Nothing the
  team had to say was interesting or amusing
  - and if by any chance it was - they weren't
  allowed to really get going. Points system,
  quite pointless!' (Clerk)

Moreover, the contestants were unequally
matched, the two men, Derek Nimmo and Clement
Freud completely overshadowing the lady
panellists, Beryl Reid and Wilma Ewart, both
of whom seemed to lack confidence or wit, thus
contributing little to the game. Nicholas
Parsons was also sometimes criticised by
those who felt as chairman and umpire he
was not always in control of the panel, nor

always quite fair in his judgments, several accusing him of having 'a bias against the female participants'. One small group wondered whether the claim that Just a Minute was a new panel game was correct as they were reminded of a programme back in the fifties called One Minute Please! which, they said, they had enjoyed more. Unfavourable comparisons were also sometimes made with such other light entertainment programmes as Listen to This Space, My Word!, The Tennis Elbow Foot Game, etc. But whether as a new idea or a 're-hash' of an old one, a considerable number of those reporting thought it might well prove successful in the long run, but had 'got off to a rather poor start'.

- 'The idea is quite a good one and the team tonight were capable and amusing, but the tendency to challenge every natural pause as a "hesitation" becomes irritating and often spoils an entertaining line of thought.' (Housewife)

- 'I don't think this idea has "sold" itself to us yet. Probably when members of the panel become more efficient it may prove more entertaining. Tonight it became a contest between Derek Nimmo and Clement Freud. The women hardly ranked as "also rans".' (No occupation)

For two in every five of those reporting, this was a lively start to what promised to be a very successful and popular radio panel game ('Who but Ian Messiter could have thought up this ingenious and unusual game?') and some

thought it the best they had heard. It was
much harder than one would think, they said,
to speak extempore on a subject 'at literally
a second's notice', and the efforts of the
various contestants had resulted in 'an
immensely entertaining half-hour's listening'.
The players, though a little uncertain at
first, had soon got into their stride, with
the 'brilliantly funny', attractive voiced
Derek Nimmo leading the way to the winning
post, closely followed by the 'droll' and
quick-witted Clement Freud with his dead-pan
humour. The rivalry between the two (sometimes
venomous it seemed) had proved the high-spot
of the evening, even for many of those who
were not particularly enthusiastic about the
game as such, and the women, though a little
hesitant about challenging, had done quite well
whenever they had had the chance to speak,
which it seemed was none too often ('Beryl
Reid often cut off in her prime'). Nicholas
Parsons ('a bright and bold chairman') had,
they thought, kept the game moving at a brisk
pace and adjudicated fairly, though he had had
a difficult task. In the words of one satisfied
listener, a Market Gardener, this was 'a
delightful new enterprise with openings for
all kinds of fun and games'. It had been, some
said, uproariously funny! ('In spite of being
in the throes of an acute virus infection, I
just sat giggling quite helplessly.') Though
this enthusiastic response was not shared by
everybody, it was frequently felt that if
improvements could be made, Just a Minute had
'distinct possibilities for the future'.

Copyright of the BBC Audience Research
Department
1st February 1968

For the pilot, Ian had partly integrated one particular aspect from *One Minute Please!*, the idea of the studio audience (similar to the jury concept in *OMP!*) deciding on the merits of borderline challenges. As the audience report indicates, that met with a mixed reaction.

Ian was one of the most imaginative individuals I have ever met, and by show seven he had decided that further embellishments to the basic rules were required to add some spice to proceedings. Once again he referred back to *OMP!*, introducing the idea of 'penalty rounds'. The first of these arrived with the subject 'Gate Crashing', on which Derek Nimmo was asked to speak without using the word 'I'.

Derek clearly found it intimidating, stumbling after only a few words, while Clement, who had challenged for hesitation, adopted a very clever approach, substituting 'we' for 'I' and sailing through to the end of the minute.

More followed in the same show: 'What to Sell at a Jumble Sale' without using 'no' or 'and'; 'This Audience' without saying 'the'. It continued through the remainder of this and the next series: 'Hollywood' without 'the'; 'Toothpicks' without 'and'; 'Relations' without 'to', 'too', or 'two'; 'Getting a Break' without 'of'.

On paper these penalty rounds look like good ideas, adding an extra element of skill and offering the opportunity for more challenges. However, in reality I think they proved to be inhibiting, especially for non-regular players.

Although Derek, Clement and then Kenneth Williams, who joined *Just a Minute* in Series 2, soon conjured up their own methods to work around the imposed restrictions, other players found them too stifling. *Just a Minute* is a difficult enough game to play without an extra inhibiting factor. Back then panellists were not even allowed to repeat the words on the subject card, although a certain amount of indiscriminate leeway was permitted in this respect. Clever and entertaining challenges, and the banter that follows them, are the core of the game; too many stops and starts, based purely on verbal errors, interrupt the flow too severely.

No matter how clever the regulars were, however, they too often found themselves caught out by these rounds, as in this example from a Series 1 broadcast of 15 March 1968, featuring a very sharp challenge from Charmian Innes.

Nicholas: Now, Derek Nimmo, it is your turn to begin and I think it's about time we had a penalty because you're all playing the game so well. So I'll mention the subject first to give you a moment's thought about it, 'Writing Thank You Letters'. We want you to talk about it for just a minute and never mention the word 'and' if you can, starting now.

Derek: Writing thank you letters is a curious English invention. It causes great misfortune to small children just before Christmas because they know that immediately after they've received those lovely inviting presents underneath the tree …

    BUZZ

Nicholas: Clement Freud.

Clement: Mistake. No, I'm sorry.

Nicholas: Right, 'Writing Thank You Letters'. I won't penalise anybody at this point. With, oh, a lot of time left, no 'and's, Derek Nimmo, starting now.

Derek: And …

    BUZZ

Nicholas: Clement Freud did press his buzzer!

Derek: Now, may I just justify that?

Nicholas: All right, you'll have to be clever again though.

Derek: *And*rew is a friend staying with me!

Nicholas: Now, Derek, we only have your word for that!

Derek: Well, I presumably laid this trap for old Freud!

Nicholas: Yes! As I get brickbats from the other three if I give a point to somebody else, I'm not going to be the final judge of this. I'm going to let our delightful audience sitting here decide whether you think he was going to say 'Andrew' or not. If you agree, if you think he was going to say 'Andrew' will you cheer. And if you don't think he was, boo. And do it now.

[CHEERS AND BOOS FROM THE AUDIENCE]

Nicholas: The cheers have it! So you were going to say 'Andrew' and you have a point. You have the subject of 'Writing Thank You Letters', with no 'and's, and no more *Andrews* either! Starting now.

Derek: And …

BUZZ

Derek: … drocles and the Lion … [BIG LAUGH]

Nicholas: What did you say?

Derek: Androcles and the Lion!

Nicholas: Right!

Derek: You asked me to clarify!

Nicholas: Charmian, you challenged.

Charmian: Because of Androcles 'and'! I didn't think it was Androcles *Andrew*!

Nicholas: Very clever! Androcles and the Lion. You're quite right, there is an 'and'! Um, Charmian Innes, there are 40 seconds left for 'Writing Thank You Letters', no 'and', no *Andrew*, no *Androcles*, starting now.

Charmian: The trouble with writing these letters is when you do, you've usually forgotten what present people gave you. And … ahhhhhh!

BUZZ

In introducing these penalty rounds Ian must have thought he had devised a clever gimmick that would be tremendous fun. What Ian did not possess, however, was a natural performer's instinct. It just was not how his brain worked. As a result, he did not quite realise that he had already produced the ideal stage, in the form of the basic concept of the game, on which entertainers could entertain. No further embroidery was required. With the addition of the penalty rounds, Ian had overcomplicated the show, and risked damaging it.

Ian, of course, was too clever, and cared far too deeply about *Just a Minute*, to allow that to happen. By our third series he too had come to the conclusion that the penalty rounds were unnecessary and began to use them very sparingly. In Series 4 they had gone altogether, although occasional appeals for audience adjudication did continue through into the 1980s. Perhaps these should have been dropped earlier as well. Kenneth Williams certainly seemed to think so, and I have considerable sympathy for the opinion (if not his critique of my performance!) he sets out in the following letter to our then producer Simon Brett.

4/11/69

Dear Simon,

Thank you for your letter. Yes I did go quite 'numb' on that second show I remember. I'm afraid it ALWAYS occurs when the chair gets weak. Decisions should be made and points awarded, without these ENDLESS holdups where the justice of the thing is discussed. It is just boring.

On that game he kept asking the audience to vote for everything and it just SLOWS you down. It destroys the momentum of the game. Its essence is speed. Once you LOSE it, you lose everything. All the playing of the game goes …

K

When David Hatch received the call from his BBC bosses informing him that they wanted a quick, six-show second series, it came too late for Derek Nimmo to take part. He had already committed himself to a filming schedule. A replacement had to be found, and it is here that David produced a stroke of genius in booking Kenneth Williams.

I had known Kenneth for many years – we had appeared together in repertory in Bromley back in the late 1940s – and although I had no input into his engagement I thought it was a very good idea. Surprisingly, it was something of a risk on David's behalf. Kenneth was well known to radio audience from his work with Kenneth Horne on *Beyond Our Ken* and *Round the Horne*, and on film and television from, of course, the *Carry On* films plus *Hancock's Half Hour*, and as the host of the weekly *International Cabaret* programme. His experience of panel games and quizzes, however, was sparse. He had been seen as a panellist on *Juke Box Jury*, heard as a celebrity voice on that radio favourite *Twenty Questions*, and appeared as a guest on Frank Muir's team in the first series of the newly formed BBC2's word-definition guessing game, *Call My Bluff*. However that was virtually all he had done until standing in as captain for an unwell Frank Muir in 1967 for another six episodes of *Call My Bluff*.

For David, however, that was more than enough. His stint on *Call My Bluff* had proved, if indeed proof were needed, that Kenneth possessed a unique talent when it came to words and improvisation.

With Kenneth on board to accompany Clement, and David very much aware that my preference was still to sit on the panel, he decided to experiment.

Compared to David's choice for a third panellist, Kenneth's panel-show experience was considerable. Geraldine Jones was the first female president of the Oxford Union, and as a result had been the subject of numerous press profiles, but she had never appeared on radio or television. Once again David's instincts were very much in tune with his audience – Geraldine proved to be a first-rate player of the game. She possessed an easy, friendly personality, slotting in seamlessly with everyone involved in the show. In terms of how she projected herself in the game, she did not attempt to compete with Kenneth and Clement in the battle to dominate airtime but instead relied on her considerable intellect to interject with clever challenges and take the given subjects down interesting and entertaining avenues.

That is where David chose to leave it. Perhaps forced by budgetary restraints he decided to try out a three-person panel, and to add to the experimental nature of the series he chose to rotate the chair for the first four shows. From the letter below, which I received from David after the first recording with me once again as chairman, it is clear he believed my skills were best suited to that role; at the same time he wanted to give me my chance.

16/9/68

Dear Nick,

If anything was likely to change my mind for this series, it was your super performance on Friday. You have never been so in command and so authoritative on the programme – it was a superlative performance. Notwithstanding, I would still like this coming Friday to try Clement in your role, but I am quite prepared to return to the status quo if it doesn't work out.

Yours, David

David may or may not have been flattering me when he wrote that I had put in a 'super performance' in the chair, but I am certain he would not have said the same about Kenneth on the panel, who frankly struggled. He stumbled over his delivery, rarely putting more than a couple of sentences together before hesitating or repeating himself, and when he did manage to build up any momentum he appeared to forget the rules of the game. Here is Kenneth during his debut, broadcast on 30 September 1968, speaking on the subject of 'Making Friends'.

Kenneth: I have made friends all over the place, I really have. I've made friends on park benches and I've made friends on ships. And I think that's a very interesting way to make friends on a ship, because then you get off the ship and you don't see them again. So you're not *bored* by them! [AUDIENCE LAUGH] Otherwise you tend to be rather *bored* if you overdo the friendship. At first, like everything else, it needs rationing, you might understand. What is friendship, one might ask oneself. Well, I mean, you could say it's taking the chaff and the grain together and sifting it all out and with a breath of kindness blowing the unpleasant things away. On the other hand, of course, some friendships can become, as I say, a great bore. This is largely because you overdo it from the start. It should be *rationed*, you see. Friendship should be *rationed* ...

BUZZ

Nicholas: Clement Freud. Yes, he's back in the war, isn't he? He's on his rations! [BIG AUDIENCE LAUGH]

Clement: Yes.

Kenneth: Are you allowed to repeat anything?

Clement: Not as often as that! [AUDIENCE LAUGH]

Whether he was initially intimidated by the sharp intellects of Clement and Geraldine it is hard to say. Kenneth did pride himself on his self-taught knowledge, but up against the education of his fellow panellists he may have experienced some nervousness. A little later in the show he certainly appeared to ... quite visibly.

Nicholas: Geraldine, you're only one point behind Clement Freud now and Kenneth Williams is four points behind Clement Freud ... So you've taken out a cigarette, you're getting a bit tense are you? [BIG LAUGH]

Kenneth: Oh yes! I'm throbbing here, I really am!

Massaging Kenneth's sometimes precarious ego in order to help draw him out of the shell into which he occasionally retreated became a key element of my chairmanship over the years. It was necessary even during that first appearance when, as we entered the final round with Kenneth 'a little way behind' the others, I sensed he required some encouragement.

Nicholas: Kenneth, it's your turn to start. The subject, which no doubt someone with your horticultural background, your thinking on the artefacts and all of those things, can discourse on at great length, but just a minute will do, 'Puffballs', starting now.

Kenneth's concerns that he may not shine in the company he was keeping could have been part of why he took three or four shows to relax into the game, but more pertinent, I believe, is the fact that the show was a new concept to him. It was not the type of performance he had done much in his career up to then. The discipline of thought required in *Just a Minute* was new to him. There is no question Kenneth was extremely quick-witted and very funny, and although we play for laughs in the show, the rules on which the game is constructed are actually the antithesis of how a comic usually operates.

If you tell a funny story, you *pause* for effect, you *repeat* for emphasis and you *deviate* for surprise. On *Just a Minute* we disregard these basic rules. Instead, the show's success is based on improvisation and ad-libbing by bright, intelligent and witty people sparking off each other. At first this opposite approach seemed to hamper Kenneth, but once he had grasped it, and found a way to play the game on his own terms, he soon began to sparkle.

David Hatch clearly recognised that Kenneth found that first show difficult and must have written to him with words of encouragement because Kenneth makes reference to such a letter in his response, in which he also acknowledges his faltering start.

18/9/68

Dear David,

Well I certainly meant it – I felt absolutely useless at the run through but Nicholas and Clement were marvellous and you kept telling me it would be alright and I actually got thro' it.

I had no idea a game could be so difficult.

Bless you for writing. If only people knew how tiny the actor's ego actually is!

Yours, Kenneth

In those early shows Kenneth may not have reached the heights that we later became accustomed to, but the promise of what was to come – his trademark flamboyance, his asides and unique personality – did reveal itself in his first ever challenge. The audience loved it, and continued to love him through until his final show.

Nicholas: The subject is 'Learning to Fly', Clement. Would you like to try and talk for just a minute, starting now.
Clement: One would have thought that when you learn to fly you need a plane. But this is utterly untrue. You need a blackboard and a man with a white shirt and gold stripes on his shoulders who has a pointer and draws …
BUZZ
Nicholas: Kenneth …
Kenneth: Well, I challenge that. I don't see what men with gold rings has got to do with flying! [BIG LAUGH] It's a disgrace, it's deviation, isn't it? He was deviating! I could see him deviating! [EVEN BIGGER LAUGH] His eyes were deviating too!
Nicholas: Kenneth, you are pressing your point very, very strongly …
Kenneth: Thank you.
Nicholas: … but even though you are new to the show, I'm afraid that I can't uphold it. I have seen men with rings around their arms connected with flying, all flying officers have got them. So I uphold Clement Freud …
Kenneth: It's a disgrace, innit? [AUDIENCE LAUGH ENTHUSIASTICALLY AT KENNETH'S ANTICS]

By the final broadcast of that second series, on 4 November 1968, Kenneth had most definitely hit his stride, sufficiently confident by then to introduce an extraordinary friend of his who, over the coming years, we would learn more about than we could ever have imagined: Maudie Fittleworth.

Dear Maudie was a creation of Kenneth's from his days appearing in the Barry Took and Marty Feldman-penned *Round the Horne*, in which Kenneth played the character Sandy alongside Hugh Paddick's Julian. These two camp, flamboyant fellows found themselves embarking on a number of enterprises, including running a theatrical agency. Maudie Fittleworth – billed as having 'Fun with a Frankfurter' – is mentioned during the shows as one of their clients.

Kenneth's first *Just a Minute* reference to Maudie arrived during his description of 'The Things in My Wallet' when he revealed that alongside his identity card and an old ration book there was the following.

> **Kenneth:** A photograph of Maudie Fittleworth! [BIG LAUGH FROM AUDIENCE] Maudie Fittleworth, you all remember, Fun with a Frankfurter. She was the top of the bill and I adored Maudie!! And I used to go round to her dressing room after ...
>   BUZZ
> **Nicholas:** Clement Freud, you challenged.
> **Clement:** Three 'Maudies'.
> **Nicholas:** Yes we had a bit too much of Maudie, I'm afraid.
> **Kenneth:** You *couldn't* have enough of her!!! [HUGE LAUGH FROM AUDIENCE]

Having received such a positive audience reaction Kenneth knew instinctively that he was on to something that could run and run. All good comics have a sixth sense when it comes to being able to spot a gag or routine to which they can return in order to lift a show if needed.

Audiences quickly grew to love Maudie, responding with enthusiasm whenever she made an appearance. Perhaps it was because they felt in on the joke, knowing that some outlandish innuendo would not be far away when Maudie's name was mentioned. In so doing, Kenneth had created another bond between himself and his fans.

Kenneth's great skill was in sensing when to introduce Maudie, with whatever tenuous link his brain could come up with, if he felt a subject required some lightness of touch to inject humour. Then, with Maudie in the frame, he would elaborate wildly on her most recent exploits.

The following is merely a brief sample from the long list of Maudie's accomplishments and escapades. The first comes from a broadcast of 12 January 1971, with Kenneth talking on the subject of 'Christmas Party Games'.

Kenneth: Maudie Fittleworth, Fun with a Frankfurter, always said that Christmas party games occupied most of her leisure time the rest of the year. [KENNETH CAN'T STOP LAUGHING HERE] In fact she said that the other times were merely a dress rehearsal for the Christmas party games. Her favourite one was dressing up as the chimney sweep, and embracing everyone at great propinquity so that the black on her came off on them!! Much to their great embarrassment of course! [BIG LAUGH]

On 15 December 1976 we learn of Maudie's aquatic knowledge when Kenneth takes the subject of 'Porpoises'.

Kenneth: I have evidence as to the training of these creatures from a woman who is called Maudie Fittleworth who did things with a Frankfurter herself. [AUDIENCE BURST OUT LAUGHING AS KENNETH IS CHALLENGED AND LOSES SUBJECT, BUT THAT DOES NOT STOP HIM] She exfoliated before the blowpipe! [BIG LAUGH] She created history! She topped the bill *twice* at Huddersfield!! [HUGE LAUGH] And she was involved in the aquarium training of these things. She used to dive in with them just to give them a bit of encouragement!! [AUDIENCE END UP IN HYSTERICS]

Kenneth outlines 'An Average Day' on 23 March 1977, which of course involves Maudie.

Kenneth: It inevitably begins with the cup of coffee and then the phone call of which that dear friend Maudie Fittleworth, Fun with a Frankfurter, expatiates at length upon the business of her exploding bow tie and the various séances she attends. She's something of a medium. And now her ectoplasm explodes as well as her bow tie! [BIG LAUGH]

Finally, during a 20 February 1985 broadcast Kenneth reveals Maudie's adventurous side when speaking on the subject of 'Stowaways' before he is challenged for deviation by lyricist Tim Rice, who claims never to have heard of this extraordinary character.

> **Kenneth:** The most famous stowaway of all time was Maudie Fittleworth-Fun-with-A-Frankfurter. She got on board the ship dressed as a sailor, and nobody dreamed that underneath that apparently rough visage was the tender feminine form of nubile …
> BUZZ

Challenges such as Tim's were always met with incredulity, shock and outrage. How could anyone be so audacious as to suggest Kenneth's Maudie stories were untrue? *Of course* his great music-hall friend with the extraordinary act had been a stowaway, a spiritual medium and a porpoise trainer! According to Kenneth, that was only the tip of the iceberg. There were also the times she dabbled as an ardent women's libber, a magician, a confidence trickster and an escapologist. Small wonder nobody else had ever met her; the woman was too busy!

I won the first ever game of *Just a Minute* in which I appeared on the panel, despite the best efforts of Clement Freud in the chair. This was now our eighteenth show (broadcast on 7 October 1968), by which point Clement had established the personality he wished to project on *Just a Minute*, and this autocratic and slightly stand-offish demeanour did not suit the role of chairman, not as I perceived it.

In Clement's view the chairman should be nothing more than a cypher through which the other players could perform, and certainly not contributing to the entertainment.

In years to come this difference of opinion was to cause some friction between us, but even at this early stage in the show's history he seemed to regard being in the chair as an opportunity for some payback for the manner in which I undertook my stewardship. He did not want me to come out on top. Here he is in his role as chairman, with Kenneth, Geraldine and myself on the panel.

Clement: Kenneth Williams, will you talk for one minute on 'Making an Entrance', starting now.

Kenneth: Well, as the poet has it, 'all the world's a stage, and all the men and women merely players, they have their exits and their entrances'. And that is absolutely true. We come into this world naked, indeed we come into it quite naked. And after that we've got to make entrances in a different way. We can't come in naked obviously! [BIG LAUGH]

> BUZZ

Clement: Nicholas Parsons.

Nicholas: Well, there was repetition of his nakedness …

Clement: Yes! [BIG LAUGH]

Nicholas: And I would say that Kenneth …

Clement: Don't, don't, don't spoil it for yourself.

Nicholas: All right.

Clement: You have a point. You have 'Making an Entrance'. You have 37 seconds, starting now.

Nicholas: Well, I'm delighted to think that I have 37 seconds starting now in which to make a …

> BUZZ

Clement: Kenneth Williams.

Kenneth: Deviation.

Clement: You're absolutely right because I made a mistake, he has 47 seconds! [AUDIENCE LAUGH]

Nicholas: Oh! Wait till I'm back on the chair again!

Clement: Kenneth Williams, you have 39 seconds, 'Making an Entrance', starting now.

Kenneth: There are two kinds …

> BUZZ

Clement: Nicholas Parsons.

Nicholas: Deviation, because you said 37 seconds before and you said 39 now. So if it was wrong for me it is also deviation for Kenneth.

Clement: You're talking nonsense. [HUGE LAUGH FROM AUDIENCE]

At my next attempt I do successfully challenge Kenneth, but quickly lose the subject again, to Geraldine.

Geraldine: When you're making an entrance whether it's in a brick wall or at a gathering, you have to remember what materials you have. It's no use making an entrance in a stunning black dress if you're going to be going to a party where …

BUZZ

Clement: Nicholas Parsons.

Nicholas: Hesitation.

Clement: Hesitation is right, you have 13 seconds, starting now.

Nicholas: I'm horrified to think that I have … [AUDIENCE LAUGH]

BUZZ

Clement: Kenneth Williams.

Kenneth: Deviation. Whether he's horrified or not is not the point!

Clement: Nicholas Parsons, you have three seconds in which to justify.

Nicholas: I'm horrified to think that you want me to speak for 13 seconds about making an entrance.

Clement: [DEADPAN] I think Kenneth Williams has a very good point indeed. [AUDIENCE LAUGH] And you have eight seconds, 'Making an Entrance', starting now.

Kenneth: Making an entrance means …

BUZZ

Clement: Nicholas Parsons.

Nicholas: Repetition, he's made so many entrances already!

Clement: Right. Six seconds. 'Making an Entrance'. Now.

Nicholas: I don't really wish to speak about this subject …

BUZZ

Kenneth: If he doesn't wish to speak about it, why start?!

[HUGE AUDIENCE LAUGHTER AND APPLAUSE]

Clement: Under what general heading was that complaint?

Kenneth: Ehhh?

Clement: Under what general …

Kenneth: It's deviation.

Clement: Oh yes. Yes, I give you deviation.

Nicholas: Why? May I justify myself, Chairman?

Clement: Not again. [BIG LAUGH] Three seconds, starting now.

Kenneth: I once made an entrance as Nefertiti …

BUZZ

Kenneth: … and it was fabulous! They all went raving when I came in as *Nefertiti*!

BUZZ

Kenneth: I had this caped hat on me! And it was *really fantastic*!!!

Clement: Nicholas Parsons?

Nicholas: Well, he said 'entrance' again. He's already said it about seven times.

Clement: You have the subject. For one second. Starting now.

Nicholas: I will speak about making an entrance …

Bell

Kenneth: It's disgraceful! [BIG ROUND OF APPLAUSE]

Clement: You *reluctantly* get a point because you were talking when the buzzer went.

The show then progresses through to the final round, with Geraldine speaking first on the subject 'Bowling'.

Geraldine: This is a terribly technical subject which I know nothing about. When I was at school, we had to play cricket, and part of learning to play this game involved learning how to bowl. It always involved such an enormous expenditure of effort, not just running, but wheeling around with your arms as well, that I decided very early on I would never ever learn to bowl. Other people I believe do. Occasionally my father forces me to watch cricket on television as part of widening my educational horizons. When I do I always find it terribly boring and particularly the part where the man bowls. It takes such a dreadfully …

BUZZ

Clement: Nicholas Parsons.

Nicholas: That's the third 'bowl' we've had, I think. Definitely twice, when she talked about school and learning bowling.

Kenneth: Very ungallant! It's very ungallant!

Nicholas: No, I let her go for a very long time …

Clement: Yes, yes, yes! Don't go on! [GERALDINE BURSTS OUT LAUGHING]

Nicholas: You're such a hard man, as Kenneth said, I …

Geraldine: My God, he is!

Clement: Nicholas Parsons, you lose a point for repeating yourself on the challenge … [BIG ROUND OF APPLAUSE]

Kenneth: *Ye-e-e-s!* Hahahah!!

Clement: But you get the subject, 'Bowling'. You have 35 seconds to go, starting now.

Nicholas: Bowling is of course a gentle, lovely game. Upon the green swards of England you will see these delightful elderly people with their little rolled-up mats, down on one knee and passing the ball gently across the green sward until it comes up against the little white pill the other end. Sometimes they say, 'Gosh, your turn, Mabel, you see if you can beat that one because I bowled a good 'un. See if you can do better.'

Bell

Kenneth: Brilliant! Very good! I liked the bit about Mabel.

Clement: A very commendable point won by Nicholas Parsons on bowling. That is it, and Nicholas Parsons wins with 33 points. For which I think he deserves a small modicum of applause. [APPLAUSE]

Kenneth: I don't! I thought it was disgraceful! Disgraceful! All that cheating!

Clement: Geraldine Jones, who was my own particular selection as many of you must have noticed, came second with 25 points. And Kenneth Williams came last. Goodbye.

Although I was successful on my first appearance on the panel, I did not entirely cover myself with glory.

I cannot now remember the specifics, and David Hatch must have subsequently edited the broadcast, but clearly I did not act entirely appropriately during the recording.

25/9/68

Dear Nicholas

Let me re-emphasise what I said about challenging. To a certain extent I agree with you, that people should be allowed to get going. However, I think this can only apply to the first 15 or so seconds, and if your joke hasn't come up, then you must expect to be challenged. The point and fun of this game comes out of those challenges and not from a brilliant exposition of one minute.

Let me take the bull absolutely by the horns and say that if somebody does challenge you within the first few seconds, particularly if it is somebody like Geraldine, it is really unforgiveable Nick to say things like 'Ah for Pete's sake let me get started!' This worries the audience and it certainly worried Geraldine.

Forgive me for saying all this Nick, but I think you'll realise that I do it for the programme, and of course, also because of the regard in which I hold you.

Yours, David

Here David is referring to an unwritten rule between the players that they would not challenge each other within the first 15 seconds or so of a subject, to allow the speaker to get going. This no longer exists, but was necessary back then as the rules were still somewhat arbitrary, allowing too many challenges and interruptions. Not only would this destroy any momentum that was building, it could also lead to unwanted tension between the players, as David Hatch mentions in the following letter written to Kenneth.

6/1/69

Dear Ken,

    Would just like to drop you a line to congratulate you on winning the second show on Friday. I thought they were both good programmes, although I think a certain amount of acrimony began to creep in at one point. I don't know what one can do about this since every week I define the rules of playing the game, no interrupting for fifteen seconds etc., and I am sure it is when those rules are broken that ill feeling creeps in.

    However, on the whole I think and hope it is a happy programme and look forward to next Friday and making two more good shows.

    Yours, David Hatch

In the exchange with Geraldine that David mentions in his letter to me, I was clearly somewhat miffed that she had challenged within the 15-second 'rule', and reacted in a way I should not have. David was absolutely correct in what he wrote. Part of the reason I acted as I did was, I am sure, because appearing on the panel for the first time I no doubt felt the game was not being run according to the brief *as I understood it.* Had I been in the chair I would not have accepted Geraldine's challenge. That does not excuse my actions, however, about which I was embarrassed. Happily the incident was quickly forgotten, and Geraldine and I remained on very friendly terms.

Next to take their place on the revolving chair, in the show broadcast on 14 October 1968, was in fact Geraldine, who proved to be both fair and entertaining. Here she is introducing a penalty round, with Kenneth to speak first.

Geraldine: Kenneth Williams, it's your turn now. Would you talk for one minute please on 'Being Measured for a Suit', but you have to talk on the subject without saying 'to' spelt T-O, 'too' spelt T-O-O and 'two' spelt T-W-O. So no 'to's are allowed. 'Being Measured for a Suit', starting now.

Kenneth: Well, being measured for a suit can be an extremely *luxurious* experience. There is a nice feeling, I think, when people say, 'Well now, just stand there, just slip off the jacket. I'll just measure you across the shoulders. I'll measure your underarm. Measure your waist.' Of course at that time it's a bit much because you suddenly realise that you have put it on a bit, perhaps, you see. And that's not very nice. They say, 'Oh *hollo!* He was thirty last time, thirty-one here!' Have to lay off the starch, I think, and the port, and lay off the wines and all that sort of thing. That can be very embarrassing indeed. I haven't said 'to' yet, I don't think … [HUGE AUDIENCE LAUGH]

> BUZZ

Geraldine: Clement Freud.

Clement: 'To'.

Geraldine: Yes, he did, he challenged you to challenge him. So Clement Freud gains a point and has 21 seconds, starting now.

Clement: Et tu Brute?

> BUZZ

Geraldine: Nicholas Parsons? [BIG AUDIENCE LAUGHTER] Nicholas Parsons.

Nicholas: He used two words. [MORE AUDIENCE LAUGHTER]

Geraldine: No, that's not allowed.

Nicholas: He said 'to', he said 'to'.

Geraldine: Yes, but I specified, you see, how the 'to' was to be spelt.

Nicholas: But it wasn't that 'tu'. I know Clement Freud, he doesn't speak Latin normally! [BIG AUDIENCE LAUGH]

Geraldine: Well, I know that he does and even if he doesn't, the Latin is correctly spelt T-U. My education is at last being of some use to me. And so Clement Freud gains another point and still has 19 seconds, starting now.

Clement: The tailor takes his tape and runs down my inside thigh measurement which he does with tremendous ability. 'Thirty-one!', he shouts. Then, 'Thirty-three!' He then goes to my waist …

BUZZ

Geraldine: Nicholas Parsons.

Nicholas: To my waist.

Geraldine: Yes, you're right. You have one point and seven seconds on 'Being Measured for a Suit', starting now.

Nicholas: Being measured for a suit is one of the lux … urious things of life. [KENNETH CACKLING IN BACKGROUND]

BUZZ

Geraldine: Clement Freud.

Clement: Hesitation.

Geraldine: Yes, yes, he was fumbling a bit, I think.

Nicholas: Ah, Miss Lady Chairman, may I say you're so charming and so understanding and so kind to people. I was born with an impediment. [BIG AUDIENCE LAUGH] I do have difficulty with my speech. I managed to combat in my youth a very difficult stutter. And 'lux … urious' has always been one of the most difficult words.

Geraldine: With you saying I was charming, et cetera, you were saying no more than the truth. But I'm not really very sympathetic to people with impediments.

Nicholas: I realise that.

Geraldine: Clement Freud has a point and …

Kenneth: She's haaard!

Geraldine: … two second left.

The next subject is 'How to Open a Bazaar' without saying the word 'the'.

Nicholas: Opening a bazaar is a bizarre experience. The whole point is …

BUZZ

Geraldine: Clement Freud.

Clement: 'The' whole point.

Geraldine: Yes, he did. You have 55 seconds on 'How to Open a Bazaar', starting now.

Clement: Ladies and gentlemen who have come … unto … my garden this afternoon. I welcome you all most sincerely … from … a … deep down … part …

BUZZ

Geraldine: Nicholas Parsons.

Nicholas: He's getting so slow, you know, it's obvious hesitation.

Geraldine: I, I agree, you don't have to argue it. I'm surprised you didn't interrupt sooner.

Nicholas: Well, I was afraid of getting penalised …

[BIG LAUGH FROM AUDIENCE]

Geraldine: I'm always fair. You gain one point.

For the fourth show of the series, broadcast on 21 October, Kenneth was placed in charge. Mayhem.

Kenneth performed wonderfully, in a mad, anarchic manner. I am not sure he really knew what was going on. He was all over the place, larking around throughout, giving approximations of the time left in rounds, talking ten to the dozen and not listening properly, which left him frequently appealing to Ian Messiter, who sat next to him, or to the audience, for help. They loved it. It was all great fun, but it was not really *Just a Minute*. Shows of this nature could not have been sustained throughout a complete series. Excellent as a one-off, but a whole string of them would have been too much.

Kenneth set the tone of his chairmanship right from the beginning of the show, with the audience laughing throughout.

Kenneth: Thank you, yes, it is me, your own heartrendingly lovable Kenneth Williams. And here I am surrounded by buzzers, stopwatches, and a lot of rules. I also have a list of unlikely subjects for the panel to talk about for 50 … I'm sorry

… 60 seconds each without pausing, without going off the subject and without repetition.

As for concentrating on what is going on …

Kenneth: Now it's Nicholas Parsons to start and your subject this week is 'The Days of the Week', starting from now.
Nicholas: [AUDIENCE LAUGHTER BUILDS THROUGHOUT] Monday, Tuesday, Wednesday, Thursday, Friday, Saturday, Sunday. Lundi, Mardi, Mercredi, Jeudi, Vendredi, Samedi, Dimanche. Lunes, Martes, Miércoles, Jueves, Viernes, Sábado, Domingo. It's so interesting sometimes to listen to the wireless and you hear the announcer say that tomorrow will be muggy followed by tueggy, weggy, thurggy, friggy, saggy and soggy. And of course soggy are so many of the days of the week in this country – wet, miserable and eventually so, so *wet* that you sometimes wonder why you ever get up in the morning to face the British weather. Now the days of the week …
BUZZ

Kenneth: Clement Freud, on what grounds are you challenging?
Clement: Repetition.

Kenneth: Repetition, *ye-e-e-s*, well, I think you're justified there. Yes, I think there was a bit of repetition, yes …
Nicholas: What did I repeat?
Kenneth: Um … well, I can't exactly recall what [BIG AUDIENCE LAUGH] … but I know it was repeated.

Kenneth is clearly enjoying his turn in the chair, winding himself up to unleash mock outrage and revelling in his position of authority to great comic effect. Here I have just attempted to challenge Clement for hesitation, justifying my claim by saying Clement's pause before he spoke was exactly the same as mine from seconds earlier, for which Kenneth had granted Clement's challenge.

Kenneth: I will not have my authority flouted!!! [BIG LAUGH] I am the chairman! *No, don't laugh! It's wicked!* I am the chairman!!!

Clement is speaking when the bell sounds for the end of a round on 'Wine, Women and Song', eliciting effusive praise from the chairman.

Kenneth: Oh! Yes, well, at the end of that round Clement Freud is definitely in the lead. It's a *fantastic* lead, Clem!! I must *congratulate* you! You're revealing intellectual *prowesses* here I never knew you …
Nicholas: Oh shut up! [AUDIENCE LAUGH] He's got two points more than us, hasn't he?
Kenneth: It's no good revealing your chagrin, Nicholas! I can actually see your chagrin from here!!! [BIG LAUGH]

A little later, the subject is 'Blancmange' without using the word 'a' and Clement is speaking with 15 seconds to go.

Clement: Among other …
   BUZZ
Kenneth: Geraldine, why did you challenge?
Geraldine: It was a cheek, really. 'A'-mong! [MOMENTARY PAUSE, THEN BIG AUDIENCE LAUGH AND APPLAUSE AS THEY UNDERSTAND GERALDINE'S JOKE]
Kenneth: No! *Quite unjustified!* Quite unjustified! Quite unjustified, I don't think 'A'-mong could ever be construed as 'a'. No! I'm not having that! It's a challenge to the very basis of my authority, isn't it? Yes! No! Eh? No!!! You get it back, Clement.

To cap this hilarious episode off, Kenneth then closes the show in an even more confused manner than in his opening remarks. This is perhaps the most entertaining end to a programme we have ever experienced. The subject is 'Annual Reports' with eight seconds remaining.

Geraldine: The only possible way to make annual reports interesting is to invent them. There is nothing more fun than sitting at a committee meeting when you know that all the people present have been present at …

Bell [FOLLOWED BY LOUD APPLAUSE]

Kenneth: Oh, and you've won that one!! *Oooh*, well, this is fantastic! You're really creeping up, darling. Oh, this is wonderful! You are level now with Nicholas Parsons!!! Isn't that *fantastic*! Yes! *But both of you are miles behind Clement!* Next one is … [KENNETH TURNS TO IAN MESSITER] … oh, that's the end, isn't it? No, we can't have any more! No! So that's the end, I'm afraid, of *Wait a Minute*, and we'll be back …

BUZZ

Kenneth: What is that?

Nicholas: Deviation! It's called *Just a Minute*! Not *Wait a Minute*! [HUGE AUDIENCE LAUGH]

The reason I had originally approached Ian Messiter to ask whether he had any new shows up his sleeve was to find a vehicle for myself to perform improvised comedy. In this second series, my chance had come. Did I enjoy myself?

Yes, I did, up to a point. Sitting on the panel provided opportunities that were unavailable to me in my role as chairman. For instance, in October 1968, during my second appearance as a panellist I had the pleasure of introducing into the game one of my great passions.

Ever since my father read the nonsense poems of Edward Lear and Lewis Carroll to me when I was young, I have adored their use of words and escapist humour, eventually going on to write my own one-man show detailing Lear's fascinating life. I was therefore delighted to try my hand at a touch of *Just a Minute* nonsense of my own when handed the subject of 'Mumbo Jumbo' by Geraldine Jones, who was sitting in the chair. Happily, the audience seemed to enjoy my performance, laughing along throughout.

Nicholas: Mumbo jumbo, jabberwocky, come thing. This is how now. Well, I thought come along the branch and step out along the way. I thought it was. No. You can't bear the gift what gives, the gift he give us, now. I saw gum. And then again, some people say this and some say that but what would you, ha ha, not I! But then, it is a point, you say! Come now? Is it him, is it them, is it they? Is it Williams? Is it Freud? No! They're coming. This is a point and so we step forth, we take our hands, we cup them together, we look up and we look down because there is a way round. I thought perhaps it was theatre, you said no, and …

BUZZ

[HUGE AUDIENCE LAUGH AND APPLAUSE]

Geraldine: Clement Freud.

Clement: I didn't understand it! [LOUD CACKLE FROM KENNETH]

I was very happy to be a panellist on five further special editions over the years (plus one impromptu appearance in 1977 when Clement was delayed on public transport and Ian took over the chair and I sat with Kenneth, Derek and my great friend the actor Peter Jones who would become one of the show's regular panellists) but in truth I didn't relish that side of the game as much as I had anticipated.

The situation might have been different had I taken on the role from the beginning. In that circumstance I would have found a way of playing the game, just as all our regulars have, in my own individual style and I would have enjoyed doing so. Instead, it is as chairman that I have found my natural voice, which I have evolved and developed over the years into something that I hope is entertaining, humorous and contributes to the fun. It has been a joy and I wouldn't have had it any other way.

The following exchange of letters between David Hatch and myself illustrates how I felt, even back in 1968.

2/10/68

Dear Nick,

    On thinking it over and bearing in mind all you said in the pub on Sunday, I think I would like you back in the Chair this coming Friday.

    It is no accident, I think, that when we have you in the chair the programme is of its best, so let's go back to the status quo, though I am still glad we did the experiment.

    Yours, David

3/10/68

Dear David,

    I must say I am pleased at the thought at being back in the chair. Having had the experience of being on the panel, I know where I feel happiest. I agree with you it was an interesting and valuable experience, swapping us all around. I only hope my discussions with you on the topic didn't bore you too much. You are very patient and understanding. It's a real pleasure to work with you and thank you most sincerely for all you do to make the show so successful, from which we all benefit.

    Yours, Nicholas

...on the subject of *Chairmanship*

There is a significant distinction between the techniques required to succeed as an actor and those that are necessary to perform in the role of host or presenter. In my experience, there have not been many capable of switching between the two disciplines. I count myself lucky this was something I was able to achieve.

Successful actors are observers, in a way that is different from other people. They unconsciously assimilate traits, gestures, mannerisms, speech patterns, all sorts of nuances, from everyone they meet, and then instinctively draw on those elements as required for a particular role.

I first became aware of this aspect of acting back in my days performing in repertory theatre up in Glasgow during the 1940s.

My first job – semi-professional, I suppose, as we were paid only £2 a week – was working with a distinguished Scottish actress called Mollie Urquhart who had converted a disused Rutherglen church into a little theatre. One of the players in the company Mollie founded was her friend John McCrae who later changed his name to Duncan McCrae and became very successful in film and on stage. In the Mollie Urquhart days John was a schoolmaster, and he had a deep feeling for the theatre. He was extremely talented, both knowledgeable and wise in the mechanics of acting. I looked up to him. He was my mentor and we became very good friends. I listened to what he told me and learned, taking in as much as possible – how to use expressions, when to pause, the most effective way to apply make-up. All manner of essential skills required in the actor's toolbox.

It is not a question of copying, not at all, instead it is a case of absorbing the different characteristics you come across, and then honing them to best suit your own personality in the role you are about to play.

That is not how a host or presenter should approach their discipline, not if he or she wishes to succeed.

When I first took on the role of chairman in *Just a Minute* I was not an experienced host. Yes, I had fronted *Listen to This Space* on radio, but that was scripted. *Just a Minute* is the exact opposite, and to chair such a show demands very different skills in order to make it work.

In those first couple of series, there is no question I was a little stiff – more arched, if you like – than is my natural personality. It was almost as though I was playing the *part* of a chairman as I thought it should be done, subconsciously drawing on elements from other exponents of the craft. Totally the wrong approach.

As host you have to be yourself, you have to be genuine. That is the key distinction between acting and presenting. As chairman of *Just a Minute* I realised that to be successful I had to cast off the *character* of a chairman, and relax into *me* as chairman. It boils down to having confidence in who you are. When you grasp that, you switch to a different mode of performing, no longer playing a role but instead making direct contact with your audience, as yourself, with your own humour. In so doing you create a bond with that audience, putting them at ease and creating a positive atmosphere that in itself contributes to the entertainment of the show.

That is very different from playing a character on stage or screen. There are, however, similarities in the two disciplines. In both, for instance, you have to be constantly open to developing new skills to improve your performance.

For instance, one thing I have noticed is that when listening to a presentation people will follow what is being said, but when a name is mentioned out of the blue it attracts particular attention. It interrupts the general flow of everyday words. Having observed this, I now always make sure that when I mention the panellists on *Just a Minute* I do so in a very precise manner, stating their full name so that it stands out, allowing the listeners to take it in.

Resting on your laurels in either discipline is fatal. Someone said to me recently that after so many years on *Just a Minute* I must surely now be running on autopilot. Nothing could be further from the truth. I would not still be here if that were the case.

With *Just a Minute* I listen to every broadcast, not out of a sense of ego, but because I know I can learn something. During the recording I concentrate so hard to ensure the show flows that I don't always have a complete sense at the time for what is funny and what is working. Listening again in the comfort of my own home I am able to relax and spot the positive elements and others that were less successful. I then use that knowledge in future shows.

One question I am often asked, particularly when the topic of conversation turns towards the four regulars of Kenneth, Clement, Derek and Peter, is how did I manage to keep them all under control? Especially when the rules were less well defined and they had considerable scope to go off on wild tangents. Well, it was not always an easy task, and nor was it always welcomed, especially by Clement, Derek and Kenneth, as is referred to in these two much appreciated letters from David Hatch, written more than four years apart.

27/1/69

Dear Nicholas,

I think that it was unfair that the last programme of the series, the 36th that we had done, should have been the hardest to chair. I thought they gave you a rough ride and I thought you came out of it extremely well.

To me you have gone from strength to strength on this programme as chairman, tightening your control, thinking always of the listener and not the studio audience, keeping the peace. I think you have done a superlative job.

Be assured that I will let this be known where I hope it will help. I am sure there are lots more Just a Minutes to do and I am sure we will be asked for many more series. I look forward to them.

Yours, David

1/10/73

Dear Nicholas,

I was aware on Wednesday evening that you were a little incensed by Nimmo, and nearly rang you on Thursday, but thought that probably by then you would have got over it, and didn't want to blow hot air on to cold ashes. However, I have been talking to Ian this morning and he told me you were still smarting, and so I thought I would like to pour some oil on troubled waters.

I really do believe that the game is about aggro, is about anarchy, as much as it is about the contestants, and the simple rules. It is a good game simply because it has this extra ingredient, which comes from the person-alities playing it. A lot of time there is the suppressed aggression against each other, but every now and then they turn like the pack of wolves they are and tear you to bits. They are always snapping at you, but if one of them draws blood, then the rest leap on you. One of the great things for an observer is to watch you avoid getting bitten, which 9 times out of 10 you do superbly. In the larger context, it is like hitting at the establishment, and people enjoy that.

The only sufferer is your ego, but I think, if you stand back from it, you will see that even you gain, because audiences either resent what is being said and love you, and you have the ultimate comeback as Chairman. There are times of course, when it goes too far, and if you can't prevent it on stage, then I try and edit it in the channel.

The most crucial thing in the whole programme is your chairing of it, and the only reason this programme has run so long, and I hope will continue to run for as long again, is by the masterly adjudications which you give each week, sometimes playing by the rules, sometimes by the show-biz rules, speeding up, slowing down, etc, etc. Even if it seems that the Nimmos, Freuds, and Williamses are against you, it is only for the pro-gramme that they do it.

Yours, David Hatch

For me, the secret was to allow things to get a little out of hand, and then rein them in before the show was lost entirely. You had the humour of the outrage or rants, maybe even a touch of anarchy, and then I drew the players back into the game. Exactly the same approach applies today, when for instance Paul Merton, Gyles Brandreth, Sue Perkins and Graham Norton are on the panel. When I see the banter is heading in a particularly entertaining direction I let them go ... go ... go ... go, then reel them back.

Every recording is so delicately balanced because it is impossible to predict what will happen. In order for it to succeed you have to grab at every possible nuance to create humour and drama while at the same time ensuring that the game itself does not lose momentum. It may be a cliché, but it is nonetheless true: it is all down to timing. That is a skill you acquire through experience. You intuitively know when you can inject a moment of comedy and when you have to move the show forward.

For instance, none of the panellists can see the stopwatch. So when someone comes in with a correct challenge with only a couple of seconds left I make a big show of it, and the audience always gives a reaction, sometimes dismay, sometimes admiration. It is just one small thing that combines with everything else to create the sense of fun and togetherness that is the core of *Just a Minute*.

The experimentation of rotating the chair produced one further consequence, a sting in the tail to some extent. For me, certainly. When my 'replacements' received their fee they discovered that the amount paid for sitting in the adjudication hot seat was slightly higher than for appearing on the panel (by the handsome amount of no more than £2!). This titillating piece of information proved manna from heaven for the regulars over the next 20 years, with the supposed difference in reimbursement growing larger each year in direct proportion to their indignity. Here's an example from August 1982, just as Kenneth has been challenged on the subject of 'Being Photographed through a Gauze', after having spoken for 52 seconds. Peter Jones, Derek Nimmo and popular writer and comic Victoria Wood also feature.

Nicholas: Peter Jones has challenged.
Peter: Repetition of 'skin'.
Nicholas: Yes, what a pity, you did repeat the 'skin'.

Peter: You think it's a pity that I challenged?? [AUDIENCE LAUGH]

Nicholas: Yes, because I was enjoying it.

Peter: Well, I'm terribly sorry!!! [BIG LAUGH] I mean it's a curious place to come for your enjoyment! I realise you've got peculiar tastes but there you are.

Nicholas: I know, it's such a serious programme, *Just a Minute*.

Peter: You wouldn't be accepting money for it, of course ...

Nicholas: No, no ...

Peter: I hope not, otherwise you're cheating somebody! [BIG LAUGH]

Kenneth: He is accepting money for it, you great fool!! It's a sight more than you're getting! I can tell you that much for nothing!!!

Derek: You know, I always thought it was unfair that he got more than us!

[THE AUDIENCE ARE LOVING THIS EXCHANGE AND LAUGH LOUDLY THROUGHOUT]

Kenneth: *I know!* I think it is disgraceful!! What's so special about 'is job that he should get more money?? I was appalled when I heard! I'm a cult figure!! [HUGE LAUGH] I'm a *cult*! [EVEN BIGGER LAUGH]

Peter: Well, it still needn't be very much! If he's getting more than I'm getting! I can tell you, *I'm not jealous*!

Nicholas: If that is true, it's only because I have to concentrate throughout the programme! You can just concentrate when you want to!

Derek: *You don't concentrate!* [BIG LAUGH]

Then later in the same recording.

Nicholas: Victoria Wood is still in second place and she also begins the next round. And the subject is 'Choosing a Frock to Suit Me'. Will you tell us something about that subject in the game, starting now.

Victoria: Choosing a frock to suit me is a very long drawn-out process. I think it has taken up to now 20 years and I still haven't found one. But I don't mind because I'm carrying on wearing trousers and jumpers and jeans and swimming costumes like I was telling you about before. So I don't really mind too much that I can't *really* find a dress. And I said 'really' twice and nobody seems to be listening so I think I'll just carry on …

BUZZ

Nicholas: Derek Nimmo challenged.

Derek: I thought I'd help her out again.

Victoria: Thank you!

Derek: You know, 'really' twice and 'dress' twice she said as well.

Victoria: I didn't! I said 'frock' once and 'dress' once.

Nicholas: She said 'frock' and then she said 'dress'.

Victoria: I said 'really' twice actually if you want to be absolutely …

Peter: I'm sorry, I should have challenged because I did hear it but I wasn't giving it my attention. I still can't get over this business about you getting more money than we're getting! [HUGE AUDIENCE LAUGH] Baffling! Baffling!

Nicholas: Peter, I will stand you a drink afterwards and that's just about the amount of money …

Peter: No need to flaunt it!

Derek: It's the first time in 15 years, I can tell you! [BIG LAUGH]

By Series 3, which ran for 14 episodes from December 1968 to April 1969, experimentation was over. I was in the chair full time and the panel numbered four. Derek Nimmo returned and joined Kenneth and Clement on every show, accompanied by a female guest, including Geraldine on six occasions and Andree Melly on four. *Just a Minute*'s basic format had been established and would remain pretty much in place for the following 45 years.

There was still work to do, however, to define the rules better and apply them with more consistency. Just look at these examples from the show broadcast on 28 January 1969. Derek Nimmo starts off on the subject 'Striking a Fresh Acquaintance'.

Derek: Well, what I generally do is I prepare my equipment first of all. I tend to favour a Malacca cane. I take it out in the morning, make sure it's nice and flexible. And then I go out into the street. And it's curious, you know, every time you turn a corner, you come across a horribly fresh acquaintance. If they're not fresh, of course, then you can make them fresh by baiting them with various well-chosen remarks. Having got them suitably game, then you take hold of your Malacca cane and *strike* them several times across the face.
    BUZZ
Nicholas: Clement Freud, you challenged, why?
Clement: 'Several times' is repetition! [BIG AUDIENCE LAUGH]
Nicholas: Very clever, Clement! Twenty-nine seconds, starting now.

In the following round, it is Betty Marsden who starts on the subject 'What to Do When You've Ricked Your Back'.

Betty: Well, when you have ricked your back the very thing you *must not* do is attempt to lie down because this makes it very painful. Plus the fact that it is impossible to get in that position. For as one bends over as a human hairpin and the pain shoots from here up to one's head one finds great difficulty in even lifting an arm. Well, here we are then, unable to lie down because the pain is so tremendous, unable to stand up. So the only thing one can do on this occasion is to get kind husband or a friend to undo a *door*, take it off its hinges and leave it in a very, very difficult way but a slight angle, like that ...
    BUZZ
Nicholas: Clement Freud, you challenged.

Clement: An angle is deviation! [AUDIENCE CLAP]
Betty: Oh!
Nicholas: It may be deviation but it is not devious and I think therefore I am justified in giving Betty Marsden another point.

Later in the show, Derek has the subject 'Utopia'.

Derek: It's what I've always been looking for, you know. Every day when I get up in the morning, I always think, 'Will I find Utopia today?' I never do, but I always keep trying, you know. I guess one of the important things in life

    BUZZ

Nicholas: Clement Freud.
Clement: Repetition.
Nicholas: Of what?
Clement: Always keeps trying!
Nicholas: Yes!
Derek: No! It's not repetition, is it? I only said it once!
Nicholas: It wasn't that, it's the implication of the word. If you always keep trying it must be repetitious. It's a very clever challenge, I think it does deserve a point and Clement Freud has gained it and he has 25 seconds left with the subject 'Utopia', starting now.

Some 'clever' challenges are accepted, others not. Consistency would have to wait for the new decade, just around the corner.

Challenge!

Q: Who were the first male and female winners of *Just a Minute?*
A: Derek Nimmo won the pilot show and Lucy Bartlett was the first female winner, on her debut in show eight of the first series, broadcast on 9 February 1968.

Q: Except for Ian Messiter, who is the only male panellist to appear on both *One Minute Please!* and *Just a Minute?*
A: My old friend Richard Murdoch, who appeared in *OMP!* in 1951 and made his first *Just a Minute* appearance in May 1988.

Q: Who was the first female to talk for a full, uninterrupted minute?
A: Actress Aimi MacDonald, in show seven of the first series, broadcast on 2 February 1968, and the subject was 'Your Schooldays'.

Q: Who is the youngest person to appear on *Just a Minute* (excluding *Junior Just a Minute* contestants)?
A: 'My Girl Lollipop' herself, the delightful Millie Small who was 21 years old when she appeared on her only show, broadcast on 27 January 1968.

Q: Which panellist has the longest gap between their first *Just a Minute* appearance and their second?
A: The wonderful actress and *Many a Slip* regular, Eleanor Summerfield, who made her debut on 1 March 1968 and returned for a second and final appearance on 13 June 1987, a span of 19 years.

Gyles Brandreth

Nicholas Parsons has been part of my life for almost 50 years. I first heard him on the radio, hosting *Just a Minute*, on Friday 22 December 1967. I first met him just two years later, on the night of Tuesday 23 December 1969. I was 21 at the time, a student at Oxford University and President of the Oxford Union. I had invited Fanny Cradock, the husky-voiced no-nonsense television chef (Mary Berry with attitude), to be one of the star speakers at my end-of-term debate and, very generously, she had then invited me and my girlfriend to her Christmas party. I can be precise about the date and details because I keep a diary:

Tuesday, 23 December 1969. Michèle and I went to the Dower House, Grove Mill Lane, near Watford, Herts, for Fanny and Johnnie Cradock's Christmas party. It was our first 'showbusiness party': everyone was there – even Lionel Blair. The champagne flowed, Fanny's buffet was amazing (she is a *very* good cook), and at 11 o'clock our hostess clapped her hands and announced that it was 'cabaret time'. Turning to Nicholas Parsons, who was standing right beside her, she declared: 'Nicholas will now entertain you!' He did – with a very funny routine involving a lot of Scottish gobbledygook. He said afterwards that he had no idea that Fanny was going to ask him to perform.

But I reckon she must have known how brilliant he'd be. As well as the Scottish gobbledygook, Nicholas did a routine lampooning Italian and French cinema. It was beautifully observed and completely hilarious. And, amazingly, it still is. I know because, 44 years later, when Nicholas was hosting his 'Happy Hour' at the Edinburgh Festival Fringe I asked him if he remembered the routine – and there and then, in his 90th year, he reprised it instantly. Like Nicholas, it has stood the test of time.

Our paths crossed next in 1971 – at lunchtime on Thursday 24 June to be exact. By then I had a BBC Radio 4 panel game of my own to host. It was a word game based around rhyming. I devised it with the comedian and master of Odd Odes Cyril Fletcher (with a little help from David Hatch, the original producer of *Just a Minute*).

Thursday, 24 June 1971. To the BBC, Portland Place, for the press conference to launch the summer season. Simon Brett (the producer) met me in reception and took me up. It was all rather grand. I moved straight over to Cyril for security. He was wearing his wig and kept reminding everybody of the fact. He introduced me to Kenneth More and Liza Goddard and we chatted. Kenneth More told us about his technique for finding out the names of people whose name he should know but has forgotten. He says, 'It's on the tip of my tongue now, come on, what's your name?' The other party replies, 'Michael' and More comes back, 'No, no, not your Christian name – I know that. What's your surname?' He gave up the technique when he met up with an old RAF chum whose surname was John. (Clearly these theatrical types repeat the same stories *shamelessly*.) We trooped up to the roof garden to have our photographs taken and I was much chuffed to be included in the 'star' line-up: Kenneth More, Liza Goddard, Kenneth Williams (who was genuinely funny in his outrageous way), Liz Gebhardt (whose dark glasses I accidentally walked off with) and Nicholas Parsons ...

This was my first meeting with Kenneth Williams who later became a real chum. He was not part of the original *Just a Minute* line-up, but once he had joined the programme, in September 1968, he became one of its lynch-pins. I became friends with Liza Goddard, too. We appeared together in lots of game shows on radio and TV in the 1970s and 1980s: she blonde, bubbly and brilliant, me wearing colourful knitwear. Liz Gebhardt never appeared on *Just a Minute*, but she should have done. She was very funny and delightful and best known in 1971 as one of the stars of the school sitcom *Please, Sir!*

I am not sure exactly why Liza and Liz and the film star Kenneth More were on the BBC roof that lunchtime, but I know that Nicholas was there to promote his new Radio 4 chat show, *Look Who's Talking*. On 3 September 1971 I was a guest on the show, alongside Paul Raymond, magazine publisher and promoter of sex shows.

Throughout the 1970s I kept appearing on Radio 4 panel games and crossing paths with Nicholas, but without being invited to take part in *Just a Minute*. Nicholas and I met in unlikely places. Once – on 20 May 1975 – at the London Palladium where assorted personalities gathered to encourage people to vote 'Yes' in the forthcoming referendum on Britain's entry into the Common Market. Nicholas turned up looking immaculate. (He always looks immaculate.) Not so Andrew Lloyd Webber. According to my diary, Andrew wore 'an open-necked floral shirt under a crumpled old sports jacket. Grubby trousers, belt with a huge buckle and terrible posture.'

I am not one to talk about poor posture – but I am one to talk. And so is Nicholas. And it was through non-stop talking that our friendship developed. At the time we were both supporters of a charity called Action Research for the Crippled Child and the charity had the bright idea of getting different people to break different records to raise money for the cause.

Monday, 17 May 1976. At the Mayfair Hotel, London, this

evening I established a new world record when I talked non-stop for four hours nineteen minutes and thirty-four seconds. Yehudi Menuhin and Elizabeth Beresford each sent £10, ditto Bob Monkhouse. Terry Jones, Janet Suzman, Sinéad Cusack, William Franklyn and the Marquess of Londonderry each sent £10, too. Bernard Miles sent £2. Nicholas Parsons gave £10.

Nicholas was not just there to lend his support. He was there to size up the competition. Soon he had taken my record from me – talking non-stop for seven hours, eight minutes and thirty-four seconds. Eventually the charity organised a play-off:

Tuesday, 14 February 1978. Last night, at 6.30 p.m., I arrived at the Hyde Park Hotel to make my second attempt on the world record for the longest-ever after-dinner speech. Nicholas and I, in adjacent rooms in the same hotel, vying to see which of us could speak the longer.

My real anxiety had been the matter of going to the loo. I was confident I could talk through the night, but could I survive the night without needing a pee? That was my dilemma – resolved by Action Research who sent me to John, Bell & Croydon to be fitted with a surgical appliance. As JB&C's kindly Mr Park explained, when he produced the extraordinary contraption, 'This isn't just for the incontinent. This is used by generals and field marshals on parade grounds when taking the salute. Wear this and you can stand out in the freezing cold for hours without having to worry about a thing. The Duke of Edinburgh has one. They're invaluable.' Essentially, the device is a lengthy piece of rubber tubing that you attach to your member and then strap to your leg. It has a four-pint capacity and a 'no spillage' guarantee.

All strapped up, ready and willing, a little after 7.30 p.m., Nicholas and I shook hands, smiled for the cameras, bowed to the toastmasters and adjudicators, and moved into our separate dining rooms. We were out of earshot of one another, but the audience could mingle between the rooms. It began well. It continued well. My voice held. I paced it nicely. At about two in the morning I began to feel the need for the loo. I began to think, 'When am I going to do this? What will it feel like? How much is four pints?' The more I thought about it, the more eager I was to pee and the more inhibited I became. The problem, I think, was knowing that I would be peeing *in front of people*. Of course, they wouldn't be able to *see* what was happening, but would they be able to *tell*? And would there be a noise – a terrible swooshing?! I thought I'd 'go for it' at the end of a story, on the punchline – letting it happen 'masked' by laughter or applause ... Anyway, the moment came. I finished the story: there was laughter, a smattering of applause and I said to myself, 'Now – *now*, Gyles – *now*! Let it flow.' Then I looked down and suddenly saw it – a long, thin sausage-skin of pale white rubber tubing snaking its way from my left trouser-leg and slowly moving across the floor. My contraption had shifted its moorings and come adrift. At once (and, oddly, without difficulty) I put the notion of peeing right behind me and forged on with the speech. (Interestingly, it's now 12 hours later: I am writing this at 2.00 p.m. and *still* I haven't been for a pee. Perhaps I never will again?)

But the pee that didn't come in the night was not the worst of it. The worst of it was this. At about 6.00 a.m. one of the Action Research people passed me a note asking, 'How are you doing? Are you ready to stop?' I read it out loud and declared I was just warming up. Another note came, then another. Apparently, Nicholas was still going strong and so was I. The organisers had therefore decided we should both stop, simultaneously, at seven o'clock and share the new world record: 11 hours.

And we did.

We shared the record – and a place together in *The Guinness Book of Records* – until the night of 3/4 April 1982 when my naturally competitive nature (and a different charity) had me reclaim the record for myself, talking non-stop for twelve and a half hours. Nicholas, Derek Nimmo and Kenneth Williams all came along to support me. And by then I had made my first appearance on *Just a Minute*.

Wednesday, 2 December 1981. Went to the BBC Paris Studio in Lower Regent Street at lunch-time to record two editions of *Just a Minute*. Nicholas Parsons said the only reason they hadn't asked me before is that I sound too like Derek Nimmo and they didn't want to 'confuse the listeners'. The truth is I was only there because Kenneth badgered them on my behalf. He is a good friend – and a good son. He arrived for the recording with his mother in tow – he calls her Louie – and installed her in her 'usual seat' in the third row. The other panellists were Peter Jones (wonderfully droll) and Sheila Hancock (sharp and good at the game). Kenneth stole the show (of course) but I acquitted myself reasonably. Indeed, I won the first game, though I know that's not the point. Being funny is the point. (People don't necessarily like you if you win.)

From the start I loved playing *Just a Minute*. I have taken part in scores of panel games on radio and TV over the past 40 years, and even devised a few, but *Just a Minute* is by a long way my favourite. The trouble with most shows – e.g. *Have I Got News for You* and *QI* – is that they record two hours and more and then edit it down to 28 minutes, so when you are doing it somehow it doesn't feel 'real'. It doesn't matter what you say because most of it will be cut anyway. With *Just a Minute*, every word counts – and, of course, by definition, you've got just a minute. The show is recorded in real time. When you listen you don't hear edited highlights: you hear what happened.

That makes it a fun show to listen to and an exciting game to play.

When I play *Just a Minute* I play to win. I can't help myself – even though I know that, sometimes, I should. Clement Freud also always played to win – and usually managed to win, too, by fair means or foul. Clement was the master of coming in with a challenge with just three seconds to go. He was also a master of gamesmanship. More than once, sitting next to him, he'd find a way of distracting me just as I was about to make a challenge. Once, deliberately, he spilled a glass of water onto me just as I was hitting my stride. He was an odd cove, incredibly funny, alarmingly intelligent, but quite difficult to know. Because we shared an interest in politics now and again Clement and I met up to have lunch. He was entertaining company, but not easy company, if you know what I mean. He had certain obsessions – you could not smoke anywhere near him, for example – and he used to pretend that he hated Nicholas. I don't think he hated him at all. I think he may have hated himself a bit. By all accounts he was an excellent constituency MP and he was kind and generous (he remained loyal to his party leader Jeremy Thorpe when Thorpe was charged with conspiracy to murder and he sent my son one of his children's books and a lovely letter from the House of Commons), but I think he may have felt that he had in some way wasted his talents and not realised his potential.

Kenneth Williams used to feel that, too. I worked with Kenneth on all four of his best-selling books – including his autobiography – and he certainly felt that by the end of his life he had painted himself into a corner professionally. He had once been a 'proper actor' – appearing with Laurence Olivier and Orson Welles. By the end he was known for his funny voices, his funny stories, the *Carry Ons* and *Just a Minute*. He told me he had wasted his life 'making a noise that floats up into the air and disappears'. I told him that he had made millions of people very happy. He was so funny. And so brilliant on *Just a Minute*. The show suited his peculiar gifts perfectly: he could mix his amazing erudition (all self-taught) with his amazing voices and his genius as a raconteur. At the end of his life, I reckon that *Just a Minute* was the one thing he still really enjoyed.

The great thing about Derek Nimmo was that he managed to enjoy life completely. He was always lovely to be with because he always seemed so happy to be alive. My wife and I got to know him and his beautiful wife Pat quite well. We both worked with him on the books he wrote and I did a couple of TV series with him, too. Amazingly, Derek would bring his own footman to the studio with him – truly: a fellow in knee britches would come to the green room after the recording and serve Derek proper wine in a proper silver goblet while the rest of us were quaffing warm white plonk from paper cups. Derek was a true bon viveur. He knew his stuff. According to one of my diary entries about an evening with Derek, 'The Château Batailley 1961 really *was* outstanding.' I am not sure where he got his plummy voice and dandified manner from. He hailed from Liverpool and lived in a caravan when he was a young actor. I think he told me that his turned-up silly-ass nose was the result of a nose-job that went wrong. Like Kenneth, he died far too young. On his gravestone he is summed up in four words: 'Actor, wit, life enhancer'. That's exactly what he was. 'The best kind of evening,' he once said to me, 'is the one you spend eating with beautiful people, drinking with beautiful people, and sleeping … with a clear conscience.'

Appearing on *Just a Minute* in the 1980s I had fun and made some good friends – Martin Jarvis, Tim Rice and Barry Cryer among them. In the 1990s I gave up panel games (and woolly jumpers) to concentrate on my political career. It did not last long. I was an MP until the people spoke – the bastards!

In some ways it was a relief to be out of politics. It was certainly good to be back on *Just a Minute*. What surprised me about the show when I returned to it was to find that it was as good as ever – if not better. I had rather assumed that the likes of Kenneth Williams, Derek Nimmo and Peter Jones were irreplaceable. Not so. A whole new generation of funny folk were now playing the game and it was being produced by bright young things who hadn't even been alive when I first tuned in in 1967. There were two constants, of course. One was Ian Messiter's simple format of genius. The other was Nicholas.

Jimmy Edwards was slated as the original chairman for the show. If he had been available, I think the programme would have lasted a couple of years at most. 'Professor' Jimmy Edwards was quite a character: outspoken, rumbustious and a heavy drinker. He would have been entertaining to listen to – he could be very funny – but he would not have been able to control the game as Nicholas does, encouraging newcomers, disciplining the obstreperous, and getting his own laughs while never failing to listen (with incredible care and remarkable accuracy) to everything that everybody says on the show. Let me say without hesitation (and it bears repetition): Nicholas is the true secret of *Just a Minute*'s longevity. I am hoping that both the show and the chairman will prove immortal.

The Seventies

The decade through Just a Minute

Sales

Sales are something I try to avoid because I never seem to get bargains. Last year I went for a winter coat and came out with a silver lamé catsuit that I didn't really need at all. Living on a farm in the middle of Sussex amongst cornfields, I don't quite know when I'm going to wear it.

AIMI MACDONALD
18 NOVEMBER 1974

Crossing the Channel

Last time I went was in a hovercraft. It was like travelling the M1 in a thunderstorm!

DEREK NIMMO
19 JANUARY 1970

Moon dust

What has happened to it? We haven't heard anything in the newspapers, on the radio, or television about this substance which caused so much trouble and expense with the time they took getting it and bringing it back in the capsule. And then it was advertised as being sent to various universities all over the world, studied in laboratories by scientists. And I hoped that there would be some advantage to the human race in all this fuss and kerfuffle that went on. But as far as I am concerned, nothing has happened! The quality of the bread has steadily got worse. It still takes ages to get from Oxfordshire to Piccadilly.

PETER JONES
6 JANUARY 1975

Slang

One of the methods employed by cockneys is to use rhyming slang. 'Up your apples and pears' for stairs. 'Shout and holler' for collar. And so on. 'Farmer Giles' is used, but I will not explain what that means.

KENNETH WILLIAMS
2 NOVEMBER 1971

Profits

Government unfortunately seems to feel that profit is a dirty word. As a result of which they nationalise almost anything which is even remotely profitable, take it into public ownership and by virtue of employing many hundreds and thousands of civil servants, make quite sure that whatever it is accumulates vast losses. As a result of which taxation goes up and the audience for *Just a Minute* doesn't turn up because of the high price of coming in and listening to the rubbish that we have to talk.

CLEMENT FREUD
5 JANUARY 1977

Home movies

You find your husband shouting at you, 'Say something funny for the movie!' Then when it's repeated at home in front of gaping friends you discover that you have, in fact, uttered something totally inane, usually a swearword such as meaning, 'go away, I want to enjoy myself, without having that rotten camera pointing at me every time'.

SHEILA HANCOCK
2 FEBRUARY 1977

Digital watch

Well, the digital watch, like the Venus de Milo, has no hands.

PETER JONES
25 DECEMBER 1979

'They shouldn't have women on the show!'
This often repeated anguished cry from Kenneth Williams was first uttered during a broadcast of 12 October 1971, when the actress Andree Melly challenged Clement Freud for hesitating on the subject of 'Surprises'. Clement had been relating the rather bizarre tale of how he had been surprised when a listener to the show bequeathed him the mineral rights beneath the crown bowling green at Rotherham.

Kenneth was clearly engrossed in Clement's extraordinary story and was outraged when Andree pressed her buzzer.

> **Kenneth:** I was loving it! I was getting quite worked up about that bit! I was enjoying it! You cut us off! Should never have had women on the show! It's all wrong! [BIG LAUGH]

The audience reacted with great delight to the explosive outrage, Kenneth knew he was on to something and a catchphrase was born. From then on Kenneth was more than happy to call on this favourite line whenever the opportunity arose, as in this exchange with Andree in the following week's show as she began speaking on the first subject 'Playing with My Yo-yo'. Peter Jones and Clement Freud are also on the panel.

> **Andree:** My yo-yo is small and golden and furry and I keep it in a little box in the pantry.
>   BUZZ
> **Nicholas:** Kenneth Williams, you've challenged. Why?

Kenneth: Oh, I'm so *bored*!!! Awfully boring! Gold and fur!

Nicholas: Well, obviously you're not a yo-yo …

Kenneth: What a load of rubbish! We know it's all lies! Deviation I say.

Nicholas: Well, I'm sorry. As bored as you may be, Kenneth, you're obviously not a yo-yo fan. I disagree with your challenge so Andree keeps the subject, she gains another point and there are nine seconds, Andree, for 'Playing with My Yo-yo', starting now.

Andree: A charming little hamster, delightful company …

BUZZ

Nicholas: Kenneth Williams, why have you challenged?

Kenneth: First of all we had a description, when she's supposed to be playing with it. And now we're getting hamsters!! What's it got to do with playing with yo-yos? It's deviation and you know it!

Nicholas: All right, she's gone on to hamsters, away from yo-yos …

Andree: But that's its *name*!

Nicholas: What?

Andree: 'Yo-yo'!

Kenneth: The subject is playing with it, not the names of hamsters, dear! [BIG LAUGH]

Nicholas: Actually I do see her point. She was going to tell us …

Kenneth: You may see her point, but I *certainly don't*!! We should never have had women on the show in the first place! Ludicrous!!! [HUGE LAUGH]

Such is the impact of the phrase that later in the same show Clement joins in.

Kenneth: It's that Andree Melly jumping on people before they've even had a chance!

Peter: Yes, quite!

Kenneth: We should never have women …
Clement: We oughtn't to have women on the show!
Peter: It's got nothing to do with being a woman!
Clement: Or men! [BIG LAUGH]

A week later Kenneth was at it again, with Andree once more in the firing line for challenging Kenneth. On this occasion Kenneth chose to add even more hilarity by supplementing his routine with a classic from one of his *Carry On* films.

Kenneth: [SHOUTING AT THE TOP OF HIS VOICE]
How dare you!!!
Nicholas: Sit down!
Kenneth: It's disgraceful!! What behaviour!
Nicholas: Sit down!
Kenneth: We should never have had women on the show!
Nicholas: Her first challenge was an incorrect one because it didn't make sense within the rules of the game …
Kenneth: Yes, it's infamy! It's infamy! Yes!
Nicholas: So you have another point, Kenneth …
Kenneth: She's got it in for me! [HUGE AUDIENCE LAUGH]

All this was great fun, and certainly did not unsettle Andree. She, like everyone else, knew it was merely part of Kenneth's act and did not represent any genuine feelings of antipathy towards women. This was abundantly clear even during the show in which his famous phrase made its first appearance. Having already pronounced his supposed opinion on women panellists, Kenneth then cleverly twisted his own words following an excellent challenge from Andree while Clement spoke on 'Coconuts'.

Clement: Sitting in a pool in Rio de Janeiro the other week, I was amazed to find that coconuts are …
BUZZ
Nicholas: Andree Melly, you've challenged, why?

Andree: He's showing off. [BIG AUDIENCE LAUGH]
Kenneth: 'Course he is! Absolutely! You're absolutely right! I
thought that, Andree! Very good having women on the show,
isn't it! [MORE LAUGHTER, WITH CLEMENT LAUGHING
LOUDEST] Very good! Astute! Intelligent girl!

While he enjoyed comically berating the fairer sex, Kenneth was also
often generous in his praise of female guests. When Geraldine Jones
cleverly won a round with some sharp thinking, for instance, he burst
into effusive congratulations. 'I thought she was really wonderful!
Isn't that wonderful! Yes, and more power to your elbow, darling!'

One female guest with whom Kenneth socialised was the comedy
actress Betty Marsden. They had worked together on the radio
shows *Beyond Our Ken* and *Round the Horne*. Betty was a talented actress
and revue artist, skilled at voices and impersonations (she used to
perform wonderful routines mimicking TV personality and cook
Fanny Cradock), who appeared in four *Just a Minute* shows. The final
one was broadcast on 28 January 1968, during which Kenneth must
have loved Betty's audacity in slipping a touch of Polari into the
show.

Polari is British theatre slang used by the gay community, and
a form of speech Kenneth knew well – he too had utilised it on
radio, during his Julian and Sandy sketches on *Round the Horne*. When
Betty used a couple of Polari words while speaking on the subject of
'Slang', Kenneth would have enjoyed the joke immensely, I have no
doubt.

Betty: You see, and your eeks [faces] are shining and your
lallies [legs] are weak by the time you've pushed down all this
scrumpy. And the whole thing is a language understood only by
deep friends of yours to whom you've written small notes in this
particular language.

No, Kenneth certainly did not have any real issues with women
appearing on *Just a Minute*, although I did sometimes detect a certain

edge to his scathing outbursts when aimed at one female panellist in particular, Aimi MacDonald.

With the return of Derek Nimmo for our third series, a pattern was established which would remain in place up to Series 6, in which three regular male panellists were joined by a female guest.

The majority of women who appeared on *Just a Minute* in those first few series – with the notable exception of Geraldine Jones – were known to Ian Messiter from appearances on one of his other radio shows – the discussion programme *Petticoat Line* and the panel game *Many a Slip*. Some of these performers only joined us for a handful of appearances, but three in particular were to establish long and successful associations with our show – Andree Melly (54 appearances), Sheila Hancock (92 and counting) and Aimi MacDonald (34).

Aimi was a talented and likeable performer who had begun her show business career as a dancer and musical artist. She first came to wide public attention in the satirical television series *At Last the 1948 Show*, which featured a stellar cast of John Cleese, Marty Feldman, Tim Brooke-Taylor and Graham Chapman, with Aimi sending herself up playing the natural dumb blonde to great effect.

With her high-pitched voice, infectious giggle, charm and seeming vulnerability (all of which she had also portrayed during her stints on *Petticoat Line*) Ian was clearly drawn to Aimi as a perfect foil for the combative men on *Just a Minute*. Aimi worked out very well on the show, just being herself, but as she became more of a regular guest during the early 1970s, I believe Kenneth initially found her persona irritating.

Aimi would greatly enjoy flapping and fluffing, mishearing and misunderstanding, which regularly drew laughter and applause from the audience. I am not sure Aimi always understood exactly why. In this example from November 1975 Peter Jones is speaking first on the subject of 'Gorillas'.

Peter: Well, there are various types of gorillas. There's the eye-level griller and the infra-red griller.

BUZZ

Nicholas: Aimi MacDonald has challenged.

Aimi: *We-ll.* I mean. He's talking about an oven. [LAUGHTER FROM AUDIENCE] What does that have to do with a gorilla?

Peter: Oh, well, I'll change the whole tack altogether. There were two gorillas walking along Regent Street. [HUGE LAUGHTER FROM AUDIENCE AND PANEL] And one said to the other, 'It doesn't seem like a Tuesday, does it?' 'No,' replied the other. 'There are not many people about.' [BIG AUDIENCE LAUGH]

Derek Nimmo then challenges Peter and takes the subject over.

Derek: Well, today we can have urban guerrillas, and presumably rural guerrillas as well! They're all over the place, shooting around and causing disturbances, standing outside …

BUZZ

Nicholas: Aimi MacDonald has challenged.

Aimi: That's just not true, is it?

Nicholas: Yes, but he's taken the word 'guerrillas' in the sense of people who fight, underground fighters.

Aimi: Oh, of course! Oh, I'm sorry. [STARTS TO LAUGH]

Nicholas: I know it's spelled differently. G-U-E-R-R- …

Aimi: Oh, yes. Aaah, yes.

Nicholas: … -I-L-L-A-S. But it's pronounced the same and it's the way it's pronounced that you take it.

Aimi: Is it … ? [AIMI CONTINUES LAUGHING AT HER GENUINE CONFUSION, WITH THE AUDIENCE LAUGHING ALONG WITH HER]

During this classic show from March 1976, Clement is speaking on 'Epicureanism', a subject that also confuses Aimi considerably.

Clement: An epicureanism is *in fact* the science, or following if you like, of happiness as opposed to the absence of pain which is what every other philosopher of those days advocated. Now, epicureanism in present-day times is sort of connected with high life, good living and food of great quality, which is *totally* wrong.

    BUZZ

Nicholas: Aimi MacDonald challenged.

Aimi: I thought 'epicureanism' was that thing where they stick pins in you! [HUGE LAUGHTER FROM PANEL AND AUDIENCE]

Kenneth: You're thinking of *Acker Bilk*.

Nicholas: Acupuncture, love!

Clement: [STILL LAUGHING] I think she ought to get it! I do think …

Nicholas: All right. For such a good challenge, for the pleasure it gave the audience and after all, you know, the definition …

Kenneth: She is a great epicurean!

Nicholas: Yes, of course! Where have we got to? Aimi MacDonald has been given the subject by Clement Freud of 'Epicureanism' which she thinks is acupuncture! So four seconds left on 'Epicureanism', starting now.

Aimi: [WITH A GIGGLE] Isn't it silly, I thought it was acupuncture!

[WHISTLE FOLLOWED BY APPLAUSE]

While the audience and listeners certainly found Aimi's approach entertaining, it did sometimes irritate Kenneth. This was especially true when he wanted the show to keep moving forward as a vehicle for either himself or one of the other regulars to demonstrate their skill and intelligence, as these two extracts from the 28 December 1971 programme illustrate. In the first, Aimi has just successfully challenged Peter Jones who had been speaking for 41 seconds. Kenneth is not impressed with my decision and in a stage whisper mutters 'She's well in with him this week, ain't she?' Then Aimi begins to talk on the subject 'How to Win *Just a Minute*'.

Aimi: I really wish I knew! Unfortunately …

> BUZZ
>
> **Nicholas:** Kenneth Williams has challenged, why?
> **Kenneth:** Well, if she doesn't know, shut up! Shut up!!

In the final round of that show, I hand Clement the subject of 'The Horse' to speak on.

> **Clement:** A poet whose name escapes me said, 'I know two things about a horse, and one of them is rather coarse.' There are other makers of verse who have used this quadruped, this equine thing with four legs, to symbolise all that is best in this country. My horse … our horse … my kingdom for the horse. If you said …
>
> BUZZ
>
> **Nicholas:** Aimi MacDonald has challenged. Why?
> **Aimi:** Repetition.
> **Nicholas:** Of what?
> **Aimi:** 'Horse, horse, my kingdom …'
> **Kenneth:** You're *allowed* to!! It's the subject, you silly thing …
> **Nicholas:** All right, Kenneth. You're allowed to repeat the subject on the card, Aimi.
> **Aimi:** Are you? All right.
> **Nicholas:** And the subject is 'The Horse'.
> **Aimi:** Sorry.
> **Nicholas:** No, don't apologise.
> **Kenneth:** *For goodness sake, get on with it, girl!!!*

When he would exclaim on air during episodes featuring Aimi that 'We shouldn't have women on the show', I think what he really meant was that we should not have people like Aimi on the show. By then his catchphrase had been established, but with Aimi, for a period at least, I do not think he was only pitching for the laugh. Here is the first occasion when Kenneth actually says the words in relation to Aimi, from 5 December 1972, after she has challenged him for elongating his words to eat up the seconds.

Aimi: Well, it's sort of cheating really, isn't it? I mean, he's drawing out all these words so that it takes …
Kenneth: Isn't it marvellous?
Aimi: … fewer words to speak a longer time.
Kenneth: *Innit marvellous!!*
Peter: Yes, and he does it every week, you know!
Kenneth: [IMPERSONATING AIMI] She can hardly talk herself!
Nicholas: Kenneth …
Peter: But Aimi doesn't come in here very often!
Kenneth: I don't care if she comes here often, or *if she comes here at all*!!!
Nicholas: Kenneth! We'll send you back to King's Cross.
Clement: [DEADPAN, ECHOING KENNETH'S FAMOUS PHRASE] I think it's a mistake having women on the programme.
Kenneth: We should never have had women on this programme!!! Never! Never! [AUDIENCE LAUGH LOUDLY AT KENNETH'S ANTICS]

Aimi dealt with Kenneth's verbal onslaughts in a very professional manner, perhaps not always realising there could be an edge to some of what was being said. She viewed these moments of highly vocal antipathy as an opportunity to use her intuitive comic skills to generate laughs, just by being herself and acting either sweetly innocent or kind and generous. Here she is in a broadcast from 28 December 1971, speaking on 'How to Influence People'.

Aimi: If I wanted to influence Kenneth I would play *Just a Minute* with him, without buzzing him for anything like hesitation, deviation or repetition. And I would let him ramble on to his heart's content, talking about anything and everything from doing his nut to the King of Siam. And he'd be very, very pleased with me.

Four years later, in November 1975, the subject of 'Putting on Your Tights' offers Aimi plenty of opportunities to counter Kenneth's rude comments. Kenneth is talking with 46 seconds on the clock, again stretching out his words to fill in the remaining time.

Kenneth: While playing in eighteenth-century costume, this has *frequently* happened to me. And I found a favourite device was to sprinkle *talcum* inside the stocking before I actually *peeled* it, so to speak, over a *very* shapely foot and a *lovely*, almost velvet-like ankle. And spectators passing the dressing room were wont to *pause*, quiver with excitement and say …
BUZZ
Kenneth: … 'Oooh! What a beautiful pair o' legs!' Who's interrupting me???
Nicholas: Aimi MacDonald.
Aimi: Me!
Kenneth: Oh, it would be her, wouldn't it? I don't know why they have women on this show, I really don't! I mean, it's a man's game, isn't it, Peter?
Peter: Not the way you're playing it! [BIG AUDIENCE LAUGH]
Nicholas: [I AM STRUGGLING TO SPEAK THROUGH THE LAUGHTER, WHILE AIMI GIGGLES IN THE BACKGROUND] Aimi, why did you challenge?
Peter: All this business about tights.
Kenneth: What's she on about? What's her challenge???
Aimi: Because you've got a very high opinion of yourself. I don't think you've got shapely legs.
Kenneth: That is your challenge, is it?
Aimi: Yes. Deviation.

Kenneth retains the subject on this occasion, after I put it to the audience to judge whether Kenneth does indeed have shapely legs, but Aimi wins it back a little later, with two seconds remaining. Kenneth is not pleased.

Kenneth: [RANTING IN OVER-THE-TOP MANNER] Two seconds?? *That's disgraceful!!!* That's just giving her this subject which I worked on like ... I mean, I've worked, haven't I? I've *worked!* *You've seen me work!* The sweat's *pouring* off me, and now with two seconds you're going to give it to that numbskull over there?
Aimi: [LAUGHING]: Oh, shall I give it to him?
Derek: We don't want it to be said that he plays to the gallery!
Nicholas: No, no.
Aimi: I thought that was a beautiful piece of comedy business, that. Shall I give it to him? [THE AUDIENCE ARE NOW IN HYSTERICS AND I DECIDE TO LET KENNETH FINISH OFF THE ROUND HIMSELF]

Aimi resolutely did not take anything Kenneth said personally even though he continued to fire shots in her direction into the mid 1970s, such as this moment when Aimi challenges correctly and then admits that she did not really want the subject: 'Ah, well you got it, dearie!!! Yes, she didn't want it! See, she's been asking for it all night and now you've got it, right in the mush!' Then later and in the same show: 'I wish they'd get rid of that female impersonator over there, I really do!' Around the time of these outbursts, however, it was clear that Kenneth had changed his opinion and had begun to appreciate just how much Aimi brought to the shows. I believe he even grew to respect her and such 'insults' no longer contained their previous edge.

Here is an example during an exchange in a March 1976 show, with Clement Freud speaking first (as a French croupier) on 'Roulette'.

Clement: '*Faites vos jeux*' and '*rien ne va plus*' are the most ...
BUZZ
Nicholas: Aimi MacDonald!
Aimi: Do they only say that when they're doing the *chemin*?
Nicholas: No, they don't! [KENNETH CACKLING LOUDLY IN THE BACKGROUND]

Kenneth: She's quite right! She's absolutely right!!!
Nicholas: They say that when they're playing roulette!
Kenneth: She's been to these places! You don't know anything about it! [BIG AUDIENCE LAUGH]

While Kenneth and Aimi certainly entertained the listeners with their sparring, the heavyweight bouts in the 'Battle of the Sexes' took place between Kenneth and his great friend Sheila Hancock.

Sheila and Kenneth knew each other well, having worked together in the theatre and revue before *Just a Minute*. Sheila tells a lovely story of when she used to give Kenneth a lift back to his lodgings on her moped. As she drove through the London streets, with Kenny sitting behind her, he would be shouting out outrageous remarks to pedestrians as they flew by. A wonderful image of the fun and freedom of the 1960s.

They both had respect for each other's talent, and in turn respect for each other as people. That is the reason, I believe, that their barracking of each other proved to be so entertaining – they liked each other and they both knew they were putting on a performance. Nevertheless, Sheila clearly felt it important to stand her ground when confronted by theatrical 'chauvinism'.

The first sign that Sheila and Kenneth's 'rivalry' would become a feature of *Just a Minute* for many years occurred during Sheila's fifth appearance, in December 1969. Here is Sheila talking on the subject of 'Waffles'.

Sheila: This is something at which this team is expert, waffles. It is a way of talking to fill in time which is a load of rubbish and at which Kenneth Williams is particularly adept.
      BUZZ
Nicholas: Kenneth Williams has challenged.
Kenneth: Deviation! Have I got to sit here and be told I talk a load of rubbish? [BIG LAUGH] One of the greatest *illumina* ...

Oh, I mean, no …

Nicholas: So why are you challenging?

Kenneth: Because it's a disgrace! Deviation!

Nicholas: No, no, I'm sorry. She wasn't deviating from the subject, is the way I see it. Because she can interpret …

Sheila: [REFERRING TO AN EARLIER ROUND] You passed your opinion on General Mao, I'm passing my opinion on you!

Kenneth: You're extremely rude! You want to shut your cake hole!

Sheila: There you are!

Kenneth: I think that was extremely rude! I don't have to come here to be insulted!

Sheila: You could be insulted anywhere!

Kenneth: *Y-eees!*

As we approach the last round, Kenneth asks me whether he is in the lead. He is not.

Kenneth: How many *marks* have I got then?

Nicholas: You've got four and so has Sheila Hancock.

Kenneth: Aaah! Who's winning?

Nicholas: Derek Nimmo's still winning. Clement Freud's in second place. And actually if Sheila hadn't been helped by the audience, you would have won.

Kenneth: That's true! *Yesss!* She's a *conniver*!

From then on, the good-natured verbal jousts between the two became a much-loved element of our show, possibly because it was clear to all that they held each other in considerable affection. Kenneth, for instance, was genuinely pleased in January 1970 when Sheila spoke for a full minute on the subject of 'Saving Money'. 'Brilliant! Brilliant!' he exclaimed when Ian blew his whistle. 'Oh, good for you, girl! She's gorgeous!'

Sheila and Kenneth's popularity had not escaped the notice of Ian Messiter who regularly chose subjects specifically in the hope that they would ignite the fireworks. He was seldom disappointed. In this broadcast from 22 February 1972, Ian first introduces the subject 'Qualities That Make up the Ideal Woman'.

Sheila: Well, I think she should be about five foot eight tall, have nut brown hair and be ...
BUZZ
Nicholas: Kenneth Williams has challenged, why?
Kenneth: Deviation, the subject is woman, ideal woman.
Nicholas: Yes, what about it?
Kenneth: Well, obvious deviation, she's no objectivity about it at all!
Nicholas: She can still talk about what qualities she thinks would make up the ideal woman. She's a woman, she's entitled to an opinion.
Kenneth: [SCREAMING] *How can a woman have any objectivity about that subject!!* It's obvious, the whole thing should be handled by a man! You'd better give it to me. I'll discuss it!
Nicholas: You'll be saying in a minute we shouldn't have women on the programme again.
Kenneth: Yes! There shouldn't be women on this show! It's a disgrace!!! Quite right! It's doing half the blokes out of work, isn't it! Out of a job! We could all do with the money! [BIG AUDIENCE LAUGH]

Kenneth eventually wins the round and I then hand Ian's follow-up subject to Sheila, 'Qualities That Make up the Ideal Man'.

Sheila: Well, it wouldn't be any of this lot, I can tell you that! I think the qualities that would make up an ideal man are exactly the same as those that make up a woman. Because I don't think one should differentiate between the sexes. Humanity, compassion ...
BUZZ
Nicholas: Kenneth Williams has challenged, why?

Kenneth: Well, deviation, you have to differentiate between the sexes! I mean … goodness gracious me! They both look very different, dear! Haven't you noticed? [BIG LAUGH]

Sheila: I was talking about the qualities that go to make up the *ideal* one!

Nicholas: Actually she was not, in saying it, deviating from the subject on the card. So she has a point and she has 44 seconds left, starting now.

Sheila: Intelligence, forbearance, a sense of humour, looking after your looks, but if you're not pretty it really doesn't matter …

BUZZ

Nicholas: Kenneth Williams has challenged.

Kenneth: This is obviously all about me! And I think … [HUGE LAUGHTER FROM SHEILA AND AUDIENCE] … it's quite wrong … it's quite wrong, you know, to draw attention to me in this way!!!

Sheila: He's obviously dying to tell us about his ideal man! So … [MORE AUDIENCE LAUGHTER]

Kenneth: [SOUNDING QUITE DISTRESSED] Oh no! Oh no! No, no! [KENNETH DOES TAKE THE SUBJECT, HOWEVER RELUCTANTLY, AND CLEVERLY DIVERTS ATTENTION AWAY FROM ANY PERSONAL MATTERS BY DISCUSSING MAHATMA GANDHI]

In February 1976, Ian's chosen subject which he hopes will spark off proceedings is 'Sex Equality'. Sheila starts, and after an initial challenge from Kenneth for deviation ('I don't know what all this claptrap is about'), she has 20 seconds remaining to talk on the subject.

Sheila: In fact it is a terrible subject on which to talk for a short time because it is so deep and you can only skim the surface. However, I would think, though I will get lots of letters to the contrary, that there shouldn't be anybody in the world who objects to equal opportunity for women with men. Whether they choose to work or stay at home is their own choice but I want my daughter ...

[WHISTLE]

Kenneth: Load of rubbish! *What a load of rubbish!* Load of propaganda! *Propaganda and rubbish!*

Nicholas: No, I'm sure we all heartily endorse ...

Kenneth: Of course we don't! They can't do loads of things half as well as we do! Can you imagine a woman in a boxing ring doing what Muhammad Ali does? [BIG AUDIENCE LAUGH]

Having seen it work once, two years later Ian reintroduces the same subject in a broadcast from February 1978.

Sheila: Oh dear! I shall get done for this! Oh God! This will give Kenneth an opportunity to insult me! ... I consider myself to be very privileged to be alive today where we have made so much progress in the equality of the sexes. And because of that reason, I'm happy to have two daughters. A more exciting period to be alive there couldn't be! Because I think one of the most hopeful things for the future of mankind is that everybody should be equal. And that women's ...

BUZZ

Nicholas: Kenneth Williams?

Sheila: [ANTICIPATING WHAT IS COMING] Here we go! Here we go!

Kenneth: Deviation, I mean! *Deviation!!* It's patently obvious to anyone that could look around any street where they are standing or any house where they are sitting that everybody is not equal! So to talk about everybody being so is absolute rubbish! I mean it's a logical impossibility!

Nicholas: Kenneth has got a legitimate challenge within the context of the game. So I have to give him a point and ask him to take over the subject ...

Kenneth: Quite right! Quite right!

Nicholas: ... of 'Sex Equality' with 37 seconds left, starting now.

Kenneth: In fact my taking over the subject demonstrates the obvious superiority of the males ...

BUZZ

Nicholas: Sheila Hancock has challenged.

Sheila: Not at all! It demonstrates that you are a sneaky, nasty, ill-mannered little man!

Kenneth: *This girl is mad about me!* Seriously! Things have gone on between us in dressing rooms that would embarrass you to hear! [AUDIENCE LAUGHTER AND APPLAUSE]

Ian then closes that show with the subject 'Sporting Women', on which Sheila is speaking right at the end.

Sheila: Any woman that agrees to appear on this panel of *Just a Minute* has to be pretty sporting to put up with the insults and vilification and pinching of bottoms that goes on ...

[WHISTLE AND APPLAUSE]

On occasions Kenneth could appear to have gone too far, making personal remarks about Sheila's appearance, as in this broadcast from 11 April 1978. Sheila had recently been to her hairdresser and had a fashionable perm. Kenneth was not impressed. Sheila, of course, took all of Kenneth's mocking taunts in the light-hearted manner they were intended. The subject is 'How to Stop Hiccups' and Kenneth is speaking.

Kenneth: I went to this doctor and he *shoved* a great load of stuff down my earhole and pulled out all this wax and said, 'That's what's making you hiccup.' I said, 'I'd never have *dreamed*! I thought it was an obfu ... obfuscation ...'

BUZZ

Nicholas: Sheila Hancock challenged.

Sheila: [LAUGHING] Hesitation.

Kenneth: Well, I was trying to say 'obfuscation'.

Sheila: Yes, it did have something to do with that.

Kenneth: *You would pick on me, wouldn't you!* [SHEILA LAUGHING IN THE BACKGROUND] She won't let me get any marks, you've noticed that? She just picks on people.

Nicholas: Oh, I don't know …

Kenneth: She's determined to win! It's her vaulting ambition. Overleaps itself, isn't it! Have you noticed that with her!

Sheila: Yes …

Nicholas: There are 24 seconds for Sheila Hancock, 'How to Stop Hiccups'.

Kenneth: Is that a wig she's got on? [BIG AUDIENCE LAUGH]

Sheila: [IGNORING KENNETH'S REMARK] The best thing is to put your head down between your knees and drink out of the back of a glass. Or let somebody give you …

BUZZ

Nicholas: Kenneth Williams …

Kenneth: I'm not having this kind of rubbishy advice given to people listening to the radio. Put your head between your legs and drink out the back of a glass! I mean, you'd have to be a contortionist, quite apart from the fact you'd end up very, very ill!

Sheila: Do you want me to do it?

Kenneth: You'd probably ruin your spinal column, I should think!

Sheila: I'll show you, I'll show you …

Kenneth: *Oh, shut your row!* You don't know what you're talking about!

Nicholas: [TRYING TO REIN KENNETH IN] Kenneth …

Kenneth: Silly great twerp!

Nicholas: Kenneth …

Kenneth: Sitting there with that awful wig on! [SHEILA LAUGHING IN BACKGROUND] Isn't it terrible! She must have had all her hair cut off, I suppose.

Nicholas: Kenneth! You only play into their hands if you start going off like that. Sheila's winning hands down in this battle of the sexes between you and her. [I WAS CORRECT, AT THE END OF THE GAME SHEILA BEAT KENNETH BY QUITE A FEW POINTS]

Sheila's ongoing 'clashes' with Kenneth offer ample proof of her competitive nature, a trait she inherited from her father as she explained during a broadcast in February 1980 when speaking on the subject of 'Winning'.

Sheila: I have a deep instinct to want to win. I think it was ingrained in me by my father, who when I used to come home from school and say I was second in an exam, would always say, 'Who was first?' And I then decided that that was the thing you should be. But I now believe that that is a stupid way to face life.

I am sure Sheila did feel that always having to come first is a 'stupid way to face life', but in *Just a Minute* terms, her will to compete rarely dimmed. In this example from March 1978 Sheila is talking determinedly on the 'Deadliest of the Seven Sins'.

Sheila: Because I think that wanting things that are not your own has probably been the downfall of our civilisation!
Kenneth: Hear, hear! What a true point!
Sheila: We are geared …
Kenneth: Hear, hear! Very well said!
Sheila: … towards always wanting things we can see.
Kenneth: Hear, hear!
Sheila: I'm keeping going, you notice, I'm not hesitating despite Kenneth Williams' avarice of wanting to get the point from me!

A couple of years later, in February 1980, she uses the peculiar subject of 'How to Encourage Salmonella' as a rallying cry to demonstrate her competitiveness.

Sheila: Well, I would say, 'Salmonella, pull yourself together. Go on, girl, you can do it! I believe in you, Salmonella, there's nothing you can't do if you attempt it. The world's your oyster, Salmonella. I am encouraging you to succeed, to win against Derek Nimmo and Peter Jones and Kenneth Williams, Salmonella, because I believe in you!' [AUDIENCE LAUGH AND APPLAUD]

In the early 1980s Sheila's appearances on *Just a Minute* grew less frequent, mainly because she was so busy with other acting work, but also partly, I suspect, because she had grown a little tired of the squabbles between Kenneth, Clement and Derek. Sheila is highly intelligent and offered much more to the show than merely to spark a reaction in Kenneth. Her contributions were always entertaining and interesting and when the other three were too busy arguing amongst themselves to allow the game to flow, she would say things like, 'Oh God, the boys are at it again', and scold them like naughty schoolchildren.

Sheila would want to get on with the game but when that proved almost impossible, some frustration crept in. Not, I am happy to say, to the point that she abandoned *Just a Minute* altogether. Far from it. Over recent years she has clearly enjoyed her appearances very much.

Sheila has revealed a considerable amount about herself on the show, although how much she has been deviating from the truth is impossible to gauge. Glimpses of her childhood have made for fascinating listening, such as when she told us about 'Finding a Caterpillar in My Salad' on 8 February 1972.

Sheila: Well, actually this reminds me of an absolutely traumatic experience in my childhood. I had school dinners, and one day I really did find a caterpillar in my salad. And being a very shy child, I hardly dared mention it. And I nibbled a bit of it, trying to disguise the fact that it was there, but it made me feel so sick that eventually I did attract the attention of my teacher and say, 'There is a caterpillar in my salad.' Whereupon she didn't believe me and said, 'You will stay there until you have finished that salad.' And I honestly had to sit there for the entire lunch hour and eat the salad, caterpillar and all.

On one memorable occasion in a March 1985 broadcast Sheila also provided the *Just a Minute* audience with an unwitting snapshot of her life with husband John Thaw of *The Sweeney* and soon-to-be *Inspector Morse* fame. The subject is 'Beaujolais'.

Sheila: Presumably what Ian means in the district from which this wine comes, of which there are many different areas that I don't know the name of. Beaujolais is a lovely red wine which actually gives me a migraine so I don't have it very often. But my old man likes a drop of the Beaujolais, mind you he likes a bit …
   BUZZ
[MUCH LAUGHTER FROM PANEL AND AUDIENCE]
Nicholas: Clement?
Derek: Oh really! How rude!
Sheila: You will cut that! You will cut it, won't you? You will cut that! Or when it's going out I'll have to make sure he's not listening!
Nicholas: Don't you know that nothing's ever edited out of *Just a Minute*?
Sheila: I know! I shall have to keep him occupied!

Just a Minute has enjoyed a long relationship with Sheila; in fact no other panellist comes near to the length of Sheila's connection with the show. She made her debut in our second ever broadcast (29 December 1967) and in January 2014 made a very welcome appearance for two recordings of the new series.

She remains as sharp, competitive and entertaining as ever. Having missed all of the two previous series as a result of her commitments in the theatre, Sheila made an immediate impact on her return. Given the very first subject she spoke uninterrupted in an interesting and amusing manner for the whole minute, receiving heartfelt and well-deserved applause. Quite brilliant.

...on the subject of *An Eccentric Astronomer*

Every player of *Just a Minute* brings his or her own unique style and approach to the game. It is this variety that contributes to the ongoing success of the show. Over the years, however, there have been three guests who stand out because of their particularly wonderful idiosyncrasies.

Patrick Moore was a household name in the UK when he made his debut in October 1975. First and foremost, Patrick was a highly regarded astronomer who since 1957 had brought the solar system into our living rooms each month with his programme *The Sky at Night*. Sporting a monocle and a light-ning-fast presenting style, Patrick soon became a personality beyond the sphere of stars and planets. Famous also for play-ing the xylophone, he made numerous television appearances on programmes such as *Morecambe and Wise*, *Parkinson*, *This is Your Life* and *The Goodies*. Patrick was also a regular on Ian Messiter's radio quiz *Fair Deal*.

In all of his 11 *Just a Minute* appearances, between 1975 and 1980, Patrick was brimming with knowledge and had a rocket-propelled delivery that often reduced his fellow panellists and myself to fits of laughter.

Over the years Ian introduced a number of specially cho-sen subjects for Patrick, including 'Is There a Copy of This Universe', 'Flying Saucers', 'Absolute Gravity' and in recogni-tion of the fact he had composed an opera score, 'Wagner' and 'Writing an Opera'. Perhaps the strangest of these sub-jects was unveiled in Patrick's debut, resulting in a great deal of laughter and a very funny closing line from Patrick himself.

The subject is 'Speaking Venusian' and alongside Patrick

are Kenneth Williams, Peter Jones and Clement Freud. Patrick begins 'speaking'.

Patrick: Speaking Venusian is of course talking the language of the planet Venus where the people are very advanced. When they go up to each other, to give a morning greeting, they do not say, 'Hail fellow, well met,' as we probably would. They say … [AT THIS POINT PATRICK PRODUCES A STREAM OF GIBBERISH WITH NO DISCERNIBLE WORDS]
BUZZ
Nicholas: You've been challenged, you've been challenged by all three of them in succession.
Kenneth: That's not true, I haven't pressed anything.
Nicholas: No, it's about time you did, that's all I can say.
Kenneth: I'm just sitting here absolutely fascinated. I loved it! I didn't want it to stop. Who stopped it anyway?
Nicholas: Clement Freud was the first to press his buzzer. Your challenge, Clement?
Clement: Repetition of [COPIES PATRICK'S GIBBERISH] [AUDIENCE LAUGHTER]
Kenneth: That's nonsense, that's nonsense!
Patrick: I didn't say. [PRODUCES A VERY STRANGE NOISE] I said [A SLIGHTLY DIFFERENT STRANGE NOISE. AUDIENCE AGAIN BURST OUT LAUGHING].

Clement then takes the bizarre subject and manages to talk for almost 30 seconds before losing it. Eventually Kenneth has it, with three and a half seconds to go. He starts off trying to explain when he heard Venusian being spoken.

Kenneth: Well, of course this was done in that remarkable fashion …
BUZZ
Nicholas: Patrick Moore.
Patrick: It was not done, it has never been done!

Kenneth: I was going to say it's been done in a remarkable fashion by you! That's what I was going to say!

Patrick: Oh, but if you only knew it. I wasn't speaking Venusian at all, I was speaking Martian! [HUGE AUDIENCE LAUGH]

Patrick's skill at the game resulted in him achieving a rare three-point uninterrupted 'minute' when talking on the non-scientific subject of 'Popular Misconceptions' in April 1978. His reinterpretation is brilliant and results in what I regard as a classic moment in the show's history. Patrick is sportingly allowed to continue by his fellow panellists because of the comedy he is creating, with Ian Messiter interjecting at the end.

Patrick: I knew a Spaniard once. A very nice chap. He lived in Barcelona. His name was *Concepcion*. Which of course, if you like, you can pronounce 'Conception'. He had three daughters. They were extremely pretty and they were known as the Popular Miss Concepcions! [BIG AUDIENCE LAUGH] Now all these had different views on life. The first of them went over to – so far as I can remember – to somewhere in the North American continent and became an expert pilot. She was flying over the North Pole of the world and therefore she did establish that the Earth is not in fact flat. There are some people who believe that our planet [PATRICK'S PACE PICKS UP DRAMATICALLY] upon which we live and where we spend *all our lives* is in fact … shaped like a gramophone record with the central point in the middle – naturally, it couldn't be anywhere else [BIG LAUGH] – and probably a wall of ice all around! [LAUGH] Now Miss Concepcion successfully managed to disprove this theory! [BIG LAUGH] Her second sister who was also a Miss Concepcion – also highly attractive, I may say – and she did not take up a career in the air force! She became a naval navigator. She could hardly become anything else of course! [LAUGH] When one has two both entirely different characters in the same family – and this very often happens! – then quite clearly one must follow a different career. And she proceeded to do so! [LOUD LAUGHTER THROUGHOUT AS PATRICK BEGINS TALKING EVEN FASTER] On the third occasion, the third Miss Concepcion, whose name unfortunately was Ermintrude! Now this was a handicap to her throughout her life. If you have a name like that, what can you do? One is bound to be inhibited and she was terribly inhibited and I'm very much afraid …

[WHISTLE AND TUMULTUOUS AUDIENCE APPLAUSE, CHEERS AND LAUGHTER]

Nicholas: I'm sorry, Ian Messiter couldn't find his whistle! You actually kept going Patrick for a minute and a half. [BIG LAUGH]

Patrick: Do I earn two points then?

Nicholas: You get two points, yes. One for not being interrupted and one for speaking when the whistle should have gone.

Ian: And a third point because I didn't blow it.

[APPLAUSE]

The contrast between Aimi and Patrick – 'the dumb blonde and the scientist' – was played up by the two of them to produce several very entertaining moments over the five programmes in which they both appeared. They enjoyed a warm relationship that transmitted itself to audiences and listeners. Kenneth Williams by this stage has begun to see what Aimi brings to the show and is certainly enjoying appearing with her on this broadcast from 13 March 1979. The fun created by the three of them, plus Peter Jones, is an excellent illustration of how important it is to have a varied panel with strong chemistry.

The first subject is 'Foolishness' and Aimi is speaking. Since the beginning of the show, Kenneth has been so unusually quiet that the listeners may have forgotten he was there. That does not last for long.

Aimi: Well, I mean foolishness is so *silly*! I mean one has to be *sensible* about life! It's so ridiculous to go through the whole shebang being absolutely uncontrollably impeccably stupid. It's much better to be irr-irrecably … aahh [BIG LAUGH]
    BUZZ
Nicholas: Patrick Moore has challenged.
Patrick: Hesitation.
Aimi: I nearly said it, I was trying to say irri … irri … irrevocably?
Patrick: [ENJOYING AIMI'S STUMBLE] I appreciate what you were trying to say, but you hesitated in d-d-d-d-doing so.
Nicholas: Yes, she not only hesitated, I think she deviated from correct English. But anyway, Patrick …
Peter: And I didn't think it was all that interesting either! [AUDIENCE BURST OUT LAUGHING AT REFERENCE TO AN EARLIER COMMENT FROM AIMI IN WHICH SHE SAID PETER WAS BEING BORING]
Nicholas: Patrick, you have a point for a correct challenge and you take over the subject of 'Foolishness' and there are 29 seconds left, starting now.
Patrick: Foolishness is indeed the characteristic of civilisation going back to ancient times. Consider for one moment if you will the ancient Athenians …
    BUZZ
Nicholas: Aimi MacDonald.
Aimi: Ah … two things.
Nicholas: Two 'ancients'. Not two 'things'.
Aimi: Two 'ancients'. Yes, quite.
Nicholas: Aimi you have the subject back with a point for a correct challenge and 21 seconds left, starting now.
Aimi: I think foolishness can be actually quite fun at times! I

mean Kenneth Williams would not understand that because he's always so incredibly …

BUZZ

Nicholas: Peter Jones has challenged.

Peter: I'm very glad you mentioned Kenneth Williams because the audience probably at home don't realise that he's with us! [BIG AUDIENCE LAUGH AND APPLAUSE]

Nicholas: Thank you very much for pointing that out.

Kenneth: I don't need you. I can talk for myself! You talk about me as if I'm some mute idiot! [BIG LAUGH]

Peter: No, no. We were just trying to coax you out of your shell! [AIMI STARTS TO GIGGLE]

Kenneth: Oooh. I was fascinated by that woman there! I'm fascinated by her! I think they should have more women on this show! [HUGE AUDIENCE LAUGH] … Give 'em enough rope they hang themselves!

Later in the show I ask Patrick to speak on the apt subject of 'The Curvature of Space'.

Patrick: Space can in fact be curved. If you look at space anywhere in this world, or outside it for that matter, you will find it is by no means straight. And by this I mean linear, non-curvature, the Einstein-Riemannian complex, as described way back in the year 1924, not by either of these gentlemen whom I didn't in fact meet, but by another whose name was Lobachevsky. He was naturally a Russian, he could hardly be anything else with a name like that. And could he be anything except a member of the …

BUZZ

Nicholas: Aimi MacDonald.

Aimi: I didn't want to stop you, darling, because you were so *beautiful* but you said 'anything' twice.

Nicholas: Yes, he did, you were listening very well, Aimi, and there are 33 seconds … for … 'The Curvature of

Space'. [AS I SPEAK AIMI IS PULLING A FUNNY FACE, CONVEYING SHE DOES NOT WANT THE SUBJECT. I CANNOT HELP LAUGHING AT THE THOUGHT OF WHAT SHE MIGHT SAY, AS DOES THE AUDIENCE AND PANEL, INCLUDING AIMI]

Kenneth: She walks right into it, don't she? [HUGE LAUGH AND APPLAUSE]

Eccentric characters with idiosyncratic approaches to the game often provide excellent ammunition for regular players to fire off witty comments. Patrick Moore, with his high-speed expositions on matters astronomical, certainly falls into that category. Here are just a handful of examples on which to finish.

Patrick has challenged Peter for hesitation, when there really was none: 'Anybody who speaks normally he thinks is hesitating, you see!'

Clement's challenge for deviation against Patrick: 'He's not going as quickly as normal.'

Peter on the contrast between Patrick and Clement's styles of delivery: 'Is Patrick under the impression that he's being paid by the word!'

Peter again after Patrick has 'complained' that he has been prevented from being able to explain 'the wild duck star cluster' because of challenges: 'Is this show the proper vehicle for you, I ask myself??'

By a large majority, the female panellists who appeared on *Just a Minute* during the 1970s were a match for the male regulars sitting alongside them, each guest bringing with her a unique style and approach to combat the idiosyncrasies and competitive tricks of the other three. One guest in particular during that period stands out in my memory for the manner in which she took the 'fight' directly to the boys.

It was a brilliant idea of David Hatch to invite Labour MP Barbara Castle on to the show in 1971. At the time she was shadow secretary of state for employment, and when in power during the previous year she had been responsible for putting the Equal Pay Act through parliament, following her involvement in the Ford Dagenham strike in 1968 over the unfair treatment of the machinists.

Barbara was a passionate advocate of women's rights and she revelled in the opportunity of making her views clear when faced with Kenneth, Derek and Clement. This combustible mix made for a highly entertaining programme, with the right honourable member for Blackburn emerging marginally on top. Here Barbara is talking on the subject 'Parties I Enjoy'.

Barbara: Well, there are two parties I enjoy. One is a Labour one and the other are the … ah … entertainments that I give at home. I always enjoy my own more than anybody else's partly because my food is better and also because I can control who I invite and therefore I can keep out bores and also loudmouths.

BUZZ

Nicholas: Kenneth Williams has challenged.

Kenneth: Well, she's being insulting about the guests she's inviting. [BARBARA STARTS LAUGHING] She said she can control her guests which is a disgrace because it infers her guests are uncontrollable. *It's disgraceful!*

Nicholas: Kenneth! You can have a party, insult your guests and do what you like as long as you don't deviate from the subject, 'Parties I Enjoy'. For some reason Barbara Castle might enjoy having parties and then insulting her guests. It is a very strange idea but in this game, you've got to keep going, and whatever you say, provided it doesn't deviate from the subject, is legitimate. So, Barbara, the challenge is not accepted.

Barbara: Thank you! Thank you! I'm glad there's some justice in this situation! I wasn't talking about my guests, I was talking about the people I hadn't invited.

Kenneth: *Oooh!*

Barbara: As a matter of fact I was making an oblique reference to you! [BIG LAUGH FROM PANEL AND AUDIENCE APPLAUD]

Later, Barbara again has the measure of Kenneth.

Nicholas: Kenneth, the subject is 'Chance'. You've gone all miserable. Can you talk to us about 'Chance', 60 seconds, starting now.
Kenneth: [ELONGATING HIS WORDS] Well, of course Shakespeare uses this word quite *bea-uu-utifully* when he *sa-a-a-ys* … the sun …
    BUZZ [FOLLOWED BY LOUD LAUGHTER FROM CLEMENT]
Nicholas: Barbara Castle has challenged you.
Barbara: Hesitation! Shakespeare could have written a sonnet between his words then! [HUGE LAUGH AND APPLAUSE]

Barbara's keen sense of fair play and equality is evident here, after she is correctly challenged by Clement for repeating the word 'box' which she originally mentioned when talking at the beginning of the round. The subject is 'Misunderstood' and an atmosphere of fun and teasing permeates the entire exchange.

Barbara: Well, I'm always misunderstood physically. People say to me, 'Well, when I've seen you on the box, I've always thought you were very small … '
    BUZZ
Nicholas: Clement Freud, why have you challenged?
Clement: It's the next repetition of 'box'. You remember …
Nicholas: To be perfectly fair you did start off by saying at the very beginning …
Barbara: You don't start again then?
Nicholas: No, no.
Barbara: Ah! Well, how am I to know? These fellers can pull all

the tricks they like!

Clement: Quite right! She didn't know!

Barbara: This is just totally weighted against women!! You're all anti-feminist, that's the trouble!

Clement: Quite right!

Barbara: I knew it before I came on the programme! I just had to take one look at them, I knew they were women haters to a man! I could tell! [AUDIENCE LAUGH AND APPLAUD] They make up rules!

Nicholas: They mumble as well, don't they?

Barbara: Yes, they were saying why don't we think up a new rule we never told her about, poor soul! So that the men can win! That's right!

Nicholas: You never knew about that, did you?

Barbara: Of course I never knew about that!

Nicholas: Of course! Well then we can't allow it! She gets another point for that. Yes.

Barbara: Thank you very much …

Nicholas: Eight seconds …

Barbara: *You're* not a woman hater! As a matter of fact …

Nicholas: I love women, yes …

Barbara: I think you're rather nice looking, as a matter of fact.

Nicholas: Yes, yes …

Barbara: I think you're rather sweet, yes. [LAUGHTER FROM AUDIENCE AND KENNETH]

As a result of a mix-up in her booking, Barbara Castle could only join us for one of the two recordings we made that evening. The misunderstanding meant that for the second show we went with a three-man panel, an occurrence that has not happened since.

This unusual recording was the last in that series, and there is a distinct end-of-term feel about the show. With no guest to keep them in check (or 'somewhat in check' would perhaps be more accurate), Kenneth, Derek and Clement take full advantage of their unexpected freedom to be at their naughty schoolboy best. This episode must go down as one of the most anarchic ever. It is also one of the funniest in my opinion. The disintegration begins as we enter the penultimate round, with the subject 'Getting into Debt'.

Clement: Getting into debt is invariably occasioned by having insufficient money or means which can raise loot of any kind, which Americans now refer to as 'bread', an unpleasant term I think …
  BUZZ
Nicholas: Kenneth Williams, why have you challenged?
Kenneth: Because the subject is getting into debt, not the colloquialisms used by Americans. We're not here to discuss that.
Nicholas: He had established he was talking about getting into debt and then …
Kenneth: He was going off about the Americans' way of *defining* getting into debt, which is nothing to do with the subject. *It's deviation! In any language!* Now look here!
[AUDIENCE LAUGHTER AT KENNETH'S HIGHLY ANIMATED OUTRAGE]
Nicholas: [FIGHTING TO REGAIN CONTROL] Now listen … Clement, listen … I mean Derek … I mean who are you? You over there!! Now listen, Kenneth, stop getting me going like that!
Kenneth: *Ooooooooh!* [KENNETH'S PLAYING UP TO THE AUDIENCE IS GENERATING BIG LAUGHS] Someone should get you going, get you out of your apathy!
Nicholas: Kenneth, you cannot possibly talk about getting into debt without discussing money.
Kenneth: But he wasn't discussing that, he was discussing Americans.
Nicholas: Yes, he was discussing money, and he said the Americans refer to it as 'bread'. Ten seconds with you, Clement, 'Getting into Debt', starting now.
Clement: An auctioneer in Belfast to whom I entrusted several cases of wine got into …
  BUZZ

Nicholas: Kenneth Williams, why did you challenge?

Kenneth: Deviation! We've gone from the Americans now to auctioneers in Dublin. It's nothing to do …

Derek: Belfast.

Kenneth: … with getting into debt.

Nicholas: I think he was just about to say he got him into debt. He actually said 'got'.

Kenneth: Well you could be *just about* to be doing *anything*, couldn't you, in the game???

Nicholas: Not on this programme. [MUCH AUDIENCE LAUGHTER AS I SPEAK IN A STERN VOICE] I must be fair, because I do get letters about this. He really didn't have a chance to establish the connection between his remark about the …

Kenneth: Well what do you think, Derek?

Derek: I agree with you, Ken! Totally!

Kenneth: *Aaah!*

Nicholas: You'll always disagree with the chairman, any of you! No, all right then, if you feel like that, I will put it to the audience. Do you feel … I must point out that I definitely don't think that he deviated.

Clement: [LAUGHING] That's the way to get them!! I wish you'd stop saying that, Nick! If you wouldn't say to the audience what you personally thought first, I'd occasionally win the cheers or boos.

Derek: Just put it as a straight question!

Clement: Yes!

Derek: If you were in a law court you couldn't say, 'This is what we want you to do, please find him guilty.' [HUGE AUDIENCE LAUGH] A man is innocent until he's proven guilty in this country.

Kenneth: *Ooooh!* We're going to have a riot!!

Nicholas: We're not going to have an argument about it. After all I am not a judge … *Shut up, the two of you!* Now listen! If you think that Clement Freud was deviating will you boo, and if you don't think he was deviating will you cheer. And will you all do it together now. [CHEERS AND BOOS FROM THE AUDIENCE]

Nicholas: Clement Freud was not deviating which is exactly what I thought! Thank you! [APPLAUSE AND LAUGHTER FROM AUDIENCE] And as we always play this game like little boys, I will now say to Derek Nimmo and to Kenneth Williams, 'Sucks to you!!!' [SURPRISED 'OOOH'S AND 'AAH'S FROM AUDIENCE AND HUGE LAUGHTER]

Derek: Interesting … When there's not a lady on the show, it all comes out, doesn't it?

Kenneth: Yes! It certainly does! Talk about Freudian!!!

Nicholas: Steady on. Steady on. We've had quite a lot come out in this show, we don't want any more! Five seconds left for you, Clement, with 'Getting into Debt', starting now.

Clement: As a result of this perfidious villainy on the part of the Northern Irish wine merchant …

[WHISTLE]

Nicholas: And at the end of that round Clement gained an extra point for speaking when the whistle went, he's now clept up … oh …

Kenneth: 'Clept up'! What a joke, isn't it! He's got no diction even! He's got no diction!!

Nicholas: Who would have, at the end of 26 shows left with these three to *battle* with? It's only one against three up here, I can tell you. Clement Freud has crept up, one point on … even Ian Messiter's fighting me! He pulled the score away before I had a chance to read it! *Heaven's sake!* He's crept up one point on Derek Nimmo who's still in the lead … [SHOUTS AND CHEERS FROM THE AUDIENCE AS DEREK STANDS UP TO ADDRESS THEM. HE CLEARLY BELIEVES I MISREAD THE EARLIER AUDIENCE RESPONSE]

Kenneth: The audience are appalled …

Nicholas: Sit down, Derek! Stop haranguing the audience! You brought up the court of law before and once the sentence has been passed, there's nothing more to be said.

Kenneth: What, we're all going to be executed or something?! *Good gracious me!* You're going to put a black cap on next! He is!!!
[LAUGHTER FROM EVERYONE]

At the close of this Series 5 finale, there was a touching moment from Kenneth which in many ways sums up his character, certainly as he revealed it on *Just a Minute*. After all the banter and exclamations of outrage at my rulings and general chairmanship, and a rendition from Kenneth of, 'Goodbye-ee! Goodbye-ee! Wipe the tear, baby dear, from your eye-ee!' I began to wind up the proceedings.

Nicholas: There are some people who are listening still, we hope, who might like to hear what the final score is. And I think it's a very apt one. This is the last one in this present series which makes us all very sad. And the three who played it most regularly have come out very, very close. Kenneth was only just in third place, just three points behind Clement Freud who was just behind this week's winner who was Derek Nimmo!
[AUDIENCE APPLAUSE]
Kenneth: And what about, what about a cheer for the man who never gets a clap, that wonderful man who chairs this show every week, Nicholas Parsons! [LOUDER APPLAUSE]
Nicholas: Thank you very much indeed! And I must tell the listeners that even Clement Freud clapped then!

That interjection from Kenneth was heartfelt. Throughout his time on *Just a Minute*, Kenneth was the only player of the game who would regularly pay me compliments.

Yes, absolutely, what a very good chairman. Hear, hear, very good. Thank goodness there's some democracy left with somebody like him in the chair. Yes! Thank you, Nicholas, very kind of you. You combine dignity with fairness, may I say.

In almost the next breath, however, Kenneth could just as easily launch an attack if he felt he could create some humour and laughter, especially if I did not rule in his favour.

> A chairman? He ought to be in a bath chair, that chairman! He's an invalid! They wheel him in here at night! They wheel him in! Before the show! They give him an injection before he starts! Queen's Royal Jelly, they give him! To get his adrenaline flowing! Hahahaha.

That was Kenneth, complex and unpredictable, and undoubtedly the first star of *Just a Minute*. Although he faltered slightly during his initial appearances, once he had found his voice the confidence he achieved allowed him to relax and I am certain he soon grew to love being on the show. Backstage he would regale us all with outrageous stories and anecdotes, but when the time came to take his seat his focus shifted entirely to the audience and the performance he was about to give.

I always introduced him last. He would walk out from behind the curtain, stick out his little bottom and strut across the stage while the audience applauded and laughed with great enthusiasm. He was acting up the whole time, playing to his public and finding ways to invite laughs through his gestures as well as in his words.

Kenneth came from a very humble background, one which offered limited opportunities for formal learning. He was, however, a highly intelligent man and set about educating himself through his voracious appetite for reading. He was rightly proud of the depth of knowledge he had acquired on a broad range of subjects, and was a great admirer of the intellect of others, in particular his sparring partners Derek and Clement.

When Derek Nimmo stepped in to save a floundering Peter Jones, who could not remember the origin of the quote about 'hunting' being the unspeakable in pursuit of the uneatable (it is Oscar Wilde, as Derek informed us), Kenneth was full of admiration. 'That's not showing off. That's a literate gentleman there, enlightening us all. A literate gentleman! Wish they had *more* of them in the world!'

Equally, when Clement in a show from December 1971 stopped Andree Melly in her tracks with a sharp challenge, Kenneth gushed in praise. 'Ah, brilliant! Oh, you aren't half clever! He's clever though, innee! Blimey! There's no flies on him, eh! Oh, that was brilliant, you should have been a barrister! Oooooooh he'd have the Old Bailey rolling, wouldn't he! Incredible, isn't it! Oooooooh! *Really incredible!*'

If Kenneth did feel inadequate in any way, he need not have. Once he had found his own way to play the game, and realised that it was an opportunity to show off his acquired knowledge, he contributed many wonderful moments of erudition, while always remaining hugely entertaining. Ian Messiter quickly recognised the value these expositions of Kenneth's brought to the show, and would introduce subjects about which he knew Kenneth had knowledge and would be able to speak with authority when asked.

Over the course of his 20 years on *Just a Minute* Kenneth spoke on almost 300 of these specially chosen subjects. After I had announced the topic, Kenneth would nod sagely, lick his middle finger, preen his eyebrows, settle himself, poised and upright in his chair, and then launch himself into what he hoped would be a magnificent oration. In this example from March 1977 Kenneth is clearly delighted to be given the subject 'Tiberius Sempronius Gracchus', stretching out many of the words in an attempt to complete the full 60 seconds. He does not quite manage it on this occasion, but it is a valiant effort, drying up with 15 second remaining.

Nicholas: So, Kenneth, look to your laurels in this game and it's your turn to begin. A subject specially chosen for you. 'Tiberius Sempronius Gracchus'.
Clement: Do you mean the other subjects are not specially chosen for us?
Nicholas: I do not mean that …
Kenneth: No! *Because I'm special! I'm the one that's special!* And get it in your head now! Or I shall go stark raving mad! Because I am special, aren't I Nicholas?
Nicholas: Right, Kenneth! 'Tiberius Sempronius Gracchus'.

Kenneth, can you tell us something about that in just a minute, starting now.

Kenneth: One of two known, of course, as the Gracchus. What an illustrious pair of sons they were to that great city of Rome! And as a tribune representing the Plebeians (don't forget, who were opposed to the Patricians) he sought the alleviations of worse wrongs in the small holding area of the populace. And with the great legacy of Pergamon said to the Senate, 'Give these wretches to the people!' *And* was brutally murdered by those who held power! (Oooh I'm getting carried away! Really I am!) [HUGE LAUGH FROM THE AUDIENCE] And of course he died and that's it, do you see!

Kenneth's enthusiasm to show off the depth of his erudition is sometimes unstoppable. Earlier in that 1976–77 series he is given the subject 'Pyramus' on which he has a lot to say, far more than even Kenneth can fit into a full minute which he does manage to complete here, with much stretching of words.

Kenneth: Well, of course we all know about this from the play by William Shakespeare. That incredible scene with Bottom and his friends who re-enact this charming *old story*. It actually had its birth in the east and tells of this young Babylonian who was hopelessly in love with Thisbe. And they could only exchange vows between the walls of adjoining houses, talking through a chink. But arranged, *conspiratorially*, to meet by the Tomb of Ninus under the *mulberry tree*, which was white! Thereafter followed the most *strange* saga! For Pyramus arrived first, and saw this lion withholding a …
[WHISTLE]
Kenneth: I mean, I meant, I meant to get to the point where the mulberry tree turned red, because it turns red after that …
Nicholas: Yes, I know. We were all holding our breath at the end, wondering whether you'd make it before you collapsed at the winning post!

Kenneth: [TALKING VERY FAST TO AVOID BEING INTERUPTED] But the whole point of that was to tell them that the mulberry tree after the murder, well, really not the murder, the suicide, went red. And thereafter the mulberry fruit has always been red, you see. That's the explanation of the myth and it's a charming … it's like the Echo, her in love with the boy, you know, Narcissus, and wasting away because he fell in the water, as you know. And in her wasting away only the voice was left! And so when the voice comes back to you disembodied today you still say 'echo'. And so you use a word from Greek mythology to describe a modern state. Which is extraordinary like the Oedipus complex. It's extraordinary that in our twentieth-century position we have use of an ancient word like that! [HUGE ROUND OF APPLAUSE]

Often when these specialist subjects arose the other players would conduct themselves in a very sporting manner, sitting back to relax and enjoy Kenneth's performance, ignoring occasional hesitations and repetitions because they recognised how much entertainment he was generating (and possibly because they did not wish to have to speak on the subject themselves!). Such generosity could only go so far.

Just a Minute works so well as a game because the rules are simple and easily understood. A certain degree of leeway in order to generate good comedy is to be welcomed, but when Kenneth occasionally paused too long for dramatic effect right at the beginning, repeated himself (favourite expressions such as 'do you see' and 'so to speak' would crop up regularly), or talked so fast that he eventually stumbled over his words, the others would quite correctly challenge. If this occurred during a topic on which he really wanted to show off, he would not be happy.

In such instances Kenneth would do his best to cover up his disappointment and irritation by playing up to the audience, often exclaiming along the following lines. 'Oh, you've ruined it now. You've ruined a good story. You are fools to yourselves! Fools!' The audience would roar with laughter but it was clear to me that he meant what he was saying. There would be real frustration in his voice, as illustrated in this extract from February 1971 on the subject of 'Frederick the Great'.

Kenneth: Well, he was renowned for welcoming at his court some men who were perceptive indeed. Among them Voltaire. In fact one morning they were walking in the grounds and he said, 'What is democracy, dear?' Because he was very, very affectionate towards him. And he said, 'Well, it means that you must say to them I disagree heartily with what you say but will defend …
BUZZ
Nicholas: Clement …
Kenneth: … to the death your right to say it! *Don't dare to interrupt!* Who's interrupted?
Nicholas: Clement Freud has interrupted.
Kenneth: Oh, what a nerve!
Nicholas: Clement, why have you challenged?
Clement: Repetition.
Nicholas: What of?
Clement: Three 'said's and two 'say's.
Kenneth: That's neither here nor there! Ask them! They were interested! Look at him! [POINTING TO A MEMBER OF THE AUDIENCE] He was throbbing! He was liking it! He was loving it!
Nicholas: We were all loving it!
Kenneth: He was loving it! Look at him! He don't want to be deprived!

When this happened, Kenneth would go into a sulk. He recognised this trait in himself, as this letter to our producer at the time, Simon Brett shows, but he was incapable of doing anything about it.

27/9/69

Dear Simon,

I am sorry about the second show on Friday – I know I was lousy. I felt very resentful about the way it was all getting like a slanging match without being amusing but admit that doesn't excuse going off into a great sulk – which is what I did.

Apologetically, Kenneth

When it became clear that Kenneth had allowed himself to slip into one of his sulks, it was my job to coax him back at the earliest opportunity, by perhaps engineering a situation so that he could once again take up the subject. 'Oh, I don't think that's a good challenge. I think as Kenneth had the subject originally, I think it's only fair that it goes back to him. So, Kenneth, this audience they care for you, they want you to go on this subject, they are dying to hear from you, they love you so gird your loins, take a breath, and off you go!'

Really I was restoking his ego, and it usually worked. He would jump straight back in where he had left off, happy to be centre stage again on that particular chosen topic. The other players would recognise what was happening and were happy to play along because they understood that the show benefited.

...on the subject of *Subjects*

The choice of subjects on *Just a Minute* is an important element of the game.

Not every subject will take off, and it is impossible to predict accurately those that will fly. What is critical, however, is to try to ensure that each subject has the potential for success. A lot of thought goes into this.

Some subjects are selected because they are multilayered, offering varied routes down which the players can take them.

For instance, 'Taking the Mickey'. That can relate to making a joke at someone's expense, but equally the speaker could go down the route of, 'Oh, my friend Mickey, when I take him out … ' or 'Bananas' could be about fruit production or going a little crazy. Subjects with multiple interpretations like this are very important when the topic changes hands, because ideally you do not want the next player merely to continue along the same lines as the one before. Variety is crucial in a spontaneous show such as *Just a Minute*.

Topical subjects also work well, as they appeal to younger listeners and also ensure the game is relevant in the modern world. Recently we have discussed 'Arm Candy', Taking a Selfie' and '3D Printing' to great effect, and a great deal of laughter.

There is one element we do have to be aware of, however, with regard to topical matters. A general subject such as 'The London Olympics' will work whenever the particular show in which it features is broadcast, as such a big event has relevance at any time. However, the inclusion of subjects that are date- or season-specific can be problematic as they run the risk of sounding very strange when the show is finally aired. Christmas specials are an exception because we know that show has been earmarked for a particular slot in the schedule. That does not apply to most of the other programmes we record. So introducing a subject of, say, 'Shrove Tuesday' may work well in front of the theatre audience during the spring, but does not quite work for listeners if the show is broadcast in November.

One aspect we do not have to worry about is introducing even faintly saucy subjects. With players such as Gyles Brandreth, Julian Clary and Graham Norton now appearing regularly, they can skilfully take any subject down an amusing and risqué direction if they so desire.

Originally Ian supplied all the subjects, but that had to change when ill health intervened and he could no longer be so actively involved. Ian's son Malcolm then took over the selection process. In more recent years our producer (who always makes the final selection) has been involved, as have I, contributing suggestions based on my experience of what may spark players' imaginations to produce funny or interesting rounds.

Ian regularly included topics with Kenneth Williams' specialist knowledge in mind. He also selected serious and erudite subjects for other players if he knew that person enjoyed a particular interest, such as this example from a broadcast of 4 November 1975. Ian must have realised that Derek Nimmo had strong views on politics and introduced the subject of 'Democracy' accordingly, hoping to spur on Derek. I think this is a very good example of how unpredictable *Just a Minute* can be. Amidst the laughter and sometimes anarchy, there can also be moments of fascinating insight. Joining Derek on the panel here are Kenneth Williams, Peter Jones and Aimi MacDonald.

Derek: Democracy, government for the people by the ditto. I think we can often think in this country today that some of our democratic freedoms are being eroded from pressures within and also from outside. Something which I think we must work hard to prevent. I think one of the things that we do notice is that the system we employ is not necessarily fair. If, for instance, we had proportional representation in this country, then we would feel the people were more democratically represented in parliament than they are at present. For instance, in our …

BUZZ

Nicholas: Peter Jones has challenged.

Peter: Repetition of 'for instance'.

Nicholas: Yes, there was, yes.

Kenneth: It was very interesting. I was moved.

Nicholas: Yes, it was very interesting.

Aimi: Oh, it was super.

Kenneth: I think we could all do with a bit of this seriousness. *Nooo*, I think there's too much levity. I mean, I would rather hear him out.

Aimi: Yes.

Peter: You ought to be on *Thought for the Day*. [BIG AUDIENCE LAUGH]

Continuing with such thought-provoking subjects is part of the ongoing success of *Just a Minute*. Over the past couple of series we have ruminated on a broad range of interesting topics, including 'The Nobel Peace Prize', 'Marcel Marceau', 'Sebastian Faulks', 'Edgar Allan Poe', 'Victoria Falls' and 'Oliver Cromwell'. Yes, the game is absolutely about entertainment, which will always remain at its core, but introducing subjects that have the possibility of eliciting a knowledgeable response from the panellists adds depth to the show. Mixed in with the more everyday topics, the inclusion of these more reflective subjects provides unexpected diversity and ensures we do not slip into the trap of becoming frivolous and inconsequential.

Self-criticism is a common trait in our business, and Kenneth could suffer as much as anyone from the debilitating feeling that he had failed to perform to the best of his ability. David Hatch in particular was aware of this depressive streak and would make sure to give Kenneth encouragement whenever necessary.

21/1/69

My dear Ken,

I must just write and say how absolutely brilliant I thought you were on Friday. They were two excellent programmes, and this was very largely due to you.

It seemed to me that you suddenly realised how best to play the challenging rule, this is really why you won the first game, but you did it without seeming acquisitive for points, and at the same time being funny all the way. It was absolutely masterly, and I haven't been so pleased since

I persuaded you that time to be Chairman.

This coming Friday sees the end of the run, and I am hoping that after the show I can organise a little hospitality from the Corporation for which I hope you will stay, and any friends you have of course, are invited. In case you should feel unable to come, and because I am rather shy of praising people to their faces, let me just say on enormous 'thank you' for all your work on this series, how very pleased and privileged I feel to have you in the company, and hope that should we be asked to do more, as I am sure we will, you will be with us again. I am sorry this has turned into a fan letter, but I am afraid it is unavoidable.

Yours, David Hatch

Kenneth's appreciation of how David helped him is clear from his response.

22/1/69

My dear David,

You can't imagine how welcome your letter was! I've been in a lousy state for some time, due to the same old trouble and everything culminated in a dreadful BLACK MONDAY which was all pain and worry.

Landed up on Tuesday with the surgeon who originally operated and he handled everything superbly. So this morning I was feeling tentative etc. and then your letter came through the box. I honestly think that praise is like medicine for an actor – and needless to say, your words acted like a tonic for me.

My unspeakable thanks for all you say about my work on the series and for your kindness and understanding the odd psychological difficulties we have encountered.

Old Guthrie used to say the first criteria for a director was 'one who could create an atmosphere in which the cast is uninhibited' and I think this is why I enjoyed it so much, working with you – you seem implicitly to understand this.

Look forward to seeing you Friday,

Gratefully, Kenneth

As the above letter makes clear, Kenneth was sufficiently self-aware to recognise the precarious nature of his ego, but he also had the ability to use that knowledge to great comic effect. Here, in a recording from March 1980, featuring the comedian Bob Monkhouse, Kenneth has begun to talk very ponderously and deliberately on the subject of 'Advice to a 21-Year-Old Girl'.

Kenneth: It has already been set down by one of our greatest writers. Neither a borrower nor a lender be. And this above all to thine own self …
BUZZ

Nicholas: Bob Monkhouse has challenged.

Bob: I've been listening to this show for 13 years and that's repetition. He always goes on like that!

[KENNETH DELIBERATELY PLAYS UP HIS OUTRAGE AT BEING INTERUPTED WITH ONLY A HALF A SECOND TO GO]

Kenneth: That's lovely, isn't it! Charming, isn't it! How you get treated, you see! You end up with your ego round your ankles! It's wonderful, isn't it! He's supposed to be a friend! *Marvellous!*

[BIG AUDIENCE LAUGH]

Despite such moments of self-awareness when he is happy to make fun of himself, Kenneth could be very self-critical, and when he felt like this he turned to David Hatch for support. The depth of his regard for David can be seen in this exchange of letters, in which David announces that he will be stepping aside from this producer role for a time (he subsequently returned).

22/9/69

Dear Ken,

You were quite absolutely, devastatingly, amazingly, brilliant on Friday. They are the best two Just a Minutes you have done, whenever you opened your mouth the Playhouse erupted.

It was wonderful to watch and to listen to. It is almost enough to make me regret that I am leaving the show after Oct 17th.

    See you Friday,

       Yours, David Hatch

Dear David,

    Well there was certainly a sting in the tail of your letter! You leaving the show on Oct 17th. You never let on before! It's obviously a well concealed plot.

    I think it's disgraceful. The Corporation don't tell you this when it starts. Who is going to take it over? Will the atmosphere be like the one you have done so much to create – think of the troubles and bad feeling that CAN ARISE – oh dear, I wish you'd never told me. I was supposed to be at the Centre today and the writer's thing and rang to say I'm ill. And now this – into each life a little rain must fall, but this morning I seem to be drenched.

    Yours, Kenneth

Kenneth's mother was another source of strength. He endured a difficult relationship with his father, which is perhaps best illustrated by a story Kenneth used to tell of when his dad gave him a pair of boxing gloves for his birthday. 'What are these for?' Kenny asked, to which his father replied, 'They are for you to put on to start fighting and become a man.' Kenny said that he remembered vividly just dropping them on the floor, turning around and walking upstairs to his room.

His mother Lou, on the other hand, worshipped her son. She was a sweet, diminutive woman who attended as many *Just a Minute* recordings as she could, always sitting in the middle of the front row, eyes glued on her son, basking in his success. I think his mother's unwavering support mattered enormously to Kenneth and he was very protective of her, paying for her flat near to his, which was not far from Great Portland Street so that they could be close. This proximity allowed her to do what she could to look after Kenneth, which I suspect was not always an easy job. Sometimes when he was low and wouldn't answer the door she would be forced to shout through the letterbox, trying to persuade him to eat.

All regulars on *Just a Minute* develop their own quirks and styles of play in order to generate laughs and earn points, and Kenneth was no exception. In addition to his, 'They shouldn't have women on the show', he developed a number of other oft-repeated lines, all delivered with perfect comic timing and over-the-top flamboyance to the great delight of the audiences and listeners over the years.

When he disagreed with a challenge or one of my rulings, he would exclaim in mock outrage, 'I haven't come all the way from King's Cross [later 'Great Portland Street' after he moved upmarket] to be treated like a load of rubbish!' If he felt he was being harshly treated he would defend himself with, 'How dare you! I'm a cult. I'm a cult figure I am ... I am ... I'm one of the biggest cults around here I can tell you!' When 'unjustly' interrupted he would proclaim that 'You've interrupted my flow! My flow's gone!' These utterances were so well known that more than 20 years after Kenneth's death Sheila Hancock and the comedian Paul Merton, who nowadays is one of our most regular and best players, were able to pay an entertaining tribute to Kenneth by recalling his famous lines.

Nicholas: Paul, you've got in with five seconds to go, 'Celebrity Spotting', starting now.
Paul: Celebrity spotting, well, I just look in the mirror and there I am!
BUZZ
Paul: Who buzzed that! Who buzzed that!
Sheila: Me! Me!
Paul: Who buzzed then! Who buzzed then!
Nicholas: Sheila.
Paul: Outrageous!
Sheila: He was so pleased with himself then, there was a long

pause after 'am'!
Paul: There was no long pause.
Sheila: There was a long pause.
Paul: Rubbish!
Sheila: There was!
Paul: I've come all the way from Great Portland Street to do this show!
Sheila: They shouldn't have women on the show!

As Barbara Castle quickly noticed during her *Just a Minute* encounter with Kenneth, his favoured tactic in the quest for gaining points was to stretch out some of his words in order to eat up valuable seconds. So accomplished did Kenneth become at this that when the wonderful American actress and musical star Elaine Stritch appeared on the show in 1982 she claimed that he could make 'one word into a three-act play!'

I found myself regularly having to adjudicate on challenges of hesitation whenever Kenneth began his verbal elongation, some of which I agreed with although more often than not he skilfully managed to remain just within the bounds of proper speech. Often these challenges led to moments of great amusement, such as this exchange and sharp pay-off line from Peter Jones after Kenneth had been talking on the subject of 'George Eliot'.

Kenneth: She was married of course to *Ge-o-rr-ge* Lewis, a *re-m-m-arkable* gentleman and his work on the French Revolution was of great interest to her *a-a-a-nd* she caused several emendations *t-o-o-oo* be …
BUZZ
Nicholas: Aimi MacDonald challenged.
Aimi: Hesitation.
Nicholas: Oh no, no, no, no, no. He managed to get it out all right. He did *elongate* it, but he …
Aimi: But that's hesitating!
Nicholas: No, if we challenged on that …

Peter: No, it's just cheating, Aimi. That's what it is! [BIG LAUGH]

Nicholas: Well, it's one of those little cheats that they all indulge in. You've got to find your little gimmicks, and the regulars have got them. It's not so easy as …

Peter: But those of us who don't know any long words, we can't do that! [EVEN BIGGER LAUGH]

There was without doubt a great deal of theatre to Kenneth Williams' appearances on *Just a Minute*, but that should not obscure the fact that he was also a very clever player of the game, who could listen intently when others were speaking, ready to come in with a sharp challenge. Here he is in January 1977 during a rather unusual recording. Clement had been delayed on a train and as a result Ian Messiter took over the chairmanship (the only occasion this happened) and I replaced Clement on the panel. Derek Nimmo is speaking on the subject of 'Hong Kong'.

Derek: It seems to me to be totally ludicrous that they have a rate of inflation there under two per cent per annum. When England takes …

BUZZ

Ian: Kenneth Williams.

Kenneth: Two per cent per annum, two 'per's. Repetition.

Ian: Two per cent per annum. Yes, yes, you've got it. It's a bit niggly. It's only a three-letter word.

Kenneth: Never mind about that, dear! It's repetition. So shut your mouth!

Nicholas: A brilliant, a brilliant challenge!

Kenneth: Yes! Thank you! Thank you! You're lovely! *Ohhhhh!* I'm on form tonight! Oh, the adrenaline's really flowing through the old veins tonight, isn't it!

Although Kenneth was a very private man, on *Just a Minute* he seemed able to open up more than perhaps he did in other areas of his life. From relatively basic subjects he could launch into astonishing anecdotes from his past with such enthusiasm that nothing could stop him from completing his tale. Here he is talking on the subject of 'Coconuts' in October 1971.

Kenneth: Well, just outside Kurunegala which was in the *ancient* times the capital of Ceylon, I sat in a coconut *grove*. And one of these things fell down quite *near* to a friend of mine. He said, 'Do you know, it's *awfully* dangerous, these coconuts.' And I said, 'Quite right. We ought to get a chopper and cut them down.' So we went up this trunk. I'm *very good* at scaling up trunks, you see …

> BUZZ

Nicholas: Clement …

Kenneth: I don't care! Shut your row! We went to cut down this coconut and what do you think happened?!

Nicholas: What?

Kenneth: [AT BREAKNECK SPEED] An *'orrible* cobra come out! I *fle-w-w-w*!!! And I shot off to the commanding officer and said 'There's a cobra up this *tree*!!' And he said 'Wait a minute, I'll get my Webley.' [RETURNS TO NORMAL VOICE] And he got his Webley and we were all standing and he said, 'Stand back!' And he shot this cobra, stone dead. What about that? *Isn't that fantastic?* Right in a coconut grove. That actually happened.

Nicholas: Well, thank you very much. That was absolutely delightful, we thoroughly enjoyed it and I'm glad you're here to tell the story. About half a minute ago you were challenged, by Clement Freud. What was the challenge?

Clement: Repetition of 'trunk'.

Nicholas: Yes, there were two trunks.

Kenneth: Ahhh, that was referring to the elephant that was there at the time. [HUGE LAUGH]

Even if occasionally Kenneth's flow was interrupted with a correct challenge, his stories were so entertaining you just had to find out what happened. In May 1987 the subject 'Cards' leads to a most amazing tale.

Kenneth: It led me into the most *extraordinary* adventure.
I was walking along and she produced these cards, *ostensibly*, you know, the kind of cards that identify people, you know. And it said 'Pose Plastique'. And I thought, oh hello, you know, that seems an amusing exhibition. And I found myself with three other people in this back *roooom* in Birmingham, round a *be-d* on which these people were displaying various kinds …
of anatomical …
BUZZ
Nicholas: Clement challenged.
Clement: Repetition of 'people'.
Nicholas: Yes, I'm afraid you did repeat people.
Kenneth: Well, it was jolly good, don't you think?
Nicholas: Yes, and we'd just got to the 'anatomical'.
Clement: Do go on a bit, I'd like to hear the end of this.
Nicholas: I know! We'd just got to the anatomical part, didn't we!
Clement: Yes!
Nicholas: What happened after the anatomical bit?
Kenneth: So we were all round this bed, you see, watching. And this woman was supposed to get into this plastique pose, pose plastique, you know what it is, they … you know, do one of these … But she got the *cramp*! And she started screaming, 'ahhhhhh ahhhhhh!' you know, like that. It was murder and we all started, you know, we all took a step back. Well, actually, ha, I fell over the chair because I had actually stood up to get a closer … look, you see. Because I do think it's very healthy to be curious, don't you? Yes, I'm sure you do too. But anyway there came an awful banging at the *do-o-r*, you see. And this landlord said the room was being used for *improper* purposes, not apropos the display but because they were *charging* admission, you see. And he said that constituted a *trade*.

Nicholas: Well, we're very interested to hear the sort of work you did before you became an actor. [BIG LAUGH FROM AUDIENCE]

The reference I make there to Kenneth's profession is important in helping to understand why he flourished in *Just a Minute* as much as he did.

Kenneth regarded himself as an actor and he was a very good one. I remember seeing him as the Dauphin in Bernard Shaw's *Saint Joan* at the Arts Theatre back in the mid 1950s, and he was remarkable. Kenneth was clearly proud of his performance because he brought it up on *Just a Minute* on a couple of occasions, such as this wonderful example from March 1971 when talking on the subject of Joan herself.

Kenneth: Well, of course the Archbishop of *Rheims* is reputed according to the memorabilia in the *Louvre* Museum, to have said to her, 'You will stand alone. The Bastard of Orleans will disown you. The Dauphin will do the same.' And she replied, 'Even if you turn against me and I am burned, I will go through the flames to the people's hearts forever and … ' then she said the word again! [HUGE AUDIENCE LAUGHTER AND APPLAUSE] 'And so God be with me.' And that's a very noble sentiment. And I once was in a restaurant with an actress who played the character of Saint Joan. And in the bar, she was discussing the role. And the gentleman that was serving us …
BUZZ

After an unsuccessful challenge from Clement, Kenneth does not have time to finish his story before the whistle sounds, but once again everyone is very keen to hear the ending.

Kenneth: It was Siobhán McKenna who played Saint Joan and the waiter served her in the bar, and it was the same waiter who later served her with the meal. And she said to him, 'Oh, are you doubling?' And he said [ADOPTS AN IRISH ACCENT] 'No, Tipperary!'

As a result of Kenneth's acting ability, in 1955 he was approached by the producer of *Hancock's Half Hour*, Dennis Main Wilson, and asked to join the cast for the second series. Throughout his time on that show, Kenneth produced a marvellous range of distinctive voices that helped bring his imagined individuals to life. He was a fine character actor.

Kenneth's performances were very popular, but Tony Hancock thought the people he was portraying were not real enough, he described them as caricature, and eventually decided to drop Kenneth. That is when he moved in to the *Carry On* films, in which he also acted very well, playing a succession of eccentric characters in a wide variety of comic situations. However, Kenneth felt that these roles strayed into the world of broad comedy, too far over the top to be believable, which did not satisfy his creative instincts. As a result he did not fully respect his own work in those films.

In contrast, *Just a Minute* provided a platform from which he was able to showcase his wide-ranging talents, in a style he developed to suit himself. That's why I believe Kenneth grew to regard *Just a Minute* as his favourite job.

Inevitably, of course, not everyone appreciated Kenneth's performances, as the following letter of complaint to the *Radio Times* illustrates. The editor of the letters section forwarded the note to our producers David Hatch and Simon Brett, enquiring whether Kenneth would reply. What is key here is David and Simon's robust response, understanding perfectly how important Kenneth was to *Just a Minute*.

12/10/72

Title: Come now, Mr Williams.
    Just a Minute, Radio 4, is such a good programme; why must it be spoiled by Kenneth Williams? It is tempting to suggest you get rid of

him completely, but perhaps it would be kinder to suspend him until he promises to play fair, obey the chairman, adapt a sporting attitude, refuse to play down to the baser elements in the audience, and stop interrupting other people and trying to monopolise this programme, as it seems that his attitude springs from being childish and spoilt, and he might grow up.

The speaker is sometimes exhorted: 'If you cannot strike oil after three minutes, stop boring.' Kenneth Williams could note this, substituting seconds for minutes, but unfortunately he is boorish as well. Please restore to us the happy atmosphere that could exist in this programme without him.

Reply:

We regard Kenneth Williams as a brilliantly funny performer. In Just a Minute his many changes of mood and direction are very skilfully timed and his bursts of childishness are all part of the performance. We regret that [the listener] dislikes Kenneth but feel sure that the show would be much less lively without him.

Of the four established regulars during the 1970s, Derek Nimmo proved the hardest to pin down for recordings. Theatre, film and television commitments forced him to miss all of Series 2 and 6, plus his fondness for travel, pleasure and business (he owned a theatrical production company which he took on tours around the world) resulted in Derek missing many other recordings throughout his long career on *Just a Minute*.

Derek's numerous trips abroad may have been the reason he now sits in fifth place when it comes to the overall tally of appearances for players of the game (Clement easily claims first place, with Kenneth, Peter and Paul Merton following) but he utilised his experiences to great effect when he was available, regularly calling upon his unparalleled knowledge of foreign countries to entertain audiences and listeners. Over his 32 years on *Just a Minute*, he referenced over 100 locations, taking in Sri Lanka, Kuala Lumpur, Hamburg, Hispaniola and Bombay, with excursions to Northern Cyprus, Bali, the Caspian Sea and Hong Kong, together with expositions on the wonders of Rome, Venice, Dubai, Corfu, Alice Springs, Amsterdam and Albania, to name a handful.

It seemed that whenever possible, he would take a subject and introduce an element of travel. On 'Sharks' he began with, 'Skin diving off Kemaman in the Straits of Malaysia ...'; on 'Cats' he launched into, 'Last week I was in Bangkok and the curious thing was that as I wandered around the capital of Thailand as it's now called, I could not see one Siamese cat ...' and on 'Punch', 'I was once in Las Vegas and there I met Muhammad Ali ...' (Did I mention the name-dropping? Derek enjoyed that enormously as well.)

You could never predict where and when Derek would find an angle to embark on a travelogue, and as this wonderful exchange from April 1978 on 'Keeping a Watch' illustrates, one could never know where it might lead. The popular actor Bernard Cribbins was on the panel with Derek that evening.

Derek: Last time I was in Bombay I watched my poppadoms [LAUGHTER FROM KENNETH] very carefully most of the night. And it was ...

BUZZ

Nicholas: Kenneth Williams has ...

Kenneth: I don't understand it! How can you *wash* your poppadoms?

Derek: Watch your poppadoms! *Watch!!!*

Kenneth: Oh, I thought he said he washed his poppadoms! I was going to *say*! Mind you, his diction's terrible, isn't it!

Bernard: So is his poppadom!!

Sheila: [LAUGHING ALMOST UNCONTROLLABLY] Washed his poppadoms ... !!!!

Kenneth: I knew he ... I knew he had a chapati in Clapham but I never knew he ... [DISSOLVES INTO LAUGHTER]

Derek's travel and his passing mentions of famous names he had (or had not, you could never quite tell what the truth was) met, proved to be the source of great comedy over all the years that he was with us, although his peripatetic lifestyle did occasionally interrupt the flow of a show. On the day of the recording in which he 'inadvertently' mentions the greatest boxer of all time, Derek had just flown in from the other side of the world and was obviously keen to catch up with what was happening at home. At one point he actually picked up a newspaper and began reading. 'And, Derek, your turn to begin. If you'd like to put the daily paper down and join the show again! I know you've just come back from Australia but there's nothing much been happening that doesn't normally happen!'

Derek was too canny an entertainer to overuse his wealth of travel tales, but he did recount them with sufficient regularity that once his fellow players had latched on to this tactic, they never let go. Kenneth's inventive mind in particular found a rich vein of laughs in pulling Derek's leg, adopting one of two personas: boredom (when Kenneth would say things like: 'Oh, he's off again. We don't want to hear about all that. We've heard it before. He's always on about his travels.'), or outrage:

Derek: When I went into Cartier in Paris, I went to the jewellery …
    BUZZ
Nicholas: Kenneth Williams challenged.
Kenneth: Oh, deviation. We're not interested in him going into *Cartier* in Paris. That's nothing to do with us!! We're not interested in him name-dropping this posh shop he goes to! *Cartier* in Paris indeed!!! Half of us are lucky to get into Woolworths in Oxford Street! What a nerve! Coming here, showing us all up! I've never heard anything like it! It's disgraceful, isn't it! Isn't it disgraceful in this age of equality?!

Kenneth's reactions to Derek's stories were produced entirely for comic effect, but behind this I used to wonder if there was just a degree of admiration from Kenneth. There was a man, after all, who found physical contact, and anything remotely unclean or unsanitary, difficult to cope with. These are hardly the character traits of a great explorer.

This aspect of his personality slipped out once during a brief but illuminating exchange in March 1985 between Kenneth and Sheila Hancock, sparked by another travel tale from Derek, set up by Ian Messiter's choice of subject.

Nicholas: The next subject is for Derek to begin and it's 'A Strange Thing I Saw on My Travels'. Oh, we're going to have more of all this name-dropping and place-dropping, aren't we now? So, Derek, there are 60 seconds, starting now.

Derek: I think probably one of the strangest things I've seen on my travels takes place at the Batu Caves outside Kuala Lumpur in Malaysia. These great limestone rocks tower into the sky. And at four o'clock in the morning on this particular day of the year with the Thaipusam Festival, you hear the drums beginning to beat. These Hindu tom-et ceteras that bang away the rhythm into the night. And slowly a great black line of figures crosses the ground towards the caves …

BUZZ

Nicholas: Clement Freud challenged.

Clement: Repetition of 'great'. And hesitation! And a few other things. And he didn't drop any names! Deviation!!

Nicholas: Well, I hope you get the subject back, Derek, and we hear more about it. But in the meantime I must be fair because Clement has a correct challenge and he has 30 and a half seconds on 'A Strange Thing I Saw on My Travels, starting now.

Clement: One of the strangest things that I ever saw on any travel of which I have partaken was Kenneth Williams, who I caught out of the corner of my eye, leaning behind me on an aeroplane, bound for the Middle East …

BUZZ

Nicholas: Derek Nimmo challenged.

Derek: Deviation, Kenneth's never been to the Middle East.

Kenneth: On the contrary!

Derek: Not with Clement Freud, you haven't!

Kenneth: I'm a habitué around Cairo cafés and have been known, I've been known …

Derek: With Clement Freud?

Kenneth: I'm a cult! I'm a cult! I'm a cult! I'm a cult! They say I'm one of the biggest cults in the Middle East, don't they, Clement!

Nicholas: Yes, wherever you go in they say, 'Ah I caught Kenneth Williams out of the corner of my eye!'

Kenneth: Yes! Kenny the cult they say!! Many's the time we've seen him sipping the mint tea!

Sheila: A few years ago you wouldn't go abroad. You thought it was dirty!

Kenneth: I know. *Isn't it funny?!*

The persona Derek created fascinates me. He spoke in a manner that could almost be regarded as the antithesis of Kenneth Williams's – laid-back, lilting even, with barely a trace of his Liverpudlian roots. Derek's style of delivery projected a sense that nothing bothered him, that he could cope with absolutely anything. To some extent that was true – he was a relaxed, easy-going man – but lurking behind that laissez-faire image lay a strong personality. There was a rod of steel running through his spine.

Derek was very competitive, especially with Clement who pushed him intellectually, and also extremely well organised and professional, all of which contributed to his great success as a theatrical entrepreneur. Despite their rivalry in the show, Derek and Clement were good friends, not that this prevented Derek from latching on to opportunities for witty one-liners at Clement's expense. In this extract from a broadcast of 15 December 1970, Kenneth is talking first on the subject of 'Henry VIII'.

Kenneth: Well, of course it is extraordinary. This

beautiful-looking young man should have become such a *gross monstrosity*! And should have resulted, having been given the title …

BUZZ

Nicholas: Derek Nimmo, why have you challenged?

Derek: Well, deviation. I think it's totally unfair him talking about Clement Freud! [BIG LAUGH]

On *Just a Minute* Derek chose to play down much of his competitive personality by projecting an image of the amiable, quintessential English gent, peppering his speech with words and phrases such as, 'Oh golly gosh!', 'delightfully', 'what-ho', 'frightfully', 'awfully' and 'really'. To be precise, Derek would have most likely pronounced these last two words as follows, 'awww-fullly' and re-ahhlly'. Similar to Kenneth, Derek had a wonderful ability to stretch out a single word to eat up vital seconds. Here he is on the subject of 'Laughing' in August 1973.

Derek: Well, *a-ll s-o-r-t-s* of things can make you laugh, can't they *re-ahhlly*! It's *ve-r-r-r-y ex-tra-or-din-ary*! I mean look at this audience tonight! I'm in positive *hoooo-ts*! And *the-r-r-e*'s a great *wel-ter* of peo-ple *co-ming* up on this wonderfully *wa-a-a-rm eee-ve-ning, sweltering a-w-a-yy*! And I look at them and I *la-a-u-g-h ou-t loud*! 'Ho-hee', says I. Because I think, 'They must be a lot of old chumps and mugs! They've got better things to do than *ha-nging a-round* and sitting on these seats! They could be out *w-a-a-ndering* along the banks!'

Derek was a gifted and entertaining raconteur, very adept at playing the game, but even he could occasionally be tripped up by his trademark phrases, as in this example from 11 March 1969 on the subject 'What Socrates Said'.

Derek: Socrates said many things of tremendous import and fascination. One of the things, I suppose, that he's most remembered for really, one of the things he said just before he died, when he said, 'Before I take this poison I'm going to bath myself to spare the women the toil of washing me down when I'm dead.' Which I really think is a terribly nice thing to do, don't you? Most considerate and kind. Also, every morning when he used to get up, he used to look across the water and say, 'Oh, look at the wine-dark sea this morning.' It was quite a catchphrase of his, terribly popular it was. Other things he used to say were, 'hello', 'what-ho' and the …

BUZZ

Nicholas. Clement Freud, why have you challenged?

Clement: Deviation.

Nicholas: Why?

Clement: [LAUGHING] He didn't say 'what-ho'!!! He really, really didn't!

Derek had a tendency to blur fact and fiction, a trait that became perhaps most pronounced when he chose to provide an 'insight' into his family. Here's what we learned about his 'Great-Uncle Augustus' over the course of a round that included numerous challenges and different speakers.

Derek: My great-uncle Augustus lived in Bayswater when it was not necessarily the wrong side of the park. He was an unemployed organ grinder. But fortunately left a large sum of money by a distant cousin on the other side of the family. He formed a liaison with a chambermaid, and one day took her to Skindle's Hotel near Maidenhead, where he was observed by a Mrs Poppington-Green who reported him to his brother George, who told Mother, who told Father … He went to India, starboard out, and married a Mrs Vindaloo who was very hot stuff …

And as for the role his grandfather's whiskers played in Britain's military past – well, I am sure it came as a revelation to serious historians!

Derek: My grandfather had the most extraordinarily *lonnng* whiskers! They were *frightfully* useful for him when he went to fight in the Boer War … During the Siege of Mafeking … he piled up the sandbags, dragged his rifle and getting hold of the whiskers he draped them over his head! And this is the first example (this is totally true!) of camouflage use in the British Isles!

There was far more to Derek Nimmo in *Just a Minute* than merely his travel experiences or the personality he projected. For instance, he had a very quick brain that he used to produce many humorous challenges. Here Clement is speaking on the subject 'Giving a Short Address' in January 1970, setting himself up for a put-down.

Clement: When I was 19 years old, I was passionately in love …

BUZZ

Nicholas: Derek Nimmo, why have you challenged?

Derek: Deviation, he was never 19 years old!

His image may have been that of the polite, bowler-hatted, butter-wouldn't–melt-in-his-mouth fine fellow, but that did not inhibit Derek from producing moments of broad, sometimes *quite* broad, humour. Even in our very first show, when asked to speak on 'Things to Do in the Bath'.

Derek: I had a girlfriend called June with whom I …

Promptly Beryl Reid challenges for 'deviation', which I think is a cunning challenge, given what it appears Derek is about to say. The audience, however, want to hear more and the topic remains with Derek, back in his bath.

Derek: The young friend that I mentioned that I used to have my bath with, we used to sit together, and I used to play with her rubber duck and she used to play with my sponge. Alas she grew up and went to nursery school and I never saw her again! Since then, I've had all sorts of interesting experiences in baths. I have at home a family bath. And I think it's terribly important to have a family bath. I have a wife and two children. We have a large bath which we all gather together in, on cold winter evenings. And it's one way of getting to know your family *awww-fullly* well.

When given the subject 'Jokes' in February 1991 Derek skilfully manages to work in a couple of really rather racy gags which receive a huge laugh at the end.

Derek: I tend to get most of my jokes from *The Times* on a Thursday. From a column written by Sir Clement Freud. And he has jokes such as, the dyslexic atheist who tried all his life to prove that Dog doesn't exist. And I always thought that was a very good joke. And also the one about the Scotsman who took part in a pornographic movie and was so mean he always ran it backwards to see the prostitute giving *him* the money! And I think that's awfully good. Other people who do have particularly good jokes are comedians like Terry Scott. Now he has a different kind of jocular manner. And a joke of his which I would like to give to you, is a man going into a kitchen finding it *absolutely* filthy. And he sees the chef going round the tart with his false teeth! He said, 'That's absolutely disgusting, you ought to have a tool for that!' He said, 'Yes, I save that for the doughnuts!'

Inhibition was not something from which Derek suffered. Here he is indulging in a spot of 'toe-twiddling' in January 1974, as poor Aimi MacDonald tries in vain to begin talking on 'How to Think'. Kenneth does not exactly help Aimi's cause either.

Aimi: Oh, ask Kenneth to stop laughing at me now!
Nicholas: Well, I must say Kenneth Williams, who sits opposite Aimi MacDonald, he's being very naughty. He's putting his

hands over his eyes and trying to dry her up! Kenneth, behave yourself, let Aimi try to talk on 'How to Think'. Sixty seconds, starting now.

Aimi: This is very difficult to do … [AIMI DISSOLVES INTO LAUGHTER WITH THE AUDIENCE VERY QUICKLY JOINING HER]

Nicholas: I will explain afterwards what the laughter is. Now keep going because no one has challenged you.

Aimi: Well, it's especially difficult to do when you've got Derek Nimmo's toes floating around in front of your face. However if you really want to concentrate the very best thing to do is to shut your eyes and block everything out of your mind and really meditate. [CLOSES HER EYES] This takes an awful …

BUZZ

Nicholas: Derek Nimmo has challenged.

Derek: Well, she's either hesitating or meditating, I wasn't quite sure! [BIG LAUGH]

Nicholas: Well, I think she was probably asphyxiated actually from the … I mention that last thing because obviously the listeners could hear. The huge laugh at the beginning was Aimi looking at Kenneth, worried that she would dry up. And Derek very quietly got his shoes off and shoved his toes under her nose, and she suddenly looked down and there was his toes wriggling away inside his socks. And she just couldn't go …

Aimi: [ATTEMPTING TO SPEAK THROUGH HER LAUGHTER] I could see his legs!! And it looked like an animal, you know!!!

Nicholas: I know! His toes do look like animals. I know it's very embarrassing because there's a little hole in the desk where they sit, and they came shooting up there just like two black sinister animals! [AUDIENCE ARE IN HYSTERICS THROUGHOUT]

Seven years after 'Toegate', Derek's mischievous nature led to an incident that delayed the recording and, I think it is fair to say, did not meet with universal approval from his fellow regulars, although his antics did cause a great deal of amusement. The following extract (which incidentally the BBC repeated in full as a tribute to Derek when he died) tells its own story. I will set it up merely by explaining that the original broadcast was on 18 April 1981 and the opening subject is 'The Best Game', with Clement speaking first.

> **Clement:** Quite a good game, which just could go for the best game, is to approach the chairman of *Just a Minute* with a stink bomb. [LOUD KNOWING LAUGHTER FROM AUDIENCE] You step on it, and the smell is so absolutely foul that the entire programme has to be put back by a quarter of an hour, causing enormous distress and inconvenience to the competitors who had appointments for dinner and were in fact moving to Cambridgeshire in order that elderly ladies with nothing better to do than wait for their member of …
> BUZZ

Clement loses the subject here for deviation and the show then progresses to the fourth round, for which Ian Messiter improvises cleverly by changing the original subject.

> **Nicholas:** Peter, the subject is 'Stink Bombs'. [BURST OF AUDIENCE LAUGHTER] Which got a nice reaction from our audience! Maybe they've had some experience of them, I don't know. But obviously it's set them alight. And they would like to hear you being set alight by the subject and going for 60 seconds if you can on 'Stink Bombs', starting now.
> **Peter:** I think they're vicious and cowardly weapons and they're quite indiscriminate, making those suffer who are perfectly innocent, not just the people to whom they are directed. I wouldn't ever, ah … I would denounce anybody [BIG LAUGH] who used … ah … stink bombs … eh … as a means …
> BUZZ
> **Nicholas:** Derek Nimmo has challenged.
> **Derek:** Hesitation.

Nicholas: I agree with your challenge, so you now very aptly take over the subject of 'Stink Bombs' and there are 42 seconds left, starting now.

Derek: I am ashamed to tell the great British public that I let off a stink bomb in this studio this evening. It has caused tremendous distress and I'm very apologetic about it. Please can I have your forgiveness, Nicholas Parsons? I promise I will never set off a stink bomb ever again … [THERE IS A SUDDEN EXCLAMATION FROM CLEMENT, A BURST OF RAUCOUS, SUSTAINED LAUGHTER FROM THE AUDIENCE, AND A CRY OF 'HE'S GOT ANOTHER ONE!', FOLLOWED BY LOUD 'OOOH'S, WHICH ALL BUT DROWN OUT WHAT DEREK IS SAYING.] You see, I happened to go to a cheap joke shop [DEREK AND PANEL BEGIN LAUGHING AS DEREK TRIES TO CONTINUE] and what I found was all kinds of different tricks. And sometimes you find that at the end of the day, stink bombs do produce a certain amount of merriment and mirth. And that is why I really quite like it. You see, ladies and gentlemen, I am sitting here with a needle through my nose and a stink bomb in my pocket …

BUZZ

Nicholas: I must explain, the hilarity in the audience was caused by the fact that Derek Nimmo, apparently he was saying something about going to one of these joke shops. And in the middle of his conversation, sitting there with an angelic look on his face and a safety pin though his nose, he suddenly brought out a thing and showered himself with sort of plastic snow, as far as I could see.

Derek: Two pounds fifty in the joke shop! Very nice!

Nicholas: As Derek Nimmo obviously feels that his life as a serious actor is drying up, he's now going over to tricks and the conjuring.

Peter: I think he's trying to get this game on to television, that's what he is doing! [BIG LAUGH]

Derek did not make a habit of bringing along his joke-shop purchases, in fact it was a one-off, but he was in the habit of scribbling down the exact wording of each subject as I announced it. It was a ploy that occasionally backfired on him if he was not paying sufficient attention, as in this instance from August 1973, which also features disc jockey David Jacobs.

Nicholas: And, Derek Nimmo, your turn to begin, the subject, 'Old Wives' Tales'. And there are 60 seconds, starting now.
Derek: Hang on! I haven't got it written down.
BUZZ
Nicholas: David Jacobs has challenged.
David: I thought he hesitated.
Nicholas: I think he did, David.

The reason Derek did this was not, as Peter Jones once suggested, because he worried about forgetting what he was talking about. Rather, Derek's intention, where possible, was to cleverly link previous subjects later in the game. In this example from April 1984, also featuring Kenneth and Sheila Hancock, Derek combines previous rounds of 'The Most Loveable Points of a Rhinoceros' and 'Florence' with the current topic of 'Space Shuttles' and ends up causing me all sorts of problems.

Derek: I've always wanted to take Florence on a space shuttle, particularly if I could take along with me some powdered rhinoceros horn – which is a wonderful aphrodisiac.
BUZZ
Nicholas: Kenneth Williams challenged.
Kenneth: Well, we've had wonderful aphrodisiacs and powdered rhinoceros horns, nothing of which is anything to do with space shuttles. I think it's deviation.
Derek: I said I'd like to take them on a space shuttle. You don't know what kind of space shuttle I'm going to go on. [AUDIENCE LAUGH]

Kenneth: Deviation – taking horns on, this is all deviation, nothing to do with space shuttles!

Nicholas: Kenneth, it's a good challenge but I'm afraid I must disagree, because he was …

Kenneth: You're a great fool! That's all I can say! Mad!

Nicholas: So if I agree with Derek, I'm a great fool. If I agree with Kenneth, I'm a great hero.

Kenneth: It's a joke, isn't it! A joke! People like me, a great cult sitting here …

Sheila: And you've come all the way from Great Portland Street! [BIG LAUGH]

Kenneth: *I know!* You're right! You might well ask! It's an insult I'll have to swallow!

Nicholas: Because he might have … er … been having … er …

Kenneth: 'Er er er!' Hark at him! 'Er er er!' Can't get it out of him! Terrible diction! Terrible diction!

Nicholas: A flight of space fantasy I was trying to conjure out of my rather feeble … feeble …

Sheila: Oh Nick, come on!!

Derek: Just get on with it!

Sheila: Pull yourself together, dear!

Nicholas: Oh, it's all this white rhinoceros stuff! It's got through to me, you see! [BIG AUDIENCE LAUGH]

Sheila: He's going to pieces!

Nicholas: I'll tell you how fair I am. I agree entirely with you, you keep the subject and you have 20, no, 39 seconds left. Let's start again! Derek …

Kenneth: He can't even add up!

Nicholas: It's not adding up, it's subtracting! You don't realise that! That's the great thing I have to live with! [I CAN'T STOP LAUGHING AT THIS POINT] I've always been coming along to *Just a Minute*! We've been going for 15 years! And they still haven't given me a clock that can go forwards and then backwards! And I have to subtract the time every time they challenge! [PLAYING UP TO ALL THE CONFUSION, I START TALKING NONSENSE UNTIL IAN MESSITER RESCUES ME WITH A BLOW OF THE WHISTLE!]

I hope that the above examples go some way to illustrating how much fun it was to be in Derek's company. He was a delightful man, someone of whom I was very fond. We became friends through *Just a Minute* and quickly grew extremely close, socialising regularly in each other's homes where he was consistently great company around the dinner table.

Our friendship did not mean I was spared any of Derek's withering one-liners, not at all. There was never anything nasty in what he said, however. We knew each other far too well for that. In fact, it was our closeness that allowed him to send me up at times, because he knew I would not be offended and instead would play the role of the straight man and enjoy the humour. If I had not joined in it would have killed the laugh, but it was always clear that I was participating in the joke.

Derek constantly looked for ways to contribute positively to the show, and regularly found opportunities by taking these witty swipes in my direction, such as this very inventive clerihew conjured up on the spot in 1975.

The chairman of this game,
Is always the same.
The fact that he's a clot,
Matters not a jot.

In May 1989 Derek seizes the subject 'Sales' to make reference to one of my previous jobs, as host for more than a decade of the popular television quiz show *Sale of the Century*.

Derek: I remember on the television there used to be a programme called *Sale of the Century*. And on it there was a very curious fellow! He used to … I can't remember his name. I have no idea what happened to him actually!

During a recording in Guernsey in 1999, Derek is unsure about a challenge that has just been made against him.

> **Nicholas:** Don't look so surprised – you did actually say it again. They try and bluff me out of it, I must explain, they look at me sometimes with shocked surprise …
> **Derek:** I'm not! I'm looking at you with total contempt!
> **Nicholas:** [WITH AN EXPRESSION OF MOCK OUTRAGE] And that's one of my friends speaking! [BIG AUDIENCE LAUGH]

With Derek Nimmo unavailable for any of the Series 6 recordings, scheduled for broadcast between October 1971 and April 1972, and David Hatch keen to retain the format of three regular players plus a female guest, a replacement had to be found. Peter Jones, best known then for his role as the harassed factory manager in the BBC sitcom *The Rag Trade*, was invited to be a regular player.

Peter already had direct experience in working with a number of the *Just a Minute* team. He and I had known each other for years, appearing together on stage during the early 1960s in *Doctor at Sea* and co-starring in a BBC series *Night Train to Surbiton*; Sheila Hancock had played one of the workers in *The Rag Trade*; and both Derek and Clement had been guests of radio show *Call My Bluff*, on which Peter was a team captain.

Peter was one of my best friends, a genuinely lovely man, courteous and kind. He was also the least competitive actor I have known. He did not exhibit any of the aggression that is common to many people in our profession, which may have hampered his career to some extent. He never quite achieved the level of success in the business that his talent justified, which always saddened me.

Peter's style was in sharp contrast to the other two ever-present panellists in that series. Where Kenneth was frenetic and combustible, and Clement highly accomplished, skilful and determined to win, Peter approached the game in a far more laid-back manner. Hesitant you could almost say, which on the surface would appear far from ideal in *Just a Minute*. In fact it took Peter 16 shows to register a joint first place with Clement, and a further eight to achieve victory outright. Not that Peter would have worried in the least. He was there to entertain, not to win.

...on the subject of An Eccentric Scientist

The second of the Great British Eccentrics to appear on *Just a Minute* was Magnus Pyke. Sporting his trademark moustache and glasses, and gesticulating wildly, Magnus became a household name quite late in his life, as a panellist on Yorkshire Television's *Don't Ask Me* on which he and his fellow experts tried to answer all manner of science-based questions. His infectious enthusiasm and clear love of science brought overnight success … in his seventies.

Magnus was a natural communicator, through books, radio and television, with a passion to explain science in terms that everyone could understand. With his flailing arms, rapid-fire manner of speech and considerable intellect, Magnus very quickly entered into the public's affections. In fact, in the year before his *Just a Minute* debut (a broadcast of 17 November 1976) Magnus came third in a *New Scientist* poll to discover the best known and most charismatic scientist of all time, beaten only by Einstein and Newton.

He was a natural on *Just a Minute*, and although he only made four appearances, he made a lasting impression. Magnus brought all of his many qualities with him on his debut, which acts as an excellent illustration of his delightful and engaging personality.

Ian Messiter, of course, chose the subjects for that show very carefully, to ensure Magnus had the best possible platform on which to perform. In so doing, Ian provided an excellent opportunity for me to inject some humour from the beginning.

Kenneth Williams, Peter Jones and the actress and impressionist Janet Brown joined Magnus on the panel that evening and as I introduced the very first subject on which Magnus was asked to speak I deliberately struggled with the pronunciation to generate laughs. Kenneth latched on to this, much to the amusement of the audience.

Nicholas: Magnus Pyke, will you take the next round. The subject that Ian Messiter's thought up for you is 'Magnet … ' Oh no! 'Magnet-o-hydrodynamics' Is that … ? Magnet-ho?
Ian: Magnetohydrodynamics.
Nicholas: Oh *Mag-nee-to*-hydrodynamics!
Kenneth: Marvellous, innit, when the chairman can't even pronounce it! [BIG AUDIENCE LAUGH]

Surprisingly, given the very specialist nature of the subject, Magnus did not keep it all to himself, falling to a Peter Jones challenge for repetition after 34 seconds. A reluctant Peter Jones challenge, I should say. As is often the case when knowledgeable eccentrics such as Magnus are on the show, it leads to some very funny comments from the bemused other players. Peter's contribution here is beautifully judged and timed.

Peter: On the other hand I don't particularly want to talk about, em …
Kenneth: You've got it now, mate!!! Go on, Nick! Go on!
Nicholas: You've hoisted yourself on your own magnetohydrodynamics, Peter!
Kenneth: That's right, Nick! Show your authority! Go on, Nick!
Nicholas: There are 26 seconds left, Peter, on

'Magnetohydrodynamics', and you start now.

Peter: When my mother taught me about this subject … [BIG AUDIENCE LAUGH]

BUZZ

Nicholas: Magnus, you challenged.

Magnus: Yes, there was a lot of hesitation, he said his mother told him about it and then he was sort of hesitating.

Nicholas: Oh no! No, there wasn't!

Magnus: You don't think so?

Nicholas: There was just a natural pause, no more than yours.

Peter: Has he had a stimulus of some kind? He's very quick off the mark!

Nicholas: Yes, he's very quick off the mark. He's very good in this game. There are 20 seconds left, Peter, a wrong challenge, you have a point for that. 'Magnetohydrodynamics', starting now.

Peter: She explained to me that she didn't really know very much about it. She had a friend in Bechuanaland, a pen friend I should have said, who was corresponding with her and these tragic lines that she wrote when she came to the end of her entire knowledge of this subject which was extremely disappointing for me …

[WHISTLE FOLLOWED BY APPLAUSE]

Nicholas: So the subject that Peter Jones didn't want of 'Magnetohydrodynamics' gained him a considerable number of points and he's taken the lead at the end of that round. He's one ahead of our authority on the subject, Magnus Pyke.

Magnus: I'm sorry about that because I was going to tell you a lot about hydrodynamics. It's very interesting, how one little fellow with his finger can raise a whole motorcar. But I can't tell it to you now because …

Peter: And one little fellow with his buzzer BUZZ can stop you dead! [HUGE AUDIENCE LAUGH]

Peter claims there that a simple buzzer could stop Magnus in full flow, and while that is correct within the rules of the game, putting it into practice was not always easy. The subject here is 'Hard Lines'.

Magnus: [AT BREAKNECK SPEED] Yes, well, the hard lines on your face are to do with wrinkles which is to do with *senility*. As you get older you get smaller and your skin gets bigger. And you can tell how old you are by lifting up a piece of skin like that and the length of time it takes to go down …
BUZZ
Magnus: … you see it takes a very long time with me because I'm quite old. If you're young it goes down 'ping!' Just like that! It's very interesting how your hard lines disappear …
BUZZ
Magnus: … when you're young.
BUZZ
Nicholas: Kenneth Williams has challenged you three times.
Magnus: Good! Well, it's an interesting matter, isn't it? [AUDIENCE LAUGH]
Kenneth: *Yeee-s*, absolutely fascinating, but you did say 'skin' twice.
Magnus: You can see all the ladies in the audience picking up their skin and letting me see. And you can tell if you have a girl, if she's not as young as she might be if she goes down very slowly she's much older than you think.
Peter: Yes, with horses you look at the teeth! [BIG LAUGH]
Magnus: Yes, but I so seldom go out with a horse!!! [HUGE LAUGH]

Magnus's enthusiasm to communicate interesting facts is the reason his own broadcasts were such a success, and he most certainly brought the same attitude to *Just a Minute*. Here he is talking on the subject 'The International Candle', exhibiting his determination to pack as much information as possible into the time available.

Magnus: Well, the international candle is a way of measuring illumination and funnily enough the light you see is different whether you look at it with your eyeball or with a photoelectric circuit … And then there is the 'Pachinchi' effect – you mustn't forget about that – which shows that when you look at different colours you see them in different illuminations. And wait a minute! I've got some more things …
BUZZ

Magnus: Oh yes. Carrots, carrots, carrots, I want to outline this because carrots are …

Nicholas: I'm sorry, it's too late, Magnus.

Magnus: Oh, is it?

Nicholas: Yes, so while …

Magnus: There's an interesting thing about that …

Nicholas: While you're referring to your mental notes …

Magnus: Well, the airmen used to eat carrots before they went up shooting down bombers because …

Nicholas: Yes, I know. I believe during the war it was thanks to you, you started that …

Magnus: Well, there was something … but maybe I'll get back, who has got the point now?

Nicholas: Your colleague beside you, Peter Jones.

Peter: Well, I think so, I came to a conclusion he was hesitating because he used the phrase, 'wait a minute'!
[HUGE AUDIENCE LAUGH AND APPLAUSE]

Moments later when Peter Jones is talking on the same subject.

Peter: It's probably on sale in Hong Kong, that great melting pot where all the countries …
BUZZ

Nicholas: Magnus …

Magnus: If it was in a melting pot the candle would have melted and we wouldn't have it. [BIG LAUGH]

Nicholas: [HERE I FEEL IT IS IMPORTANT TO BE GENEROUS TO OUR GUEST AFTER HIS CHALLENGE] Oh, we give you a point for a very good challenge on that …

Magnus: Oh thank you.

Nicholas: … but he wasn't actually deviating from his international candle. He has 22 seconds to continue, starting now.

Peter: No doubt all the various nations of the world …

Magnus: Very well, it's like this, you see, when you look … [HUGE AUDIENCE LAUGH AS MAGNUS THINKS HE HAS THE SUBJECT]

Nicholas: No, no, I'm sorry …

Magnus: Oh, I'm so sorry.

Peter: That's quite all right. I do understand.

Nicholas: You got a bonus point for a good challenge but I left the subject with Peter.

Magnus: Oh, I didn't understand you.

Nicholas: No, I know you didn't.

Peter: You're being very fair to him, I think, Nicholas.

Magnus: I'm still trying to get back with this carrot thing …

Peter: Yes, I know you are. Yes, it's Muhammad Ali and Norton all over again! [HUGE AUDIENCE LAUGH]

Peter Jones' first few shows were reminiscent of Kenneth's early appearances in as much as they both required encouragement and gentle assistance from the chair. Kenneth understood my interventions on Peter's behalf, but he still latched on to them in order to create laughter. Clement, however, was less amused, I think. He thought we should play strictly by the rules, allowing the adept players to shine with clever discourse and challenges, with very little input from me.

Here is an example from Peter's second show, illustrating both his relaxed approach and my attempts to help him by pointing out possible challenges and being generous in my adjudications until he found his feet. The subtle difference in tone between Clement and Kenneth is also noteworthy – Kenneth is having fun while Clement seems genuinely aggrieved when I offer the newcomer some gentle assistance, a fact I feel necessary to point out.

Andree Melly is about to begin on the subject of 'Friendship'.

Kenneth: She won't know much about that, mate! I can tell you! Hahahaha!

Nicholas: You'll get your chance, Kenneth. 'Friendship' – Andree, can you talk for just a minute on that subject, starting now.

Andree: This is something we all need and value. The kindness and generosity of spirit of one fellow being for another. When you are speaking on a difficult subject like playing with your yo-yo, to feel that somebody by your side is in sympathy, and wants you to win and get that extra point. *This is real friendship.* And I feel that I … we … ehhhh … [AUDIENCE LAUGHTER]

BUZZ

Nicholas: Clement Freud, you've challenged.

Clement: Hesitation.

Nicholas: Hesitation. Actually, Peter Jones, I would have challenged her then. She said the man sitting beside her is in sympathy, wanting her to get the extra point. You weren't, you were trying to get one off her!

Peter: I know, but I thought she was going to say something very interesting and I wanted her to go on! [AUDIENCE LAUGHTER]

Nicholas: Clement Freud, I agree with your challenge, so you gain a point, you take over the subject of 'Friendship', there are 37 seconds left, starting now.

Clement: Friendship has been described as 'fellow feeling'. Or to put it another way, having Kenneth Williams' hand on my knee, again. [BIG AUDIENCE LAUGH AS THEY REALISE KENNETH IS TOUCHING CLEMENT'S KNEE] This I find very pleasant and endearing. And many's an evening …

BUZZ

Nicholas: Peter Jones, why have you challenged?
Peter: Deviation.
Nicholas: Yes!
Kenneth: [JUMPS OUT OF HIS SEAT IN OUTRAGE] *Nothing devious!!!!*
Nicholas: Kenneth, sit down!
Kenneth: You've had it on yours as well, so come off it!
Peter: Well, he must be deviating, describing his hand on his knee and everything!
Nicholas: He's going further than friendship, isn't he! [LOUD LAUGHTER FROM AUDIENCE] I quite agree with Peter Jones' challenge so he gains a point and he takes over the subject of 'Friendship' and there are 24 seconds left, starting now.

BUZZ

Peter: Oscar Wilde said …
Nicholas: No! Clement Freud, you challenged.
Clement: Hesitation.
Nicholas: No, because he hadn't got going and he's new to the game.
Clement: Of course he hasn't got going, that's why it's hesitation! If he had got going it wouldn't be hesitation!
[AUDIENCE LAUGH]
Nicholas: This is only his second appearance …
Clement: Oh, I see. There are different rules, you mean?
Nicholas: Yes! At this moment there are different rules.
[AUDIENCE LAUGH]
Clement: Oh fine!
Peter: I'm supposed to start speaking when you say now, is that right?
Nicholas: Peter Jones has only been with the show once before, you've been with it for three years now.

Kenneth: Well, let's have hearts and flowers in a minute!
[CLEMENT AND AUDIENCE LAUGHING]
Nicholas: [REGAINING CONTROL] Peter Jones has a point.
He keeps the subject 'Friendship', 23 seconds left, starting now.
Peter: Oscar Wilde said that there is no friendship between
men and women, there is love, enmity and passion, but no
friendship. And I always think there is a great deal of truth in
that. Though after what Andree Melly has just told me about
her feelings about … er … what she's thinking and what I'm …
um … saying …
BUZZ
Nicholas: Clement Freud, you challenged, why?
Clement: I would have said with anyone else it would have
been hesitation. But … [LOUD LAUGHTER FROM PANEL AND
AUDIENCE FOLLOWED BY CLAPPING]
Nicholas: I hope, Clement, that you are playing for a laugh
and that round of applause and not showing the unsporting
feelings that you're displaying. Because I agree with your
challenge, there was a very definite hesitation.
Clement: Oh good.

Then later in the same show:

Nicholas: The subject is now with you, Peter, your turn to
begin. The subject is 'Cannons'. Can you talk on that subject for
60 seconds, starting now. [SILENCE]
Peter: … They are the most …
BUZZ
Nicholas: Kenneth Williams challenged you.
Kenneth: Hesitation.
Nicholas: Yes, I know, but I'm not going to allow it, because it's
only the second time he's played the game.
Kenneth: *Oh, don't mind me. Just kick me as you pass!*
Nicholas: Can I wait till after the programme? [AUDIENCE
BURST OUT LAUGHING AS DO I, REQUIRING ME TO

TAKE A DEEP BREATH TO CONTINUE] Peter, next week I'm
afraid I can't be quite so lenient. You do have to begin as soon
as I say …

Peter: You mean I'm coming next week? [CLEMENT LAUGHS
LOUDLY AND AUDIENCE APPLAUD]

Nicholas: I'll put it to the audience. Shall we have Peter Jones
next week? ['YES' FROM THE AUDIENCE]

Peter: I don't want charity, you know. I mean, you're
humiliating someone in my position …

Kenneth: Well, what are you holding that begging bowl for
then??? [HUGE LAUGH]

The final broadcast of Series 6 aired on 4 April 1972, and two weeks
later I received a letter from David Hatch, informing me that the
listening figures had been high and looking to establish dates for the
next series, which would begin recording in August. I knew Derek
Nimmo would be making a welcome return, but even still I did not
expect to read David's final sentence. 'Please don't mention this to
Peter yet, because no conclusion has yet been reached on who will
occupy the third male chair.'

Why would the BBC have doubted Peter? After a slow start his
contributions had been wonderful and the banter between Peter,
Kenneth and Clement highly entertaining and good-natured. It was
hardly a surprise Peter had proved to be a success. After all, in the
early 1950s he had been a big hit as half of a duo – alongside Peter
Ustinov – in arguably radio's very first improvised comedy show, *In
All Directions,* playing dodgy characters Dudley and Morry Grosvenor,
driving around the country looking for a fictitious address. Never
before had the BBC sanctioned an unscripted show, and it proved to
be very funny. Naturally a performer with such a background would
be a perfect fit on *Just a Minute.*

Fortunately the correct decision was made when Peter was re-
engaged for the next series, completing what many people regard
as *Just a Minute*'s classic line-up – Williams, Nimmo, Freud and
Jones. These four regulars first featured in a show broadcast on 26

September 1972 and would go on to make a further 37 appearances together through to 23 June 1988.

Over the years fans of *Just a Minute* have often said to me that Peter was their favourite player of the game, and I can understand why. While the others might be vying for points, Peter would sit back, waiting to pounce with a perfectly judged one-liner or clever challenge. Here he is in great form during a show broadcast on 4 November 1975 that also features Kenneth, Derek and Aimi on the panel. The subject is 'Snap'.

Derek: The snap of a twig in the forest. Red Indians walking towards the plantation where the young settlers are there with their young children …
BUZZ
Nicholas: Aimi MacDonald.
Aimi: Two 'there's. Oh, *definitely*.
Nicholas: Two 'young's.
Kenneth: What are you doing there, helping her or being a chairman?! [AUDIENCE LAUGH]
Nicholas: I'm being, doing both.
Kenneth: 'I'm being, doing both'?! [LAUGHING] He gets worse every week.
Nicholas: Yes. A Freudian slip: 'I'm being, doing both', yes. And as he can't be with us this week, he did send all his love to all his many fans who listen to *Just a Minute*, but he said he had other business.
Peter: You mean he had a job! [BIG AUDIENCE LAUGH]
Nicholas: I think it's more fun with Aimi MacDonald than Clement Freud, anyway!
Peter: I've never tried it with Clement Freud! [DEREK AND AIMI LAUGHING LOUDLY AND JOINED BY AUDIENCE]

Later, Peter manages to get the better of Kenneth with one of the most entertaining pieces of gamesmanship I've ever witnessed on *Just a Minute*.

Nicholas: Kenneth, you have the subject and you have 17 seconds on 'Snap', starting now.
Kenneth: It is a fact that when somebody of a *sub-lunary* talent is faced with a general incomp …
BUZZ
Nicholas: Peter Jones has challenged.
Peter: What was that again? [AUDIENCE LAUGHTER]
Kenneth: It is a fact that when someone of a *sublunary* talent …
BUZZ
Peter: Repetition. [HUGE LAUGHTER FROM EVERYONE, AND CLAPPING]
Kenneth: [LAUGHING] *I've let myself be led!!* I was led like a lamb to the slaughter.

Another reason for Peter's popularity was his honest charm. He once admitted that, 'Well, I'm not winning because of course I can't really play the game,' and on another occasion, when challenged for repetition, 'I never listen to what I'm saying'. Peter certainly had no concerns about poking fun at himself, and sometimes even his own career.

In 1960 and again in 1974, Peter hosted television versions of the popular radio show *Twenty Questions*, but on both occasions a second series failed to be commissioned. At the end of this extract from November 1976, which features Sheila Hancock, Peter provides an explanation for this unfortunate setback.

Nicholas: Peter, you have 13 seconds left for 'What I Put into Life', starting now.
Peter: I think perhaps what I put into life is appreciation. Now Kenneth Williams is an acquired taste and I'm still trying to appreciate even him.
BUZZ
Nicholas: Sheila.
Sheila: Oh! No, that was a mistake. I thought it was 'appreciate' and 'appreciate' but he wasn't.

Peter: No, it wasn't.

Nicholas: No, but I'm afraid he gets a point for that. It was a wrong challenge. You did press your buzzer and the light came on.

Sheila: I put into life a certain generosity. I've given him a point. [AUDIENCE LAUGH]

BUZZ

Peter: [FLABBERGASTED THAT SHEILA SEEMS TO BE TALKING ON HIS SUBJECT] Wh … , wh … , wh … , what?

Nicholas: It's all right, Peter, I've given you the point!

Peter: So why is she rabbiting on like that?

Nicholas: Because everybody seems to rabbit on in this game, you know. [BIG LAUGH]

Peter: But I thought I got the subject back.

Sheila: Yes, you did! Get on with it!

Peter: Well, what are you talking about?

Nicholas: You haven't got it back. You haven't lost it.

Peter: That's how I lost the chairmanship of *Twenty Questions*, going on like you are! [HUGE AUDIENCE LAUGH AND APPLAUSE]

Peter's self-deprecating lines were sometimes delivered with a sting in the tail, often aimed at Kenneth. Here he is talking on the subject of 'Losing Money in a Telephone Box' from a broadcast of 18 September 1982.

> **Peter:** Well, it's one of the most frustrating ways of losing money that I know. Because unless you write to the people, or they take your name and address, the operator, then you can't get your money back. And this does seem to be very unfair. Now if …
> BUZZ
> **Nicholas:** Kenneth Williams challenged.
> **Kenneth:** Deviation – he's telling the audience something that's utterly not true. You simply get the operator and say that you've

lost your money. She gets you the call free. I mean it's rubbish
to say ...

Nicholas: But you can't actually get your money back! That's
what he said.

Kenneth: You don't want your money back, you want your call,
don't you?

Nicholas: Yes, but you may not get your call, then you still can't
get your money back.

Kenneth: Well, anyway, I should have the subject. He was very
dreary about it and I think ...

Nicholas: I know he was dreary, I don't think he was actually
deviating.

Peter: Well I ... I admit to being dreary, but that's never been
any hindrance on this game! As Kenneth Williams has proved
time and again! [HUGE LAUGH]

Over the years, perhaps because of their opposite approaches
to playing the game, Peter and Kenneth built up a wonderful
understanding, bouncing gags off each other to create many laughs.
In this extract from February 1980, comedy actor and scriptwriter
John Junkin is the guest, and Kenneth is speaking on 'Getting a
Good Start'.

Kenneth: What immediately springs to my mind is the training
I underwent in the army. And an assault course was presented to
us. And believe me, we had to get a good start ...

BUZZ

Nicholas: John Junkin has challenged.

John: Hesitation, I think.

Nicholas: Oh no, no, no.

John: Believe me we ...

Kenneth: *It's unbelievable!!* A guest! A guest! He's not even on the
show regular! And he's accused *me* of hesitation! There was no
hesitation there at all! None whatsoever! Not one suspicion was
there!

John: I dozed off in the middle of one of the pauses!

[AUDIENCE LAUGH]

Kenneth: Listen, I'm going to take you outside, I'm not going to sit here …

Nicholas: If we challenged for such small hesitations, I think we'd never get going at all, John.

Peter: I think, John, you should make allowances for his curious delivery. And for his age! [BIG LAUGH]

Peter then acquires the subject and appears to have decided to pay Kenneth a compliment on his fine acting ability, but with devious intent.

Peter: And in all seriousness I can say that when I went to the Garrick Theatre (was it really two decades ago?) and saw a show called *Share My Lettuce*, with a person I thought was perhaps one of the most remarkably gifted performers as …

[WHISTLE AND APPLAUSE]

Nicholas: Well, Peter Jones kept going until the whistle went which tells us that the 60 seconds is up, and whoever is speaking at that moment, do I need to remind you, gets an extra point …

Peter: I knew Kenneth wouldn't interrupt me! [BIG LAUGH]

As with Derek Nimmo, my close friendship with Peter did not protect me from his disparaging comments. During one show he claimed I was being patronising when I gave him a point, to which I replied that I was just trying to be fair. 'I know! And you fail most of the time!' On hearing this, Derek could not contain his laughter and had to take a few moments to gather himself before exclaiming, '*I like that!* It makes me laugh anyway, I can tell you!' On another occasion, Clement Freud had been waxing lyrically on a subject that had quite captivated both Kenneth and myself, as I tried to explain to Peter while we debated a challenge. 'I thought that was magnificent. I was like Kenneth Williams, I was carried away.' In an instant came Peter's retort. 'I wish you were!'

As the years passed, Peter began to slow down a little and found, I believe, the competiveness of the others more difficult to deal with. As a result he adopted a slightly different approach to the game, sitting back even more, listening while the others did battle, ready to strike with a late, wonderfully witty or acerbic comment.

Peter was aware of this slowing down with age, and being the clever, talented man he was, he used the fact to create laughter. In February 1992 Paul Merton had been speaking on the subject of 'First Baron George Jeffries', lost it, and picked it up again.

Paul: First ... Baron ... George ... Jeffries was a pub round the ...
   BUZZ
Nicholas: Peter Jones challenged.
Peter: He said that already!
Nicholas: That's the subject ...
Peter: Very slowly.
Nicholas: Yes, he said that, that's the subject on the card. You can repeat the subject on the card. I know you've only been playing the game 25 years, Peter ... [LAUGHTER FROM AUDIENCE AND PAUL]
Peter: Yes ...
Nicholas: ... but sometimes things do slip your memory, I realise.
Peter: Thank God, it's merciful in that way! [LAUGHTER AND APPLAUSE]

Six years later, and again with Paul Merton, Peter treats us to a line that was diametrically opposite from the truth, but somehow summed up the self-effacing, quick-thinking humour that had entertained *Just a Minute* fans for so many years. He is talking on the subject of 'Doric Columns'.

Peter: Frankly there's really nothing more to say about them. [HUGE LAUGH] And it seems to me rather boring to rabbit on, when there's nothing to say.

BUZZ

Nicholas: Paul challenged.

Paul: Well, 'nothing to say'. Repetition of 'nothing to say'.

Peter: This is an attitude that's hampered me for 32 years!

[HUGE LAUGHTER AND APPLAUSE]

Regular winner Clement Freud once commented that 'Peter Jones is very good at losing at this programme'. In many ways what Clement said was true, and Peter was perfectly happy for that to be the case.

Clement was paying Peter a compliment, I have no doubt, recognising the fun Peter brought to the game without the need to be competitive. If anyone had said the same about Clement, he would have been horrified.

My relationship with Clement stretched further back than with any of the other players. In the 1950s I regularly performed my cabaret act at his Royal Court Theatre Club, situated on the top floor of the Royal Court Theatre on Sloane Square, London. Clement had trained as a chef in the Dorchester before launching the club, at which he offered fine dining and entertainment from an array of performers. As host, Clement stepped into the role of compère, initially introducing each act in a very succinct manner, but as his confidence grew, so did the length of his introductions. I do not think it is too much of an exaggeration to say that the groundwork for his later success on *Just a Minute* was laid during those years. Back then he was not known to the wider public, but to all those who worked with him during that period it was clear that he was a man with multiple talents.

My first engagement at Clement's club was in 1954, but my first encounter with him happened long before then – at public school. We attended St Paul's at the same time, a fact not lost on Derek Nimmo and Kenneth Williams.

During a show broadcast on 22 May 1979, Ian Messiter selected the subject of 'Parbuckle'. Derek was first to speak and, perhaps wisely, given what was to happen, chose to interpret this rather archaic word as referring to a housemaster at his son's school, 'Pa' Buckles. He kept this going for 35 seconds before a correct challenge of hesitation from Clement. From there, mayhem ensued.

Clement claims a parbuckle could be a knot, eliciting outrage from Kenneth.

Kenneth: Parbuckle is a rope, it can't be a knot!!! It's a rope! It's got to go up and down! A knot can't go up and down! What are you talking about?! A knot's for tying, you great nit! He's an idiot! He doesn't know anything!! He's never read a dictionary!

Peter: Well, it doesn't matter, it's not er ...

Kenneth: Why, it matters to me! It matters very much to me! What do you mean it doesn't matter! I think it's important that these people here are given an accurate account of these things, otherwise they're going out of this place, full of misinformation! Is that what you want, a nation of illiterates walking round not knowing, not having any idea all their lives, what a parbuckle is! They want to know, they're throbbing with it, aren't they! That lady there, she's dying to know what a real parbuckle is and I happen to know!

I rule Kenneth's challenge incorrect and the round continues.

Clement: In a ship's chandler's shop in Leyton Buzzard ...

BUZZ

Nicholas: Derek Nimmo challenged.

Derek: Repetition of 'ships'.

Nicholas: Yes, you did mention the word 'ships' before.

Clement: Not *ships* chandler, ship-apostrophe-s chandler.

Nicholas: You're quite right, yes it was 'ships' before and this was 'ship-apostrophe-s'. I'm sorry, Clement, ten seconds ...

Derek: Oh for goodness sake! Really!

Nicholas: ... on 'Parbuckles' starting ...

Derek: Since he was a prefect at school you've always been terrified of Freud, haven't you! [BIG LAUGH]

Kenneth: Yes! He's right! Yes! Right, yes! That's true, isn't it!

Derek: If anybody else on the team had said 'ships' twice …

Nicholas: I try to be …

Derek: 'Ships-apostrophe-s'! A load of rubbish! You ought to resign!

Kenneth: *Resign!*

Derek: *Resign!*

Kenneth: *Resign!*

Derek: Shall we ask the audience if Parsons should resign?

Kenneth: He's a rotten chairman! [ANOTHER BIG AUDIENCE LAUGH]

At this point I turn to Ian Messiter to ask his opinion. Ian agrees the inclusion of an apostrophe constitutes a different word, and much to Kenneth's consternation Clement keeps the subject and the round continues to its conclusion

I am still none the wiser as to the meaning of 'parbuckle', however.

I still regard Clement as a friend. I was very fond of him, but we did have a difference of opinion as to how the game should be played. A difference of opinion that simmered over the years and eventually led to an unfortunate incident in Edinburgh, which I will come to later.

Initially *Just a Minute* was regarded as a more formal panel game. As the show developed, however, my approach also evolved. I grew to see Ian Messiter's creation as a wonderfully inventive vehicle that can generate a lot of laughter created by *everyone* involved. In this regard, Clement and I disagreed.

As we were finding our feet, the show was rigid – more old-fashioned, if you like – a simple game where intelligent people came to talk on a subject to demonstrate their intellect and wit. The humour produced from challenges and interplay was secondary to the players being given an opportunity to display their individual talent. As for the chairman's role, Clement saw that as a passive activity, someone whose input should be restricted to, 'Correct challenge. That's a point to you. Carry on.' This is how he phrased it in his autobiography *Freud Ego*: 'A good chairman is one who steers the game with a minimum of interruptions, encourages the contestants and makes correct decisions.'

In Clement's opinion, the show should have been preserved in aspic, unable to evolve. If that had happened, if the rules had not been refined and defined over the years while still remaining absolutely true to Ian Messiter's original concept, I am convinced *Just a Minute* would long since have died a natural death. Stuck in a time warp, it would have withered away, falling victim to the evolution of comedy styles and viewer preferences.

Clement was a highly intelligent individual, intellectual and a polymath – raconteur, writer, broadcaster, restaurateur, chef, lover of sport and a politician – and he brought all his varied skills and abilities to every edition of *Just a Minute* in which he appeared. To great effect. No one in the history of the programme has won more games.

From Clement's love of cooking, we learned of his opinions on a wide variety of dishes, including dripping ('delicious'), boar's head ('It's a very odd thing that the more patriotic food is, the more disgusting it is.') and cock-a-leekie soup ('You would think it would be a slightly incontinent condition, but is in fact chicken broth with leeks and prunes.').

Over the years, we were also treated to some mouth-watering recipes, such as this quite marvellous sounding 'Omelette' which is on the menu in April 1983. Midway through, Clement is challenged for repetition of 'into', eliciting boos from the audience who clearly want to hear the remainder of the recipe. I agree, and Clement continues.

Clement: A concoction of eggs, often containing some fish or meat or vegetable inside. Even cheese, I venture to say. You take half a dozen of these hen fruit, put them into a bowl, and whisk them with a fork, if possible iced water, cream, and little pieces of butter. At which time you get a pan very hot indeed, put a miniscule amount of fat into it, and swish the mixture into the fryer … Parsley and mint are other useful ingredients to wrap into the mixture about which we have already talked. Now it is terribly important, I would like none of you to forget, that when an omelette is served, the plate should be hot.

[WHISTLE AND VERY ENTHUSIASTIC APPLAUSE]

Clement's culinary interests, however, could sometimes become the target of a funny challenge. On 3 February 1976 he outlines the 'Things I Keep in My Freezer'.

> **Clement:** The things in my deep freezer are cockroaches mostly, which come creeping crawling out …
>   BUZZ
> **Nicholas:** Peter Jones has challenged.
> **Peter:** I don't think he should be allowed to advertise his hotel on the air! [BIG LAUGH]

From the world of literature, Clement had favourite writers whom he enjoyed quoting, such as Ogden Nash, and in this instance Rudyard Kipling whose poem 'If' made a number of appearances, much to Kenneth's disgust. Here Clement is speaking on 'Conjuring' in November 1971.

> **Clement:** If you can keep your head, while all around you …
>   BUZZ
> **Nicholas:** Kenneth Williams challenged.
> **Kenneth:** Repetition! We're always having this bit of old rubbish crammed down our … *A load of old rubbish!!* He just resorts to it at every juncture, Nicholas! And it's simply not good enough, Nicholas!

Kenneth is in fact being somewhat disingenuous (imagine!) in his outrage here, as this extract from 11 March 1969 proves. Kenneth has the subject 'A Common Touch'.

Kenneth: This is a phrase which I take to mean, if you can keep your head when all around are losing theirs and still retain the common touch. These are of course the words of the poet …

BUZZ

Nicholas: Clement Freud, why have you challenged?

Clement: Deviation. If you lose your head you have nothing to guide your hands! [BIG AUDIENCE LAUGH]

Perhaps inspired by his days running the Royal Court Theatre Club, Clement exhibited an excellent knowledge of old-time music hall and variety material. This is a classic song from the nineteenth century to which he referred on three separate occasions, but only once were we blessed with the full chorus, during a September 1973 broadcast.

Clement: 'Does your mother take in washing?
Has she sold her mangle?
What's become of the old piano your sister used to strangle?
Has your father plenty of work?
Does he still get boozed, too?
Tell me all the particulars
And stop as long as you used to.'

In 1998, in a programme recorded at Blenheim Palace, Clement professes his appreciation of more modern music (well, more modern than the nineteenth century) when talking on the subject of 'Two of a Kind' which he eventually loses because of his deliberate pauses, which produce a great deal of laughter.

Clement: The Ink Spots, of whom I was extremely fond, had a song called, 'I Hates You Because Your F … E … repeated … T Are Too Big.' 'Down at Harlem, at a table for two, there was four of us. Me, your big … and you,' were the lyrics. [BIG AUDIENCE LAUGH]

Sport was another of Clement's passions, with cricket references featuring in a number of his *Just a Minute* appearances. He once claimed that while watching village cricket in Walmersley, a French person approach him and said, '*Excusez-moi, monsieur, qu'est que c'est a "googly"?*' to which Clement replied, 'It was an off-break bowled with a leg-break action,' confusing the poor fellow terribly.

Clement's sporting interest extended well beyond cricket. He knew, for example, that footballer Matt Le Tissier had been born on Guernsey and also revealed he enjoyed watching the pipe-smoking world bowls champion David Bryant. Perhaps Clement's greatest love in sport, however, was reserved for Plymouth Argyle Football Club, of which he had been a fan for many years and may even have featured in some of his daydreams. It certainly seemed that way in 1976 when he was given the subject of 'Beef' and instead of launching into the expected cookery-related anecdote, he surprised us all with the following.

> **Clement:** In my sporting autobiography, which of course was called 'Beef, Booze and Birds', which related my arrival at Home Park to play for Plymouth Argyle dressed in green and white, I raced around the pitch. I was at centre half at the time but with no sense of balance or direction. [BIG LAUGH]

In July 1973 Clement Freud won a by-election in the Cambridgeshire constituency of Isle of Ely to become a Liberal MP in the House of Commons. This was potentially a problem for the BBC. Clement's appearances on *Just a Minute* during elections could have been deemed to provide an unfair political advantage, which would be against the charter. There were rumours around the time when Clement first entered parliament that he might be dropped from the show. Thank goodness these proved unfounded.

Clement's Westminster career did, however, have an impact on the show. He contested five further general elections (I actively supported him in some of his campaigning), winning four before suffering defeat in 1987, and in the month or so preceding each of these elections *Just a Minute* programmes featuring Clement were not broadcast. In fact we were generally taken off air for those weeks. Whether this was something Clement recommended, or whether it was a BBC directive, I am unsure.

As a sitting MP, Clement refrained from mentioning this aspect of his career during his shows, although a heartfelt passing reference did creep in while he spoke on the subject of 'My Favourite Place' on 9 March 1977.

Clement: The constituency of the Isle of Ely generally is very, very near to my heart …

BUZZ

Clement: … very near!

Nicholas: Kenneth Williams has challenged.

Kenneth: 'Very, very near!'

Nicholas: 'Very, very near!' Kenneth there are 32 seconds …

Clement: I do think sincerity is more important here than the minutiae of this game. [BIG LAUGH]

Such reticence did not extend to Kenneth Williams, however, who saw Clement's recent re-election in May 1979 as a source of entertainment. Clement is speaking on 'Smash and Grab'.

Clement: To be a successful smash and grab operator, it is homework which counts …

BUZZ

Nicholas: Kenneth Williams has …

Kenneth: Deviation! I don't think an MP's got any right to broadcast stuff about … how to be an efficient smash and grab man!! *Absolutely disgraceful!!!* Very devious! Most devious!

Nicholas: On the basis that it is devious for an MP to put forward those sort of recommendations …

Kenneth: Hear hear! Hear hear! Very glad you picked that point up, Mr Chairman! Very good! Very glad! I'm glad we've got an astute chairman here! Very glad!

Following the loss of his seat, Clement was more than happy to introduce the topic of his time in the Commons, sometimes with considerable candour, and on other occasions purely to tell a good story or deliver a funny line (on the subject of 'Oxymoron' Clement offers the following definition: 'a juxtaposition of two words, the whole of which beggars belief, like "a heavyweight Liberal"'.).

Serving as an MP would also appear to have provided Clement with some advantages, or so he amusingly claimed in April 2005 when given the subject 'The Best Excuse I Ever Had'.

> **Clement:** When I was a member of parliament, and drove home, or to my constituency, I was frequently stopped by police who decreed that I was going too quickly. And I made the excuse that I was speeding for no other reason than to go to Westminster in order to vote for a pay rise for policemen!

Clement Freud was without doubt the most competitive player of *Just a Minute* there has ever been, even more so than his great rival, Derek Nimmo (and that's saying something!). The will to win was part of Clement's DNA and he was proud of it. 'Winning in *Just a Minute*,' he said, 'is something I am fairly accustomed to, mostly because the other people lose with unrelenting frequency.' What made Clement so effective as a player of the game was the fact that he was able to combine his deep competiveness with intelligence, a confidence in his ability and his own brand of dry humour, as demonstrated by this fine example of a full minute from March 1972, on 'Why I Am Seldom Wrong'.

> **Clement:** The only possible answer to the question why I am seldom wrong has got to be because I am invariably right. And the reason for this is the wealth of knowledge I have acquired in what could be called a long life. If you ask me to explain Pythagoras, I would do so readily. Anyone who wishes information about differential calculus has only to come to me. Why am I seldom wrong? Here you have it. Education,

erudition, intellect and a brain power second only to Kenneth Williams who is about to buzz but will now, I hope, refrain from being so beastly as to interrupt this flow of rhetoric which I have worked upon.

[WHISTLE AND APPLAUSE]

To win, Clement employed a number of clever tactics. His ability to replace words in order to avoid repetition was first class. Here he is in July 2003 with the subject 'Ballroom Dancing', coping wonderfully well with the tricky words before falling to the repetition of 'again'.

Clement: Ballroom dancing tends to take place in palais or halls, and there is music to which people go, slow, and that word again, quick, monosyllable repeated, and then the first one again.

Listening intently, with sharp focus, was one of Clement's methods, forensically scrutinising each word said in the hope of spotting an opportunity to engineer a challenge and earn a point. In January 1970 Derek Nimmo has the subject 'False Teeth'.

Derek: It's a very embarrassing subject for me. I must confess, actually, that I do happen to have a couple of little ones, really, which I had knocked out, the real ones, when I was at school, and I then had a little plate made, which stuck in on two little wire hooks round corners really. And then one day I remember, I swallowed them. [AUDIENCE LAUGH] And I was sent home from school, and there were long, anxious moments while relations foregathered, waiting for them to reappear. Eventually ...

BUZZ

Nicholas: Clement Freud has challenged. Why?

Clement: Repetition.

Nicholas: Of what?

Clement: Of the teeth, if they reappear! [I BURST OUT LAUGHING AS DO THE AUDIENCE]

Clement's level of concentration seemed to intensify the closer the 60 seconds drew to completion. He would lean forward, buzzer at the ready, poised to pounce on any misdemeanour. Some guests who were less familiar with the game could find this a little intimidating, and in some cases it caused them to hesitate. Even more regular players, knowing full well Clement's intentions, would occasionally react. In the same show just mentioned, Sheila Hancock performs wonderfully well under such pressure, turning Clement's tactics to her advantage as she speaks for the full minute on 'Saving Up', with some leniency granted to her by the other players.

> **Sheila:** This is something that now I am patently bad at. But when I was young I was very good at it. My father was a very frugal man and I used to have so much pocket money every week, above which sum he *would not* allow me to go. When I was very young it was sixpence and then I think it was increased to a shilling. All of which I had to work for. And out of that money I had to save money for Christmas presents and birthday presents. So as soon as I had saved up for Christmas, I then had to start all over again for birthdays. In fact the whole of my youth was spent saving up. Which probably explains why I am an extremely extravagant person now. If I want something and if I have the money *I get it immediately*. And this I think is why I will never teach my child to save up. Also I save up my emotions. If I feel angry with somebody, if I dislike somebody, *if I feel spiteful like I do towards Clement Freud, I am saving up for one dirty great scene in which I will tell him exactly what I think of him when he comes in in the last few seconds of my thing, which he is waiting with his finger on the buzzer to do now! I will save up the biggest …*
> [WHISTLE FOLLOWED BY APPLAUSE]

Such was Clement's desire to snatch the subject in the dying seconds that if he realised too late that he had overlooked a chance he could find it hard to accept. In this example, Derek is coming to the end of a round on 'Great Paintings' in a broadcast from 18 April 1981.

Derek: Canaletto, I suppose, the great Venetian master, is of all the painters that I have ever seen probably the one with the most ... [WHISTLE AND APPLAUSE]
Nicholas: So ...
Clement: *Where* did you see Canaletto?
Derek: [CONFUSED] Sorry?
Clement: [IN A STERN VOICE] Where did you *see* Canaletto? [AN AWKWARD SILENCE DESCENDS] Oh, it doesn't ... He's *dead*! [UNCOMFORTABLE LAUGHTER FROM AUDIENCE BUILDS]
Nicholas: [LAUGHING IN ORDER TO LIGHTEN THE MOOD] You try very hard sometimes, Clement!

The above miss was a rare occurrence for Clement. He really was an expert at pinching the subject with only a second or two remaining. He could not see any clock or stopwatch to provide an indication of how long remained (none of the panellists can); Clement, however, had a secret weapon.

He always sat next to the whistleblower and he had noticed that sometimes, as the seconds counted down, that person would pick up their whistle in preparation to signal the end of the round. Clement knew then that if he were going to make a move, it would have to be done quickly. Fortunately for the other players, our whistleblowers did eventually stop this habit, much to Clement's disappointment.

Another technique Clement employed was to take a subject and cleverly reinterpret its meaning, which always produced a burst of appreciative laughter from the audience, in itself eating into the time remaining. For instance, on the subject of 'Youth' Clement began with, 'Youth is the first syllable of "euthanasia", something which I'm desperately against because it is inhuman ... ' and on 'The Midas Touch, 'My da's touch was much warmer than my mum's touch!'

Of all the tactics Clement employed in order to win points on *Just a Minute*, one stands out above the rest. Clement was an expert at constructing lists. It is perfectly within the rules, and it is an exceedingly difficult task to perform without hesitation or repetition. Listing became Clement's trademark and he was without question the master. It was a particularly useful skill in the first few series when Ian Messiter introduced his gimmick rounds. Here's Clement in February 1968, talking on 'The People Next Door', with the word 'and' prohibited. 'I've got new people next door. An awfully nice couple from Scotland consisting of a man, a woman, a child, three dogs, two cats, a snake, a parakeet.'

One of the trickiest aspects of creating a list is to know when to stop and head down a different track. Clement was generally very accomplished at this, but occasionally he did try to push things a touch too far, as in this list of 'Nursery Foods'.

> **Clement:** Nursery food is a sort of portmanteau name given to cobbled and scrambled eggs and mashed potatoes, bubble and squeak, cottage and shepherd pies, corn beef hash, kedgeree, puddings such as semolina and rice, tapioca and vermicelli, syllabubs, custard creams and mousses, Welsh rarebits, anchovies on toast. They all qualify as nursery food. And there is …
> BUZZ
> **Nicholas:** Peter Jones challenged.
> **Peter:** I don't think anchovies … [BIG LAUGH]
> **Nicholas:** No! I would agree, Peter! I can't see any children in the nursery eating their anchovies very rapidly!

This is an unusual example of over-extending on Clement's behalf, as he was always very careful not to allow his lists to become boring. As accurate as that statement is, I am positive *EastEnders* star Wendy Richard would disagree. She found the technique infuriating and would often exclaim, 'He's listing again! You have got to stop him!' As far as I was concerned, I rather admired Clement's skill, especially when he chose to be inventive, such as this creation of a family from 'Whiz Kids' on 4 September 2000.

Clement: Hamish and Ophelia Whiz at Ashby-de-la-Zouch have a numerous family, and the kids are called Adam, Bernard, Charles, David, Eric, Ferdinand, Frank, George, twins Harry, Isaac, James, Kenneth, Leonard ...

Where Wendy was genuinely annoyed, Kenneth Williams would use Clement's listing as a launch pad for one of his own trademark routines – the indignant and outraged fellow player – which often led to highly entertaining exchanges. Here Clement is speaking on 'Flat Hunting' in November 1969.

Clement: Essex is perhaps the best county for doing this, because all you need is a terrain without hills or mountains, without undue depression and a fair amount of game such as grouse, hare, buffalo, tigers, rabbits ...
BUZZ
Nicholas: Kenneth Williams, why have you challenged?
Kenneth: Repetition! An endless list of animals and we want to listen to the subject.
Nicholas: No, I think we've got to establish one thing. If you go on, you can have a list of anything and call it repetition. But unless you actually repeat the word, I don't think that in this game we're going to get anywhere if ...
Kenneth: That's true!! We've got to have the *rules*. You've got to have rules!! You can't get on without them. Quite right!
Nicholas: So I'm not going to give any points for that, I'm going to ask Clement Freud to continue with 44 seconds left, starting now.
Clement: Horses, cows, chickens, bantams, worms, hamsters ...
BUZZ
Nicholas: Kenneth Williams, why ...
Kenneth: Deviation! It's all *boring*!
Clement: I'm always boring!
Kenneth: Well, that's deviation, you see!

Clement: I'm always boring, that's not deviation!!! [BIG
AUDIENCE LAUGH AND APPLAUSE]

Despite the arsenal of tactics at his disposal, Clement did not use
them to saturate *Just a Minute*. He recognised the importance of
entertaining the audience and listeners. Ours is a show designed to
produce laughter, and even though Clement and I did not always see
eye to eye on exactly how that should occur, he did not lose sight of
why the game was so popular. He wanted to win, certainly, but had
the wit to link that desire with his ability to tell a funny story or joke,
pause to soak up the audience reaction, and *still* keep the subject.
Here he is working in a funny joke when talking on 'Inspiration' in
August 1998.

Clement: This man telephoned the hospital, asked for
'maternity' and said, 'My wife is having contractions every
two minutes.' And the nurse who answered requested the
information, 'Is this her first child?' And he said, 'No, *you bloody
stupid woman*, it's her husband! [AUDIENCE AND PANEL BURST
OUT LAUGHING AND THERE IS SUSTAINED APPLAUSE
DURING WHICH A BUZZER IS PRESSED]
Nicholas: Clement, you just pressed your buzzer. Have you
challenged yourself?!
Clement: I didn't want to be challenged for hesitation.
Nicholas: So you've challenged yourself for hesitation?
Clement: Yes.
Nicholas: Well listened. There are 28 seconds, starting now.

Clement was an award-winning after-dinner speaker and would
obviously have been used to performing in front of a wide range of
audiences, some of whom must have expected more adult-themed
material than would be appropriate for *Just a Minute*. I am sure he
was very adept at meeting such expectations, but he never introduced
any of that body of material into the show. He did, however, relish
the opportunity to relate a few risqué tales, which with his deadpan

style and serious, deliberate voice, often came as a surprise, and always received an enthusiastic reaction.

In January 1993 Clement once again demonstrates his love of football by recalling a very funny story involving the Newcastle-born England footballer Paul Gascoigne who also played for Spurs and Italian club Lazio. The subject is 'Geordies' with eight seconds remaining.

Clement: I'd like to tell rather a nice story about Gascoigne who is known as 'Gazza', a footballer who plays for Lazio and was asked by a coach whether …
[WHISTLE AND APPLAUSE]
Nicholas: And we'll never know! Was it worth finishing or not, Clement?
Clement: I think it probably is, yes. When Gazza played his first game for Lazio, the coach said to him, 'Do your best, and we'll pull you off at halftime.' And Gazza said, 'Oh, that'll be a change. At Tottenham they gave us oranges.' [HUGE AUDIENCE LAUGH]

In a broadcast from 3 August 1998, Clement introduces us to an alumni from Uppingham school, Rutland, in order to set up a funny gag, the punchline for which he is determined to deliver regardless of Derek Nimmo's challenge. The subject is 'The Experiment'.

Clement: Norman Douglas, who went to Uppingham, as did Stephen Fry, wrote a very interesting treatise on aphrodisiacs. Oysters, we all know, are such. In fact, I once ate a dozen, which were so powerful that if I didn't …
BUZZ
[AUDIENCE LAUGHTER AND SHOUTS OF 'NO!']
Nicholas: Derek?
Clement: [CONTINUING AS IF UNINTERUPTED] … swallow them quickly …
Derek: Hesitation.

Nicholas: That's right, yes.

Clement: … I got a stiff neck! [LAUGHTER AND APPLAUSE FROM AUDIENCE AND PANEL]

Clement and Kenneth quickly developed an excellent rapport on *Just a Minute*, which I think may have been down to a degree of mutual admiration. Kenneth (who often affectionately called Clement 'Clem'; Derek Nimmo used 'Clay') certainly admired Clement's education and erudition and enjoyed testing himself against it, while Clement, I am sure, had respect for Kenneth's showmanship and the warmth he created between himself and his audience. The following is a good example, from 16 November 1971, with Clement hijacking Kenneth's catchphrases while Kenneth is determined to argue his case.

Nicholas: There are nine seconds for 'Poetry', Clement, starting now.

Clement: There was a time when poetry consisted of verse, and each …

BUZZ

Nicholas: Kenneth Williams, why have you challenged?

Kenneth: Because this is deviation. The statement is totally incorrect.

Nicholas: Why?

Kenneth: Because poetry has always been poetry. It's never *consisted* of anything else.

Nicholas: I disagree, I mean poetry can be verse. It depends on which way you look at it. [KENNETH AND CLEMENT PROCEED TO SHOUT OVER EACH OTHER, MUCH TO THE AUDIENCE'S AMUSEMENT UNTIL I EVENTUALLY PULL THEM BOTH BACK INTO LINE]

Kenneth: He said there was a time when poetry …

Clement: Don't argue with the chairman!

Kenneth: … was classified …

Clement: He's a very good chairman!

Kenneth: … there's never been anything like that!
Clement: I don't know why we have Kenneth Williams on the
show in the first place! [BIG AUDIENCE LAUGH]

With Kenneth, any comments made at my expense were all about
showmanship, putting on a performance. There was no malice. With
Derek and Peter, the lines they threw my way were delivered and
received from a position of friendship and respect. With Clement,
however, there certainly could be an edge whenever he took a swipe
in my direction. Which was fairly often.

If you did not know him you would think it was all part of the
banter. Clement was very clever and could construct a comment in
such a way that it was not obvious there was more to it. I understood
the reality, however; I could sense it and recognised what lay under
the surface of what he was saying. It can all be traced back to our
differing opinions on the role of the chairman and the evolution
of the game, and it meant I had to be on my toes with him and
concentrate very intensely, far more than with anyone else. It required
strength, and quick retorts, to stand up to Clement's brilliant mind.
If I showed any weakness, he would take the opportunity to make
me look foolish, and enjoy it.

The following examples speak for themselves. In the first, from
23 February 1971, the subject is 'Plastics' on which Clement had
just been talking, claiming that the word meant a bomb in common
usage. Kenneth challenges this on grounds of deviation, and my
ruling does not please Clement.

Nicholas: I quite agree with you, Kenneth, that is not
the definition of plastics. So you take a point and you have
50 seconds. [CLEMENT POINTEDLY CLEARS HIS THROAT IN
THE BACKGROUND] What do you want to say, Clement? You
look shocked. Oh, that's all right, just acting, were you?
Fifty seconds for 'Plastics' …
Clement: I ceased to be shocked by your decisions about four
years ago!

Kenneth: Well, shut your row then and let's get on! [I LAUGH
AT KENNETH'S COMMENT AS DOES THE AUDIENCE]

In September 1974 it seems that Clement has not been listening as
intently as normal when he challenges Derek Nimmo, who is speaking
on the subject 'Don Quixote'. Once again Clement disagrees with
my adjudication.

Derek: Charles Parker, make-up man extraordinary, had the
task of making up Peter O'Toole to play Don Quixote. Sancho
Panza, his great chum, once said to him, 'Those who have ...'
and I can't repeat any more because ...
    BUZZ
Nicholas: Clement Freud has challenged.
Clement: Deviation.
Nicholas: Why?
Clement: Well, he hasn't mentioned Don Quixote and he's
trying to make us think that Sancho Panza was a friend of the
make-up man ... [LAUGHTER FROM AUDIENCE AND PANEL]
... who is the only person he has mentioned to date. And that is
devious.
Derek: No, I mentioned Don Quixote.
Clement: No. No.
Derek: He was making him up to play Don Quixote.
Nicholas: He was. I know, you established that he was in my
mind. And after all Sancho Panza is the ...
Clement: [TURNING TO ME] We're going by *your* mind now,
are we? [LOUD BURST OF LAUGHTER FROM DEREK]
Nicholas: It's better than going by yours, Clement! [AUDIENCE
LAUGHTER AND CLAPPING]

I respected Clement enormously and we enjoyed many happy times
together, but he could be difficult because I was never sure quite how
he was going to react. Here he is at his unpredictable best, setting
up a very funny challenge from Andree Melly in October 1972 while

speaking on the subject of 'The Minute Waltz'.

Clement: As a dance the Minute Waltz has particular appeal to me because it seems to me to have movement which combines deviation of step with repetition of direction, combined with a hesitation of tempo. And therefore could not have been invented for a better panel game than that to which Ian Messiter lends his name which is so very ably judged by you, Nicholas Parsons …

BUZZ

Nicholas: Andree Melly, you've just challenged.

Andree: Deviation.

Nicholas: Why?

Andree: Because I do not believe that Clement Freud thinks that Nicholas Parsons judges this particular game with …

[LOUD LAUGHTER FROM AUDIENCE AND KENNETH]

Nicholas: Before you said it, I was about to give Clement Freud two points for his nice compliment! But I'm inclined to believe that you are accurate in what you've just said, Andree Melly.

[FURTHER AUDIENCE LAUGHTER]

Series 8, running from July 1973 to January 1974, saw an enforced change in the structure of the *Just a Minute* panel.

3/5/73

Dear Ken,

I am mortified to hear that you must go into hospital. Not because of what it will do to Just a Minute (where frankly you are irreplaceable) but for the ill-timing in terms of all your other commitments, the theatre, etc.

Poor old Ken, it will be no comfort to you whatever, but I too will be confined to hospital barracks as of May 9th – we have always had a lot in common.

I will write at more length when I get a second, but at the moment I

must try and somehow find someone to replace you on Just a Minute. Let's face it there is no-one in the world who can do that adequately.
   Yours, David

With Kenneth only able to record 14 of the 26 shows, David Hatch, before he also was hospitalised, had to secure replacements, and the decision was made to engage male guests – actors Warren Mitchell, Ian Carmichael and Alfred Marks, disc jockey David Jacobs and writer Barry Took. This established a format that would remain pretty well in place for every series until the late 1980s: a scattering of episodes featuring the four regulars, with the remainder comprising two or three of them joined by guests. Over this period there were never more than five shows in a series with the four regulars together, and in two series there were none. In the tenth this was down to other work commitments and in the seventeenth Clement and Kenneth each chaired an episode rather than appearing on the panel. Impressively, Kenneth appeared in every show broadcast from 9 March 1977 to 2 June 1988.

...on the subject of *Seating*

Having launched their *Just a Minute* careers in a particular seat in which they grew comfortable, regular players of the game tend to return to the same seats whenever they appear. During the 1970s and '80s, the four regulars always occupied the same position on the panel. The order never changed. Kenneth Williams would be out on my far right (where Paul Merton now sits) and next to him was Clement Freud, which on the surface was a strange pairing given their very different demeanours and personalities but they built up a strong connection. On the other side, Derek Nimmo sat out far left (Gyles Brandreth today) and Peter Jones was next to me. For the shows in which only two or three of them were

> present, the invited guest or guests would take the unoccupied
> seats.

~~~~~~

The inclusion of more guests from Series 8 onwards meant that over the remainder of the 1970s we enjoyed the company of some outstanding British talent. I cannot do justice to them all here, so I am only going to pick a small handful that particularly stick in my memory and which I hope is representative of the wonderful cast of character who entertained us in that decade.

For a broadcast in March 1977 our producer who was then John Browell had decided to invite a fairly specialist form of comic entertainer on to the show, an act one might have thought better suited for television – a ventriloquist, famous for his sidekick, Lord Charles.

This was actually Ray Alan's second appearance on the show (the first of this double recording was broadcast on 8 December 1976, and he joined us twice again in 1979) and it worked wonderfully well because of Ian Messiter's astute choice of subject ('Gread and Gutter'), Ray's willingness to play for laughs and the tacit agreement of the other players not to challenge. Great entertainment.

Ray: What a ridiculous phrase this is. It's always attributed to bad ventriloquists although I must confess I have personally never heard anyone say 'gread and gutter' and mean it seriously. It is a sort of burlesque on … my particular art. And when people get up there with a dummy on their knee they usually say 'gread and gutter' or they say 'gottle of geer' or 'who's a naughty goy' or 'isn't it nice to see all the geople'? And 'here we are at the London Galladium!' Or at the 'Gee Gee Cee!' Where everygody's having a 'gnargellous time'! Because 'Nicholas Garsons is the chairman'! With 'Geter Jones', they've got 'Kenneth Nilliams'! And they've got 'Glement Freud!' And then they have the guzzer and they intergrupt you when you start regeating yourself! Why do you allow this, that's what gread

and gutter is all agout! It's galking without saying a gee for a gee! And if you can all do it when you aglause at the end of this giece you'll gind that gread and gutter …
[WHISTLE, CHEERS AND APPLAUSE]

The actor Bernard Cribbins appeared on two shows in 1978, with a laid-back, witty style that together with Sheila Hancock's charm complemented the chaos created by Kenneth and Derek. Bernard's first contribution was to wonder aloud whether I was wearing a wig – we were friends so I didn't take offence – and then to hand out mints to his fellow panellists, a first for *Just a Minute*.

By Bernard's second show, broadcast on 11 April, he had worked out how best to play the game on his terms, not trying to out-talk the others but listening carefully to make clever challenges and amusing comments. Here Derek is talking on the subject 'Customs'.

Derek: In the middle of the Australian desert they recently found some Aboriginal tribesmen who had never seen another human being before. And when they were taken back to Darwin …
BUZZ
Nicholas: Bernard Cribbins?
Bernard: Deviation, because they must have seen each other. That is another human being!
Kenneth: Ah, hahahaha!
[LONG AUDIENCE APPLAUSE]

The following subject is 'Why Elephants Can't Jump', which in itself generates a laugh from the audience as I ask Bernard to speak first.

Bernard: I suppose the most obvious reason why elephants are unable to jump is because they're really too heavy. And also they do have to carry this large trunk with them which, as you know, could contain a lot of clothing, heavy weights [AUDIENCE LAUGHTER], furniture, sand, rocks, bits of granite, boulders.

Anything of this sort which would obviously restrict their height from the ground if they put a great physical muscular effort into raising themselves above the aforementioned … terra firma.

   BUZZ

Nicholas: Derek Nimmo challenged.

Derek: An 'er'.

Nicholas: No, it was in 'terra' firma and, Bernard, you keep the subject for an incorrect challenge and another point of course. And 29 and a half seconds left, starting now.

Bernard: Another reason that elephants are unable …

   BUZZ

Nicholas: Derek Nimmo challenged.

Derek: Repetition of 'reason'.

Nicholas: Yes, you did mention the word 'reason' before.

Bernard: Did I? I've lost my reason, yes! [BIG LAUGH]

Sheila eventually completes what proves to be a long round, and I give a quick round-up of the scores, which produces some entertaining banter thanks to Bernard's interjection.

Nicholas: So Sheila Hancock now has the lead at the end of that round, she's one ahead of Bernard Cribbins and Derek Nimmo. And Kenneth is trailing a little. And Sheila, will you begin the next round and the subject is …

Bernard: Trailing a little what? [LAUGHTER FROM AUDIENCE] Sorry, no, sorry!

Nicholas: I didn't say 'a little what', just 'a little'!

Bernard: No, I did!

Nicholas: A little behind actually! [SHARP INTAKE OF BREATH FROM KENNETH IN MOCK SHOCK AT MY COMMENT FOLLOWED BY A BIG AUDIENCE LAUGH]

Finally, to finish off the decade, Miriam Margolyes. Miriam, who is now best known for her performance as Professor Sprout in the *Harry Potter* films, only ever appeared in one *Just a Minute*, broadcast on

8 May 1979. What a show it turned out to be. She took to the game as though she had been playing it for years, matching Kenneth and Clement blow for blow from the very first round and, quite frankly, keeping me firmly in the palm of her hand.

The show seemed to have everything. It was riotous and hilarious and I found myself swiftly carried away with the atmosphere, committing the chairman's crime of interrupting one of the players in full flow, for the first time ever! Broadcaster Kenneth Robinson was the fourth member of the team and he made excellent contributions, but it was Miriam who stole the show.

The first subject is 'Hotch Potch', which Clement has claimed is an alternative name for Lancashire hot pot. Kenneth is not convinced.

Kenneth: Deviation! This is *nothing* to do with what's on the card. Hotch potch is nothing to do with cooking, and nobody's ever ordered a hotch potch in a restaurant or in a house in their *lives*!

Clement: They have!

Miriam: [LOUDLY SHOUTING OVER TO KENNETH] You be quiet! You be quiet!

Kenneth: You shut your row! [AUDIENCE BEGINS LAUGHING, WHICH CONTINUES THROUGHOUT THE EXCHANGE]

Miriam: You be quiet! Be quiet!

Kenneth: [OUTRAGED] Shut your row! They should never have had women on this programme!

Miriam: You're a disgrace!

Kenneth: There's a woman here!

Miriam: I should think so too!

Nicholas: Yes, well, I think I may have some support at last. We have a guest who doesn't like to have the chairman rattled by Kenneth Williams like that.

Miriam: *Yes*! You go on, dear! Yes, go on! *Yes*. [AUDIENCE CONTINUING LAUGHING]

Nicholas: Thank you very much, Miriam. And Clement Freud will also continue with 35 seconds on 'Hotch Potch', starting now.

Clement: Hotch potch can also be a mess. Just any disorganised, rumpled, crumpled, unregimented …

Nicholas: Like *Just a Minute*! [I START TO LAUGH]

> BUZZ

Miriam: [DIRECTED AT ME] You be quiet too! Hahahaha!

Kenneth: Yes, I don't think it's in the rules of the game that the chairman is supposed to interrupt somebody!

Nicholas: Well, after 13 years I suddenly wanted to. I've never done it before.

Kenneth: We're not here to satisfy your occasional whims! [BIG AUDIENCE LAUGH]

Miriam: Oh, I don't know!

Kenneth: You take your proclivities somewhere else! I've never heard anything so disgraceful!

Kenneth Robinson then wins the subject from Clement and resolutely attempts to stand up to Kenneth Williams' subsequent challenge and tirade.

Kenneth R: Hotch potch, of course, comes from the Russian, 'spodge'. It is really 'hod-spodge'.

> BUZZ

Nicholas: Kenneth Williams challenged.

Kenneth: Hesitation.

Nicholas: I'm afraid there was, Kenneth, it was such a …

Kenneth R: No, no, it was a hyphenated word, 'hod-spodge'.

Nicholas: Yes, but it did take some getting out and so you hesitated.

Kenneth R: But a hyphen has to be spoken …

Kenneth: Don't argue! The chairman's ruling is final. [AUDIENCE BEGIN LAUGHING] And he's a very fine chairman! I mean he's a wonderful man! He never interrupts people …

Kenneth R: Kenneth!

Kenneth: … when they're under way! You know when they've started to play the game … He's very good!

Kenneth R: Kenneth Williams, if you ever find …

Kenneth: [SOUNDING HYSTERICAL] *You shut your row!* Don't argue with me! I'm a regular!

Kenneth R: … your way to literature you'll realise that a hyphen takes some *doing*!

Nicholas: Well, now that we've all got a little bit off our chest and we've got the audience warmed up, because after all, they're not used to *Just a Minute* …

Miriam: I've still got a lot on my chest! [HUGE LAUGH]

Nicholas: Well, if you have, I would keep it to yourself, Miriam!

Miriam: You didn't say that last night! [SUSTAINED AUDIENCE LAUGHTER]

Kenneth: *Aye aye!* 'ello!

Nicholas: It's developing into quite a different show this week!

Miriam: *Yes!*

The round continues, with Clement ending up speaking as the whistle goes. The second subject is for Kenneth Williams, 'Why I Am So Well Informed'.

Kenneth: Because I have had the good *fortune* to mix with the erudite and the *lear-ned* of this world. And as Emerson rightly remarked, we have as many …

BUZZ

Nicholas: And Miriam Margolyes has challenged.

Miriam: It's boring! [BIG AUDIENCE LAUGH]

Kenneth: I think it's disgraceful!

Nicholas: Miriam, it frequently is on *Just a Minute*!

Kenneth: I've come all the way from Great Portland Street! *I'm insulted! I mean that is insulting! That's really insulting!*

Miriam: It's true though! It's true!

Kenneth: I don't know how you're sitting there *takin' it*! I'm amazed you haven't got up!

Nicholas: Kenneth! *I try to be just and fair!* It was a wrong challenge. You keep the subject, you have 47 seconds …

Clement: Oh. Is that your New Year's resolution?

[AUDIENCE LAUGH]

Shortly after, Clement takes up the subject.

Clement: Principally I am so well informed because I read an extraordinarily large number of boring documents which Miriam Margolyes really ought to come and join me in the perusal of. Hansard …

BUZZ

Nicholas: Miriam Margolyes.

Miriam: Bad grammar! You ended your sentence with a preposition.

Kenneth: Yes!! Yes!! Deviation! Deviation! Yes!!! [APPLAUSE]

The banter and clever challenges continue throughout the following rounds, and as we reach the final one it is Miriam's turn to speak first. I very much doubt Ian Messiter anticipated the fireworks that his choice of subject, 'The Contents of My Handbag', would produce.

Miriam: [AT BREAKNECK SPEED WITH AUDIENCE LAUGHING THROUGHOUT] *How dare you ask me to reveal the contents of my handbag!* I think that's the most appalling liberty I've ever heard! It's none of your business what's in my handbag! In fact I don't have a handbag. I have a pantechnicon which I carry around and I park outside. I don't think it's anything to do with you what I carry with me. As a matter of fact, of course, I have a diary and that is … [BECOMES BREATHLESS] … where your telephone number is, Nicholas, as I don't have to tell you. [NORMAL VOICE] And I shall shortly be collecting it from all the other gentlemen in the audience [KENNETH CACKLING IN BACKGROUND] if they're very lucky. Another thing that should be in a woman's handbag is a penknife. Now I find the Swiss Army knives quite exceptional. There's something for taking stones out of horses' hooves, and something for taking horses out of stones' hooves. And if you haven't …

BUZZ

Nicholas: Kenneth Robinson has challenged.

Kenneth R: Repetition of 'horses' and of 'stones'.

Nicholas: 'Horses', 'hooves' and 'stones', yes.

Miriam: Quite right.

Nicholas: That's perfectly right. So you do realise now that Miriam Margolyes doesn't receive money for appearing in the show, she gets telephone numbers instead. [AUDIENCE LAUGH] Kenneth, you came in there and I'm afraid Miriam started before we could set the watch going, so we don't know how long she's been going actually. [AUDIENCE LAUGH] So we'll estimate it was 40 seconds …

Miriam: You see, that's what happens when men are in charge. Don't you agree with me, ladies? It's ridiculous! Absolutely! [CHEERS, CLAPPING AND SHOUTS OF 'YES' FROM THE WOMEN IN THE AUDIENCE]

Nicholas: Yes, the more light-hearted, easy approach to things! The less regimented idea than with women at the helm!

Miriam: [COCKNEY ACCENT] *You wait for it, mate! We'll get there one day!* [NORMAL VOICE] Won't we, girl-chaps? Won't we?

Nicholas: Will you be in the vanguard or the rearguard?

Miriam: Tell you tonight! [BIG AUDIENCE LAUGH]

As I said, what a show it turned out to be, eventually won by Clement. What an excellent way, also, for *Just a Minute* to demonstrate its rude health in the final series of the decade.

Challenge!

Q: What is the longest subject ever used, by number of letters?

A: 'Llanfairpwllgwyngyllgogerychwyrndrobwllllantysiliogogogoch', the Welsh town on Anglesey, which has come up three times, the first being in 1973.

Q: Which subject has come up most often in the radio version of *Just a Minute*?

A: 'Magic', on seven occasions. First in 1970 and most recently in 2005.

Q: Which player has achieved the most uninterrupted minutes?

A: Kenneth Williams, with over 60. More than twice his nearest rival, Clement Freud.

Q: Who was the first male guest panellist to appear on *Just a Minute?*

A: David Jacobs in 1973.

Q: Name the five politicians who have appeared on *Just a Minute* (radio and television)?

A: Clement Freud, Gyles Brandreth, Barbara Castle, Michael Cashman and Tony Banks.

Jenny Eclair

I first did *Just a Minute* back in the 1980s, before my daughter was born, so I would have been in my mid to late twenties. Young and thin!

The first recording I did was in Scarborough; Derek Nimmo was on the panel, along with Peter Jones and Clement Freud.

I recall very clearly that Clement refused to sit next to me because I smelt of cigarette smoke and he was violently against smoking. Unfortunately, back then I was a compulsive nervous smoker and I'd probably inhaled an entire packet of Silk Cut on the train journey up (yes, we're going back to the days of being allowed to smoke on public transport).

Anyway, I was terribly intimidated by the whole thing and at one point I had to go to the bathroom to rest my head on the cold white tiles, as I felt I might faint with the stress of it all. To be honest, I was pretty lousy at playing the game but Nicholas gave me 'the benefit of the doubt' on a couple of occasions and I survived the recording, even receiving a gruffly mumbled 'well done' from the frankly terrifying Mr Freud.

Afterwards we went out for a meal to the sort of place where they insist on giving long-stemmed roses to 'the ladies' and I remember Clement sending his starter, main and pudding back. You could see the owner of the place having a semi-nervous breakdown in the kitchen.

I remember sitting next to Peter Jones, who was magnificent company and very kind. He told me a filthy joke at dinner, which I can still remember but won't commit to paper as it's a bit un-PC!

The next day I was exhausted and a bit hungover and when I saw Derek Nimmo on the train platform, I hid behind a pillar until I saw which carriage he got into and promptly got into another one down the other end of the train. I was just spent by the enormity of the situation, and my confidence had been completely used up. Like an over-excited child I'd worn myself out and I slept all the way back to London.

Over a quarter of a century later, it's still one of the few jobs that ties knots in my stomach. *Just a Minute* brings out my slightly ugly competitive side and deep down I've never played the game without wanting to win it.

However, over the years I've learned that actually enjoying the game is the trick to scoring more points. The less het up I get, the better I do, and anyway the laughs are what really count.

In recent years more and more women have been invited onto the teams. *Just a Minute* has always been ahead of its time in terms of female voices and these days it's not unusual to have two women playing (shock horror). This is definitely for the good, and for me it's always a massive relief to see another woman in the green room, as sometimes the conversation pre-show can be a bit cricket-heavy! Seriously, once I was the only contestant who hadn't spent the earlier part of the day at Lords!

When we play the game in London, we record it in the radio theatre at Broadcasting House. I love this venue dearly, but I still miss the Paris Studios where the game was recorded back in the 1990s, a lovely little underground Art Deco theatre with black-and-white photos of radio stars lining the walls. Radio seemed to be a lot more glamorous back in the 1950s than it is today.

That said, before the show the BBC provides a smörgåsbord of Scandinavian food. I've no idea where this tradition came from, (some say it was Sandi Toksvig's idea) but as I'm a big fan of smoked salmon and chopped beetroot, it's one

I approve of most heartily. After the show we tend to gather back in the green room for a gossip and a drink and I continue to hoover up the Swedish meatballs.

Of course the mainstay of the programme has always been Nicholas. One of the most civilised men in showbusiness, Nicholas is a gent right down to his Lord Tavernor tie pin. He's an exquisitely dressed, beautifully mannered man who must have a hell of a picture in an attic somewhere!

I'm very proud to be a *Just a Minute* player and even after all these years, when I hear myself playing it on the radio, I still can't believe I was legitimately invited onto the show and didn't have to gate-crash it.

The Eighties

The decade through Just a Minute

Package holidays

The trouble with a package deal holiday is that you're surrounded by the English, who are so terribly boring, the last people you want to see when you're going on to France.

DEREK NIMMO
6 FEBRUARY 1985

Oil

I was on a television show in New York when the host said that unless there was more oil in America, they were seriously considering invading the Emirates, to which I asked whether if they ran short of whisky, would they wage war against Scotland?

CLEMENT FREUD
29 JANUARY 1980

Fads

I've fallen under the spell of so many fads, it's almost impossible to list them. From skateboarding to sucking kumquats.

KENNETH WILLIAMS
28 AUGUST 1982

Video games

Happily the popularity of video games seems to be in decline. It seems to me the most enormous waste of time to stand in front of a Space Invaders machine, pressing buttons, trying to stop these little things hitting the bottom line. In fact I'd rather talk to Kenneth Williams than play video games and that's saying quite a great deal.

DEREK NIMMO
27 FEBRUARY 1982

Microwave ovens

There was a case reported in the paper of a lady who purchased one of these things. And while it operated it leaked its rays, and she suffered greatly in the process. Now then, what she done was to sue the manufacturers and a large sum of money was paid out in court. I read this, and I thought, 'Hello, there'll be trouble with them microwave ovens when it gets around.' But to my amazement, they are sold openly without malice aforethought, over the counter!

KENNETH WILLIAMS
13 MARCH 1982

Supermarkets

Is a supermarket trolley in your garden a status symbol? Because there are lots of them in our road!

PETER JONES
25 APRIL 1989

Rules

Rules are made to be broken by geniuses. Michelangelo is a case in point. So, of course, is John McEnroe.

KENNETH WILLIAMS
27 JULY 1987

Keeping fit

I've never quite understood the attraction of keeping fit. But whenever I watch television, somebody in the morning seems to be shouting at me saying, 'In, out, up, down, upwards, downwards, inwards, outwards,' and all that sort of stuff. And fat and unappetising ladies and gentlemen cavort themselves around my 17-inch screen, showing what I would very much not like to do, which is to be svelte and slim and have bad breath, wet feet and tennis elbow.

CLEMENT FREUD
24 JUNE 1984

The 1980s represents a decade of arrivals and departures.

Lyricist Tim Rice joined us for the first time in a show broadcast on 15 January 1980, sitting alongside Kenneth, Derek and Peter. I think it would be fair to say that Tim was just a touch over-eager during that first outing. Rather than allowing momentum to build, and letting other players go when they were being humorous, Tim was initially a little 'buzzer-happy' in his keenness to make a mark. Part of the reason for that may have been that Tim was less used to sitting centre stage in a performing role back then. He had not yet fully developed his entertainer's instinct. It did not take him long to hone his skills, however, and he is now both good at the game and popular with listeners.

Tim's rush of challenges did not detract from the entertainment value of what was an outstanding debut. He was clearly comfortable with the game from the very beginning, perhaps not surprisingly given that language and words are the tools of his trade. It might have come as a surprise, however, if you were unaware of who Tim was and tuned into *Just a Minute* as he made his first ever challenge. Peter Jones was speaking on the subject of 'Carrier Bags'. I put it down to nerves on Tim's part.

> **Peter:** Carrier bags! My goodness, you've touched a nerve there. Now I was talking to Ian about that only the other day because I think these supermarkets, what's *super* about them?
> BUZZ
> **Nicholas:** Tim Rice has challenged.

Tim: I would like to say that I believe he repeated the word 'super'.
Nicholas: Yes, but 'supermarket' is all one word.
Tim: Is it really?

It did not take long, however, for Tim to find his confidence. From his debut game he built relationships with the other players whom he obviously respected and whose company he enjoyed. (He would later describe them as follows: 'The erudite Mr Nimmo, the flamboyant Mr Jones, and the undescribable and indescribable Kenneth Williams.') Here he is challenging Derek, who is telling a rather racy story on the subject 'Overwhelming the Audience'.

Derek: I remember sitting in the MGM Grand in Las Vegas and there was a huge tank filled with water, dolphins and whales swimming around these lovely ladies taking off their bras and panties for the delectation of the people so assembled. Suddenly the whole thing burst, water came tumbling …
BUZZ
Tim: I think repetition of 'water'.
Peter: Absolutely right! Well done, Tim! Good old Tim! Well done! [LOUD AUDIENCE APPLAUSE]
Tim: It wasn't actually a sensational mental achievement, Peter.
Peter: No, I don't want to …
Tim: I thought you were over the top with your praise there.
Nicholas: Tim …
Peter: Oh, I'm terribly sorry.
Nicholas: You're learning the rules very fast …
Tim: Yes.
Nicholas: Ignore the chairman.
Tim: Who is the chairman?
Nicholas: I've often asked the same question myself.
[AUDIENCE LAUGH]

Tim's ability to fit quickly into the rhythm of the game was important if he was going to make a big contribution. Newcomers to the show can feel overwhelmed and inhibited on their maiden voyage, especially if they find themselves up against three experienced players who are extremely comfortable bouncing off each other. The following example from Tim's debut, featuring Kenneth and Peter, illustrates the strength of their rapport to great effect. Kenneth had begun to tell a story about an Orson Welles production of *Moby Dick*, a subject on which he was very knowledgeable, having appeared in the show.

Kenneth described how a boat had been launched into the stalls of the theatre. However, before he can complete his tale Kenneth is interrupted mid flow with a correct challenge from Derek Nimmo. He is not pleased and withdraws into himself. At the end of the round I try to coax Kenneth back into the game.

Nicholas: I think the audience would like to hear the rest of Kenneth Williams' story.

Kenneth: [WITH A SULKY TONE] I'm here to play games, not to tell anecdotes, dear.

Nicholas: So you don't want to …

Kenneth: [POINTING AT DEREK AND SHOUTING] *He challenged me! He stopped the story!* I'm not going to say it now. No!

Nicholas: He's hurt!

Kenneth: I'm not hurt at all! I'm not hurt! I'm not hurt!

Peter: Oh be quiet! [AUDIENCE LAUGH]

Kenneth: You can't just say, 'Jump! Go on! Go on!' It's like a thoroughbred! It's got to be taken at the moment when the *muse alights upon my shoulder!*

BUZZ

Nicholas: Peter Jones has challenged.

Peter: I wish he'd sulk for a bit and be quiet!

[BIG AUDIENCE LAUGH]

Ian Messiter chose Tim's first subject with great care, knowing full well that as Tim had written the lyrics for *Evita* he would be well versed in the life of her husband Juan Domingo Peron. Tim does not disappoint.

Tim: Juan Domingo Peron is a fascinating character. Perhaps not a very likeable individual but somebody who has given a lot of people a very different perspect, or if that's the wrong word, perspective, on society throughout Argentina in the 1940s and also the following decades. Let us go back in time, if you will bear with me to 1890, which is about the moment that the aforesaid Juan Domingo Peron was born. Yes, he first saw light of day in those far-off moments of the nineteenth century. He was born about 150 miles from Buenos Aires, the capital of that South American country which I mentioned before. And when he was five years old, his family moved down south to Patagonia. Not, as you might think, hot, but very cold. In fact, very parky indeed.
　　BUZZ
Nicholas: Peter Jones has challenged.
Peter: Well he said 'very' twice.
Nicholas: Yes, he did.
Tim: Oh you cad! You rotter! [AUDIENCE LAUGH FOLLOWED BY APPLAUSE FOR TIM'S EFFORTS IN KEEPING GOING FOR 51 SECONDS]

Tim plays up very well to Peter's late challenge in the above example, but it is with Kenneth in particular that Tim seems to make an instant connection. They are both strong characters who enjoy trading blows, much to the delight of the audience. The subject for the following round is 'Table Mountain' and Kenneth is speaking with 47 seconds to go.

Kenneth: Tables shouldn't be ever taken to mountains because as you have a rocky, crevasse-like structure, it is unlikely that the equilibrium which the rectangular object needs will ever be …
　　BUZZ

Nicholas: Tim Rice has challenged.
Tim: Can you challenge for boredom?
[AUDIENCE LAUGH AND APPLAUD]

In the next round Kenneth hits back, but only after Tim offers a unique interpretation of how the game should be played.

Nicholas: Tim, you have 50 and one half seconds on 'Morse Code', starting now. [TIM DOES NOT SPEAK AND INSTEAD BEGINS TO TAP OUT A MESSAGE IN MORSE CODE ON THE DESK]
BUZZ
Nicholas: Derek Nimmo challenged.
Derek: Repetition of … [TAP TAP-TAP TAP]
Tim: Not at all, Mr Chairman! I was in fact doing my talk on Morse Code in Morse, which was …
Nicholas: I know, but you were repeating the dots. [AUDIENCE LAUGH]
Tim: No, no, they were different letters.
Kenneth: This game says *speak* for 60 seconds. It doesn't say tap out messages for 60 seconds! [BIG AUDIENCE LAUGH] *It's ridiculous!!!* I mean! It's like he's got some board here, for the occult! You do one rap for no, and two raps for yes! You know, like, 'You'll cross water and meet a dark stranger!' I always wanted to do that!!! [HUGE AUDIENCE LAUGH]
Nicholas: He was challenged for repetition and he did repeat the thumps. And we apologise to the listeners who might have …
Kenneth: I should hope so! He should also apologise to the engineer up in the box!
Tim: I'm sorry. I was wrong! I was wrong!
Kenneth: You were wrong! *Bitterly wrong!* You should be bitterly ashamed! [AUDIENCE LAUGH]

There is an unusual and noteworthy footnote to Tim's first show.

It concludes with a unique four-way tie between the players. This strikes me as somehow a fitting start to *Just a Minute*'s new decade.

Tim's affinity with Kenneth Williams grew stronger as they progressed into the 1980s, creating much laughter and memorable moments. Here Kenneth is talking on the subject of the 'Costa Del Sol' in February 1982. Scriptwriter John Junkin is also on the panel and contributes nicely at the end.

> **Kenneth:** '*Il corno artist incompreso*' was the remark made by Arturo Toscanini when he was offered the conductorship of the National Broadcasting Orchestra which was especially *created* for the aforementioned and *brrr-illiant* …
>   BUZZ
> **Nicholas:** Tim Rice has challenged.
> **Tim:** I tried to give him every chance but this has got nothing whatsoever to do with the Costa del Sol.
> **Kenneth:** [NEAR HYSTERICAL] *He was on the Costa del Sol, you great fool!!!* He was performing in Malaga! You are an idiot! Do you know where Malaga is situated? Do you know where Malaga is situated?? Do you know?! Have you ever opened a *ge-e-o-ography book*!! I really shouldn't be here at all! I'm wasting my time you know. [BIG AUDIENCE LAUGH]
> **Tim:** I agree. I agree.
> **Kenneth:** I should be on *Brain of Britain* or something really distinguished, shouldn't I!
> **Nicholas:** Kenneth, I think you made your point [AUDIENCE LAUGH], but you don't need to be quite so rude to the other panellists.
> **Kenneth:** *Welll!!* I get so, I get so *furious!!!* I mean, I am by nature a tempestuous creature, you see.
> **Nicholas:** Yes …
> **Kenneth:** [IN THEATRICAL VOICE] We in the theatre. *W-e-e-e in the theatre*, you see, we are used to expressing ourselves!
> **Nicholas:** Unlike Tim Rice, who has got no association with the theatre at all!!! [BIG AUDIENCE LAUGH]

The three regulars in 1969. Clement Freud and Derek Nimmo standing, Kenneth Williams to my left. Ian Messiter is sitting to my right.

Our first producer, David Hatch, who put his job on the line to save the show.

Me and Kenneth in 1981 acting up for the camera, but always remaining the best of friends.

Aimi MacDonald made her debut in 1968. Her entertaining dizzy personality was the perfect foil for the male regulars.

Peter Jones joined the team in 1971. Seen here in *The Rag Trade*, the TV show with which he was most associated, alongside future panellist Sheila Hancock.

How *Radio Times* promoted the show.

September 1974. In many people's eyes the classic line-up, talking on the subject of 'Gravy'.

February 1978. The listing described the show as 'A panel game whose unruly members are occasionally kept in disorder by the Chairman'.

September 1975. Even the wonderful Kenneth Williams could be tripped up. Here challenged by Clement Freud, Alfred Marks and Peter Jones for committing all three Deadly Sins in just six words!

The three eccentrics who appeared on the show during the 70s and 80s.

Top left: Pictured here in 1982, monocle-wearing astronomer Patrick Moore always put on a great spectacle for our audiences.

Top right: Irrepressible 'mad scientist' Magnus Pyke in 1977, whose arm-waving explanations of scientific matters were often impervious to challenges.

Right: The 'master of gobbledegook', Professor Stanley Unwin, shown here in the early 80s, entertained everyone with a new language during his two appearances.

'You've got in with one second remaining!' These words were most often said to Clement Freud, who employed various tactics to successfully challenge as the 60 seconds drew to a close.

Some of the regulars as they were when they first appeared on the show …

Wendy Richard, whose charm and wit was sometimes overshadowed by her competitive streak, made her first appearance in 1988.

Paul Merton, one of our most skilled players, caused concern for producer Ted Taylor on his debut in 1989. According to Paul, Ted feared he had booked a Sid Vicious-type character.

Butter wouldn't melt in his mouth … Since his first appearance on the show in 1995, Graham Norton has loved to push boundaries, but never goes too far.

Pam Ayres has brought a charming poetic air to the shows in which she has appeared since 2003.

Sue Perkins, whose rapid-fire delivery and quick-fire wit have made her one of the game's most popular players since her debut in 2000.

Julian Clary who, since 1997, has taken innuendo to hilarious new heights, but has always remained within the bounds of acceptability.

Produced by Mike Mansfield, *Just a Minute*'s small screen debut arrived on ITV in 1994.
Here in that first series I am joined by a fresh-faced panel of Kit Hesketh-Harvey, Tony Hawks,
Tony Slattery and Helen Lederer.

Clement Freud, Sheila Hancock, Paul Merton and Graham Norton join me in celebrating our 35th anniversary in 2002, at the Playhouse Theatre, the venue where it all began back in 1967.

On stage for this special show with Claire Bartlett ready to blow the whistle when the 60 seconds are up.

After a recording at the Edinburgh Festival in 2010 with Paul Merton, Jenny Eclair and Gyles Brandreth, three of our most competitive players.

Two of show's most accomplished players, doing what they do best in Edinburgh in 2012. Paul playing to the audience ... and Gyles determined to be first on the buzzer.

On stage in Mumbai with Paul Merton, Anuvab Pal, Tilusha, Cyrus Broacha and Marcus Brigstocke during a far-flung and truly memorable recording.

With producer Tilusha Ghelani, enjoying a JAM club in Bangalore in 2012.

With Paul Merton in 2010.

Kenneth: No!

John: Nicholas, is there a challenge for overacting?

[BIG LAUGH]

Tim's status as the 'new boy' also proved to be the source of much banter with the established players. Here is Tim from a show broadcast on 11 August 1984 talking on the subject of 'Fairgrounds', which he cleverly twists while also slipping in a reference to Ian Messiter's radio panel game on which Tim regularly appeared in the 1970s. Tim is joined by Kenneth, Peter and writer and comedian Barry Cryer, who had earlier in the game challenged Tim for repeating the word 'or'.

Tim: I have fair grounds for complaint, I think, when I play this programme because I have not been treated with quite the respect a young, up-and-coming *Many a Slip* person deserves. And this has been illustrated time and occasion again, by the players such as Mr Jones over there, who had a vicious go at me very early on, when I'd hardly got settled down. My nerves were still very, very fraught. Kenneth Williams, here on my right, talented performer though he is, and long may he continue to entertain us in his dotage … [BIG AUDIENCE LAUGH] He has also been fairly unkind to me. And Mr Cryer, this man who can have a go at an innocent little fellow like me, for saying 'or' more than once. I ask you …

BUZZ

Nicholas: Barry Cryer.

Barry: How many 'I's have we had?

Nicholas: It wasn't that. I mean, when are we going to get to the fairgrounds? That's what I was wondering.

Barry: Oh, that's it! That's what I meant! Yes, that's what I meant!

Nicholas: I'm surprised nobody picked it up before.

Tim: Well, I was arguing about the 'fair grounds', which I've not had. I mean what I'm saying is I've had fair grounds for complaint.

Barry: He was, to be fair, using it in a different sense, yes.

Peter: But who was this 'up-and-coming young person' that you were talking about?

Tim: Well, I'm afraid compared with everybody else on this panel, it has to be me! [AUDIENCE LAUGH] I admit, in most companies I'm the clapped-out old wreck but …

Kenneth: Here, you're 'up-and-coming'! He's right! He's right!

Peter: Here you're a clapped-out *young* wreck! [HUGE AUDIENCE LAUGH AND TIM CONTINUES WITH THE ROUND]

As with all accomplished players, Tim has developed his own, idiosyncratic tactics. A favourite is to slice the subject into manageable segments, and to announce this intention with something along the following lines. 'I want to break my talk on supermarkets into five or six sections and I want you to follow extremely carefully. Point one …'

Tim did not manage to progress very far with his point-by-point talk on supermarkets before being challenged. This in turn led to a considerable amount of back and forth between the panellists as Tim attempted to make his point. Eventually Peter Jones had heard enough, and much to the audience's amusement exclaimed, 'Well let him get on with the first one, because we've got five more!!'

Not surprisingly, Tim regularly falls back on his extensive knowledge of popular music, once quoting perfectly Elvis's spoken section of 'Are You Lonesome Tonight?' On a separate occasion Tim again called upon lyrics from his great hero Elvis to help him out, invoking a couple of lines from 'Wooden Heart' when asked to speak on the unusual subject of 'Austrian Cakes'. Tim opened with the words '*Muss I denn, zum Städtele hinaus*', then went on to explain that this was the phrase that sprang to mind every time he ate an Austrian cake because it was the only German he knew.

Unlike this 'Austrian Cakes' example, from time to time subjects are introduced for which the music-related theme is obvious. For instance, Tim once managed, with great persistence after fighting to regain the topic following numerous challenges, to name all of the

Spice Girls when talking about 'Girl Power'.

Where Tim is particularly effective, however, is in identifying unusual angles to bring his passion to the fore, as in this example from January 1998 when given the subject 'Eyes and Teeth'.

Tim: Eyes and teeth are terrific attributes if you want to become a star. Think of all those incredible performers over the years whose eyes have made them what they are. Viz, Frank Sinatra, Paul Newman, eyes of blue, irresistible! Then there are teeth. Immediately one thinks of the Bee Gees: Barry, Robin and Maurice. Let me just recite one or two of their great hits. 'Massachusetts', 'New York … BUZZ … Mining Disaster 1941, brackets Have You Seen My Wife Mr Jones … ' I'm sorry, did someone buzz?

Nicholas: Yes as you started to go on to some of the Bee Gees hits, Paul challenged you. Paul?

Paul: Well, I didn't want Tim to recite some of their greatest hits! [AUDIENCE LAUGH]

Nicholas: So you consider that is deviation from 'Eyes and Teeth'?

Paul: Absolutely!

Tim: Well, the entire Bee Gees career was founded on brilliant songs, but also teeth.

Paul: And the hair!

Tim: And the hair!

Paul: And the medallion!!

Nicholas: You're arguing against yourself now, you know, Paul.

I agree with Paul here, that Tim has strayed too far off the subject, and Paul carries on with the round with no further reference to the Bee Gees.

It would be totally incorrect, however, to give the impression that Tim Rice's excellent contributions to *Just a Minute* revolve exclusively around music. There is an erudite side to his character that manifests itself in clever challenges and informative commentaries laced with humour. Here Tim is talking for the 30 seconds to the whistle on the learned subject of the fifteenth-century Italian preacher Girolamo Savonarola in a show broadcast on 20 February 1985. Ian Messiter originally introduced the subject for Kenneth, but Tim successfully challenged for repetition and then went on to surprise us all with his knowledge.

> **Tim:** By any standards, this guy was a few bricks short of
> a load. He was a nut! [AUDIENCE LAUGH] He was always
> standing on balconies, ranting away to the populace of Florence
> about obscure religious things that had no relevance and even
> less importance to the problems of the time. One of the greatest
> struggles that the local people had at that particular point in
> history was disease, which was rife in the papal army. And the
> popes in those days, my God, they were a nasty piece of work.
> [BIG LAUGH] In fact there were three or four of them operating at
> one moment. There was one in Avignon, which is in France …
> [WHISTLE AND APPLAUSE]

Tim's lifeblood, as he once referred to 'writing', is words, and he treats them with a great deal of respect. In a broadcast from April 1987 he successfully challenged for deviation when 'hopefully' was being used incorrectly. 'The word hopefully is misused by nearly everybody in this country. It does not mean I hope this will happen, it means it will happen and I have hope. If you say, "I'm going to Paris", or if you say, "I'm hopefully going to Paris", it doesn't mean I hope I'm going to Paris, it means I'm definitely going to Paris with hope in my heart.'

It is amazing how much you can learn from listening to *Just a Minute*!

Interesting explanations such as this always bring a welcome additional dimension to the show. Over the many years, however, it is Tim's great skill in wordplay, taking subjects in unexpected directions, that has consistently generated much laughter from an appreciative audience.

Tim on 'Unsolicited Mail': You see before you sitting humbly in this hall an unsolicited male. Never have I been approached in the street by anybody, not ever. Not an opinion poll. I have never been asked whether I watch ITV or BBC.

Tim on 'How to Recognise a Real Yorkshireman': Not many people know that Robert Mugabe is a real Yorkshireman because spelt backwards Mugabe says, 'Eee bah gum!'

Tim on 'Round Robin': Round Robin is what Batman is most of the time!

Another arrival in that 1979–80 series, in a one-off appearance, was madcap DJ and comedian Kenny Everett. When Kenny spoke on the subject of 'Marbles' in the final round he may have broken more *Just a Minute* rules than anyone else during his uninterrupted minute … and a half as it turned out. Kenny produces a tour de force of style over substance, and it is simply marvellous for it. This fact is fully appreciated by his fellow panellists, who refrain from legitimate challenges in favour of allowing Kenny to continue. That is one of the joys of our show; you never know what is going to happen next.

> **Kenny:** Marbles is a game that I last played when I was at
> St Bede's Secondary Modern School for Aspiring Twits. And
> I always used to wonder, as I got my thumb into the marbleising
> position, about to flick and ruin all the others in the circle,
> I used to wonder, how the heck they got those little coloured
> squirly bits to go through the glass. You know the … the …
> ahaaaaaaaahhh! [SOUND OF KENNY THUMPING HEAD ON
> DESK] Ahhhrrrgg …
> **Nicholas:** Keep going!
> **Kenny:** And anyway [BIG AUDIENCE LAUGH AS KENNY

SITS UPRIGHT] … um … I used to wonder whether they put them in after with a hypodermic, or whether they built the glass around the coloured squirly, and how they got all the colours all to inter-twangle with each other. All sort of mangling and tumbling in a gay abandon throughout the glass. That's what I used to wonder. And then I'd flick 'em and in the middle of the circle they'd go, scattering all the other marbles in all various directions, from east to west, north and probably south as well. And all the other kids would … would rush around saying, 'What a wonderful holly player the old geezer is', because they used to call them hollies as well, you know. And they used to call them after other things, but I've forgotten what the other things were they used to call them. Because I was very young at the time. I'm 44 now and it's been absolutely a-a-a-ages since I was at school. And so I've forgotten the whole thing. And anyway it was the coloured squirlies that caught my eye really, because I had a great eye for coloured squirlies. And I think I've done much more than a minute! [SOUND OF KENNETH WILLIAMS CACKLING IN BACKGROUND. WHISTLE AND MUCH APPLAUSE]

Nicholas: Well, I'm afraid we were very wicked. We let Kenny Everett go on talking for 90 seconds [BIG LAUGH] on the subject of marbles! During that time, he continually repeated himself, deviated, and also hesitated.

Kenneth: But didn't lose his marbles! [AUDIENCE CONTINUE LAUGHING AND APPLAUDING]

...on the subject of *One-line Gags*

It is true to say that one-liners or 'gags' are making a comeback in the world of comedy, with Tim Vine widely recognised as a supreme exponent of the genre. Tim was very funny and successful when he appeared on *Just a Minute* in

2012 but I think he would agree himself that the true master of rapid-fire jokes had already treated us to a wonderful display more than 30 years previously – a certain Bob Monkhouse in a show broadcast on 4 March 1980. The subject is 'The One-line Gag'. Bob is challenged unsuccessfully during this virtuoso performance and eventually loses the subject to Derek Nimmo with half a second remaining. However, it is best to enjoy what Bob said in full.

Bob: Never tell secrets to a peacock, you know how they spread tales. Reincarnation is a considerable surprise. Venus flytraps, do they eat the front of your trousers? It is one-line gags like these that have held back what was once a promising career. But on my way to the studios I invariably called in at the zoo, and tell my one-line gags to the hyena which gives me a great deal of confidence. But I also have to spend money on these one-line gags because I pay a schoolboy to translate them from the original Latin. Please don't laugh at these, there are people down the front who are trying to sleep. A typical one-line joke would be the one about the female hippopotamus who was pregnant for 16 months so there will be no hurry with the knitting. … Is Karl Marx's grave a Communist plot? Always try to be yourself because if you are not, someone else will be. Does unabridged mean a river that you have to wade across? These are other one-line jokes which certainly should not be extended …

BUZZ

Derek's challenge right at the end is correct and wins him a point as he is speaking when the whistle blows, but it is Bob who earns the loud cheers and applause that follow.

Producer David Hatch had been responsible for inviting both Tim Rice and Kenny Everett on to the show, having once again taken up on a full-time basis the *Just a Minute* production reins in 1979. David had originally handed over day-to-day control to the extremely capable Simon Brett at the end of 1969, following David's relocation within the BBC to the north of England. However, during that period David had remained involved with the programme as much as practically possible. In fact, Simon and David worked closely together over the years Simon was in charge, with David occasionally producing shows.

A series of first-rate producers followed Simon's departure in 1975 but nevertheless it was still welcome news to learn of David's return. He was, after all, part of the fabric of the show. David was a charming man; modest, but extremely bright. He possessed an acute sense of what to say at just the right moment to ensure those involved with the show did what he wanted, without upsetting them. Part of that, I believe, was down to the fact that David himself had been a performer and understood how performers think. It is a great skill, and one that I and many others on the team appreciated, none more so than Kenneth, with whom David had remained in contact throughout the 1970s.

In 1981 David produced his final *Just a Minute* (his 166th show), having been appointed controller of BBC Radio 2. His was the first significant departure of the decade, with Pete Atkin taking over production duties.

Pete employed a different approach to David. Pete was more used to working on shows in which he provided assistance to the performers through production notes, suggesting possible improvements that individuals could make. He continued in the same vein when he arrived on *Just a Minute*, a show by then regularly featuring five experienced performers who really did not require such guidance. Kenneth in particular found this hard to swallow.

As David Hatch proved time and time again, someone of Kenneth's temperament had to be treated with great tact. He was a seasoned and established professional who resented receiving instruction on his performances. I remember distinctly Kenneth exploding in the green room having received a note from Pete (who had left by then) '*How dare he!!* I've been in this business for years! It's a disgrace!'

From my perspective I found much of Pete's feedback from the other side of the production box perfectly valid and useful. Kenneth, however, loathed being told how to do anything.

Pete was a smart producer and recognised the value in David's policy of introducing new talent to the show, an approach Pete continued to great effect. There were, however, occasional unforeseen consequences.

For the opening two recordings of 1982's Series 16 (broadcast on 6 February and 14 August), Pete's first as producer, both the guests were late. Jazz saxophonist Benny Green did not make it at all, forcing Pete into making a quick, and inventive, decision. Leonie Lawson from the production team took over whistleblowing, with Ian Messiter moving to the panel for his first, and only, appearance in that role. 'Rotten trick!' was Ian's reaction when it was announced.

Ian entered into the spirit of the occasion marvellously, playing on the fact that he was doing the show a favour. When I disputed his first challenge, much to the audience's amusement Ian retorted with, 'If I went home now, you would be stuck!' He had a point, but not for the challenge. Rules are rules, even when the inventor of the game is involved.

As you would expect after so many years of close observation, Ian quickly found his feet, producing numerous entertaining challenges. On the subject of 'The Chairperson', Derek Nimmo has cleverly twisted the meaning.

Derek: My favourite, in fact *the* great chairperson as far as I am concerned, is Chippendale. Of all the manufacturers of chairs in this country, he probably was the most original …
BUZZ
Nicholas: Ian Messiter.
Ian: Chippendale made very fine furniture … but Hepplewhite was better!

The audience enjoy Ian's challenge here, but I do not accept it on the grounds Derek is merely expressing an opinion, and the round continues to its conclusion.

The first subject I ask Ian to speak on is 'My Great-Great-Uncle Ebenezer's Strange Habit' which prompts one of the tactics sometimes engaged in by the regulars when 'newcomers' are involved – they sit back and put down their buzzers. Well, Kenneth Williams and Peter Jones do.

Ian: My great-great-uncle Ebenezer's strange habit is something I'm delighted to talk about, because he was very peculiar indeed. He was seven foot eight inches tall and that was before he stood up. This gave him the habit of washing the ceiling. It was very easy and he would be rented out at enormous expense by lots of people. And they're all playing this thing on me at the moment, I know … [IAN BEGINS TO LAUGH]

BUZZ

Nicholas: Derek Nimmo's not playing the thing!

Derek: No, he changed the subject and was just sort of waffling. He said, 'They're all playing this thing on me, I know,' which is nothing to do …

Nicholas: Yes, that's complete deviation, yes.

Derek: What's the matter with everybody?

Nicholas: They did that on purpose.

Ian: They all put their buzzers down and refused to buzz.

Nicholas: After all these years, Ian, you must know they have all kinds of ploys.

Ian: I saw Kenneth's sneaking hand going like that …

Nicholas: That's right.

Ian: … putting his buzzer down and folding his arms.

Nicholas: And then Peter Jones followed, but Derek Nimmo didn't, you see. You can never rely on anything in this game.

Derek: I'm not only deaf and hoarse, I'm also blind, you see! So I didn't see what was going on. [AUDIENCE LAUGH]

Ian continues to make excellent contributions for the remainder of the game, as I recognise in winding up the show.

> **Nicholas:** So let me give you the final score. Ian Messiter, not having played the game before, braving everything, competing with our three regulars, did extremely well. Many congratulations, Ian.
> **Ian:** I was last!
> **Nicholas:** You were last.
> **Ian:** I thought so. Yes.
> **Nicholas:** But you were one of the best lasts we've ever had, I think. [APPLAUSE FROM AUDIENCE]

For the second recording that evening, Ian is spared further exposure when comedian Victoria Wood appears just before we are due to begin, her train having been delayed. This is Victoria's debut on the show but unfortunately her late arrival does not allow any opportunity to check that she is fully cognisant with the rules. As a result, she is immediately caught out when handed her first subject.

> **Nicholas:** Victoria, your turn to begin, the subject is 'My Plums'. I can see the relationship in Ian Messiter's mind. But you take it in whichever way you like in the game, starting now.
> BUZZ
> **Nicholas:** Derek Nimmo challenged.
> **Derek:** She didn't start, did she!
> **Victoria:** I thought there would be a noise to tell me when to start.
> **Nicholas:** Yes, yes, I am the noise.
> **Victoria:** I've only just got here! I mean I can't be expected to know whether you're supposed to start or not. I thought there'd be a noise.
> **Derek:** If you'd been on time, we wouldn't have had this problem! [BIG LAUGH]

Victoria may have been a little unclear on the rules there, but it was a one-off slip as she settled into the game. Thereafter she proved to be an extremely adept player. Victoria is a wonderfully funny and inventive performer who was certainly not overawed by the esteemed *Just a Minute* company she was keeping. She also displayed an ability to talk incredibly fast, making challenges difficult as the other three struggled to keep pace with what she was saying. It all made for a hugely entertaining debut and it is a shame that Victoria's busy schedule has not made it possible for her to appear in more than two further shows.

By the final round Victoria has clearly grasped the rules of the game, which allows her to stick up for herself admirably against Derek and Kenneth. The subject is 'Choosing a Frock to Suit Me', with 40 seconds remaining.

Victoria: I think if I had to choose …

BUZZ

Nicholas: Kenneth Williams challenged.

Kenneth: Hesitation.

Nicholas: No. Of course not!

Kenneth: Yes, everyone agreed it was hesitation.

Victoria: No, they don't! They *don't*!!! [CRIES OF 'NO, NO' FROM THE AUDIENCE] See!

Peter: Naturally just a bit slow after two and a half hours on the train.

Victoria: Yes!

Nicholas: You don't come all the way from Morecambe to be challenged for hesitation by Kenneth Williams! [BIG LAUGH]

Victoria: No!

Nicholas: So, three quarters of a second went by. So you have 39 and a quarter seconds on 'Choosing a Frock to Suit Me', Victoria, starting now.

Victoria: What I would do is if I had to choose a frock to suit me, I will go to the shop that does the biggest sizes in the whole world. 'Cos it's rather difficult for me to get a frock that will fit me, because of being 16 on the top and 14 on the bottom. Which means I really have to have a two-piece suit actually, if I'm going to get something that will actually fit …

BUZZ

Nicholas: Derek Nimmo challenged.

Derek: 'Suit', repetition of 'suit'.

Victoria: No, in two different senses, suit to suit, and suit in the costume sense.

Nicholas: She's quite right, you know, Derek. [AUDIENCE APPLAUD]

Kenneth: It doesn't matter in what sense! The word's the same, and Derek's right. It was repeated! *You great fool!!! You're not meant to use it!*

Nicholas: She's not just a pretty face, she's a very able player of the game. She's doing marvellously!

Derek: Is this a new rule? Is it, Parsons?? Another new rule?

Nicholas: No, it's a new guest! All the way from Morecambe! Right, carry on with it, Victoria – 25 seconds, 'Choosing a Frock to Suit Me', starting now.

Victoria: I think what would suit me best would be a very long one that covered my face as well.

BUZZ

Nicholas: Derek challenged.

Derek: Well, a third 'suit' now.

Victoria: But it's in the title! Ian Messiter wrote me a letter. He said you can say it if it's in the title.

Nicholas: Yes, you can. So you slipped up again.

Derek: Oh! That's true. I am very sorry. All right! All right! I've made an absolute mess of it! [AUDIENCE LAUGH AND VICTORIA CONTINUES WITH THE ROUND]

...on the subject of *An Eccentric Professor*

The third and final of *Just a Minute*'s eccentric guests is 'Professor' Stanley Unwin. Stanley was a charming man, eccentric certainly, with a lovely personality that made him easy to get along with. He appeared on just two shows, both of which proved to be memorable for the fun created and for the fact that almost every aspect of the rules of the game was ignored or forgotten.

Kenneth Williams described Stanley as the 'master of gobbledegook' and I doubt anyone could argue with that title. The origins of Stanley's unique method of talking ('Unwinese' as it became known) can be traced back, so Stanley used to claim, to a fall suffered by his mother.

Apparently her description of the incident was that she just 'falolloped over'. From there, a new language was born, one which Stanley turned into a career in entertainment after the war, encompassing radio, television, books, theatre, popular music (Stanley narrated the Small Faces album *Ogdens' Nut Gone Flake*) and film (he played the Chancellor of Vulgaria in *Chitty Chitty Bang Bang*).

Kenneth was a huge fan. He and Stanley appeared together in the 1961 film *Carry On Regardless* in which Kenneth acted as an interpreter to Stanley's otherwise incomprehensible character. Kenneth was clearly very taken with Unwinese, to such an extent that he would occasionally slip into his own version during *Just a Minute*.

When I first learned that Stanley was to be a guest on the show I thought it an excellent idea and I was intrigued by what might happen. The versatility of the game and the fact that Stanley was appearing alongside the seasoned regulars Kenneth, Clement and Peter, left me in no doubt the experiment would work. My assessment proved to be correct.

Stanley's first show was broadcast on 9 May 1987. By that

point in his career he had been a television regular for a number of years, and the extent to which he had been embraced by the public was clear from the moment I introduced him on to the stage. He received resounding cheers and applause, which I think quite moved him as he took his seat.

Stanley's first subject on *Just a Minute* is 'Communication', a topic he seems to take to heart as this proves to be his most coherent moment. He also chalks up more 'ers' in the round that anyone before or since, all of which are ignored by the panel in order to allow Stanley to continue. Who could possible interrupt such unique entertainment?

Stanley: The early communication, of course, was the tom-tom which is a wonderful form of communication between the natives of various continents of the world. But … um … from the so-called civilised world I think … er … the … er … early digital … early digital communication was the Morse code. Di di dee dah dee dah and so on. Er … then after that … er … we had … um … we had … er … oral communication. Now the trouble is that I find is that … er … our wonderful, our wonderful language which very few of us bother to speak properly, you know. Er … you might … but um … there's always a first time on a programme you know! But deep folly! Communication … eh … I found one day that the chap wasn't listening to what I was trying to express …
[WHISTLE AND LONG APPLAUSE]
Nicholas: Well, that was Stanley Unwin's first attempt at playing *Just a Minute* and I think he hardly erred once, did you Stanley? [HUGE LAUGH]

By the final round of his debut, Stanley has found his voice. He is first to talk on the subject of 'Art', but is challenged after only half a second by Clement, an act that outrages Kenneth. 'That is most unfair, Clement!' he exclaims. 'After all, Professor Unwin is a guest on the programme and I think he deserves a little courtesy.' I agree with Kenneth that it is an incorrect challenge and Stanley continues, with plenty of hesitations, repetitions and deviations. All of which are again quite rightly ignored. The audience are enthralled, laughing along throughout.

Stanley: Art is connoted with beauty. And beauty as you all know is in the eye of the beholder. Er … I think it was Ralph Emerson who said … er … you cannot … you must carry it with you or you'll never find it. Unquote. And … um … in order to build up a picture of art you must have some idea of linear perspective which starts at the beginning and finishes at the end. Then you must have spatial relations which are lumps in between. You see? If you also have a human being there, and there's a most spherical globule on the armpecker, they call that a circlode of confusiode. You see? Now in the spacial relakers and the liney perspectey, all this joy comes back into the individuhode. So you really must carry it with you or you'll never find it. You see what I mean? Ah, there's joy! Oh no. So you may want to manifest your art by getting a bicycle and raiding it … riding it over a lump of solid …
[WHISTLE FOLLOWED BY ENTHUSIASTIC APPLAUSE]

Stanley's appearance resulted in a funny show, mainly because Stanley himself was hugely entertaining, but also because the other three were generous in letting Stanley perform while I worked hard to make sure everything held together. It is almost *Just a Minute* played in a parallel universe; great fun, but not something that could be repeated too often. The joke would quickly wear thin. That is the reason it was another two years before Stanley returned.

On that occasion he was joined by Derek, Peter and Tim Rice, for a broadcast on 2 May 1989. Stanley's was the first in the double recording that evening, the second featuring someone of even less experience than Stanley, debutant Paul Merton.

Stanley clearly did not feel he had to ease himself into this game, as he had during his first appearance. Here he is, early in the show, having just challenged Derek Nimmo for 'intersection flection' (I took that to be hesitation). Derek had been speaking for 50 seconds on the subject of 'Openers'.

Stanley: Er … well … a poker bid is the first opener, you've got to fido and triddly out the trumps and call form. And there's deep joy, dig in the pocket. Ah, folly!
[WHISTLE AND APPLAUSE]

In the fourth round Stanley is given the subject of 'Engines', on which he seems to be an expert, although his enthusiasm for diesel proves fatal when Peter successfully challenges for repetition. The laughter of the audience is constant throughout.

Stanley: A quick mention of three engines here … er … two of them, one is the petrol, the other is the diesel and there doyo huffallo dowder with explodey at the top of the … [SNIFFS DELIBERATELY] … down and nafalode to open ladey! Right! The third one is the rotatey jet, which Sir Frank Whittle, which invented just after the war and years eshplesun throod exploding the sound barriclode and he put one on the back of a lorry … this is near after twirly tractor to snaffypoo through the window. I've got one. Now then, this lorry trickley ho forward and all the engine that was in the forwode made it right daydle! Oh folly! So now we come to the diesel, you see, because this has got …
BUZZ

These brief extracts can only offer a flavour of Stanley's two strange and very entertaining shows. It is impossible to do justice to the irrepressible Professor Unwin in print. Of all the players to have played *Just a Minute*, his style is the one that can only really be captured aurally.

That said, I think Stanley's answer to a question from Peter Jones, asked towards the end of the second show, goes some way to expressing on the page the uniqueness Stanley brought to *Just a Minute*.

Peter: Stanley, excuse me, Stanley, is it true that you're studying English as a second language?
Stanley: Yes! I have all the participles lines up: Declime! Conjugapers! All these betwoo! Pure grammatal syntax in the partis participle you could ever throwed! Oh yes!
[BIG AUDIENCE LAUGH]

Two additional debutants introduced by Pete Atkin in the early 1980s proved to be significant – one because he has gone on to be a stalwart of the game and a hugely popular player, the other because her one-off appearance led to one of my favourite shows.

Taking the latter first, I have already mentioned Elaine Stritch in passing, in relation to her lovely comment regarding Kenneth stringing out a single word into a 'three-act play'. That one line is an excellent indication of how sharp and funny Elaine was on *Just a Minute*, and the broadcast of 11 September 1982 in which she features is rightly seen as a classic.

Elaine was born in Michigan and enjoyed a phenomenally successful career on stage (plays, musicals, cabaret), as well as film and television work on both sides of the Atlantic. As recently as 2011 she appeared on Broadway in Stephen Sondheim's *A Little Night Music*. In the UK she is perhaps best known for the sitcom *Two's Company*, in which she co-starred with Donald Sinden. The programme ran for four series, between 1975 and 1979, and cemented this fine performer in the British public's affections.

The amazing thing with Elaine is that she had never heard an edition of *Just a Minute* before she joined us, but she was one of those exceptional performers who loved to accept a challenge. Pete had engaged her for one broadcast, and Elaine told us she would make her appearance on the second recording of the evening. She asked to sit with Pete in the recording booth to listen to the first.

From the moment she was introduced, you would have thought she'd been a devoted fan since the pilot episode, such was her instant grasp of the dynamics of the show. She demonstrated what I would call theatrical genius – the astonishing talent to be able to listen to one performance and then walk straight out and be natural, engaging and very funny. I remember Kenneth saying during the show, 'Nobody's ever played the game like her!' He was correct. We would have loved to have her back again but her work commitments here and in the States never made that possible.

The following can only provide a taste of both the fun we enjoyed and the infectious energy that Elaine brought to the show. Her dynamic personality certainly helped her fellow panellists Kenneth, Clement and Barry Cryer raise their performances to even greater heights than normal.

Elaine's first words, describing her thoughts on the game, are spoken through laughter after Barry has made a clever challenge against Clement. 'Oh, this is *insane*!!' she exclaims in delight. During that opening round, Kenneth is talking on the peculiar subject of 'Kangaroo Pie', and suggests at one stage that Elaine would be an excellent cook of this Antipodean dish. This causes Elaine considerable consternation, which she expresses after Clement has challenged Kenneth for making such a devious comment.

Elaine: Well, I don't know what to do in this game! [BIG AUDIENCE LAUGH] I've never been so terrified in my whole life. [MORE AUDIENCE LAUGHTER] They taught me how to play the game, or thought they did, and now I have to say whether I would be *in* a kangaroo pie … [INCREASED LAUGHTER FROM EVERYONE] or have anything to do with making it? I would not! If that's going to clear this game up! [HUGE LAUGH]

From that moment on she is in full, magnificent flow, interjecting soon after the kangaroo pie discussion with, 'When is it my turn?!' She is desperate to be involved.

The second round is 'What Makes Me Fall About Laughing' with Kenneth speaking.

Kenneth: It is unquestionably Frankie Howerd. I remember him talking about going down to Chequers. And he said [IMPERSONATING FRANKIE HOWERD], 'I was trying to get *in there* to see MacMillan. You know, it's a lovely *spread* he's got there, *beautiful* place, goes with the job, of course! And he wouldn't come out, I was shouting through the letterbox, but he never *appeared*!' And I thought it conjured up a most *won-derful* picture of …
    BUZZ
Nicholas: Elaine Stritch, you challenged.
Elaine: I can't hear you! [HUGE LAUGHTER AND ENTHUSIASTIC APPLAUSE FROM AUDIENCE] Or understand you, Kenneth! I really can't! And I think it is a cheat!
Nicholas: He did repeat the word 'there'.
Elaine: *Oh, that has nothing to do with it!* [AT THIS POINT KENNETH BURSTS INTO A LOUD CACKLE WITH WHICH THE AUDIENCE JOIN IN]
Nicholas: It has everything to do with it!
Kenneth: [EXCLAIMING LOUDLY] You can't help her! *You can't help her!!!*
Nicholas: No, you can't help her! She's so noble, isn't she!
Kenneth: I know, so truthful.

To illustrate her point, Elaine then gives an exaggerated impersonation of Kenneth's nasal delivery, stretching out her words so that they become unintelligible.

Elaine: I couldn't understand him and I don't think that's fair!

Nicholas: Elaine, he did repeat the word 'there' three times.

Elaine: Well yeah, of course! That we all know! [BIG LAUGH]

Nicholas: So therefore you have a correct challenge and you get a point for that.

Elaine: What are we talking about?

Nicholas: I'm going to tell you in a moment! You have 26 seconds to try and talk on the subject of 'What Makes Me Fall About Laughing', starting now.

Elaine: I don't think I can ever remember in all the times that I've lived in America or in this country, of ever laughing at a comedian like Tommy Cooper. One night I was sitting alone in my room at the hotel and I was watching a television show. And I think one of the strangest things in the world is to *laugh* when you're all alone, out loud. I think it really is an example of really thinking something is funny. [LAUGHTER IS BUILDING IN THE AUDIENCE AS THEY REALISE NO ONE IS GOING TO CHALLENGE DESPITE THE REPETITION] So I'm watching Tommy Cooper and he said, 'I was sitting in a dentist's office the other day.' And he said, 'I was reading a magazine [AUDIENCE LAUGHING LOUDLY NOW] and the dentist ... the dentist told me that ... ah, the secretary of the dentist ... ' Nobody's challenging me! [ERUPTION OF LAUGHTER AND APPLAUSE FROM PANEL, AUDIENCE AND IAN MESSITER WHO FORGETS TO BLOW HIS WHISTLE] I almost challenged myself! I said ... I couldn't believe it!

Nicholas: People have been known to do that and get points for it, actually! But, Elaine, you kept going magnificently for about an hour and a half, and you fully deserved the point for ...

Elaine: Well, anyway, I gotta tell you what Tommy Cooper said!

Nicholas: Oh yes!

Elaine: He said, 'hahaha!' and all that business! [LAUGHTER FROM PANEL AND AUDIENCE] And he said, 'I was sitting in a dentist's office the other day, hahaha!' And then he said, 'I had to wait two hours, hahaha!' And then there was a long pause and then he said, 'Isn't that terrible about the *Titanic*!' [BIG LAUGH FROM AUDIENCE AND PANEL] I don't know, that takes a lot of explanation. But have you ever read the magazines in a dentist's office? They're old! But anyway that's what makes me fall about laughing ... as opposed to this show! [HUGE LAUGH]

Although there is no whistle (Ian, I think, is enjoying himself so much he forgets), that proves to be the end of the round. In the next, Elaine demonstrates her mastery of the comic put-down.

Nicholas: Elaine, the subject is 'Keeping My Figure', and you have 60 seconds, starting now.

Elaine: I think keeping your figure is very important, both ...

BUZZ

Nicholas: Clement Freud has challenged.

Clement: Ah, it's keeping my figure, not ...

Nicholas: It doesn't matter, she can still say 'keeping your figure' and go on the subject. She doesn't have to say 'keeping my figure'. Start off with the words on the card. How ungentlem– ...

Clement: [DEADPAN] Direct deviation of the subject.

Barry: You cad!

Nicholas: You can't be so ungenerous and ungallant!

Elaine: I got two laughs and you're mad at me! [BIG LAUGH FROM AUDIENCE AND PANEL, INCLUDING CLEMENT]

Elaine then goes on to talk uninterrupted on the subject of 'Keeping My Figure', exclaiming midway through, 'Don't do this to me again!' when once more no one challenges despite a number of repetitions and hesitations. They are enjoying her performance far too much.

Nicholas: Well, Ian Messiter *did* blow the whistle then at the end of 60 seconds. It's an amazingly long time to talk, isn't it when you ...

Elaine: It is, but now really, be honest with me. I repeated myself, didn't I?

Nicholas: You did, yes.

Kenneth: I would complain that you're not decipherable. You can't be heard properly! [ERUPTION OF LAUGHTER ALL AROUND] You've got to be like me, you speak very *plain-ly*, you see. And *enunciate*! You've got to *enunciate*! That's what you've got to remember!

Elaine: Listen! Kenneth! I don't want to go home and have this show broadcast and say, 'How was I?' and somebody will say, 'Well, they were very nice to you.' I mean that really isn't going to *cut* well with me, so I wanna be treated just like the rest of the gang! [APPLAUSE] Right!

Nicholas: Actually I can tell you something, Elaine. They've actually treated you rather toughly because that's a *mean* thing to do, what they've done.

Elaine: Right.

Nicholas: They only do that to people that they not only love, but people that they know are good at the game.

Kenneth: We did it to Barbara Castle!

Elaine: Well, all the time I thought it was because I was attractive, Nicholas! [BIG LAUGH] And I'm going to keep that thought and go home with it! [BIGGER LAUGH] *So the hell with all of you!!!*

Nicholas: That actually goes without saying, Elaine! I didn't think I had to mention it.

Elaine: Oh Nicholas!

Kenneth: You sycophant! Look at him! [AUDIENCE LAUGH]

Elaine: Come on, let's go, I want to challenge somebody!

Finally, at the end of the show, Elaine signs off with a big laugh to complete a memorable evening.

Nicholas: Well, it's been great fun, hasn't it? And it's been lovely having such an unusual and original performer as Elaine

Stritch! Because her contribution was …

Panel: Hear! Hear! [LOUD APPLAUSE FROM AUDIENCE]

Elaine: Thank you very much! Thank you, Nicholas! Thank you. Thank you. Thank you!

Nicholas: Elaine, your contribution has been …

BUZZ

Nicholas: Yes? Elaine, you've challenged. What was your challenge?

Elaine: I repeated myself! [HUGE AUDIENCE LAUGH AS THE SHOW DRAWS TO A CLOSE]

Pete Atkin's second debutant made his appearance in a show broadcast on 7 August 1982 alongside Kenneth Williams, Peter Jones and Sheila Hancock. His name was Gyles Brandreth.

Gyles was far less of a public figure back then, known principally for his writing of word puzzle and Scrabble books, but his success in that linguistic arena made him an ideal candidate for *Just a Minute*.

I first met Gyles at a party held by celebrity cook Fanny Cradock, and we have been very good friends ever since. He is always a joy to be with, socially and professionally. At the time of the party, Gyles had only recently come down from Oxford where he had been President of the Union. He remembers the occasion clearly, even referring to it many years later during a recording of *Just a Minute*, shortly after we had celebrated the show's 40th anniversary. 'It is 40 years since I first met Nicholas Parsons who was then a matinee idol, a young Adonis, who was at a party organised by Fanny Cradock with Lionel Blair as the entertainment. They were known as Butch Casserole and the One-Dance Kid! Nicholas was there in all his glory.'

I also have a keen memory of that party because Fanny suddenly announced midway through the evening, and out of the blue as far as I was concerned, that I was to entertain her guests. Gyles says he was very impressed that I just stood up and did a turn. Fortunately it was well received. It was part of my cabaret act at the time, in which I took off the foreign films of the day by talking gibberish in the various languages, which I punctuated for laughs with English 'subtitles' and comments.

Gyles' appearances on *Just a Minute* in the 1980s were sporadic. In fact between 1982 and 1986 he joined us on only ten occasions, and thereafter not again on radio until 2002. The reason for his absence was strangely prophesised in that first show. Here is Sheila Hancock talking during that game on 'The Most Outstanding Personality in this Show'.

> **Sheila:** The most outstanding personality in this show is definitely Derek Nimmo! Because he's tall …
> DUZZ
> **Nicholas:** Peter Jones has challenged.
> **Peter:** Sorry, Derek Nimmo isn't in this show!
> **Sheila:** Isn't he? Oh!
> **Peter:** That's Gyles Brandreth over there! [BIG LAUGH]

Then later, in the penultimate round Kenneth is talking about 'Hallucinations'. The previous subject had been 'My Goodness'.

> **Kenneth:** This definitely happened to me on holiday. I was given what I believed to be a Mickey Finn. That's what I think. And in the middle of the afternoon. I felt I was floating! I had this awful sense of colours, right in front of my eyes! I thought, 'Oh, where am I? Oh my goodness!'
> BUZZ
> **Nicholas:** Gyles Brandreth has challenged.
> **Gyles:** Deviation – 'my goodness' was the last subject.
> [AUDIENCE LAUGH]
> **Nicholas:** All right, Gyles, a bonus point for a clever challenge but Kenneth gets …
> **Sheila:** Are you sure he isn't Derek Nimmo? [BIG AUDIENCE LAUGH]

Although Sheila is being funny here with her closing comment, there were some people who may well have thought she was making a valid point. Yes, the reason that Gyles was dropped from the show for a period of time was that certain decision-makers felt he sounded too much like Derek Nimmo, and as Derek was an established regular they could not feature both. This decision resulted in *Just a Minute* missing out for many years on Gyles' excellent contributions, such as the following ad lib rhyme he concocted when talking on 'What Goes in My Wastepaper Basket' in 1986, which was rewarded with howls of laughter from the audience.

> **Gyles:** As you might well guess, what chiefly goes into my wastepaper basket is my poetry. I sit at my desk scribbling away all day, and then crumple the little bits of paper and chuck them despairingly away. Today, for example, if you looked into my wastepaper basket, you would find an ode I had written to the distinguished chairman of this particular programme. Dedicated to Nicholas Parsons, it began
> *Don't worry if your job is small,*
> *And the rewards are few.*
> *Remember that the mighty oak,*
> *Was once a nut like you!*

I do not think there would be the same concerns now regarding the perceived similarity in voices. Back then, however, that was the thinking of the programme planners and it was not until after Derek's death that Gyles was asked to make a return. He is now, I am glad to say, one of the show's first-choice panellists. Gyles clearly enjoys his appearances enormously. No matter how busy he is (and he is a bit of a workaholic) he will always do his very best to accommodate the recording schedule.

Some 'rude' words also made an appearance on *Just a Minute* during the 1980s, with varying degrees of acceptability when it came to BBC sensibilities.

In a late October 1983 broadcast, Ian Messiter introduced the subject of 'Limericks', no doubt confident that the team would be able to recite some classics. As anticipated, the subject produces an enormous amount of fun as each of the panellists tries to outdo the others, often having to speak through their own laughter and that of the other players and the audience. During the round, Derek Nimmo wins the subject from cricket commentator Brian Johnston who is also on the panel, and comes out with the following, producing a riotous response from every person in the theatre. It is a good job that The Little Green Book had long since been consigned to history.

Derek:
There was an old poof of Khartoum,
Who took a lesbian up to his room.
They lay on the bed,
And suddenly said,
'Who does what, with what, and to whom?'

Derek cannot continue as he is laughing so much and begs to be given a moment to recover. I am laughing just as hard but manage to reply.

Nicholas: Lord … excuse me just a moment … Lord Reith, turn in your grave. Derek, I think you've broken new ice in the realms and history of broadcasting. If you want to write to us about them, please address your letters personally to Derek Nimmo, because you will get a personalised reply. [BIG AUDIENCE LAUGH]

In fact Brian had challenged Derek correctly on the repetition of 'what' (the least of his sins) but Derek is determined to win the round back as he has another wonderful example up his sleeve. He duly manages to do so and attempts the following.

Derek:
There was a young lady from Colesville,
Who sat herself down on a mole's hill.
The inquisitive mole,

Stuck his nose …
I'm … I'm so sorry!! [DEREK AND EVERYONE ELSE BURST
INTO LOUD LAUGHTER]

Derek cannot continue here, having dissolved into a fit of giggles
anticipating the punchline. Many years later, however, on a show
from 2003 that turns out to be Wendy Richard's final appearance,
Clement Freud talks on the subject of 'Molehills' and manages to
accomplish what Derek could not.

Clement:
The delectably lovely Miss Coleshill,
Once chanced to alight on a mole's hill.
The inquisitive mole,
Stuck his nose up her hole,
Miss Coleshill's all right, but the mole's ill!
[HUGE LAUGH FROM EVERYONE]

After the laughter subsided Clement innocently claims, 'Wendy told
me that!'

In 1985, two years on from when Derek first introduced us to the
goings on in Khartoum and Colesville, the seemingly safe subject of
'Bognor Regis' arises. Well, it would have been safe if Peter Jones
had not been on the panel. The actor Martin Jarvis is speaking first,
with 14 seconds remaining.

Martin:
When George the Fifth was lying ill in bed,
The man by his side, his doctor said,
'Don't worry, your Majesty … '
    BUZZ
Nicholas: Derek Nimmo challenged.
Derek: I don't believe the doctor was in bed with King George
the Fifth! Deviation!
Martin: No!

Kenneth: Ridiculous! 'Lying by his side!' You said it! You did!

Martin: It was 'lying' because in fact …

Kenneth: No!!!

Martin: … if you're going to listen, he wasn't, in fact, saying the truth. He was trying to cheer him up.

Derek: I don't believe he and the doctor were in bed together when he was ill! [BIG LAUGH]

Martin: Oh, I never suggested they were in bed together! He had a bedside manner, this doctor, he was *beside* the bed, and he was going to …

Kenneth: He might have done it, yes, to cheer him up! He might have gone in with him to cheer him up! I wouldn't mind a few getting in beside me! *It'd cheer me up, I can tell you!!!* Nobody wants anybody to be lonely!

Nicholas: I think that what we'll do is, as you're in the lead, and Martin is a guest, we'll give him the benefit of the doubt because it was a slip of the tongue but he didn't deviate from 'Bognor Regis' and so you have seven seconds on the subject, starting now.

Martin:

And the doctor said,

'Don't worry, your Majesty, soon it will be … '

> BUZZ

Nicholas: Peter Jones has challenged.

Peter: Repetition of 'doctor'.

Nicholas: Yes, the doctor, you mentioned him before.

Martin: Oh, did I?

Nicholas: Yes, but it was a bit devious what he was doing! But certainly enough he's been mentioned twice, that is repetition. So, Peter, you have five seconds on 'Bognor Regis', starting now.

Peter: He said, 'Bognor will do you the world of good.' And the old king replied, 'Bugger Bognor!' [HUGE BURST OF LOUD LAUGHTER FROM EVERYONE]

Peter's line brought the house down during that recording, but radio audiences were left having to guess what he had actually said because incredibly, given this was 1985, the BBC chose to bleep out the word 'bugger' for the broadcast on 6 March. In modern times the use of the word has become far more tolerated, as it is commonly delivered in an inoffensive manner. This change in attitude has proved to be good news for *Just a Minute* ... especially if Stephen Fry is on the show. Here he is speaking on the subject of 'My School Days' in a broadcast of 7 January 2002.

Stephen: My school days straddled the period from round about 1960 to 1970 ...

BUZZ

Stephen: Bugger! Two nine ... All one word!

Nicholas: Clement, you challenged, what was it for?

Clement: Repetition.

Nicholas: Repetition, yes.

Stephen: It's all one word! Nineteen-sixty and nineteen-seventy, all one word!!!

Clement: No.

Stephen: No, it isn't, you're right. I mean, a point to him.

Then later in the same show Clement makes a clever reference back to that earlier round.

Nicholas: And Stephen, your turn to begin, the subject 'Going to the Optician'. Tell us something about that in this game, starting now.

Stephen: This is something, melancholy to relate, that I have to do more and more often these days.

BUZZ

Stephen: *Bugger!!* I said 'more' twice! Damn!!! It's a trap for the unwary, this game, isn't it!

Nicholas: I know!

Stephen: Dear me!

Nicholas: Yes! Particularly with the language!

Stephen: Oh!
Nicholas: Who challenged?
Clement: I did.
Nicholas: You did, Clement. What was your challenge?
Clement: He said 'bugger' twice! [HUGE LAUGH]

The final show of Series 19 (1985–86) saw two departures, one known about at the time, the other revealed shortly before recording for the new series began.

That broadcast of 1 March 1986 was Pete Atkins' last as producer, with Ted Taylor taking over the reins. Ted was an experienced producer, and quite naturally wanted to introduce some subtle changes when he joined the team. One of these, which I learned of when discussing the forthcoming recording schedule, was to drop the announcer's voice at the beginning and end of each show. Ted felt that having an announcer was a throwback to a different era of radio, more stuffy. He was keen that we modernise our presentation to make it sharper, a decision with which I was delighted.

Ted suggested that I take over the introduction of the panellists and the closing lines concerning Ian Messiter and the producer. A small change perhaps, but it did make the programmes snappier, with a more immediate connection to the listeners. That is how we have done it ever since, as the Minute Waltz fades away.

It was around this period that I made a suggestion to the head of Light Entertainment at the BBC, with regard to the show's presentation. 'Every other comedy game show has an accredited writer,' I explained, 'who provides the presenter with some witty comments at the start of the show, perhaps throughout, and also in the closing remarks. Can I have a writer?'

He listened, then came back to me with a rather shrewd observation. 'Nicholas, we have thought about this and have come to the conclusion that as *Just a Minute* is our only completely spontaneous show, if we gave you a writer then the listeners might think that there may be more preparation in other areas than there is. That would detract from the show.'

He was absolutely right. Other programmes are improvised in their banter and jokes, but the gags in the introductions and the wind-ups are scripted. That is not *Just a Minute*. I took his response as a compliment to everyone involved in our show and have been extremely happy ever since to have no assistance.

Finally, as the decade drew to a close, there were two significant arrivals and two very unhappy goodbyes.

The arrivals first.

Wendy Richard, who I mentioned briefly with regard to Clement Freud's habit of making lists, made her first appearance in a broadcast of 12 May 1988.

Ted made a good choice with Wendy. I had worked with her back in the 1960s on *The Arthur Haynes Show* on television and knew her to be a talented supporting actress, feisty certainly, and popular with viewers. Since then Wendy had received considerable public attention playing Miss Brahms in the sitcom *Are You Being Served?* and thereafter soap stardom as Pauline Fowler on *EastEnders*.

I was very fond of Wendy. When I first knew her she was laid-back and humorous, and that side of her character came across in her early appearances on *Just a Minute*. She was full of infectious giggles at her own mistakes and clearly enjoyed the atmosphere being created by her fellow panellists Kenneth, Clement and Derek.

To help ease Wendy into the game Ian Messiter set her up with an excellent first subject, 'Soap', which she tackled in a self-effacing and likeable manner.

> **Wendy:** The word 'soap' can apply to many things. It could refer to some of these appalling American programmes that are shipped over here, i.e. *Dallas* and *Dynasty*. Or as the French say, it could also pertain to … *savon* … which is what one washes one's hands with. [BIG AUDIENCE LAUGH] Or … or it could relate to *EastEnders*, a little-known … television show …
> BUZZ

Derek: How mean! Who said that?

Kenneth: I did, because how can you say *EastEnders* is little known? It's well known! Millions watch it, don't they?

Wendy: I was being modest!

Nicholas: Yes, and this is where the boys are very generous. They do want everybody to know who's listening in this country and abroad that Wendy Richard is one of the stars of *EastEnders*. And she was so modest she dried up and Kenneth got in with a correct challenge, and he takes over the subject of 'Soap' with 29 and a half seconds left, starting now.

In the following round I feel it appropriate to lend Wendy some assistance, allowing her to revise her challenge, and clarifying the rules. This is something that I often do with newcomers to help overcome their understandable nerves and build confidence. Kenneth is talking on the subject 'Neptune'.

Kenneth: Well, of course he is the old Latin god of the sea, water to be precise. But also there is Neptune in New Jersey, where this Methodist association has a lot of tents, and they're camping all the year round. It's an *enormous* camp and they are great campers ... [HERE I CATCH WENDY'S EYE AND INDICATE SHE SHOULD CHALLENGE]

BUZZ

Nicholas: Wendy Richard, you challenged.

Wendy: Well, because he said 'camp' ... Is camping, campers and camp classed as one word or three?

Nicholas: They are three words. You can have camp and camps.

Wendy: Well ... I think then it was a deviation?

Nicholas: All that camping was a deviation from Neptune?

Wendy: Yes!

Nicholas: Yes, I think you're right, Wendy. Yes, definitely. [AUDIENCE LAUGH AND APPLAUD] So you've got your first point on *Just a Minute*. Well done.

Wendy: Thank you.

Nicholas: [PLAYING FOR A LAUGH WITH A DELIBERATE MISTAKE] So will you talk on 'Camping' now … [AUDIENCE LAUGH] No, no, sorry … will you talk on the subject of 'Neptune' with 32 seconds left, starting now.

Wendy: There used to be this wonderful fish and chip shop in Soho called the Neptune and they used to serve the best food you've ever had. And Manny, the chap who owned this premises, made wonderful batter which he used to … dip the …

   BUZZ

Nicholas: Derek Nimmo challenged.

Derek: I just didn't want to hear what he dipped. [BIG LAUGH]

Nicholas: So you're challenging for deviation.

Derek: Hesitation really, and deviation.

Wendy: I didn't know you could buzz me.

Derek: I've never tried before. [MORE LAUGHTER]

Wendy: I would have buzzed you before now. I'm sorry, I misunderstood. I would have done you before now.

Derek: This is going to be my lucky night! [HUGE LAUGHTER AND APPLAUSE]

Nicholas: I think I should explain to our listeners the reason for Wendy's remarks is that they sit in pairs either side of me, and Wendy, sitting beside Derek Nimmo, she assumed that he was her partner! And she's just discovered he's playing against her.

Wendy continues on the subject, and even if still not absolutely certain of all the rules she quickly finds her rhythm in terms of making her case in the face of a challenge. Derek shows good sportsmanship when he realises Wendy has genuinely misunderstood how to play the game.

Wendy: So he used to make this wonderful batter that he used to dip the fish in …

   BUZZ

Nicholas: Derek Nimmo challenged.

Derek: Repetition of batter.

Wendy: That's not true!

Derek: When you start again, you're not supposed to repeat the same thing in the same question.

Wendy: I was just letting them know from whence I had left off!

[AUDIENCE LAUGH AND APPLAUSE]

Clement: Quite right.

Derek: I'm sorry, I withdraw my challenge.

By the following round Wendy has clearly begun to relax. She is enjoying herself and has the confidence to make a challenge purely to generate a laugh. The subject is 'Shambles' and Derek starts off with some outrageous comments about me that we all find very entertaining.

Derek: The whole of this programme of *Just a Minute* turns into a shambles because we have such an *inadequate chairman* who never gets things right! [AUDIENCE LAUGH] And always gives the wrong decision because unfortunately he's rather deaf and terribly elderly, and …

BUZZ

Nicholas: [LAUGHING] Wendy Richard has challenged.

Wendy: I object to that remark.

Nicholas: You're absolutely correct!! So you consider that devious?

Wendy: I do. I played his girlfriend a few years ago. He can't be that old! [BIG LAUGH]

Wendy's second recording that evening was broadcast a month or so after the first, on 16 June. That particular programme has considerable significance in the story of *Just a Minute* and I shall return to it shortly.

Wendy's sense of fun in her first recording was carried over into the second, helping to create an excellent atmosphere within the panel which led to a touch of mischief.

The fact that double recordings are separated when the series is actually broadcast, in order for listeners to hear a variety of voices from one week to the next, means that the panellists should be careful not to mention events that occurred earlier in the evening. This is something of an unwritten rule … to which the players do not always adhere.

During this recording session both Kenneth and Wendy deliberately refer back to comments from the first show. In a spontaneous programme such as ours, it is natural to grab at every opportunity to generate a laugh. The theatre audience enjoy being in on the joke, and both remarks produced big laughs at the time. That is what the show is all about, but it did mean an intervention from me was required, which in itself entertained the audience.

First, on the subject of 'Nannies', Kenneth reintroduces the idea of 'Milking a [Nanny] Goat', the topic on which he has spoken in the final round of the first show. The audience bursts out laughing in such an enthusiastic manner that the following word of explanation from me is necessary for when the show is aired. 'If you were listening a few weeks ago, you may remember, if not I will inform you, that actually Kenneth finished the show talking about milking a goat. And that's what he was referring back to. That's what made us all laugh so much.'

Wendy then joins in when talking on 'Neighbours', which she calls '*yet* another soap'. As the topic of soap operas has not been raised so far in *this* recording, once again I feel it necessary to explain.

This show also sees one of the game's *actual* rules being broken. Clement successfully challenges Derek with a fifth of a second remaining on the stopwatch. I hand the subject, 'Atlas', to Clement, he opens his mouth, and Ian blows the whistle. As Clement drily points out, he has gained a point for 'not speaking' as the whistle went. A *Just a Minute* first.

If Wendy Richard had continued in the same vein in which she began her *Just a Minute* career, I am certain she would have clocked up significantly more appearances than the 41 she totalled. Unfortunately, however, Wendy seemed to drift from the persona she projected during those first couple of years on the show. It was almost as though she allowed the harder personality of her *EastEnders* character Pauline to take over, becoming more crabby and aggressive.

Many listeners appreciated Wendy's different approach to the game, and it could be enjoyable to listen to, there is no doubt. For the live audience, however, Wendy's snarky comments and miserable look created a negative atmosphere that permeated the whole show. It drained energy and inventiveness from the other players and in time our producers grew to see this as a problem.

...on the subject of Producers

Over the years I have been very fortunate to work with a succession of excellent producers on *Just a Minute*.

The most important attribute, in my opinion, that these producers share is having an ear for the show. In order to be able to cast the panellists effectively – perhaps the most important role the producer undertakes – it is essential that the person making those decisions is in tune with the comedy that *Just a Minute* generates.

Simply put, a producer who understands the show casts it well.

Having decided who they would like to feature on the panel, the producer then has to contact those people to see if they are available, and find replacements if they are not. This can prove to be a complex logistical puzzle requiring organisational skills and patience. It is likely that everyone who is approached will have other professional commitments, all of which have to be successfully juggled in order to put the show together.

On the day of recording, just before we get underway, the producer runs through housekeeping points with the audience, pointing out the fire exits etc., and then disappears into the production booth to check sound levels and observe the show.

What the producer does not do is 'direct' the performers. We are left to our own devices. The concept behind *Just a Minute* is that it is spontaneous. The producer will have ensured that there are at least two, and more often three, experienced players on each panel. They, in addition to myself, know exactly what it takes to make the game work. In a scripted drama the producer may well provide input into how the actors should perform in advance of the recording, but in *Just a Minute* the responsibility of making the show a success is down to the performers on the stage.

Once the two recordings are completed, the producer then takes over. Occasionally I may be asked to redo my introduction or closing remarks if the sound has not been quite right. Other than that, the shows that are created on the night are what the listeners hear on the broadcasts, save for some fine tuning by the producer in the editing room.

Unlike many other shows, in *Just a Minute* we do not deliberately over-record in order to be able to cherry-pick the best bits. Yes, there will be some trimming required to reach the broadcast length, and fluffs may be edited out (unless they generated laughs), but it is a case of polishing what is already there. This is where the producer puts his or her stamp on the show. Although there may only be a few minutes to cut, obviously something will be lost for the final transmission and that decision is the producer's alone.

The following is a list of all the *Just a Minute* producers since the pilot show in 1967 up until Series 68, broadcast in February and March 2014.

- David Hatch: 166 shows between 1967–75 and 1979–81 (Series 1–9 and 13–15)
- Simon Brett: 43 shows between 1968–75 (Series 4–9)
- John Cassels: eight shows between 1973–74 (Series 8)
- Bob Oliver Rogers: six shows between 1973–74 (Series 8)

- John Lloyd: 38 shows between 1974–76 (Series 9 and 10)
- John Browell: 40 shows between 1976–78 (Series 11 and 12)
- Pete Atkin: 67 shows between 1982–86 (Series 16–19)
- Edward Taylor: 46 shows between 1987–91 (Series 20–24)
- Sarah Smith: 30 shows between 1992–95 (Series 25–28)
- Mike Mansfield: 28 television shows between 1994–95 (ITV Series 1 and 2)
- Anne Jobson: 35 shows between 1994–98 (Series 28–32)
- Chris Neill: 46 shows between 1998–2000 and in 2004 (Series 32–36 and 44)
- Helena Taylor: 20 television shows in 1999 (BBC Series 1)
- Claire Jones: 191 shows between 2000–06, in 2008 and 2012 (Series 37–49, 54–56, 58, 60 and 62–64)
- Tilusha Ghelani: 86 shows between 2007–08 and 2010–14 (Series 50–53, 57, 59, 61–65 and 68)
- Andy Brereton: ten television shows in 2012 (BBC Series 2)
- Katie Tyrell: 14 shows in 2013 (Series 66 and 67)
- Elizabeth Clark: five *Junior Just a Minute* shows in 2013 (*Junior Just a Minute* Series 1)

The second significant arrival in the late 1980s was Paul Merton.

My first encounter with Paul came in Manchester – in 1988, I believe – when we were both appearing on the TV panel game *Scruples*, hosted by Simon Mayo. After filming Paul and I were talking, and he mentioned how much he loved *Just a Minute*. In fact, what he told me was that while trying to establish himself as a comedy performer he had lived in a bedsit with no television, and for entertainment he used to listen to cassette tapes he had recorded of *Just a Minute*.

I had been very impressed with Paul's performance on the *Scruples* edition on which we had appeared, the two of us enjoying trading gags, and as he was telling me how much he enjoyed *Just a Minute*, I suddenly realised that he would make a wonderful guest.

Back in London I spoke to Ted Taylor and suggested he consider

Paul for future recordings. This was the first occasion I had ever done such a thing. The casting of panellists is the responsibility of the producer. People often assume that I have some influence over who will appear, but that is incorrect. In recent years I have offered feedback when asked but the decision on who features in each show is exclusively in the hands of the producer.

That is how it should be. As chairman I believe it would be invidious for me to be in any way actively involved in casting. That could lead to favouritism, which would strike at the integrity of the game.

I am delighted, however, that I did draw attention to Paul as a possibility, although Ted's initial reaction was less than enthusiastic. Ted told me he would consider the idea but was worried that Paul was one of those 'alternative comedians' who could not be trusted. Ted was a delightful man, with great talent, but he was most definitely a traditionalist in the style of what used to be called Auntie BBC.

My response was that 'alternative' was merely a fashionable phrase and that Ted should think of Paul as just a clever comedian who loves the show. I assured Ted that I was confident Paul would do well.

Some time later, Ted telephoned me to say that a prospective guest had been forced to pull out of a recording and that he was considering Paul to fill the slot. Once again I reassured Ted that Paul would do well, to which he replied, 'Well, if he doesn't, it's your fault, Nicholas. Not mine.' Although Ted did not mean this unkindly, I did feel his response put me under a certain amount of pressure.

Paul takes up the story.

Ted's approach coincided with me posting a letter because Nicholas had mentioned that he thought I might fit into the show. I'd never written a letter to a producer before, or since, but there I was suggesting myself and enclosing a review from a show I was doing in Edinburgh. When I received Ted's call it was obvious he was quite worried about having me on the show. First of all, he wanted to know what I'd be wearing! I'm not sure but I think he saw me as some sort of Sid Vicious character or something! He then went on to explain what language was acceptable and that swearing played no part on the show. All kinds of things like that. It was clear to me that in his mind he was taking a bit of a chance on me. Thank God he did.

The chance Ted was willing to take initially extended to only one recording. Sitting alongside Paul for his debut were Derek Nimmo, Peter Jones and Tim Rice. In many respects this was a baptism of fire, and Paul came through wonderfully well. He contributed to the competitiveness of the game while at the same time he was looking for ways to generate laughs himself or to provide opportunities for others.

That sums up Paul's attitude to the game ever since. He has an intuitive understanding of what makes for a good programme, either injecting humour at precisely the right moments or sitting back when others are performing well.

In that first recording (broadcast on 25 April 1989) Derek offers Paul no leeway from the very start, perhaps sensing that here is a guest with the ability to match him blow for blow. It makes for a wonderful jousting match. The first subject is 'Pinching', on which Derek had initially spoken, with reference to the pinching that can occur after buying a new pair of shoes. Having won back the subject, Derek is now taking a different tack.

> **Derek:** So when Pinching started his factory in the Potteries near Stoke-on-Trent, he *actually* stole the designs of Wedgwood and that's why it was called Pinching. Which is a frightfully interesting fact that not everybody …
> BUZZ
> **Nicholas:** Paul Merton has challenged.
> **Paul:** Didn't Wedgwood make plates?
> **Nicholas:** He did make plates, yes.
> **Paul:** Well, how would a shoe manufacturer pinch designs …?!
> [BIG ROUND OF AUDIENCE APPLAUSE] Unless that's just me

being thick, of course!

Nicholas: I don't think he'd established that. I think that's such a good challenge we have to give it to you, Paul. And you get a point for that and you have 20 seconds to tell us something about 'Pinching', starting now.

Paul: Pinching or nicking is er, … a … term that …

BUZZ

Nicholas: Derek Nimmo challenged.

Derek: Put him in his place. 'Er'! How dare he!

[AUDIENCE LAUGH]

Nicholas: Derek, that is one of the meanest challenges! That is the first time that Paul Merton has opened his mouth on *Just a Minute* [AUDIENCE START TO 'OOOH' AND AHH' IN SYMPATHY FOR PAUL], and he had three words out and you came straight in there as sharp as a knife. And all I'm going to say is, I thought it was an unfair challenge even if it was correct!

Paul tries to continue but loses the subject to Derek almost immediately, prompting me to comment to Paul: 'You get some idea of how the game is played now. Even if you are a new boy in the show you get no quarter, I am afraid.' Derek then starts to speak with 14 seconds remaining, with Paul poised to retaliate. Their humorous exchanges contribute to an exciting atmosphere building in the theatre.

Derek: It is awfully mean to pinch …

BUZZ

Nicholas: And Paul Merton has challenged.

Paul: Repetition of the English language. [AUDIENCE LAUGHTER]

Nicholas: I don't mind what you say, Paul, I quite agree with the challenge! [AUDIENCE LAUGH AND APPLAUD AND PAUL GOES ON TO FINISH THE ROUND]

The banter continues into the third round. Derek is talking on the subject of 'Rope Tricks', dragging out his words in his own inimitable style for comic effect.

> **Derek:** I remember *be-ing* in the outer *sub-burbs* of *Bom-bay*. And there I *espied* a *fa-kir* with his rope, which he was *try-ing* to get to rise *high* into the air. He had a *flu-te* in one hand …
>   BUZZ
> **Nicholas:** Paul Merton challenged.
> **Paul:** Why is he talking funny?? [BIG LAUGH FROM EVERYONE]
> **Nicholas:** I don't know, I think that's a very good question. In other words, deviation from his normal speech.
> **Paul:** Indeed, yes.
> **Nicholas:** Yes, indeed. So, Paul, you have another point and you have 43 seconds for 'Rope Tricks', starting now.
> **Paul:** I know a magician who could do several good rope tricks. One was to make the rope go down to the shops and do the shopping for him. Er … another …
>   BUZZ
> **Nicholas:** Derek Nimmo challenged.
> **Derek:** Why is he going 'er' *and talking funny*? [AUDIENCE LAUGH AND DEREK TAKES OVER THE SUBJECT]

Throughout the game, all four panellists are on top form, realising perhaps that this show is proving to be a particularly keenly fought contest. In the next round Tim Rice is talking on the subject of 'Bimboes'.

> **Tim:** Bimboes are a comparatively recent phenomenon. If you had said to somebody, 'What is a bimbo?' five or even only three years ago they would have said, 'What are you talking about, cock?' Or words to that effect. And the reason is not hard to discover. This word was invented by politicians or by journalists following politics in the United States of America in order to do down perfectly decent politicians …
>   BUZZ

Tim loses the subject to Paul through the repetition of 'politicians', but quickly recaptures it, and falls back on one of his favourite tactics – linking a song to the subject. This proves fatal.

> **Tim:** *'Bimbo, whatcha gonna do-eo'* was the first line of a song popular in about 1954. I never discovered ...
>   BUZZ
> **Nicholas:** Peter Jones challenged.
> **Peter:** Well, he told us a minute or two ago that it hadn't been used until the last three or four years! [BIG AUDIENCE APPLAUSE AND PETER CONTINUES WITH THE SUBJECT TO THE END OF THE ROUND]

During the sixth subject, 'Sharks', Tim demonstrates that he is a match for Paul.

> **Tim:** Sharks have been the inspiration for a good many motion pictures, or movies, for our American listeners ...
>   BUZZ
> **Nicholas:** Paul Merton challenged.
> **Paul:** Name five.
> **Tim:** Jaws One, Jaws Two, Jaws Three, Jaws Four, Jaws Five.
> [AUDIENCE AND PAUL LAUGH]

In the eighth round the subject is 'Nerds', during which Peter shows wonderful comic timing. Paul is first to speak.

> **Paul:** I suppose this is the male equivalent of the bimbo. It seems to be a word that was conjured round about the same time. I know there have been films made, certainly released in America. There was one movie called *Revenge of the Nerds* which is ... A nerd is a person who wears glasses, his ears stick out ...
>   BUZZ
> **Nicholas:** Tim Rice has challenged.
> **Tim:** If all this is true, then they are in no way the equivalent of

bimboes. [AUDIENCE LAUGH] Bimboes are highly attractive …
Peter: It's not their ears that stick out, is it? [HUGE LAUGH
FROM EVERYONE]

Ted Taylor's fears that Paul would run amok in *Just a Minute*,
destroying the very fabric of the show, were clearly allayed by that
superb first recording. Paul was invited to return, beginning a happy
relationship with the programme that continues to the present day.
During Paul's second recording (which was actually broadcast out
of sync on 4 April 1989, giving the impression this was Paul's first
appearance) Paul, Derek and Peter gel wonderfully well, with some
lovely contributions from comic performer Richard Murdoch who
was on the panel for the second time.

Nicholas: And Paul Merton's turn to begin … Paul, the subject
is 'Bottle'.
Paul: Well, again, this is one of these words which means
something else. Bottle can refer to courage or nerve. For
example, a parachutist who refuses to jump out of a plane … er
… maybe because he …
BUZZ
Nicholas: Derek Nimmo challenged.
Derek: Sadly a hesitation. It's not his first time … [INTAKE OF
BREATH FROM PAUL]
Nicholas: No!
Derek: 'Er'!
Nicholas: I disagree entirely! [FAINT 'NO' FROM AUDIENCE
WHICH I MISHEAR]
Nicholas: What do you mean 'oh' in the audience?
Derek: Well, he said 'er', didn't he!
Nicholas: I don't think he hesitated, no. I think you should
keep going about the parachutist. Forty-nine seconds, we want
to hear from you, Paul …
Richard: To err is human. [AUDIENCE LAUGH]
Nicholas: … on 'Bottle' starting now.

Paul: If he was to jump out … er … without a parachute, he could be said …

BUZZ

Nicholas: Derek Nimmo challenged.

Derek: Did he do it again then? Or am I mishearing him? [BIG LAUGH FROM AUDIENCE]

Nicholas: What are you challenging for?

Derek: He keeps saying 'er', doesn't he?

Nicholas: [AT THIS POINT I DECIDE TO BE GENEROUS TO PAUL AS IT IS ONLY HIS SECOND APPEARANCE AND THE AUDIENCE ARE ENJOYING DEREK'S CHALLENGES] He didn't say 'er'. He actually repeated 'parachute' but you didn't challenge him for that. [BIG AUDIENCE LAUGH] So, Paul, you keep going with 44 seconds on 'Bottle', starting now.

Paul: I had a friend called Ernie and we all called him Er!

[LAUGHTER FROM PANEL AND AUDIENCE]

BUZZ

Nicholas: Derek Nimmo challenged.

Derek: Not hesitation, repetition of 'er'! [LAUGHTER AND APPLAUSE FROM AUDIENCE]

Paul: But hadn't we, hadn't we ruled that I hadn't said 'er ' before?

Peter: I'd like to hear what happened to the man who was about to jump out of the plane! [HUGE AUDIENCE LAUGH]

Nicholas: I think we all do.

Paul: He doesn't come round much any more!

Nicholas: So, Paul, you're going to continue with 39 seconds on 'Bottle', starting now.

Paul: Fifteen thousand feet he plummeted towards the earth. His ears were held back by the wind as he attempted to fly back up to the plane. But it was to no avail because he travelled down to terra firma at such a rate that he was splattered … out … as … flat as a pancake by the time he hit the ground! And his wife later described his condition as very satisfactory! [BIG LAUGH FROM AUDIENCE]

BUZZ

Derek: What's this got to do with bottle? Deviation!
[LAUGHTER CONTINUES]
Peter: Well, you have to have bottle to tell a story like that!
[LAUGHTER EXPLODES EVEN LOUDER WITH MUCH APPLAUSE]

This recording is an excellent example of the exciting mix of new talent and ever-sharp old-stagers that was to become an important feature of *Just a Minute* in the coming years. In the following round Paul sits back and enjoys himself as the others have fun with the subject 'Silly Songs', one of which is the children's favourite 'Mares Eat Oats' as performed by Derek.

Derek: One of the silly songs that I used to enjoy in my youth which of course was a very long time ago, is 'Maaars eat oats and does devour cereals … '
BUZZ
Nicholas: Richard Murdoch challenged.
Richard: It's 'mares' not 'maaars'!
Nicholas: That's right! It's not 'mars'. It's not either the thing you eat or your mother!
Derek: I *know* it's 'Mares eat oats'. [DEREK STARTS TO SING IN A HIGH-PITCHED VOICE, INCREDIBLY QUICKLY]
'Mairzy doats and dozy doats and liddle lamzy divey. A kiddley divey Tooo … wouldn't yooo!'
Peter: We'll let you know! [BIG AUDIENCE LAUGH]

In the penultimate round Derek is speaking first, having won the subject of 'Rag' from Peter, who comes in at the end with a very amusing comment.

Derek: One of the better-known clubs in Pall Mall of course is the Army and Navy Club, which is frequented by distinguished officers of those said forces. And that is known …

BUZZ
Derek: … as the Rag …
Nicholas: And Paul Merton challenged.
Paul: Oh, he just came to what it has to do with 'rag'.
Nicholas: I think you were just in time, Paul, because I think he began …
Derek: Everybody knows that the Army and Navy Club is called 'the Rag'!
Nicholas: Let's ask this audience. Does everybody in this audience know that the Army and Navy Club is called 'the Rag'?
Peter: They do now! [BIG LAUGH]

During the final round Paul demonstrates his dry wit when challenging Derek, who is speaking on the subject of 'My Bicycle'.

Derek: My bicycle has two wheels …
BUZZ
Nicholas: Paul Merton.
Paul: Well, there's a surprise! [HUGE LAUGH FROM PANEL AND AUDIENCE]

With Paul having displayed such a wide range of talents throughout only his second appearance on the panel, it is evident that a new *Just a Minute* favourite has been discovered. However, it is the two established regulars who bring the show to a close with a bang. Derek has the subject, 'My Bicycle', and cannot resist the temptation to sing a song, directed at his wife.

Derek: 'Patty, Patricia, give me your answer do. I'm half crazy, all for the love of you. It won't be a stylish marriage. We can't afford a carriage …'
BUZZ
Nicholas: Peter Jones has challenged.
Peter: It's better than 'Mares eat oats!' [AUDIENCE BURST OUT LAUGHING] He is improving actually!

Derek: But you're still going to let me know, are you? [THE LAUGHTER CONTINUES, AND WITH HALF A SECOND REMAINING DEREK BRINGS THE SHOW TO A CLOSE]

...on the subject of Richard Murdoch

Comedy actor Richard Murdoch made seven *Just a Minute* appearances, during which three landmarks occur that link the show's past and present. The first of these relates to *Just a Minute*'s origins. On his debut, broadcast on 19 May 1988, Richard became the only man, excluding Ian Messiter, to appear on both *Just a Minute* and the show out of which it was born, *One Minute Please!* The second event also coincided with that first appearance, the significance of which was impossible to know at the time. The show marked the end of an era as it proved to be Kenneth Williams' final recording. Richard was also present, however, at the beginning of the show's modern incarnation. On his second appearance Richard is joined by Derek Nimmo, Peter Jones and Paul Merton, who is making his broadcast debut.

Richard was in his eighties when he joined the *Just a Minute* team, having enjoyed an outstanding career. Before the Second World War he appeared with Arthur Askey, one of the biggest stars of the time, in the radio show *Band Wagon* in which Richard's character was called 'Stinker' Murdoch. During the war, Richard served in the RAF, and afterwards teamed up with Kenneth Horne in *Much-Binding-in-the-Marsh*. This was a tremendously successful radio comedy set on an air force base, written by and starring Kenneth Horne. I joined the *Much-Binding* cast in 1954 and from then on Richard and I became friends.

By 1988, however, Richard's television and radio appearances had all but come to an end, save for a role as Uncle Tom in *Rumpole of the Bailey*.

Fortunately, *Just a Minute*'s then producer, Ted Taylor, was of the same generation as Richard and well aware of his talents. Ted had written a show for Richard in the 1960s and '70s called *The Men from the Ministry*, which ran for fourteen series.

Ted invited Richard to appear on *Just a Minute*, an invitation that was happily accepted. Richard was a lovely man, warm-hearted and very entertaining, combining old-school charm with a sharp brain. My son was in the audience for one of his appearances and after the recording he referred to Richard when he asked me, 'Dad, who was that? I've never heard of him before, but he was very funny.' Richard's humour had found a fresh audience through *Just a Minute*.

Richard knew instinctively how to play for laughs, sending himself up to great effect. The fact that someone of Richard's age could prove successful on the panel once again demonstrates the versatility of the game. *Just a Minute* accommodates a wide variety of talents, which blend together to create great entertainment.

Here is Richard during a broadcast from 30 May 1989 deliberately playing up his age. Derek Nimmo is speaking first on the subject of 'Earrings'.

Derek: Actually I've never possessed any earrings, principally because I'm rather too frightened to have a hole pierced within my lobes. I know …
BUZZ
Nicholas: Richard Murdoch challenged.
Richard: [TURNING TO ME] Did you say 'earwigs'? Because I was surprised at Derek getting them up his nose! [AUDIENCE LAUGH]
Nicholas: You obviously quite haven't woken up yet, Richard. No! I said, 'Earrings'!
Richard: Ahh … yes! Well I must get an 'earing aid! [BIG AUDIENCE LAUGH]

Richard calls on his years of experience in a show on 24 March 1990, entertaining the audience, panel and listeners in a most delightful manner. No one else, I believe, could have performed two old-time songs such as these with the panache that Richard brings to his performance. The subject is 'Ditties'.

Richard: Well, talking about ditties perhaps you would like to hear one. It went something like this ...
Don't eat peas with a very sharp bread knife,
It's inadvisable,
Just use a sizeable
Thing, like a ladle or a fork instead.
Don't boil eggs in a bottomless saucepan,
They're never edible,
It's quite incredible,
How many people never get things right.
That is the end of a pretty little ditty. Cheerio ... Goodnight!
[HUGE ROUND OF APPLAUSE]

As the applause dies down, Richard comments that he knows other ditties but he is sure no one would want him to sing any more. He is, of course, quite mistaken. Wendy Richard, who is also on the panel, challenges Richard's statement and speaks for everyone when she says, 'He said nobody wanted to hear another one. I do!!!' Strictly within the rules of the game Wendy's excellent challenge is correct, for deviation, but clearly that is irrelevant. I ask Wendy if she will withdraw it in order for Richard to continue. Naturally, Wendy agrees and Richard takes up the subject again, treating all present to a wonderful glimpse of his past.

Richard:
At Much-Binding-in-the-Marsh!
We really were a very happy station!
At Much-Binding-in-the-Marsh,

You'll always find us doing something useful!
We're very fond of sausages,
We often study Greek.
Experiments in science keep us busy every day!
And when we've time to spare,
We often make up rhymes like this,
At Much-Binding-in-the-Marsh!
That's all I know about that one!
At Much-Binding-in-the-Marsh!
[LOUD APPLAUSE]

Knowing how to construct a comic story was one of Richard's great assets, as demonstrated in this last, lovely example from 28 April 1990, Richard's final appearance. The subject is 'Getting Confused' and Richard appears to be relating a recent incident that is relevant to the topic. However, he is far from being confused. Richard speaks for a full minute, although he is interrupted once with an incorrect challenge. Here is Richard's full story on 'Getting Confused'.

Richard: Well, perhaps I did a little bit last week. I went into Dickens and Jones … or was it Harvey Nichols? I forget which. [AUDIENCE LAUGH] And I said, 'I want a dozen oysters, please.' And the girl said, 'I'm sorry, we don't serve those.' So I said, 'Well, what do you sell?' She said, 'Women's things, mostly.' I said, 'All right, I'll have a dozen of those!' [BIG LAUGH] Now you may think that I was just getting confused but I wasn't. I was just doing my normal day's routine shopping! [HUGE LAUGH] Those bivalves or whatever you call them, those shellfish things, have a very good effect. And I was going to buy a see-through nightie … It wasn't for myself, it was for my wife, of course. And she looked absolutely splendid in it! And why not! And that's all I've got to say on the subject of getting confused.
[WHISTLE FOLLOWED BY CHEERS AND APPLAUSE]

Richard Murdoch died less than six months after this final appearance. His career straddled seven decades during which he saw the world of comedy evolve and change. In a way his brief *Just a Minute* career is a reflection of this. Sitting along-side Kenneth Williams he witnessed part of the game's past; with Paul Merton he saw some of its future.

Both Wendy and Paul's introduction were happy events in the *Just a Minute* story. Unfortunately, around the same time we also faced two very unhappy departures.

In the show broadcast on 30 May 1989, Ian Messiter can be heard to blow his whistle for the final time on air. Ill health made it impossible for Ian to continue with recordings although he did remain very much in contact with the show through his selection of subjects for a number of years to come. Ian had not only devised the game that had become part of so many people's lives, he had also been present at my side on all but ten of the programmes up until that end-of-May show. I missed his presence very much.

Ian fought his illness courageously for ten years before we lost him altogether. As a very old friend I miss him even more.

I mentioned previously the poignant significance of Wendy Richard's second appearance on *Just a Minute*, broadcast on 16 June 1988. The BBC announcement prior to the show explains why.

This series of Just a Minute was recorded just before the death of Kenneth Williams and is broadcast now as a tribute to that master of radio comedy.

This show was broadcast as the penultimate episode of the series, which is fitting as this was the second last occasion on which Kenneth took to the *Just a Minute* stage. The date of his final double recording was 6 March in the Paris Studios, London, the venue for the whole series. For the first of those shows Kenneth sat alongside Clement, Derek and actor Lance Percival, whose place in the second recording was taken by Richard Murdoch. Kenneth is withdrawn and uncharacteristically quiet in both shows.

At one point Kenneth resorts to reciting a limerick he had used two or three times previously on *Just a Minute*, and in his final ever two rounds he does not contribute at all (one of which is a full minute from Clement). The last subject Kenneth speaks on is 'Gold' with these words: 'Women love it. I don't know why they always want gold and diamonds. They love gold with diamonds in it, in fact …' Clement then challenges for repetition and Kenneth is not heard from again.

The double recording featuring Wendy Richard took place on 21 February and perhaps provides a better insight into how Kenneth was in the last couple of months of his life. Wendy's contributions in her first appearances are excellent and she quickly establishes a strong rapport with Kenneth and the others. This helps to create two good shows, even though Kenneth is clearly not on top form. His delivery is slurred and he is unable to reach the comic heights to which we had grown accustomed. There are, however, moments when echoes of his old self can be heard, most notably in his last uninterrupted minute.

Clement Freud has just completed a full 60 seconds himself in the previous round, and Kenneth, sitting upright in his chair, poised and ready, is obviously determined not to be outdone by his old sparring partner. The subject I hand Kenneth is 'Gobbledegook', which he attacks with relish, producing laughter from the audience throughout.

Kenneth: Once on this very *programme*, we had the *past master* at the art of gobbledegook, in the form of Professor Unwin. And he said to us, '*Rise* in the early maude, with your waking thoughts of clarity in the milode, trip over very quickly the ancient greasus marks where the wax old Ulysses stuffed in the eardrobes in order to pass the siren safely.' And I said at the time, 'Wonderful! But how should we say "*hello*"?' And he cried out, 'Goodly byelode!' which I thought was quite delightful. He described a luxury block of flats as 'Luxury flabberblock with dangly chandeleery Henry the Eighth and Catherine of Arabold.' And while I knew that Catherine of Aragon did once occupy the position of consort, I'd never heard her called Arabold, which I thought was quite delightful. And I wanted very much for him to return …

[WHISTLE, APPLAUSE AND LOUD AND PROLONGED CHEERS]

Kenneth was booked to appear in the two recordings scheduled after 6 March but pulled out on health grounds at the last minute, his place taken by Lance Percival.

When Ted Taylor informed me of Kenneth's absence I immediately wrote to my dear friend. I knew he had been suffering from stomach problems and I was worried.

Dear Kenny,

I was so sorry to hear that you are not well and could not be in the show. I realise it must be quite serious for you not to have turned up as I know how much you love the show. We missed you desperately, it was not the same without you. I hope you will soon be feeling better.

With best wishes, Nick

Kenneth was a very punctilious letter writer and I received an immediate and sweet response.

My dear chum,

What a lovely sweet letter of yours. I did miss the show terribly but I had a resurgence of my problems and am trying something new. If it doesn't go away I think it is the dreaded surgeon's knife. I don't know whether I can face it.

Your old pal, Kenneth.

Kenneth died on 15 April 1988, shortly after that exchange, having appeared in 344 editions of *Just a Minute*. It strikes me that what he wrote in his letter gives a strong indication of his state of mind. He could not bear the idea of anybody invading his body. That was too much for him. What happened next it is impossible to say for certain but he never did face that surgery, dying instead of a barbiturates overdose.

Kenneth was such a strong personality, not at the expense of the others but within the overall concept of the game, that after his death some BBC executives assumed it would mark the end of *Just a Minute*. What they overlooked is that *Just a Minute* is a team show that allows everyone to contribute and excel. It does not rely on one person for its success, not even the exceptional Kenneth Williams. He was a huge part of the show, his loss devastating, but Kenneth was not *Just a Minute*.

I, along with others, lobbied the BBC on that basis for the programme to continue, and we eventually won the day; shortly after our reprieve Paul Merton, and others, arrived to give *Just a Minute* new life.

Kenneth's final *Just a Minute* broadcast went out on 23 June 1988 and features, appropriately, the four regulars. Again, Kenneth was not at his brilliant best, but he still treats the audience to flashes of his unique and outrageous talent to entertain.

> **Nicholas:** Kenneth, we're going to hear from you now as you take the next subject, which is 'Poppadoms'. Will you tell us something about that delightful subject in just a minute, starting now.
> **Kenneth:** I had a poppadom served by this chapati in Clapham. And I thought it was questionable ...
> BUZZ
> **Nicholas:** Peter Jones has challenged.
> **Peter:** Couldn't be served by a chapati!
> **Kenneth:** His name was Chapati and he lived in Clapham, you great fool!!

Clement: He was the chapati!
Nicholas: Well, we don't know, so I think Kenneth has wriggled out of that one very successfully because he could have been called Chapati.
Kenneth: Do you want to come out to Wandsworth with me?
Nicholas: No, I would rather resist the temptation. Going to Wandsworth with you is not something I would actually feel is the height of luxury.
Kenneth: I could take you up some of the back alleys! [HUGE AUDIENCE LAUGH]

It is easy in hindsight to read too much into certain phrases. However, perhaps the words Kenneth spoke at the end of the second show featuring Wendy Richard, after the final whistle, do offer a clue as to how he felt within himself.

What prompts this curious comment from Kenneth is something I mention in passing. We have been laughing about the fact that Wendy Richard's partner Paul is in the audience and I explain the source of our amusement to the radio listeners, describing Paul as 'without doubt the love of her life at the present moment, and has been for quite a while'. Kenneth then comes out with the following.

Kenneth: What Nicholas means is that there are changes in the body. It's what they call your metabolism. And one year you might fancy a sweet sherry, another year you might say, 'Oh, what a revolting drink!' You know what I mean? And a lot of people maintain that this is the basis for the argument apropos divorce.

I don't think any of us knew quite what Kenneth was talking about. One can only speculate.

I will leave this look at *Just a Minute* in the 1980s with Kenneth's own words, spoken during a phone-in radio show, concerning how he would like to be remembered. As always, Kenneth knew exactly what to say.

I certainly would *like*, I suppose, to be thought of as someone that did, you know … what can you say at the end of the day? Was there rather less grain than chaff, you can say that you made 'em laugh. He enlivened some people's moments. He made them … well, he diverted them from … from troubles for a *little bit* of the time anyway. I would like that said, yes. I would like to have them say, afterwards, that he was funny, he did get quite a few laughs, but I would like them to *sa-a-ay*, you know, that he had a serious side. *Yeees.* Because I don't want to be thought of as a cardboard cipher thing. I would like them to say, you know, that he had another dimension.

Challenge!

Q: Where and when did *Just a Minute* take on *Tomorrow's World*?

A: During the children's television show *Star Turn*, hosted by Graham Garden, in September 1979. A *Just a Minute* team of Kenneth Williams, Alfred Marks and June Whitfield battled against *Tomorrow's World* presenters Michael Rodd, Judith Hann and Kieran Prendiville in a series of acting and verbal challenges for points. *Tomorrow's World* ended up victorious.

Q: What is significant about the show broadcast on 15 January 1980?

A: It is the only time in *Just a Minute*'s long history that the four panellists – Kenneth Williams, Derek Nimmo, Peter Jones and Tim Rice – came equal first.

Q: Who is the only person to produce *Just a Minute* and appear as a panellist?

A: Comedian Chris Neill.

Q: Which player has received the most bonus points for humorous challenges?

A: Paul Merton.

Q: Name the only two panellists who have failed to score a single point during a show?

A: Peter Jones and Christopher Timothy.

Graham Norton

I am in shock. In my head whenever I step on stage to play *Just a Minute*, I always feel like one of the new boys. I take solace in thinking that the audience will forgive my inept performance because I haven't been on the panel as much as the other people playing the game. Sadly such excuses have just come to a jarring halt. Having been asked to write about some of my memories of this great show I did a little research and discovered that I first held my buzzer in front of a crowd in 1994. For those of you a little slow at maths, let me point out that is *20 years ago*.

Two things strike me after two decades; first, I am getting quite old now and second, I must accept that I am never going to get any better at playing the game.

In the summer of 1994, of course I wasn't playing *Just a Minute* on the radio. My involvement began when David Johnson and Mark Goucher produced a live version of the show at the Edinburgh Festival. Every lunchtime fans trooped up to a large tent on top of Calton Hill to see the game being played. They knew they would see Nicholas, and Tony Slattery was a resident panellist, but the rest of the players weren't announced beforehand. David and Mark were also producing my show, a comic monologue called *Charlie's Angels Go to Hell*. My venue was a tiny attic space on the other side of town. I felt like Anne Frank, except more people found her.

The producers knew that in the late-night hedonistic whirlwind of the Festival there was the distinct possibility that many of their stellar comedy bookings might fail to materialise for a lunchtime show, or if they did, it might be best to relieve them of their duties. Looking for someone with so little going on in their life that they would be willing to show up each day just to sit on the substitute's bench, they naturally thought of me.

I didn't have long to wait. The very first day, a no-show meant I found myself being introduced to a disappointed crowd. I've no idea how many people the tent held but to a boy playing nightly to audiences often not in double figures, it felt like I was appearing at Wembley. Sitting alongside Tony and Nicholas should have been very intimidating but they were both more than helpful and generous to me. Nicholas in particular was a shining example of professionalism. A lesser man would have looked at this kid standing at the back of the tent and rolled his eyes, content to just pocket his cheque and put the whole thing down to experience. Not Nicholas Parsons. Every show, no matter who is playing or where we may find ourselves, is approached with the same desire to make it the best for the audience. We all love playing *Just a Minute* but Nicholas respects it and protects it. As the chairman he has the unique ability to look to the future and the past. Like the great man himself, the show remains forever young.

It wasn't till 1996 that I was deemed ready for the radio. My first show was in Alnwick in Northumberland and the good people of that town were so excited by the arrival of the BBC that even my presence on the panel didn't dampen their spirits. I'm sure I was nervous that night, but I wasn't as terrified as I should have been. Somehow in my head I was thinking of it as just a gig when in fact I was becoming a footnote in one of the most extraordinary pieces of light entertainment history this country has ever known.

As I scrolled through the archives to see when I had first made an appearance I was struck by the roll call of greats I had been lucky enough to work with. Sadly I was too late to meet Kenneth Williams but I've been honoured to share the airwaves with such wonderful performers as Peter Jones,

Derek Nimmo, and of course Clement Freud.

When Clement died in 2009 the funeral was held in St Bride's, the journalists' church just off Fleet Street. I squeezed in to a pew alongside a few other *Just a Minute* regulars, Tony Hawks and Paul Merton. Clement's son is Matthew Freud who is married to Liz Murdoch, and his daughter Emma is the wife of Richard Curtis. We watched in awe as the church filled up with the great and the good. Famous faces from the world of entertainment. Just before the service started, in walked Bono and the then Prime Minister Gordon Brown. Paul Merton turned and whispered to me, 'I had no idea *Just a Minute* was so popular.'

It goes without saying that repetition has no place here but I confess I will never hear often enough the phrase 'And as the minute waltz fades away …'

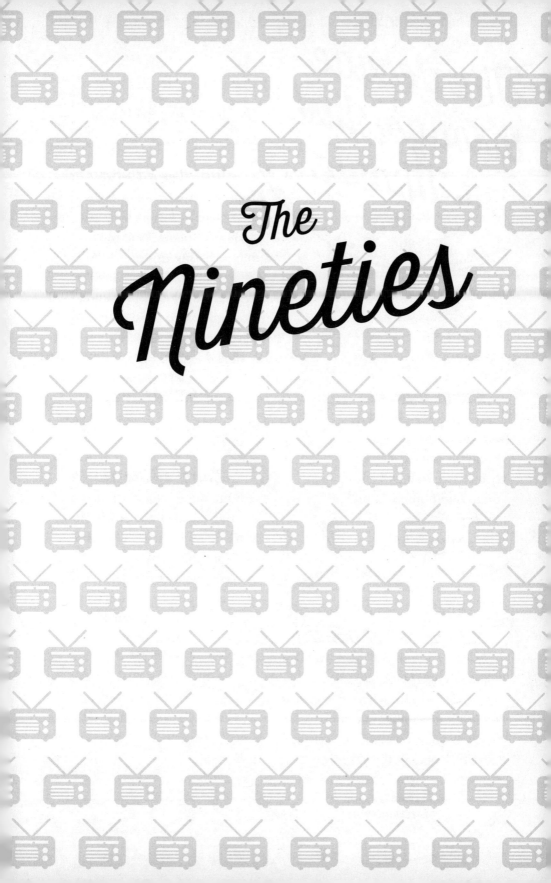

The Nineties

The decade through Just a Minute

Sun-dried tomatoes

Delia Smith, of course, raves about them. Personally I think they taste foul, of old library books. And the texture is that of bedroom slippers. And if you try to pull them out of their jar, oil dribbles right up your sleeve and all the way down the road to Islington, which is where they're mostly consumed, by Tony Blair, I should think, and his ilk!

KIT HESKETH-HARVEY
25 FEBRUARY 1995

Pump rooms

Pump room is somewhere, obviously, where you can go to pump in private. George Michael would have been good to find himself in one of those but it wasn't to be.

JULIAN CLARY
27 JUNE 1998

Angel of the North

One thing is for certain about the Angel of the North. It is definitely northern because it is out there day and night, all weathers, freezing cold, and it hasn't got a coat! In fact not even a T-shirt!

LINDA SMITH
17 DECEMBER 1999

Wrong end of the stick

It was mooted that Lord Archer's face should be on postage stamps in England. But when they gave it a test it was found that there was a lack of adhesion. And they realised that people were spitting on the wrong side!

CLEMENT FREUD
15 FEBRUARY 1999

Modern art

I'm not too keen on modern art. Every year we are treated to pictures in the paper of ridiculous things that are termed as modern art. I believe one year it was a pile of bricks. Then this year I think it was a toilet roll holder.

WENDY RICHARD
28 APRIL 1990

London Marathon

I feel the London Marathon should now be renamed the London Snickers.

TONY SLATTERY
9 AUGUST 1994

Information highway

I'm not tremendously conversant with the information highway. But for the record, if you want to email me the number is 'F R dot point slash barcode UK no comment'.

CLEMENT FREUD
22 MARCH 1999

Channel Tunnel

Well, I'm never going to travel through the Channel Tunnel because I should be denying myself the excitement of seeing France loom up over the waves. And that is one of the most exciting things one can have on a holiday, I think. Going in the Channel Tunnel would be like approaching the Continent in a submarine.

PETER JONES
5 FEBRUARY 1994

Zeitgeist

'The spirit of the age' is another definition of this word. Something like perhaps the Spice Girls could have been considered as part of the zeitgeist maybe 18 months ago. Whereas now everybody realises their career is going to dive-bomb very quickly into the sea and then disappear. I don't think there's any chance of the five of them having solo careers because who cares, really? Nobody is the answer to that.

PAUL MERTON
31 JANUARY 1998

With the team of four regulars broken up forever after Kenneth's death, followed swiftly by the welcome arrival of new players such as Paul Merton, *Just a Minute* underwent another subtle shift in its evolution. There was nothing conscious in the transition, no brainstorming by the production staff. Rather, I would call the realignment one of 'entertainment osmosis'.

In broad-brush terms, the shift was a move away from *Just a Minute* panels comprising a core of comic actors, to those featuring comedians. The distinction is not watertight. Kenneth Williams could certainly be described as a comedian as well as an actor, and there is no doubt players such as Sheila Hancock and Derek Nimmo possessed the ability to perform stand-up. Clement Freud, as a raconteur, does not fall neatly into either camp. However, in providing a general sense of how the *Just a Minute* landscape was changing, I believe the labels work.

The world of popular entertainment was in a process of transition around this period. When *Just a Minute* first appeared on the airwaves in 1967 there were a large number of prominent performers with a wide array of skills, people such as Kenneth, Derek and Peter Jones. From the 1980s onwards, entertainers cast from the same mould proved to be increasingly rare.

The situation persists today. Most people who are successful in show business now focus on one discipline (dramatic performances, stand-up, musical theatre) for a simple and understandable reason – if you demonstrate a broad range of talents the decision-makers tend to overlook your existence because it is much easier to pigeonhole performers rather than embrace the fact that someone can take on a variety of roles.

None of this is a criticism, merely an observation, and again not necessarily watertight. Of course there are exceptions. Stephen Fry springs to mind, and Gyles Brandreth, but again I believe on the whole that my statement holds up and helps explain the change in the composition of the line-ups in *Just a Minute* from the 1990s onwards.

One of the reasons that the modern entertainment world has come to favour 'specialisation' is the death of intimate revue. In the past a performer in revue was likely to have the ability to do everything: singing, dancing, sketches and jokes. That is the reason the comic actors back then were able to perform so successfully on *Just a Minute*. Take for example someone I have not even mentioned so far, Ian Carmichael. A brilliant actor who became a big star in the 1950s in 'straight' films such as *I'm Alright Jack*, *Betrayed* and *The Colditz Story*, but who began his career in revue and was able to bring the multiple disciplines learned there to the *Just a Minute* stage. Such performers are rarely found today and those that do exist often face limited opportunities to obtain profitable and regular work. The industry has moved away from broad-based acts.

This development brings with it a further consequence. Professional variety shows have been replaced on the TV schedules by stand-up programmes that feature highly talented comedians delivering material that is very different from that of the 'old-school' routines.

To my mind, the reason for this is because of the astonishing increase in the amount of comedy that has been broadcast into the nation's living rooms over the past couple of decades. Before this explosion, most comics would work on an act, polish it, and then take it on tour for many months without having to alter a word. Now, however, the ferocious appetite television has for laughter eats up material rapidly. It is no longer possible merely to tell jokes; the TV audiences have become too vast, and jokes do not last.

In order to survive, modern comedians have been forced to create a mass of new material. This is why, I believe, so much of today's humour is drawn from life experiences; it is observational. Comedians have learned to delve into their personal lives to generate laughter. They improvise around the stories and images they create, some of which are factual, some of which are exaggerated and some of which are downright surreal. They shape their own world, and by so doing each time they perform it will be subtly different as they incorporate alterations, ad libs, reinterpretations, and fly off on wild tangents.

During the 1990s, *Just a Minute* began to reflect this new approach. The up-and-coming generation was working with a broader canvas in order to develop material, each performer doing so in their unique style. Paul Merton was *Just a Minute*'s pioneer in this regard. Before Paul's arrival, generally when panellists were on a roll, what they were saying would usually be factually correct. The monologues, while certainly entertaining, became vehicles to demonstrate their erudition. Seldom did they venture into a made-up, fantasy world.

Paul changed all that. As the decade progressed, Paul's confidence in playing *Just a Minute* on his own terms grew and he began to hone his game-play in a very individual manner. His tactic of taking a subject down a surreal path is one example. Sometimes this could amount to deviation, so far had he veered off the topic, yet he would remain unchallenged. This is because when Paul is in full flow his fellow panellists recognise how funny he is being and let him continue for the sake of the show, such as in this broadcast of 4 February 1995 in which Paul talks for a full, uninterrupted minute on 'Flying Saucers'.

Paul: Well, a flying saucer landed in my back garden about 19 years ago, and I got on it and went to the planet Venus. And it's *true* because I've got photographs here of me standing on the surface of that particular planet. And anybody who says that this is false can come outside and I'll give 'em a damn good fight! Because I was trapped on that particular orb in space for *years*! I tried speaking to the Venusians and said, 'Look, it's not my fault I'm here. I was kidnapped by one of your people.' They

said, 'It's got nothing to do with us, it could have been anybody
they picked up. We had Winston Churchill about 30 years ago.
And before that Sir Stanley Matthews, the Wizard of the Wing,
spent a fortnight on this very surface.' I thought, 'Well I'm very
proud to be in such august company.' And they said, 'So you
should be 'n' all! What do you want for your dinner?' I said,
'Well, what have you got?' They said, 'Well, we can offer you
fish cakes, if that's not too fantastic for you.' I thought it's quite
an extraordinary concept, the idea of eating that particular
meal out here this far away from the Earth where I originally
came from. They said, 'Well, look, do you want it or not?' I said,
'Well, fine.' So at that point they produced a doner kebab which
to all intents and purposes was completely cold. I said, 'Why
is this not served up hot?' They said, 'We got it from a shop in
Highgate and it's a long way away to bring it all the way from
that particular part of north London to where we're standing
now.' I said, 'Okay, I go along with that. What have you got to
drink?' They said, 'Well, we've got Watney's Red Barrel.' I said,
'Oh, that is just too fantastic because nobody outside of the ...'
[WHISTLE FOLLOWED BY CHEERS AND APPLAUSE]

Almost a year later, Paul takes a surreal look at me (and my career!)
when handed the subject 'Virtual Reality'.

Paul: We have before us a virtual reality version of Nicholas
Parsons. We can see and hear him but somehow he's not quite
there! It's almost as if you could put your hand through the
ghostly shadow that we see before us and we know we will find
very little backbone or any kind of life as we understand it on
this planet. But this doesn't stop him finding regular work on
the radio! Alas, television got wind of him quite some time ago,
and his appearances there are now restricted to early afternoon
or perhaps half past four in the morning before we get the truck
racing from Idaho on Eurosport ...
BUZZ

At this point Derek challenges for deviation, claiming Paul is not talking about virtual reality and is instead embarking on a 'sustained attack on our revered chairman!' Needless to say, I agree with Derek's challenge!

Over the years Paul has continued to entertain audiences and listeners with his incredible flights of fancy, but even he sometimes wanders so far away from the subject that he has to be challenged. Such instances offer opportunities to the other panellists to create humour, such as in the following example from July 2003. Paul is talking on 'Ballroom Dancing', alongside Clement Freud, comedian and writer Tony Hawks and the voice of Brian Aldridge from *The Archers*, Charles Collingwood.

> **Paul:** Some of you may remember myself and Clement being an ideal couple when we danced for the Southern England Counties in 1948! [AUDIENCE BEGIN TO LAUGH UPROARIOUSLY] At the Blackpool Tower Ballroom. What a fantastic achievement it was! Clement was the lady!!!
> BUZZ
> **Nicholas:** Tony challenged.
> **Tony:** I think he's lying! [BIG AUDIENCE LAUGH]
> **Nicholas:** Yes, I'm sure he's lying. But on the other hand …
> **Tony:** Well, it's certainly deviation, them dancing together! That's for certain! [AUDIENCE LAUGH]
> **Paul:** Not at all! Not at all!
> **Clement:** I led!
> **Paul:** We danced beautifully!!! [AUDIENCE LAUGH EVEN LOUDER]

I decide to give Paul the benefit of the doubt regarding the original challenge and he continues on the theme.

> **Paul:** I think the paso doble was our favourite. The judges would always mark us very high! As my partner's head would touch the floor of the ballroom … [BIG AUDIENCE LAUGH]

… only to be whisked back up into my arms, twizzled around my head and thrown straight through the public bar! [BIG AUDIENCE LAUGH] Then he'd get the drinks in! It was at that point that I realised that alcohol was affecting my ability to dance at the highest level. I then decided that perhaps the partnership should be broken up.

BUZZ

Tony challenges for hesitation, incorrectly, and Paul goes on to finish the round, receiving resounding cheers and applause when the whistle blows.

Paul has a great deal of respect for the show's history, as he has shown on a number of occasions during the 25 years he has been playing the game. Here he is in February 1996, wittily taking off Derek Nimmo's tactic of introducing an anecdote from his many travels whenever possible. Although Paul is quickly challenged for deviation, the knowledgeable audience in the theatre recognise exactly what he is doing and applaud his brief homage to Derek.

Nicholas: Right, eight seconds, 'Salad Days' with you, Paul, starting now.

Paul: I was eating a Caesar salad on the Greek island of Lesbos some 48 hours ago and as I …

Eleven years later, in September 2007, Paul makes a similar nod to the antics of Kenneth Williams by echoing one of Kenneth's famous phrases. Tony Hawks is speaking first, on the subject of 'Lily of the Valley'.

Tony: I'm growing a lily of the valley in my back garden. I planted it last Thursday. Not interesting information for you, but using up valuable time from my point of view. I'm hoping it will grow large …

BUZZ

Nicholas: Paul challenged.

Paul: Deviation, he's talking about wasting time from his point of view, not giving valuable information. He's come off lily of the valley, he's talking about how much time he's got left. Complete deviation, absolutely outrageous!!! I've come all the way from Great Portland Street, I don't have to listen to this!! [BIG AUDIENCE LAUGH]

Paul's love of playing *Just a Minute* is very clearly demonstrated by the fact that he goes out of his way to make himself available for recordings. I think one of the major reasons he enjoys the game so much is because it suits his many talents — quick witted, inventive, innovative, knowledgeable – allowing him considerable freedom just to have fun. During the celebrations marking our 40th year on radio, Paul took the opportunity to declare openly this deep affection and admiration he holds for the show. The subject is 'Behind the Times'.

Paul: *Just a Minute* is 40 years old this year and if you listen to the very early recordings, you can hear Clement and Kenneth and Peter Jones and Derek Nimmo and of course Nicholas indulge in this magnificent game. And in fact it hasn't dated whatsoever. I was listening …
BUZZ
Nicholas: Clement challenged.
Clement: Absolutely right! [LAUGHTER AND APPLAUSE FROM AUDIENCE]
Nicholas: Paul, you were interrupted, you get a point for that, you keep the subject, 'Behind the Times', 35 seconds, starting now.
Paul: It's fascinating to listen to it, and it is incredibly extremely fantastic to think that this programme is still running after all this length of time.

Once when talking on the subject of 'Slogans' Paul claimed that the one he lives his life by is, 'If you can be kind, honest, sincere, and you can fake all those elements, you have a career in show business!' That could not be further from the truth.

Paul is one of the most sporting and generous players of the game. If he thinks he has been dominating in a show he will take a step back, giving others the opportunity to entertain and be heard. He is more concerned with *Just a Minute* being a success than he is with shining brightest.

Accomplished players of *Just a Minute* have the ability to think on their feet to produce sharp, witty comments. That Paul possessed this skill was clearly evident from his first appearance on the show. Then, as he gained experience, Paul began to develop a very particular approach to this aspect of playing the game, viewing common words or phrases through the unique prism of his comic brain. For instance, given the subject 'Spying' in February 1996, Paul plays on our basic knowledge of the British intelligence community and leads us to a clever and entertaining surprise.

Paul: A couple of years ago I was asked by MFI to spy for them. And they were particularly keen to find out more about a certain Swiss furniture maker that was importing put-together wardrobes at a price that they couldn't match, quite frankly! [BIG AUDIENCE LAUGH]

In July 1998 it is the punctuation of 'Man-Made Fibres' that comes under Paul's scrutiny.

Paul: When I see the phrase 'man-made fibres', I immediately think this is a newspaper headline. '*Man Made Fibres!*' Or is it a bit like '*Chicken Fried Rice*'? [BIG AUDIENCE LAUGH] Is that a dish, or is it something that a bird actually did?

Keen listening is another of Paul's core skills that his years on the show have helped sharpen to a fine point. In this example from September 2009 he combines attentiveness with his quick wit to produce a very funny challenge, as Charles Collingwood begins to speak on the unusual topic of 'Three Things You Should Know about Salt'.

Charles: Can you think of anything harder than to talk about salt and three things you know about it?

BUZZ

Nicholas: Paul challenged.

Paul: Four things you know about salt!! [LAUGHTER AND APPLAUSE FROM AUDIENCE AND PANEL]

Paul has such an inventive mind that he can create situations that have never occurred previously on *Just a Minute*, through which he generates humour himself and sets up opportunities for others to contribute. Silence is not something that is normally associated with the game, but in February 1997 Paul uses it to produce a genuinely surreal moment, with the stand-up and improv comedian Neil Mullarkey taking full comic advantage. The subject is 'The Supernatural'.

Paul: I would like to take this minute to think about something in my mind. A household object and if you, the audience, can pick up what that particular thing is, that would be indeed some kind of psychic phenomena. So here we go! [PAUL STOPS SPEAKING AND THE AUDIENCE START TO LAUGH AND APPLAUD]

BUZZ

Paul: You've just ruined an experiment!!!

Neil: Repetition!

Nicholas: Repetition?

Neil: Yes, he was thinking the same thought twice! [BIG LAUGH FROM AUDIENCE]

Paul: It was one continuous thought!

Nicholas: Neil, you have a correct challenge, you have 'The Supernatural', 42 seconds, starting now.

Neil: The supernatural can be blamed for many things. The rise of *The Shane Ritchie Experience*. The demise of the Nolans. The success …

BUZZ

Nicholas: Paul Merton challenged.

Paul: An awful lot of 'the's in there: 'the' Nolans, 'the' demise, *'The' Shane Ritchie Experience.*

Nicholas: We let it go once, maybe twice, but if it's consistent we say repetition. Thirty-three seconds, back with you, Paul, on 'The Supernatural', starting now.

Paul: Allow me to pick up from where we left off … [PAUL STOPS SPEAKING AGAIN, SHUTS HIS EYES AND PRETENDS TO BE CONCENTRATING HARD IN AN ATTEMPT TO SEND A PSYCHIC IMAGE TO THE AUDIENCE] … Did anyone see a house then? Petunias? [AUDIENCE BURST OUT LAUGHING]

Eight years later, almost to the day, Paul returns to the use of silence in a very different scenario. This time he combines his surreal imagination with some acting to produce a hilarious scene. This again allows one of his fellow panellists – here it is Clement – to come in with great effect. The subject is 'Pulling Someone's Leg'.

Paul: Pulling someone's leg is another way of saying you're gently teasing somebody. For example, the microphones weren't working particularly well when we did the sound check for this programme, but now they're … [PAUL PRETENDS TO CARRY ON SPEAKING BUT THERE IS SILENCE FOR A NUMBER OF SECONDS, WHICH IS FILLED WITH AUDIENCE LAUGHTER] … and there was half a pound of mince left at the end of the show! [VOLUME OF LAUGHTER CONTINUES TO GROW] I've always taken that as a parable for our modern times. Indeed, if you look today at the state of the church you can see that the Archbishop of Canterbury, when he said just before … [PAUL AGAIN PRETENDS TO TALK BUT NO WORDS ARE HEARD AS AUDIENCE LAUGHTER INCREASES]

  BUZZ

Nicholas: Clement has challenged.

Clement: Repetition of microphone failure! [BIG LAUGH]

During a recent recording Paul found himself having to fall back on his ability to adapt in order to complete the second show. In fact we all had to be inventive that evening. The recording took place in a cinema in Evesham that was in the process of being converted to accommodate a stage.

The renovations were ongoing, and the backstage area had not yet been completed. This meant we were unable to make our normal entrance of stepping from behind a curtain to greet the audience. Instead we had to make our way down the aisles and then climb up some steps onto the stage. Not a very elegant or a professional way to begin a show.

Problem number one: quite simply, our entrance took too long. By the time we had all made it up to our seats, the atmosphere in the auditorium was slipping away. With the help of the others I managed to gag about the long walk and how difficult it was for us to climb such steep steps, and we managed to lift the mood again. What we did not know was that we were soon to encounter problem number two.

Our seating area was no more than a narrow platform in front of where the screen would have been, with a sheer drop down to the front row of the audience. Not a huge issue under normal circumstances.

Except, Paul Merton suffers from vertigo.

Sitting on that strip of stage, which did feel as though we were performing on the edge of a cliff, was torture for poor Paul. Somehow he managed to make it through the first recording. At the break, however, he made it clear it would be impossible for him to continue if he had to remain seated where he was. 'Could I please get down from the stage. I'm really feeling quite unsettled up here,' he explained to us. 'Of course. No problem at all. But how do we ...'

We made it work. Paul sat in the front row of the stalls; we could not see him and he could not see us. He listened carefully to what we were all saying, making his usual excellent challenges and contributions, while the rest of us had to find ways of reacting to a disembodied voice. It is surprisingly difficult to interpret what someone means or says when you cannot see their facial expression.

Clearly all those present in the audience that evening were aware of what was happening, but such was the team's skill and professionalism that no one listening on the radio was any the wiser. Until now, that is. The fact that we could pull this off successfully is, I believe, an excellent illustration of the simple strength of the show and the talent of the performers.

As anyone who has followed Paul Merton's career will know, he has a great fondness for 'old-style' comedy in general, and in particular he possesses an encyclopaedic knowledge of comics from the silent era. Throughout his career on *Just a Minute*, Paul has treated listeners to many informative and entertaining expositions based on this great passion. Here he is in a 30 January 1993 broadcast, correcting Derek Nimmo's grasp of 'Custard Pie Humour'.

Derek: Custard pie humour really came into vogue, I suppose, during the silent movies with Buster Keaton and Charlie Chaplin. Because you could throw …
> BUZZ

Nicholas: Paul Merton has challenged.
Derek: What's the matter?
Paul: Deviation. Buster Keaton never used custard pies.
Nicholas: You're quite right! Buster Keaton didn't, no.
Derek: 'Era', I said! 'Era'! If you'd been listening …
Nicholas: I was listening and so were the audience and so was Paul Merton, and I agree with Paul's challenge. So Paul, 35 seconds on 'Custard Pie Humour', starting now.
Paul: It's certainly true to say that within the silent screen era there were very few examples of custard pies. Perhaps the most famous one was *The Battle of the Century*, a short film made by Laurel and Hardy in 1927 which took the concept of custard pie throwing to its ultimate ridiculous level. A company was supplying the custard pies, I believe there were 15,000 of them that were used over the course of the five-day shoot …
> BUZZ

Paul hesitates when he realises he has repeated the word 'film' and Derek continues to the end of the round.

Derek finds himself again on the receiving end of Paul's extensive knowledge in a broadcast on 8 June 1998, when he attempts to introduce a quote in relation to 'The Press'.

Derek: Noël Coward was once asked by the *Sun* newspaper what he would like to say to them and he said, 'Shine'. Which always seemed to me to be a reasonable remark …

BUZZ

Nicholas: Paul, you challenged.

Paul: Deviation. That's the wrong story.

Derek: What is then?

Paul: It was a paper called the *Star* and they said, 'Have you got anything to say to the *Star*?' And he said, 'Yes. Twinkle.'

Nicholas: That is absolutely correct! That is what he did say and he's quoted as that. So you were deviating, in fact you were misquoting …

Derek: It is actually a true quote.

Paul: You mean he used the same joke twice? [BIG LAUGH]

…on the subject of *The Minute Waltz*

Written in 1847 by Polish composer Frederic Chopin, Waltz in D-flat Major, Opus 64 No. 1 is known by the misnomer of the Minute Waltz, a fact spoken of during the two occasions on which it has been a subject on *Just a Minute*.

In 1972 we learned from Andree Melly that she was confused as to why that piece of music has been chosen as our signature tune because, 'you cannot get through it in 60 seconds. It takes a great deal longer.' In fact, it takes about two minutes to play from start to finish.

Then in 2001 we received a warning from Jenny Eclair not

to confuse our waltz with 'the *My-newt* Waltz', which according to Jenny is apparently, 'a dance for very small people under 5 foot 2!' Interestingly, it seems this is indeed the derivation of the common name. Not as a dance for small people, but 'minute' in the sense of being short. Over time the pronunciation of the name, and therefore the meaning, has changed.

Back in 1967 it seemed like a good idea to have this as our theme for obvious reasons, but in truth it is hardly the music you would automatically link with a new radio programme played for laughs. By around the third or fourth series I suggested that we might be better served with a different tune as the Minute Waltz did sound somewhat pompous for what was now clearly a broad comedy show. Ian Messiter and David Hatch discussed the possibility and came back with absolutely the correct decision. '*Just a Minute* is now identified with that piece of music. It is instantly recognisable. And the title fits well with the game. We are keeping it.'

Thank goodness we did. The music is catchy, and with my introduction and sign-off now spoken over the fading music, I think it works very well indeed.

'Nick-baiting' is a phrase first coined by Sheila Hancock in a broadcast from 11 April 1978, in relation to Kenneth and Derek haranguing me over whether the subject of 'Why Elephants Can't Jump' was a question or a statement. Derek was convinced elephants could jump and the wording of the topic was wrong. 'It's like saying why can't Nicholas Parsons speak? We all know he speaks endlessly about all manner of subjects!' To which Sheila then exclaimed, 'Oh dear! I didn't think it would be long before we were Nick-baiting!' A new expression had been born for a source of humour that has been enjoyed by many players of *Just a Minute*.

As I mentioned previously, when Kenneth and Derek took swipes in my direction it was always in a spirit of entertainment and friendship, while Clement's comments often had more of an edge.

In this aspect of the game, Paul Merton resides very firmly in the former camp.

Paul has the ability to make outrageous comments about me while always conveying that there is absolutely no hidden agenda. Whatever remarks he comes out with, they are said entirely in jest. Yes, they are at my expense but they are never spiteful, and I can be just as cheeky back to him. The secret is laughter. When the audience can see me enjoying myself, laughing along, they know I am not in the least offended and in fact I find Paul's gags as entertaining as everyone else.

Paul and I forged an immediate connection when we first met, and as our friendship grew through the 1990s and into the new century, so it seems did the frequency of his good-natured ribbing! The following is just a handful of examples, all of which produced huge laughs from the audience. The first occurs in an August 2002 broadcast from Edinburgh. When I announce the first subject, 'The Chairman's Darkest Secret' and ask Paul to begin, I know I am in for trouble. He certainly does not disappoint.

> **Paul:** Nicholas, or as close friends know him, Susan, is the first transsexual to successfully host a panel show in this country! Looking at him now, it's hard to believe that, yes, he used to be a man! The transformation is extraordinary! As he wafts through Edinburgh, the scented air behind him, the various wisps of pillow cases hanging around his ears. He's come from the hotel where he is fêted and starred in many productions in the bar. They know him there as Lily, because he can't use his own real name. As they see a stiletto heel print on the carpet, they look knowingly towards one another. They say, 'He has been here, who was once a "she", and has now become a "he" again.' [CONTINUOUS LAUGHTER THROUGHOUT HIS OUTRAGEOUS COMMENTS]

The following extract takes place at the Cities Varieties theatre in Leeds during a recording that would air as the opening broadcast of our 2004 series. We are approaching the end of the first show and I have been joking with the audience about how I hope they come back to see us again a second time. Then I set myself up for some 'Nick-baiting' by mentioning that I had performed there previously. Paul, Charles Collingwood and the excellent writer and entertainer Kit Hesketh-Harvey duly oblige.

> **Nicholas:** Oh thank you, audience, you're so lovely, I'm definitely coming back again! You're almost as good as when I did my one-man show here actually. You were lovely then too!
> **Charles:** It wasn't quite this full though, was it Nicholas? [BIG AUDIENCE LAUGH]
> **Paul:** Does the 'one-man' element refer to the stage or the auditorium? [MORE AUDIENCE LAUGHTER]
> **Nicholas:** They're so mean to me, aren't they? [AUDIENCE LAUGH THROUGHOUT] And I take it in good grace. Because I know that the audience know, because many of them were here, and that's why you've come back again.
> **Kit:** Because they've died! [BIG LAUGH]

Still in 2004, Tony Hawks is talking on 'Texting' when a system malfunction leaves me vulnerable. Charles Collingwood is also involved.

> **Tony:** This is something which goes on an extraordinary amount now, particularly outside schools. Kids with these mobile phones texting each other, that wouldn't have happened 25 years ago, largely because those kind of things weren't kicking around so they couldn't …
> BUZZ
> **Nicholas:** Tony challenged.
> **Tony:** Did I???
> **Nicholas:** Yes …
> **Charles:** No!!! No, he didn't. I think you'll find he was speaking!

Nicholas: I have a number of little lights in front of me, and whoever's buzzer is pressed …

Paul: One of them's a life-support machine! [HUGE LAUGH]

Here the talented entertainer Graham Norton is speaking on the subject of 'Clubbing' in a December 2008 show, when Paul buzzes in with a challenge. I can sense very quickly where this is going.

Graham: Any Saturday you like, Soho in the centre of London will be full of young kids going clubbing. And I can't help …

BUZZ

Nicholas: Paul challenged.

Paul: I choose a Saturday in 1787.

Graham: And I think you'll find it's full of some people going clubbing.

Paul: I don't think Soho in 1787 was full of people going clubbing any Saturday you like!

Graham: I say it was!!

Paul: Nicholas, can you remember? [BIG LAUGH]

My age continues to provide rich pickings for Paul's mischief, as in this example from February 2013. Gyles Brandreth is speaking on the 'Globe Theatre' and there is some confusion from comedian Alun Cochrane as to which venue Gyles means.

Gyles: In fact the theatre I am thinking of is in Shaftesbury Avenue, called after a …

BUZZ

Nicholas: Alun challenged.

Alun: Deviation. It's a different theatre.

Gyles: No, it isn't!

Alun: Oh, is it??

Gyles: No, it's the same theatre. Changed its name.

Alun: Oh, I feel a fool!

Nicholas: The Globe Theatre, yes, I worked there. Years ago.

Paul: Shakespeare gave you the job, didn't he? Shakespeare gave him the job! *They were looking for somebody who could play older parts!!!* [HUGE LAUGH]

The only person on *Just a Minute* who did not appreciate Paul's humour and generosity was Wendy Richard. It was a very unfortunate situation and one that I never fully understood. For some reason, Wendy seemed to develop an antipathy towards him which she did not always manage to conceal.

The following is a series of exchanges found in one single broadcast, from 24 March 1990. The building tension is evident and it is compounded by the fact that Wendy allows her feelings not only to be heard but also to be seen. It is obvious, from her narked expression, that Wendy is annoyed. This happened on several occasions, poisoning the atmosphere and inhibiting the audience. They cannot understand why Wendy is not enjoying herself.

Wendy has just successfully challenged on the subject of 'Garden Worms' and has nine seconds remaining. It is the first time she has spoken during the show.

Wendy: I haven't got any worms in my garden. I wish I had because I believe they're very good for the soil because they aerate it, don't they, as they go through it. Actually I haven't even …
[WHISTLE AND APPLAUSE]
Nicholas: Wendy, you have a point for that and you're now in the lead at the end of the first round. And we would like you to take the second round, which follows this theme. We've got 'Garden Gnomes'. Will you tell us something about those in this game, starting now.
Wendy: I don't have any garden gnomes. In actual fact I don't have a garden, I have a patio on which …
BUZZ
Nicholas: Paul Merton challenged.
Paul: Well, deviation, because you had a garden in the last

round and now you don't!

Wendy: Ah! If I hadn't have come to the end of my minute, I would have said that! I'm continuing on with me gnomes from the worms.

Paul: But the serial started off with a lie because you said you had a garden.

Wendy: It wasn't a lie! If you'd have ... if I'd had more seconds I would have *told* them I haven't got a garden!

Paul: But you said you had a garden!

Wendy: Yes, well, she blew the whistle, didn't she! I didn't say that!!

Paul: Have property developers moved in in the last minute??

Wendy: I think I'll go home now if he's going to be like this.

Peter: You were, Wendy ... you were whinging on about not having a garden ...

Wendy: Oh all right!!

Peter: ... and then you continued whinging by saying you didn't have any gnomes and people were beginning to look quite upset about it.

Wendy: Oh all right then!

Paul finishes that round with no further incident. It is not long, however, before the sparks are once again flying. Wendy has just successfully challenged Richard Murdoch who was speaking on the next subject of 'Coincidences'.

Wendy: I was at a charity ball a couple of years ago when by some dreadful coincidence two ladies turned up wearing the same frock. I ...

BUZZ

Nicholas: Paul Merton challenged.

Wendy: I knew it would be him!

Paul: Were they wearing the same frock or identical frocks?

[BIG LAUGH]

Wendy: If he's going to nit-pick I'm going home!!!

Nicholas: I think it was a very good challenge …

Wendy: All right, all right.

Paul: Because if it's the same frock that's not a coincidence, they're just very good friends!

Wendy: I'm not going to tell you! It's a secret!

Nicholas: It was such a good challenge, this picture of these both ladies in the same frock. I think maybe the fair thing is to give Paul a bonus point for his lovely challenge but leave the subject with Wendy …

Wendy: I don't want it! Let him talk about it! He wants the point, he can have the subject 'n' all!

Finally, Wendy has challenged on the subject 'Choke' with 49 seconds remaining, and lets slip her feelings regarding Paul.

Wendy: I don't drive but I do believe a choke is a very important part of the motorcar. You have to pull it out to start the engine in the cold weather, or indeed if you have a vehicle …

BUZZ

Wendy: What?

Richard: She said 'have' twice. Too many haves. You did actually say have … have …

Wendy: As it's you, Richard, I don't mind. If it's him I get annoyed!!! [AT THIS POINT THE AUDIENCE LAUGH UNEASILY AND FALLS QUIET]

Paul found such exchanges very difficult and eventually he made it known that if Wendy was going to be on the panel, he would rather not be included in that recording. I can understand why. Although these clashes sometimes came across as entertaining banter on the radio, during the actual performance it would be all too clear from the look on Wendy's face that there was genuine friction in the air.

I often found myself falling back on my professional experience to rescue those particular shows. I had to find ways in which to lift the mood by making light of whatever had occurred and then moving on as swiftly as possible. 'Wendy, darling, I don't know what is going on with you today. I think it was a very funny challenge and the audience enjoyed it as well. I am sorry if you were upset but I think you were the only person who was! Paul, you have the subject …'

During the period between the end of Series 28 in 1995 and Series 40 in 2002, Wendy disappeared from radio broadcasts, although she did feature in ten *Just a Minute* television programmes. When Wendy made her radio return in a broadcast of 11 February 2002, alongside Tony Hawks and comedians Sue Perkins and Ross Noble, I very much hoped that she would have softened her attitude. Indeed, in her first show back she seemed to have done so, demonstrating a similar character to that which everyone enjoyed when she made her debut. She was warm, engaging and played up her *EastEnders* role to great effect, which allowed Ross to introduce Wendy's *EastEnders* rival, Peggy Mitchell, into the exchange.

> **Nicholas:** And Wendy's turn to begin. The subject, Wendy, 'Laundrettes'! [BIG LAUGH FROM THE AUDIENCE] I wonder why they thought of 'Laundrettes' for Wendy Richard? Anyway, Wendy talk on the subject in just a minute, starting now.
> **Wendy:** My local laundrette does not have a charming friendly person like *Pauline* to help you with your service washes. Oh no! We have a chap called Jeff …
> BUZZ
> **Nicholas:** Ross Noble challenged.
> **Ross:** I'm going to go for deviation, because you were very, very nasty to Peggy. And that's not charming at all! [LAUGHTER AND APPLAUSE FROM AUDIENCE]
> **Wendy:** I've never been nasty to Peggy in the laundrette! *She* had the *cheek* [AUDIENCE LAUGHTER BUILDING] the other week to come in and complain … [AUDIENCE LAUGHING AND APPLAUDING LOUDLY]
> **Ross:** [IN A GRUFF EAST END ACCENT] Leave it out! You're

bang out of order! [BIG LAUGH]

Unfortunately Wendy soon allowed flashes of her more bitter side to re-emerge, which was such a shame. I continued to be very fond of Wendy but when she insisted on repeatedly bringing up her bête noirs of listing and being challenged too quickly (Wendy would claim rather stridently to be just 'taking a breath'), the situation again grew difficult. There was even an awkward moment during my introduction on her second show back, which thankfully Tony helped to retrieve.

Nicholas: Thank you, thank you, hello, my name is Nicholas Parsons. And as the Minute Waltz fades away once more it is my pleasure to welcome our many listeners, not only in this country but in all the other countries around the world who listen to us on the World Service. And we also welcome to the show this week four exciting, talented, intrepid and really experienced players of the game who have come together just for your joy and benefit. And in no order of seniority, let me introduce to you Wendy Richard, Sue Perkins, Ross Noble and Tony Hawks. Please welcome all four of them! Beside me sits Janet Staplehurst who's going to help me keep the score, and she'll blow a whistle when the 60 …

Wendy: Nicholas, can I just ask you something?

Nicholas: Yes.

Wendy: Just then, you said …

Sue: Seniority!

Wendy: Yes! Are you implying …

Sue: Thank you! Tony's older than me!

Wendy: Are you implying that I'm older than this lot? Because I take exception to that!

Nicholas: No, I put you top of the bill, because in showbiz seniority, I thought you were top of the bill.

Wendy: Right, as long as you're not … as long as you're not being ageist!

Nicholas: All right, I'll do it the other way round! Wendy, because you are very experienced and very highly established, I thought it would be a nice courtesy …
Wendy: All right, thank you. That's fine, lovely! Thank you!
Ross: Can I just ask why was I last?
Sue: Why was I second?
Nicholas: Because you are the highly talented new kids on the block, you see.
Sue: So he gets to be young and virile? And I get to be second!
Tony: Listen, if we're quibbling over the introduction, we'll never get through the show! [AUDIENCE LAUGH]

In a broadcast from the following series, in August 2002 after the World Cup, Wendy is again joined by Tony Hawks and Sue Perkins, plus Kit Hesketh-Harvey. This proves to be a rather difficult recording, and Wendy only appears in two further shows. The subject here is 'The Changing of the Guard', with Tony speaking.

Tony: In one sense, I suppose, the England football team are going to have to have a changing of the guard, if you think of the goalkeeper as having that role. And David Seaman, of course, is approaching the end of his career. But if he does retire …
  BUZZ
Nicholas: Wendy challenged.
Wendy: I'm sick of football! [BIG AUDIENCE LAUGH AND APPLAUSE]
Nicholas: Well, you've struck a raw …
Wendy: People are listening to this because they want to get *away* from football!
Nicholas: So what is your challenge within the rules of *Just a Minute*, Wendy?
Wendy: Well, he's deviating, going on about football.
Nicholas: Well, actually, Wendy, I've got to say he's not deviating. You may be bored by it, and you may have struck a

chord in this audience …

Wendy: Well, I'll tell you what then, Nicholas, I think that's really unfair of you, because that's a definite deviation!

Nicholas: No, it wasn't. Though you may hate your football, and a lot of other people are bored by football …

Sue: Make them stop, Mum! They're frightening me!

[AUDIENCE LAUGH AT SUE'S INTERJECTION]

Midway through, Wendy is given the subject of 'Reality TV'.

Wendy: Apparently it's this *Big Brother*, which *thankfully* I have never *clapped* eyes on! How you can call that entertainment, watching a load of people living in some house. And doing all their ablutions and other bits and pieces that they get on with …

BUZZ

Nicholas: Kit Hesketh-Harvey challenged.

Kit: Isn't that *EastEnders*? [AUDIENCE LAUGH COMBINED WITH GOOD-NATURED BOOS]

Wendy: No!

Nicholas: Kit, you didn't win many friends with that one.

Kit: No, I'm sorry … I'm getting the look of the basilisk from the left!

Nicholas: I know! Kit is sitting next to Wendy Richard and if looks could kill, I mean, Kit would be a dead man now …

Kit: I Love *EastEnders* and she's magnificent in it! And long may she continue! [AUDIENCE LAUGH AND CHEER WHICH HELPS LIFT THE ATMOSPHERE]

Going into the last round, Wendy has the subject 'Cheating' and displays some lovely flashes of humour which the audience enjoy, but she also snaps at Kit, which leaves me having to find a way to release the tension.

Wendy: I see no point in cheating when one is playing games. I enjoy playing crib. And it really drives me daft when people come up, and look over your shoulder, and go, 'Oh, you're cheating again!' or 'You've got the cards up your sleeve!' I mean I really want to pick the board up and whack them one with it! Because what is the point? You enjoy the whole …

    BUZZ

Nicholas: Kit Hesketh-Harvey.

Kit: An awful lot of 'enjoy's, weren't there?

Nicholas: She did enjoy it before.

Wendy: You see that's the problem with people! They hate to see me having a good time! [BIG AUDIENCE LAUGH]

Kit: I'm sorry …

Nicholas: Oh, she knows how to win her audience! Kit, you've got a correct challenge, you have a point of course, you have 41 seconds on 'Cheating', starting now.

Kit: There's a lovely story about a wedding rehearsal, where the male fiancé slipped a tenner to the vicar and said, 'Can you leave out the bit about … loving and honouring …'

    BUZZ

Nicholas: Wendy challenged.

Wendy: Well, not only was it hesitation, *but honestly*!!! If you go into another one of those appalling jokes again! This is *Just a Minute*, not *Variety Bandbox*!

Nicholas: *Variety Bandbox* does date us a bit, Wendy! I mean that does go back into the annals of the past.

Wendy: Well, you used to be on that, didn't you, Nicholas! I used to listen to it when I was in my pram! [AUDIENCE LAUGH]

Wendy's penultimate show, broadcast on 3 February 2003, does in fact feature Paul and Clement. This proves to be a combustible mix. It is Clement who challenges Wendy here.

Nicholas: So, Wendy, you've got 'Pulling Power' back and you have 36 seconds to tell us something about it, starting now.

    BUZZ

Wendy: Listen!! You're always doing that to me on this

315

programme! You are at least allowed to *draw breath* before you start.

Nicholas: No, no, no, Wendy, actually in this game I always give a pause before the 'now', so they can draw the breath before that and I say, 'And you start … now.' So everybody goes straight off or otherwise they will be at it like knives. And I'm afraid it was a long pause.

Clement: Within a half an hour!

Wendy: Well, I have to take a big breath!!!

Later, Clement is speaking on 'Market Traders' with 47 seconds remaining.

Clement: I'm very fond of Berwick Street Market in Soho, where my favourite trader has now gone because the 'Weights and Measures' man has overpowered him with red tape. It's very sad because one used to get all kinds of cheeses: Gorgonzola, Gruyère, Cheddar, Cheshire …

Wendy: Oh …

BUZZ

Nicholas: Wendy challenged.

Wendy: Look, he's listing again.

Nicholas: I know he is!

Wendy: I heard it the other day, that's all he does, is *list*!

Nicholas: He does a lot of other things. He's very witty and clever in the show.

Wendy: I didn't say he wasn't. I'm just saying *he lists*! If I can't pause for breath, he can't list! [AUDIENCE APPLAUSE]

Nicholas: Wendy, I'm sorry, darling! They're only clapping your effrontery! You can't come in the show and institute a new rule! Anybody can list if they want to. Actually it is an extremely difficult thing to do. You try it some time.

Wendy: I will. Next time it's my turn, I'll have a list! [SHOUTS OF 'OOOH' FROM THE AUDIENCE]

Clement continues with the round, cheekily explaining that the market trader he had spoken of earlier then gave him 'a list' of his wares, 'cream, milk …' Quite what Wendy thinks of this, I don't know, as Paul fortunately challenges for repetition and takes the subject to its conclusion.

In the end it was all rather sad. Wendy was confused and upset as to why she was no longer being invited on to the show because she loved *Just a Minute*. Wendy blamed her exile on the producer at the time, but I knew that was not true. Whenever we subsequently met, Wendy would ask me what was going on. How could I explain to her that she had to relax much more and start enjoying her appearances? More to the point, she had to *act and sound* like she was enjoying herself. How do you tell a fellow professional that their approach is wrong?

'Do you know, it's a lot more difficult than it seems when you're listening on the radio!'

These are the words of writer, actor, comedian, broadcaster, presenter, quiz-show host, and all-round talent Stephen Fry on 11 January 1992, his debut on the show. Stephen has one of the finest brains in the business, and for him of all people to recognise so openly how hard *Just a Minute* is to play was very generous.

Stephen slotted into his first show like a regular, sitting alongside Paul, Derek and Wendy. He asked for no quarter and, given his fearsome intellect, his skill with words, and his razor-sharp wit, he received none. Especially after his very first challenge, successfully made against Derek, gave him the subject with one second to go. Derek Nimmo was not about to take that lying down.

The next subject, given to Stephen, was the composer and conductor 'Wilhelm Furtwängler'.

Stephen: Well, Wilhelm Furtwängler, as it should properly be pronounced because there's an umlaut on the 'a' in his name,

was a great Germanic com … er … conductor … er … of …
BUZZ

Stephen: Oh dear!

Nicholas: And Derek Nimmo's challenged.

Derek: It's unfair but there were rather a lot of 'er's.

Stephen: Yes, there were!

Derek: I mean, somebody so bright as he should be able to speak properly.

Nicholas: But he's never played the game before.

Derek: Oh, all right. [AUDIENCE BEGIN TO SHOUT IN SYMPATHY WITH STEPHEN]

Wendy: Aaaw, that was mean.

Nicholas: Yes. Stephen, I'm not going to allow that.

Stephen: Well, you're an old sweetie!

Derek: Nobody's ever called him that before!

[BIG LAUGH]

Having successfully established he was worthy of his seat, in his second show Stephen went to town, combining his acting skills, erudition and humour, while throwing in literary references, scientific explanations and drawing attention to grammatical errors. If he felt any twinges of nerves during his first appearance, I think it is safe to say he had overcome them by his second.

First he poked fun at Derek's travelogues and then treated everyone to a splendid impersonation of the *Just a Minute* stalwart.

Next he introduced the novelist Simon Raven into the show, informing us that his books dealt with matters of 'time and chance', before explaining to an awestruck audience the meaning of 'Morphology', cut short only by a challenge from Paul for repetition of 'kind'.

Stephen: There are two distinct meanings to morphology. The first is a kind of biological natural history word. It means the science of form. The Greek *morphos* means 'shape', as in metamorphosis. And of course that morphology describes the

way things are structured in some manner or other, doesn't it?
The other kind is grammatical and is used as an assignation …

We then learned that Stephen was a fan of Gregorian chants; I was given a lesson in pronunciation; and Wendy was accused of something truly awful-sounding when she spoke about her 'fellow compatriots on this programme'.

Stephen: What's all this drivel about fellow compatriots? 'Compatriot' means a fellow countryman anyway so it's a *deviant tautology*!

In addition, Stephen still had time for a funny, political joke.

Nicholas: Stephen Fry, would you take the next round, the subject is 'Cows'. You can take it as 'Cowes', with an 'e', or 'Cows' without an 'e'.
Stephen: Oh, how sweet of you! How nice!
Nicholas: I wish I hadn't said it now! You have 60 seconds, Stephen, starting now.
Stephen: Edwina Currie and Margaret Thatcher were both, I believe, in power at the time of bovine spongiform encephalitis, which indeed struck cows, which may strike some people as being remarkably relevant and germane …
    BUZZ
Nicholas: Derek Nimmo challenged.
Derek: Well, said Edwina Currie wasn't in power at the time.
Stephen: Wasn't she?
Derek: She was gone quite a long time before. The eggs, the eggs before the cow, you see.
Stephen: Yes, I always wondered which came first, the egg or the cow. Now I know! [BIG LAUGH]

Anyone possessing even a passing familiarity with Stephen's extensive body of professional work could not be surprised that he proved to be a natural at the game. In 2009, however, we discovered another reason to explain how he attuned himself so quickly to the rhythm of the show.

Stephen has been given the subject 'Blogging' and proceeds to entertain the audience with a routine that mystifies Paul Merton.

Stephen: Well, the word 'blog' is a contraction of 'weblog', and blogging really is a *kind* of logging. It's basically a form of diarising or journal keeping, but online, on the web if you prefer. It was coined [STEPHEN SUDDENLY, AND INEXPLICABLY, BEGINS TO TALK IN A VERY DEEP VOICE, MUCH TO THE AMUSEMENT OF THE AUDIENCE] *about seven years ago.* [NORMAL VOICE] I don't know quite why my voice did that. And it's taken on an enormous popularity …

BUZZ

Nicholas: Paul's challenged.

Paul: Has Stephen been channelled by the ghost of Elvis Presley? [AUDIENCE LAUGH AND APPLAUD, WHILE STEPHEN BRAYS WITH LAUGHTER]

Paul: What's happened there? [PAUL THEN BREAKS INTO AN ELVIS IMPERSONATION BEFORE RETURNING TO NORMAL VOICE; AUDIENCE IN HYSTERICS] What's going on? Is it *Just a Séance*? What's going on?

Nicholas: I should explain to our listeners, that peculiar laugh is coming from Stephen actually.

Paul: It could be coming from Glenn Miller! We don't know!! [EVEN MORE AUDIENCE LAUGHTER … AND BRAYING]

Stephen: [THROUGH HIS LAUGHTER] I'm sorry … it's the only way I can keep going … it's odd, sorry! When I was a boy I used to come and watch Kenneth Williams doing this, you know …

Nicholas: He used to go into different voices.

Stephen: … and somehow you absorb it, listening over the years, of suddenly having … I don't know … I'm sorry …

Nicholas: It sounded more like Kenneth Williams than Elvis

Presley actually.

Stephen: [AS KENNETH] *Y-e-e-es*, I know.

The depth of Stephen's erudition can be intimidating to his fellow panellists. People assume he is always correct, and of course Stephen is not about to dissuade anyone of that notion if it can win him points. This is evident from an incident during a recording in 2009, which must count as one of Stephen's finest moments on *Just a Minute*.

While speaking on 'Shopping Online' Stephen is challenged by Jenny Eclair. Stephen then proceeds to defend himself with such authority on the existence of a particular word that Jenny does not pursue her claim with any vigour and I accept Stephen's assertions on face value. The incident then led to a unique moment in the history of the game when the episode was broadcast on 7 September.

Stephen: Ocado is one of the rather weird names of an online shopping service. There are many others of course. Amazon is well known, *far* too celebrated for me to expand on it much further. Howmever, Play dot com is another site …

> BUZZ

Nicholas: Jenny challenged.

Jenny: Well, it was 'howmever' he said.

Stephen: It is a real word.

Jenny: It's deviation.

Stephen: Whomever and howmever, they're both poetical uses of the word. I promise you. Look at it in a dictionary! Whomever, howmever. [APPLAUSE FROM AUDIENCE] I wouldn't have said it otherwise. It's a nice … I've always said it … my favourite.

Jenny: But I'm at a disadvantage having not been educated at all.

Stephen: Ah, well, I'm sorry. I had literally no idea. Howmever, howsomever, in fact.

Jenny: I'm hoping you might catch some of my thickness by osmosis and halfway through the show crack up completely.

Paul: [TO JENNY] How are you speaking English? Is it sheer guesswork every word? [BIG LAUGH]

At the end of the broadcast, listeners heard the following official statement. This had never happened before, and it has not happened since.

BBC Announcer: Now, just in case you were taken in by Stephen Fry, Radio 4 can now confirm that there is no such word as 'howmever'. A post-programme disqualification may be in order.

Stephen's ability to combine his numerous talents is perhaps best exemplified in the following extract from January 2002. Here he draws on his wit, his politics, his irreverence and his knowledge to produce an unforgettable magic minute. The subject is *'Schadenfreude'*.

Stephen: Not the daughter of one of our panellists, but a German word that comes from two separate meanings. *'Schaden'* means 'shame' or 'disgrace'. *'Freude'*, 'joy', as in Shelley's famous ode to that emotion. It really betokens that pleasure we take in other people's misfortune. For example, I suppose everyone can remember Michael Portillo losing his seat. There was a great surge of national *Schadenfreude*, whatever our political feelings. Somehow I think almost every single member of the plebiscite or electorate, in some way, joined in with great enjoyment at that moment. However, *Schadenfreude* seems a very Teutonic kind of quality. It's therefore no accident that there is no English phraseology or nomenclature for it. But we use instead the Tedesco, as they say in Italy, the Germanic if you like, but I personally don't. *Schadenfreude* of course also means something more sinister or unpleasant which is a genuine delight in real misfortune. That I think is unforgivable ...
[WHISTLE FOLLOWED BY HUGE ROUND OF APPLAUSE]

One month after Stephen made his debut, one of the show's most popular and ongoing regular guests made his first appearance – comedian, best-selling author and pop star (well, 'one-hit wonder' might be more accurate, although he does enjoy reminding *Just a Minute* listeners from time to time of his success with Morris Minor and the Major and their Number 4 smash 'Stutter Rap') Tony Hawks.

Tony has a wide range of interests – sport, music, travel – which he combines with an astute eye for the modern world, a surreal streak and the ability to pull them all together to produce some very witty one-liners. Sometimes he strays near the edge of BBC sensibilities, but he never oversteps the mark, which is one reason he is so popular with the *Just a Minute* audiences and listeners. Tony is one of the guests guaranteed to produce multiple moments of comedy whenever he appears on the show.

Here he is playing expertly to the Cardiff audience on the unsurprising subject of 'Rugby' in February 1995. With perfect timing he draws them in and then lands a comic punch.

Tony: Rugby is a fantastic game! [ENTHUSIASTIC CHEERS AND APPLAUSE FROM AUDIENCE] This is because it gives you the opportunity to bury your head in someone else's bottom. That can't be sniffed at! [BIG AUDIENCE LAUGH]

A year later in Ayr, Tony is handed the subject of 'Mensa' and gives that organisation a new meaning before bravely taking a gentle swipe at one of the most widely read entertainment journalists of the time.

Tony: I used to think that 'Mensa' was an acronym for Mentally Enhanced Nerds Sit Around. [BIG AUDIENCE LAUGH] I am not a member of Mensa. I was sent the application form but was unable to reassemble it in the shape of a rhomboid in the allotted 40 seconds! [MORE AUDIENCE LAUGHTER] Garry Bushell, however, the TV critic of the *Sun* is in this magnificent society! Which goes to show that intelligence and good writing don't necessarily go together! [EVEN BIGGER AUDIENCE LAUGH] He will not give me a good review the next time I appear on the television!

In the same show, Tony manages to work in an extremely funny joke, which I very much doubt would have made it past The Little Green Book had it still been in existence.

Nicholas: Tony, you got in with 30 seconds on 'Digits', starting now.
Tony: There is an old joke connected with digits. Can I use your Dictaphone? No, use your finger like everybody else! [LOUD LAUGHTER FROM THE AUDIENCE]

In February 1999 listeners are treated to a classic Tony Hawks play on words, seemingly heading in a safe direction on the subject of 'Contortionists' before suddenly changing course to produce a big laugh.

Tony: Someone told me if you want to be a contortionist, it helps if you are double jointed. Because you can smoke both the joints and then you don't feel any pain as you move your body into a different position.

Finally, in July 2003 Tony is happy to share one of his most cherished 'Tips' which I am sure will have subsequently stood everyone who heard it in good stead.

Tony: I was given a tip some years by a very wise man who said, 'Tony, it's never a good idea to try and leapfrog a unicorn.' And I've stuck with that ever since. [BIG LAUGH]

The introduction of both Stephen and Tony was not the only important milestone that occurred in the *Just a Minute* story in 1992.

Three other factors came together to launch an aspect of the show that continues to this day, one that I think is both wonderful and important for the continuing appeal of the game.

First, 1992 marked our 25th anniversary.

Second, we welcomed a new producer, Sarah Smith, who took over responsibility for our silver anniversary show.

Third, a new initiative had just been given the green light at the BBC.

These three elements came together to send *Just a Minute* on the road.

For the first 24 years, all of our recordings were central London-based, in BBC-leased venues, the most commonly used being the Playhouse Theatre, near Embankment (where we recorded the pilot show), and the Paris Studio in Lower Regent Street.

That all changed when we reached our 25th year, with producer Sarah Smith deciding to record two shows from Highgate School in north London to commemorate the occasion. It was the first time we had ventured outside the centre of the capital. The shows were a great success, leading Sarah to suggest we take the next series further afield.

Sarah's cause was helped by the fact that within the BBC an initiative had recently been launched that would have a major impact not merely on *Just a Minute,* but also on many of the Corporation's radio shows.

Sandy Chalmers was head of BBC Radio publicity at the time, and it was Sandy who was the driving force behind a movement to take the various BBC networks out of London on a more regular basis. Sandy persuaded her boss, a certain David Hatch who was then managing director of BBC Radio, that a travelling roadshow should be created that would send selected programmes around the UK. From there, *Radio Goes to Town* sprung into life, and *Just a Minute* became one of its integral components.

It was not long before we were on the move. In May 1992 Sarah produced the first double recording of *Just a Minute* to take place outside of London, in Bury St Edmunds, with Clement, Paul,

Wendy and newcomer Tony Slattery, who was by then a well-known improv comedian. Our next stop took us out of England altogether, to Llandudno in Wales. These four shows were broadcast as part of the 1993 series.

The show's London venues have also changed over the years. After the BBC decided not to renew the Paris Studio lease, when not on the road we have most commonly appeared in the Mermaid Theatre, the Drill Hall and in recent years at the Radio Theatre in Broadcasting House.

I very much welcomed the decision to take the show to different locations in the country. Not only was it another element in the evolution of *Just a Minute*, but it also infused each of those shows with a slightly different atmosphere, especially as Ian Messiter would be sure to include subjects that he knew would prompt a reaction from the audience: 'Landslides' in Scarborough (they had suffered such an unpleasant experience the previous summer); 'Dragons', 'Leaks' and 'Choir' in Cardiff; 'Robin Hood' in Nottingham; 'Burke and Hare' and 'Tattoos' in Edinburgh.

There was an additional reason that I was so happy to move away from what had become almost a residency in the Paris Studio. The fact that we recorded in the same venue on such a regular basis meant that ardent followers of the show would be found there queuing for tickets for every performance. Such fans help enormously in creating a good atmosphere. They understand the in-jokes and historical references that panellists sometimes introduce which produce immediate and positive reactions. However, thanks to one fan in particular, I found myself acquiring a reputation for being mean-spirited.

The woman in question was an engaging but over-enthusiastic supporter who was always there early in order to ensure a position at the head of the queue. When I arrived she would detach herself from the line and rush over for a chat. This was flattering but at the same time quite uncomfortable. 'Oh Nicholas,' she would gush, in front of the dozens of people queuing, 'lovely to see you, how *are you*? Are the family well? Good. Hope you have a lovely Easter. Give my love to your wife. And the children. Oh yes, give my love to the children.' I did not know the woman at all, but was always courteous and happy to go along with her, swapping pleasantries before excusing myself to enter the theatre. These exchanges were disconcerting enough in their own right, as I really did not have anything to discuss with her, but became truly embarrassing on one occasion. I had just arrived backstage after one of these encounters when one of the members of our team turned to me and said, 'Nicholas, I really do think you are rather unkind making that relative of yours queue up for every show!'

Between 1994 and 2008, the majority of *Just a Minute* recordings took place outside of London, which was very enjoyable. We always received an excellent response wherever we went, enjoying many different audiences. Such unpredictability was exciting, and a huge positive for an improvisation show such as *Just a Minute*.

Since 2009, however, budget considerations had reduced the travel remit considerably. In my opinion, that is a shame. It is good to take the show out to the public and not confine it to a London-orientated audience. Not only has taking *Just a Minute* on the road produced many high-quality shows, it has also been responsible for a number of memorable moments.

It is 1995 and I am on a train pulling into Alnmouth station, Northumberland. Next to me is *Just a Minute* producer Sarah Smith and opposite sit Peter Jones and Derek Nimmo. Across the aisle is Graham Norton. This will be Graham's first *Just a Minute* appearance on radio. This is our stop, the nearest to our destination, Alnwick. We stand up, collect our bags from the overhead compartment, and leave the train. As we are walking down the platform I glance into the next carriage and spot Tony Hawks sitting there.

I wave. Tony waves back.

I turn to Sarah. 'Isn't it strange that we were on the same train as Tony Hawks and we didn't know. It's a pity really, as it would have been nice if he had sat with us. I wonder where he is headed? Scotland for a gig, I suppose.'

Sarah looks at me in alarm. The train is pulling out of the station. 'What do you mean Tony's still on that train! He's on the show tonight!'

Later Tony told us what happened. Having seen me, he suddenly realised he too should be getting off. Alnwick station, which he had been looking out for, does not exist. By the time he pulled himself together it was too late. In a panic Tony spoke to the train guard who contacted the driver. What a story Tony pitched to them, I don't remember, but he achieved what he wanted. 'They were amazing,' Tony said. 'They agreed to make a brief, unscheduled stop at the next station. The place was deserted but somehow the guard managed to arrange for a door to be unlocked, allowing me to run up to the local town, find a taxi, which delivered me to Alnwick in the nick of time!' Throughout all this Sarah had been working out how she could do the show with only three players. Fortunately we did not have to find out.

Tony, of course, did not survive the show unscathed.

Graham has just completed his first uninterrupted minute and is understandably pleased when I explain that he gains two points for his achievement.

Graham: Oh hip hip hooray …
Tony: So you don't get a car or anything like that? Because really, frankly, a car would be more useful than an extra point!
Nicholas: Especially for you, and your experiences with trains!
[BIG AUDIENCE LAUGH AS THEY HAVE ALREADY BEEN INFORMED OF TONY'S TRAVAILS]

Later Peter joins in on the fun. Tony has just made a rather convoluted challenge against Peter regarding which city has the largest crime rate. Peter defends himself by explaining that he has done his research. Tony attempts, forlornly, to make his point but is quickly cut off by Peter, much to the amusement of the audience.

Peter: After I'd observed you through the train window, senseless, you know, absolutely blotto, and tried to get you to get yourself together. To come here and try and malign me in this way I think it is very unfortunate! [BIG LAUGH]

The *Just a Minute* team is together in a restaurant in Jersey in 1996. The booking has been made by the people who organised the two recordings we have just completed. Both shows went very well. We are upbeat and looking forward to dinner. On the menu is lobster, offered at a reasonable price. Almost everyone at the table orders it for their main course.

Time passes, but there is no rush as we are enjoying a glass or two of wine and lively conversation. No one has anywhere else to go. Suddenly there is a commotion at the other end of the table. Clement has stood up and thrown down his napkin.

'This is ridiculous! I know how long lobster takes to cook! God knows what they are doing out there but I am not wasting any more time in this place. I'm off to bed!'

With that he disappears out of the restaurant. No one bats an eyelid. We have seen similar outbursts from Clement before. Moments later, our lobsters appear, with an extra one to share.

It is 2002 in Bradford. I've been concerned about this recording. It is taking place in the magnificent Alhambra Theatre, one of only a handful of such handsome venues remaining in Britain now. It is a large theatre, one of the biggest in the country, and that is why I am concerned. Is it too big for *Just a Minute*? My worries have been somewhat put to rest by a chap at the stage door who spoke to me in a strong local accent.

'Nicholas, this is amazing. We get a lot of shows coming here but we've never had a show fill every seat in the house. Even the panto doesn't do that, and that does well. You've got something really special here. Absolutely *bloody* marvellous.'

Later I am thinking about the two shows that we have just completed. The audience had been excellent, very receptive and upbeat, but I had been correct in my concern. *Just a Minute* works better in smaller venues. In large auditoriums such as the Alhambra there is an infinitesimal delay in the laughter reaching the performers from the back of the dress circle or stalls. With a scripted production that does not matter because you are not playing to the audience for laughs, you are playing to the situation on stage. You are interacting with the other actors.

Regardless of how the audience responds the script or the action carries on, save perhaps for a momentary pause to give space to the laughter generated. In *Just a Minute* we are interacting directly with the people in front of us and that requires an immediate response if the show is to be successful. We feed off the audience. That's the difference. If there is even a minute disconnect between delivering a line and receiving the laugh, we lose something.

Backstage at the City Varieties theatre, Leeds, 2003, and there is a problem. Chris Neill, our producer, is explaining.

'Our fourth member can't make it. He's ill. It's too late now to get someone from London. But I have been in touch with Charles Collingwood who is recording *The Archers* in Birmingham. He's free this evening and is going to jump in a car as soon as he finishes work and drive up to join us. He should make it in time for the 7.30 start.'

Half past seven comes … and goes. No sign of Charles. We cannot keep the audience waiting very much longer. They will grow bored. Then Paul Merton has one of his moments of inspiration.

'Let's go out and start the show anyway. When Charles gets here we can just slot him in.'

This fires my imagination. It's living dangerously, I know. Who knows when Charles might arrive? I am sure we can make it work, though. One of the joys of *Just a Minute* is that it can push you professionally to experiment in ways you have never tried before.

'Brilliant idea, Paul,' I say. 'We'll improvise around the fact that we have a fourth player who isn't there!'

Moments later I am on stage, introducing the panel. The audience of course can see that we are one panellist down, and I have explained that Charles is on his way. The introductions always generate a loud reaction from the audience, but today the response is even more boisterous and energetic than normal as I make them a little longer, playing for time. They are laughing throughout.

'Thank you, thank you. Hello, my name is Nicholas Parsons. And as the Minute Waltz fades away once more it is my tremendous pleasure to welcome our many listeners, not only in this country, but throughout the world. Also to welcome to the programme four attractive and talented players of this game. I mean who can resist the spontaneous humour and brilliant repartee of Paul Merton? Who can resist the charm and personality of Liza Tarbuck? Who can resist the wit and clever enunciations and observations of Kit Hesketh-Harvey? And who can *resist* the *engaging personality* of that fine actor, Charles Collingwood? Would you please welcome all *four* of them!'

I give the first subject, 'Music Hall', to Paul who begins talking about the time when Charlie Chaplin appeared in this very theatre, but he stumbles on the word 'Lancashire'. Liza takes up the topic but she soon repeats the word 'barrel' and is challenged by Kit. I make an innocuous sounding comment about hearing from 'three of them in this round', and this receives a loud burst of laughter from the audience. It is time to come clean.

'Perhaps I should explain to our listeners that frisson of laughter that occurred then,' I announce. 'Because only three of them are here at the moment! Charles Collingwood, who works in another show on Radio 4 called *The Archers*, has left his production in Birmingham to come up here to Leeds and unfortunately the traffic is so bad, he is still on his way. We hope that he'll be here before we finish!'

Charles, who has obviously yet to score, is due to take the next subject and Paul suggests that we leave it like that to see how 'Charles' manages. 'All right, Paul. Very good idea,' I say. 'Charles, the subject is "Slippery Slope". Would you talk for 60 seconds on the subject, starting now.'

Kit buzzes. 'Repetition!'

'Of what?'

'Because he didn't say anything last time.'

Paul cuts in. 'I think that was a harsh challenge, Nicholas. I think we should give Charles another go.'

I agree, and so clearly do the audience who have been laughing all the way through. I give Charles a point for an incorrect challenge and ask him to continue with the subject. This time the unavoidable silence is interrupted by a challenge from Liza, who cleverly claims that Charles is guilty of deviation by not paying attention. The audience again burst out laughing. I give Charles another point and ask him to speak again.

Silence.

Paul challenges, brilliantly taking this bizarre scenario to yet another level. 'Repetition of zoological gardens!'

Another point to Charles for an incorrect challenge. He still has the subject, and it is Liza who then challenges for a second time. 'Hesitation.' I agree, and the game continues in its normal vein for a few minutes. Midway through the next round, Liza suddenly cries out, 'Excuse me, who's this??'

I look up, and as the cheers and applause ring out I see Charles walking through the theatre towards the stage. He has done well. Three points already in the bag.

Just a Minute's very existence came under threat twice during the 1990s. Threats, Ian informed me at the time, which originated from within the BBC itself.

The first instance occurred in 1993 when Ian Messiter, who controlled all commercial rights in the show, decided to try out a stage version at the Edinburgh Festival.

Ian gave permission to two young impresarios, Mark Goucher and David Johnson, to produce the show, and they in turn engaged me as chairman, and Tony Slattery as the resident player. According to Ian, the BBC were not impressed, although quite what their fears were I do not know. Perhaps they were worried about losing a degree of control. Whatever the perceived concerns, it seems they were sufficient for Ian to be told that if he continued the BBC would take *Just a Minute* off the radio.

Whether the threat was real, or whether the BBC were merely calling Ian's bluff, it is hard to say for sure. Whatever the BBC's strategy was, they certainly misjudged Ian. He was not a man easily cowed, and the stage production went ahead. I believe it improved the show's overall image, but it was not without its troubles.

The venue chosen was on Calton Hill, in a huge tent erected at the eastern tip of Princes Street, which could only be accessed via a steep flight of steps at the end of a long uphill walk. The location, however, was the least of our problems.

Just a Minute took to the stage at noon, and in the evening the venue hosted the *Jim Rose Circus Sideshow*, which quickly attracted all sorts of negative publicity when local councillor Moira Knox objected to its explicit content and called for the venue to be closed down. The councillor was unsuccessful, and it will surprise no one to learn that her intervention proved box office gold for the circus, with the accompanying publicity also benefiting our show.

For each panel the intention was to engage a succession of comedians who were already appearing at the Fringe but, inevitably, many did not show up. A noon appointment can seem very early if you have been partying all night. To their credit, Mark and David had anticipated this problem and brought in as cover a relatively unknown comedian who was performing in a one-man show called *Mother Teresa of Calcutta's Grand Farewell Tour*. His name was Graham Norton.

His responsibility was to step in if one of the guests failed to appear, and he took part fairly regularly during our three-week stint at the festival, and performed very well. The same, however, could not be said for all our guests. A number of those who did show up had never heard of *Just a Minute*, let alone listened to it, and they viewed their presence on the panel purely in terms of an opportunity to plug their own shows. With technical difficulties thrown into the mix (the buzzers did not always work, requiring challengers to raise their hands), the outcome was surely a disastrous theatrical run? Not at all.

Tony Slattery was an excellent choice as the permanent comedy player in the shows. Having played the game previously, he understood what was required. He quickly recognised that if the show was to be entertaining, he and I would have to interject and help the guests who were struggling. In addition, Graham Norton proved to be a natural at the game, stepping in when required and generating a lot of humour. With those elements holding everything together, coupled with the input of some very amusing young comics, we ended up with a successful three-week residency.

Just a Minute also remained on air. Perhaps the BBC eventually came to the conclusion that the stage version would have no detrimental impact on the radio series. When *Just a Minute* returned to Edinburgh the following year, it was not as a stage show however. Ian decided once was sufficient. Instead we arrived in the Scottish capital to record a number of broadcasts for the upcoming radio season, as part of the BBC's policy of taking shows outside London. We have been back every year since, with the show now staged in the BBC's own venue at the Pleasance.

It was during one of those Edinburgh trips that the simmering difference of opinion between Clement and myself boiled over.

Quite simply, Clement did not like the fact that I played the game for laughs. As I have previously mentioned, Clement saw my role as a passive adjudicator of challenges and very little else. I believed, and still do, that *Just a Minute* is all about being clever and generating fun, and everyone involved should contribute to that.

It came to a head after a double recording. Clement had clearly been frustrated by a decision I had made earlier in the evening, and he allowed himself to harbour his resentment all through the post-show hospitality and meal, and on into the taxi back to our hotel.

Whether Clement had a valid point regarding my adjudication, I cannot recall. It may well have been a borderline decision. One thing I am certain of, however, is that whatever my ruling was that sparked his anger, it will have been made with the benefit of the show in mind. If the same situation arose today I would perhaps have used a phrase I have subsequently developed to deal with such occurrences. I give one player 'the benefit of the doubt', which I then look to balance out later in favour of the player who may have felt harshly ruled against.

Back then 'the benefit of the doubt' did not really exist and Clement took my decision to heart, allowing it to fester for a couple of hours. That is the aspect that surprises me most regarding this incident; that such a clever man, who was playing a game purely for entertainment, could allow himself to become so worked up over something that ultimately was entirely trivial.

It was just as the taxi pulled up in front of the hotel that Clement erupted. 'That decision of yours, it was totally ridiculous! You had absolutely no justification. Your actions were appalling!'

Although it had been obvious from Clement's demeanour throughout the evening that he was upset about something, I had no idea that it related to what had happened during the show. I was taken aback by his ferocity but tried to calmly explain the logic behind my decision. I told him I was sorry that he did not see the ruling in the same way as I did. I then went on to say that I felt I had not been arbitrary in my thought process and had acted in the best interests of the game. On that basis 'my decision was entirely justified'.

I will not repeat Clement's response as he climbed out of the taxi, other than to say he made it plain he did not agree with me.

Peter Jones was present during all this and, bless his heart, he could tell I had been shaken by Clement's words. 'Come on, dear boy,' he said, 'let's go and have a drink.'

Over a glass of whisky, Peter's quiet counsel helped reassure me that I had acted in a professional manner although I remained unsettled when we parted. Clement's unjustified behaviour clearly continued to play on Peter's mind as well, because a short time later he appeared at my bedroom door. 'Nick, I've been going over what happened. I don't think you should be too upset by what Clement said. Look at it logically. He has achieved so much in his life, but he only has one thing left now, and that's to win points in *Just a Minute*.'

That was typical of Peter. Thoughtful to take the time to come and speak to me again, and clever to voice his opinion in such a witty and unusual manner to help put my mind at rest.

I was fond of Clement and I could not understand how such an intelligent man, playing a game for fun, could harbour so much rsesentment over something so trivial, and let it fester for so long and then express his feelings in such an aggressive manner. I am still puzzled to this day .

And to cap it all, I paid for the taxi.

...on the subject of *Final-Second Challenges*

Some people have said to me that they feel that challenges in the final couple of seconds of a round are somewhat unsporting. To an extent I understand what lies behind such a reaction. The audience and listeners become so involved with what the speaker is saying that they want that person to complete the round and gain the point.

Clement Freud was a past master at these challenges, giving himself an edge over his fellow panellists when he noticed, as I mentioned previously, that the whistleblower would sometimes raise the whistle a second or two early in preparation of the minute being completed. That changed, however, when the whistleblower held the whistle in her hand throughout and since then none of the players have any inkling of when the 60 seconds are about to come to an end.

I deliberately play up these moments when they occur, employing some showmanship to add to the drama. This often generates 'ooohs' and 'aahs' from the audience, almost as if the speaker has been robbed of their point. They haven't. If they have hesitated, repeated or deviated, and are successfully challenged, as I often say, 'Those are the rules of the game.'

In a show from March 2009 Paul Merton found a clever way to turn the audience's reaction into a big laugh.

Paul is joined here by writer, actor and comedian David Mitchell, and Clement. David is speaking first, with 19 seconds available, on the subject 'In the Stocks'.

David: In the stocks is a place you don't want to find yourself being. And in fact in the village fêtes where people are put in the stocks like vicars nowadays and have sponges thrown at them, I think it's incredibly offensive that that is a reference to a very unpleasant form of medieval torture. And those medieval ghosts … oh!
  BUZZ
Nicholas: Paul challenged, yes?
Paul: Sadly repetition of 'medieval'.
Nicholas: Yes.
David: It's a tiny little word you need in most sentences though! [BIG LAUGH]
Paul: But it represents quite a big period of history!
Nicholas: Paul you've cleverly got in with two seconds to go … [CRIES OF 'OOOH' FROM AUDIENCE] 'In the Stocks', starting now. [SILENCE]
  BUZZ
Nicholas: Clement.
Paul: Sorry, I thought I'd give succour to the people who are disappointed that I won that last particular challenge! [BIG LAUGH AND APPLAUSE FROM AUDIENCE]
Nicholas: Yes, but that's all wrong, because those are the rules of the game. Anyway, you were challenged by

Clement Freud.
Clement: Hesitation.
Nicholas: Hesitation. Right, Clement, one second to go on 'In the Stocks', starting now.
Clement: Custard tart.
[WHISTLE, LAUGHS AND APPLAUSE]

In many people's eyes, Paul is now the expert at the last-second challenge and I have heard comments that he must be able either to see a clock or he has his own stopwatch. He cannot and he does not. All Paul is doing, or anyone else for that matter who buzzes in right at the end, is playing the game.

There is no hint that can be gleaned from me either. I do not look at the stopwatch. I am too busy concentrating on what is being said. I wait for the whistle to blow just like the panellists.

Kenneth Williams, naturally, loved to go overboard in the face of such challenges, particularly if he was expounding on one of the subjects Ian Messiter had chosen specifically for him. Here he is in September 1971 overacting wonderfully well, with the audience in the palm of his hand.

The subject is 'Frederick the Great' which Clement won from Kenneth after 28 seconds, much to Kenneth's disgust. Since then Kenneth has been trying desperately to retake it, which he has achieved with 23 seconds remaining. Derek Nimmo, however, is waiting in the wings.

Kenneth: He had a *pen-chant* for *ta-a-a-ll men*, and imported some people from the Caribbean because he was told they were all over six foot. Erroneously, of course. But, they were shipped and without holes being *bored* in the boxes they were shipped in, most of them died in the process. And when he opened the boxes he said, '*Oooh!* Hello!' …
BUZZ [FOLLOWED BY BIG LAUGH FROM AUDIENCE]
Nicholas: Derek Nimmo challenged you. Why?

Derek: Repetition of 'boxes'.

Nicholas: Yes. Yes, I'm afraid you repeated your boxes.

Kenneth: Most ungallant of you!

Nicholas: I know, but it was rather clever getting in just before the whistle. So you did repeat boxes. I agree with Derek's challenge …

Kenneth: *So he's got in just before the end to get the point!!!* That's what he's done, isn't it!

Nicholas: No! He got a legitimate point because you repeated boxes and he was the first to challenge. So Derek has got a point and he has two seconds for 'Frederick the Great', starting now.

Derek: Nancy Mitford has been a great aficionado …

[WHISTLE AND APPLAUSE]

Nicholas: At the end of that round …

Kenneth: What are you clapping for?? Anyone could get in with two seconds! *What'd you clap him for?*

Nicholas: They're a very warm, generous audience.

Kenneth: Warm?! Daft apes! [BIG LAUGH] It's me that done the work and he got in and you know it with those last two seconds! *It's a disgrace!* I've got a good mind to …

[HUGE AUDIENCE LAUGH AND APPLAUSE AT KENNETH'S ANTICS]

In 1994 the future of *Just a Minute* was once again in jeopardy after Ian Messiter agreed a deal with ITV to produce a television series.

This was not the first attempt to bring the game to the small screen.

In 1968 we recorded a TV pilot in a studio run by a friend of mine, Bill Stewart, and his partner Peter Lloyd, both of whom were ex-Associated Television employees. Granville Studios, on Fulham Broadway, was a simple and sparse venue, but the recording went very well. We had three panellists – Kenneth Williams, Clement Freud and Sheila Hancock – plus myself in the chair, and there were some lovely visual moments as well as the usual verbal battles. I remember Kenneth insisting that I must have misread the time during one round and jumping out of his seat to inspect the clock that had been set up for the viewers. There was a lot of laughter and nonsense as he made a big show of this, which would have worked very well on screen. Unfortunately, having produced what we all felt was a good show, nothing more came of it. I do not know why. The idea was quietly dropped.

The next attempt came in the early 1980s and it was a disaster.

The BBC decided to record a pilot with Kenneth, Clement, Peter and astronomer Patrick Moore. We were obviously delighted, keen to make the jump onto TV, but our enthusiasm did not last long. Our first shock on arriving at the recording was that instead of the small tables to which we were accustomed, the production team had set up large imposing desks for each of us. Immediately we all recognised this as a major error. The layout physically positioned everyone too far apart, inhibiting spontaneity and banter, both essential elements of *Just a Minute*.

The second surprise was an even greater shock. They had forgotten to engage an audience. Other than technicians, the only people present in the studio were my son and half a dozen or so of his college friends who had come along to watch. The producers did not seem to be particularly worried that we in effect had no one to play to, explaining that the recording would go ahead regardless and they would add in the 'laughter' during the edit.

It does not work like that. It is the interaction of the audience with the players that makes *Just a Minute* a success. The show's strength is that it features people who have an instinct for 'comedy of the moment', by which I mean ad libbed and improvised jokes and comments that generate an immediate response from the people in the theatre. This in turn sparks more amusing comments from the performers, and thus the entertainment builds. Without that immediate reaction it is virtually impossible to produce a strong, humorous and sharp performance. My son and his friends did their best to create a positive atmosphere, but it was an impossible task.

I had never seen Kenneth Williams so angry. He was a true professional, and gave a good performance during the recording, but he felt personally insulted that the planning and execution had been so incredibly badly conceived. The moment the cameras were closed down, Kenneth stood up and stormed away. I did not blame him.

Needless to say, a series was not commissioned.

Given the disappointment surrounding that BBC pilot, it was hardly surprising that when Mike Mansfield, a highly experienced television producer, approached Ian Messiter on behalf of Carlton TV, an ITV franchise holder, an agreement was soon reached.

Once again, it seems the BBC were unhappy with Ian's decision. In conversations between Ian and myself regarding the new television show, although he made it clear that no actual ultimatum had been issued (neither Ian nor myself was hauled up to the 'headmaster's office', as it were) there was a lingering sense that the powers-that-be were considering their position regarding the forthcoming radio series. Ian informed me of the various discussions he was having with BBC executives, and assured me that nothing would come of the noises I was hearing that we might be taken off air. I did not quite share Ian's confidence. I was concerned that after all these years the show might finally be coming to an end. At the same time, I was philosophical about the situation. If the BBC did pull the plug, that decision could lead to other doors opening for me, perhaps in radio and television. That is the nature of the business.

Just a Minute, as we know, was not cancelled. Indeed, I think the BBC quickly came round to the idea that rather than taking away from their audience, the television show actually opened up the game to even more people who would then tune in to the radio. I spoke to Jonathan James-Moore, head of Light Entertainment at that time, not long after the first ITV series was aired. Jonathan had initially followed the BBC line that the television series was potentially detrimental to the radio shows, but he was at heart a down-to-earth pragmatist who understood the world of entertainment very well.

'We are going to be able to carry on with the radio, aren't we,

Jonathan?' I asked him. 'Yes,' he replied. 'As a matter of fact I think the TV is going to help rather than hinder us. More people than ever know about the show now.'

The first ITV series was a great success. It was broadcast after the *News at Ten* and featured a number of the guests who had appeared on the stage version in Edinburgh. Amongst those was Graham Norton, plus the comedians Arthur Smith, Neil Mullarkey, Nick Revell, Lee Simpson, Jeremy Hardy and a number of others. This influx of young talent heralded a new and welcome era for *Just a Minute*.

Two innovations were introduced for the television series, one of which worked better than the other. The first was a round in which I invited the audience to come up with a subject, and while this could be entertaining it did become a little confusing, with too many voices calling out, sometimes with ideas that were not appropriate. The second new element, a mystery object round, was a big success as it took advantage of the fact that we were now a visual entertainment show.

The object in question would dramatically rise out of a hole in the desk in front of me, whereupon I would ask one of the panellists to speak on what was now in front of them, without actually explaining what it was. Given the nature of the objects selected (for instance, a pantomime cat, an electrostatic collector, David Garrick's death mask) it was most unlikely that anyone would recognise its true identity. Occasionally someone would guess correctly, purely by chance, but more often than not whoever was talking would try to do so with confidence, when in fact they were bluffing entirely.

Both scenarios (the lucky guess or the blatant bluff) proved to be very effective, opening up amusing challenges of deviation from the truth. Knowing exactly what the object was, I would then adjudicate as to whether what had been said had any relevance. If the speaker had been talking nonsense, I would ask the challenger to justify themselves by explaining where the deviation had come in. This in turn led to some highly entertaining exchanges, as the challenger probably knew as little about the object as the original speaker.

One particular object sticks in my mind, perhaps for the wrong reasons. When it first appeared Graham Norton thought it was a handbag made out of an ostrich egg, comedian Ann Bryson then suggested it could be a hand grenade, and Tony Slattery came to the conclusion that it was a prop from a *Doctor Who* episode entitled 'Terror of the Unfrightening Ceramic Thing'!

In fact, it turned out to be Queen Victoria's muff warmer, to which Tony remarked, 'No wonder she was always sitting down'! This caused a huge amount of laughter from the panel, the audience and myself. As I tried to recover my composure I commented that it would have been more delicate if the explanation on the card in front of me had been 'Queen Victoria's hand muff warmer!' to which Graham retorted, 'No, it wouldn't!'

I think it is probably best if I refrain from any further detail regarding that exchange. It really did come very near to a line that should not be crossed. I will leave it to your imagination.

The mystery object round was continued into the second ITV series, but unfortunately another innovation was introduced. This was presumably because it was felt that an additional element to the game was required in order to hold the attention of a television audience. We now played in teams, with presenter Dale Winton captaining 'the Midlands' and Tony Slattery 'London'. Both captains were excellent, but *Just a Minute* is intrinsically a game of individuals competing against each other; it does not lend itself to teams, as you are either forced to sit back when your teammate is talking, or to challenge him or her, which does not really make sense. Why challenge someone on whose side you are supposed to be? Unsurprisingly, the game did not flourish under this new structure, which was not helped by the move to a mid afternoon broadcast slot. A third series was not forthcoming.

Since then there have been two further moves into the world of television. In 1999 the BBC commissioned a 20-episode series, to be filmed at their Pebble Mill Studios in Birmingham over the course of two weeks. We had an excellent producer, and a very good atmosphere on set, but unfortunately one fundamental error was made. The television side of the BBC did not consult in advance with the more experienced (when it came to *Just a Minute*) radio team.

Had they done so, I have no doubt that the first piece of advice given would have been to consider very carefully the mix of panellists. *Just a Minute* is a difficult game to play, and for it to work, for the shows to come alive, it is essential that any newcomer is supported by more experienced players.

Unfortunately, that did not happen. Part of the problem lay in the manner in which television series are made. You book the studio, camera and sound crews for a block of time, in our case two weeks, in order to construct the set and record the programmes. That was fine for me, I had a contract for the complete run, but the same did not apply for the panellists. Many of them had other commitments and their availability varied which therefore required the producers to enagage a large number of individuals over the fortnight of recordings.

This meant that although there were some wonderful guests booked, excellent names and talented people, many of those who came on the show had never previously listened to *Just a Minute*. A couple had not even heard of it. There are nuances to the game, and only people who have played it before understand what it takes to make the show work.

After two or three recordings, the production team admitted that things were not going as they had hoped. I suggested they try to find more players who knew the game, such as Gyles Brandreth and Tony Hawks. To their credit, they listened and acted on my advice, bringing in both Gyles and Tony. This did help considerably, and we managed to produce a number of successful shows, which to my mind proved *Just a Minute* had a future on television. Apparently, however, there was not enough to convince the BBC, and there was no second chance.

Had the decision been taken at the very beginning to produce a pilot show, I think a lot would have been learned, resulting in a successful subsequent series. Instead, we launched straight into the run and that killed the prospects dead.

A further mistake was also made. The series was broadcast at midday, in the slot once held by *Call My Bluff*. Now that was a very good programme, with an easy charm and gentle humour, perfect for a lunchtime viewing audience. *Just a Minute*, on the other hand, is far sharper and more incisive, and should sit, in my opinion, in the evening schedules. Putting us out at noon proved to be the final nail in the coffin.

Just a Minute eventually did return to television in 2012, with many of the mistakes of the past having been learned – many, but not quite all.

We recorded ten episodes, which were superbly produced by Andy Brereton and Jamie Ormerod, who cleverly brought on board our radio producer Tilusha Ghelani to advise on what had worked in the past and what had proved to be a mistake. That was a smart decision, as Tilusha has many years of experience with the show, and I have no doubt her input was invaluable. Technically, the series was very professionally put together and the presentation, casting and staging excellent.

Andy and Jamie also introduced some creative elements. Normally in a television studio the audience are situated behind the cameras and the crew, quite a distance from the set. This, they realised, would prove to be too passive an arrangement for *Just a Minute*, so instead they placed a section of the audience directly in front of us, with the cameras behind and then the main body of the audience further back. This unusual set-up helped to create the intimacy that the show feeds off.

From my point of view, in terms of the performance and the atmosphere, the television shows felt exactly the same as the radio, which I think was one of the reasons it worked so well.

The problem, however, was once again the time of broadcast.

The schedulers seemed to view *Just a Minute* as an intelligent show in which clever people talked and cracked some jokes. Accordingly we were put into the late afternoon *Eggheads* and *Pointless* quiz slot. That was a misconceived notion. They are both excellent programmes in their own right, but they are not the equivalent of *Just a Minute*, which is a fast-paced comedy show, requiring attention and engagement from its audience. We are more attuned to *Have I Got News For You*, and I still believe that we should be aired in the evening at a similar time.

I was not surprised to learn that the 2012 television series earned excellent appreciation figures, but disappointing viewing figures. The audience at that time of day was attuned to something gentler and more laid-back. To date, there are no plans that I know of for a second run.

How to sum up the history of *Just a Minute* on television? Well, I would say that of the various incarnations we have seen, none has failed but equally none has quite taken off as we hoped.

January 1994 saw the radio debuts of two panellists who have subsequently notched up more than 40 appearances each and have contributed wonderfully to the sense of variety that has marked *Just a Minute* since the beginning of the 1990s.

Writer, actress and award-winning stand-up comic Jenny Eclair (the year following her arrival on *Just a Minute*, Jenny became the first female winner of the prestigious Perrier Award at the Edinburgh Festival) announced her presence on the show five seconds into a broadcast on New Year's Day with an incorrect challenge of hesitation on Peter Jones. 'Too keen,' she admitted, and it is such keenness and enthusiasm for the game that has been the hallmark of her appearances ever since.

Jenny is very good at the game, clever and extremely competitive, a character trait she is very happy to display openly. Here she is during the final round of a broadcast from January 2005, three points behind Paul Merton, but having successfully challenged him on the subject of 'How to Get a Good Night's Sleep' with 35 seconds remaining.

Jenny: A litre of red wine, *Newsnight*, that's me down for nine hours! A good night's sleep should be a bit like being in a coma, nothing should wake you, not even needing a wee at three o'clock in the morning! I don't need that, that's not my problem. The old man, he's always going for …

> BUZZ

Nicholas: Paul challenged.

Paul: Repetition of 'need'.

Jenny: Need! Yes, yes! I will get you back, Paul!! You obviously wanted this subject *so* badly! [THE AUDIENCE BURST OUT LAUGHING]

Paul: What would you be like, Jenny, if you were competitive? [ANOTHER BIG AUDIENCE LAUGH]

Jenny loves to play up this side of her character, happy to demonstrate that her competetiveness extends beyond winning points. For a February 2002 broadcast, Jenny, Tony Hawks, Tim Rice, Graham Norton and myself travelled to Harrogate by train, which resulted in an incident that Jenny describes in the following extract. The subject is 'High Spirits'.

> **Jenny:** You don't have to be drunk to have high spirits, though the two things aren't mutually exclusive. I started my journey to Harrogate in *high spirits*, but British Rail put paid to that! [AUDIENCE LAUGH] Also something else that really unnerved me was how many people were asking Graham for his autograph and ignoring me. So my high spirits turned to sour grapes by the time we got to the station. [JENNY THEN BREAKS INTO A WHINY, CHILDISH VOICE WHICH THE AUDIENCE GREETS WITH A BIG LAUGH] 'Oh, Mr Norton, can I have your autograph? Oooh, I think you're *really* good …'
>
> > BUZZ
>
> **Nicholas:** Tim, what was your challenge?
>
> **Tim:** We had a repeat of autograph.
>
> **Nicholas:** We had the autograph before.
>
> **Jenny:** So did he! There were about 300!!! [LOUD AUDIENCE LAUGHTER]

Graham: I did try! When I was signing the paper put in my face, I was going [GRAHAM STARTS MOTIONING WITH HIS HEAD TOWARDS JENNY WHILE TALKING UNDER HIS BREATH IN AN URGENT MANNER], *'Ask her!* I've got her on this train for hours! She'll sulk! *Ask* her!!!'

Jenny: [PRETENDING TO BE ONE OF THE GAGGLE OF AUTOGRAPH HUNTERS] 'Who is it? Is it Su Pollard?' [HUGE LAUGH FROM AUDIENCE AND PANEL]

Such self-deprecating honesty has been a feature of Jenny's appearances, especially when it comes to describing her personal life. Jenny's writing talent is very obvious when she goes down this route, as she is able to conjure up wonderfully vivid images, made even more entertaining by the fact that she is very rarely complimentary about herself. This is one of the many aspects that Jenny brings to the show that has endeared her to audiences and listeners over the years.

During this February 1994 show, Jenny's second, I give her the subject 'At the End of the Day', and she holds nothing back. The audience adores every second.

Jenny: At the end of the day I like to sit on my sofa, slobbing around, surrounded by bottles of wine, cigarette packets, watching one of those dreary old sitcom things that make me laugh so much. And then I know I should take my make-up off because otherwise I'm going to have skin like a pterodactyl!! [BIG AUDIENCE LAUGH] But unfortunately I'm a bit of a sad old slapper and I go to bed, and it's all over my pillow – mascara, lipstick … dribble, because that's what I do at the end of the day. Lots of dribbling!!! [ANOTHER BIG AUDIENCE LAUGH] And another thing I do, I like to be able to slip into clean cotton sheets, Irish linen. But unfortunately I have to roll back a rather smelly old duvet which is full of biscuit crumbs and my rather flatulent four-year-old daughter. I have to turf her out and get her into her bed. Then I get into the bed and I like to kiss my partner good night. He goes, 'Yeuch! Why don't you go and clean your teeth???' [EVEN MORE LAUGHTER FROM AUDIENCE]

Jenny's domestic arrangements – and seemingly long-suffering partner – come under scrutiny again in July 2001, when she begins talking on 'Clutter'.

> **Jenny:** Do you know, being a slovenly old slut I have heaps of clutter in my life, beneath the bed, behind the curtains. I live with a minimalist for whom clutter is an absolute anathema. He's always following me around with his little dustpan and brush. In fact some days when I'm looking particularly untidy, he attempts to sweep me into the cupboard under the stairs which is brimming with broken hoovers, plastic buckets, empty tins of paint, and a cleaning lady that I once … killed …
> BUZZ
> **Nicholas:** Paul, you challenged.
> **Paul:** Well, I mean, I've heard of clutter, but having a cleaning lady you once killed in a cupboard, that's *very* untidy, isn't it!
> [LOUD AUDIENCE LAUGH]

Jenny's 'minimalist' partner, as she describes him above, regularly features in the descriptions she paints of her life. More often than not he is portrayed extremely positively and with great affection. Even he, however, does not always escape Jenny's brutal honesty. She once indicated that her ideal man would be one 'in a cowboy hat who sits back and shuts up, soaks up any stray bullets, and buys the drinks till bedtime! … A thick, leathery-skinned bloke that tears the hides off buffaloes for their woman!' Perhaps it is no surprise, therefore, that she dried up when describing her partner in August 2001, initially in a very upbeat manner, before allowing herself to ruminate on one of his less dynamic interests. The subject is 'The Cleverest Person I Know'.

Jenny: The cleverest person I know is my boyfriend. Because he's managed to keep me by his side for 18 years, despite stiff competition from thousands of other men! And I mean that literally!! Oh, he can put up shelves, drive cars very fast down motorways *aaand* …

BUZZ

Nicholas: Graham Norton, you challenged.
Graham: Apparently he can't do anything else! There was a pause there.
Jenny: I was having to think quite hard!
Graham: What else can he do?
Jenny: I was going to say he knows a lot about battleships, but then that made me depressed!!! I stopped talking!

Normally Jenny's revelations revolve around herself. In a broadcast of 30 July 2001 she brings the house down with this description of a teenage date. Paul actually correctly challenges mid way through for repetition of 'date', but to everyone's delight Jenny treats us to the full story before Paul takes up the subject of 'Things That Make Me Blush'.

Jenny: I was asked on a date and he took me to the recreation park because it was a posh date. It was there my pants fell out of the bottom of my jeans! You know when you wear your pants in your jeans, and you put on clean pants the next day, but those pants are still tucked in the legs! It made me blush! They ricocheted out of the leg of the jeans!!! [HUGE LAUGH]

In the same show, Jenny goes on to paint an extraordinary picture when I give her the subject of 'A Sure Sign that Summer is Here'. Looking back now I do not believe that there is any other *Just a Minute* panellist who could show such nerve. The audience absolutely loves the description Jenny provides, and laugh loudly throughout until she is inadvertently cut off by a 'Freudian slip'.

Jenny: A sure sign that summer is here is when women take off their thick woolly tights, and expose pallid flesh to the sun. I start applying fake tan, even though it smells of burning prophylactic and makes my legs that fluorescent orange of a chicken tikka. [HUGE AUDIENCE LAUGH] I don't care! It's better than looking like a jellyfish!!! The other upsetting thing is, you know when you try on last season's clothes and you look like tapioca in a string bag? [EVEN MORE LAUGHTER] And you realise that you must go back to the gym, that's another sure sign that summer is before us ... [BUZZ FOLLOWED BY GROANS FROM THE AUDIENCE AS THEY ARE ENJOYING THE MONOLOGUE]

Clement has mistakenly pressed his buzzer here, for which he apologises. Jenny continues, but only for a few more seconds before drying up and losing the subject to Clement for a correct challenge this time and the round continues to its conclusion.

Jenny is also very generous in passing on various tips she has learned over her many years in the public eye. When given the subject of 'How to Look Good in Photos' in a February 2002 broadcast from Harrogate, Jenny first pulls one of what she describes as her '37 faces', much to the Yorkshire audience's amusement (and this is after Jenny has admitted she's from Lancashire!), before going on to offer a handy hint.

Jenny: If you want to look good in a photo, stand next to something that is much uglier and older than you are! May I suggest a ruined castle or Barbara Cartland. Oh, she's dead ... [AUDIENCE AND OTHER PANELLISTS BURST OUT LAUGHING]

Jenny also brings great energy to the show, which transmits itself to the audience, often creating a raucous and wonderfully entertaining atmosphere. The following is an example from July 1999, during a broadcast from the Oxford Union. Jenny has already won the audience over with numerous funny and outrageous comments. First she offered her views on the subject of 'The Dreaming Spires'. ('Well, obviously I have a *massive* chip on my shoulder,' she explained, 'because I never went to Oxford or Cambridge University! Still I haven't done badly for a girl with no education and hardly any bosom to speak of!!!!') Jenny then produced an unusual take on the topical subject 'The Millennium Bug'. ('If I've got this right, the millennium bug sends clocks backwards. I wouldn't mind catching it because then I would be 19 again! Hurrah! Imagine that, all nubile and gorgeous once again!')

Here she has just successfully challenged Kit Hesketh-Harvey as he was speaking on 'Thinking Out Loud'. Jenny does exactly what the subject suggests, before I have asked her to begin speaking.

Jenny: [WISTFULLY] Thinking out loud … See that bloke four rows back, he's cute, isn't he! Oops, done it again! [BIG LAUGH]

Kit: You are shameless, Miss Eclair!

Jenny: Absolutely! I can't concentrate actually.

Nicholas: I haven't given you the chance to start yet.

Jenny: Oh dear.

Nicholas: I do have to say there are 38 seconds, 'Thinking Out Loud', starting now.

Jenny: Can I say what I just said again?

Nicholas: Yes.

Jenny: So he knows I'm serious!!!! [JENNY CANNOT STOP HERSELF BURSTING OUT INTO WHAT CAN ONLY BE DESCRIBED AS A VERY LOUD 'FILTHY' LAUGH AS THE AUDIENCE APPLAUD WILDLY]

Kit Hesketh-Harvey, who appears in the above extract, was *Just a Minute*'s second 1994 virgin, although to be accurate, by the time Kit's first show was broadcast on 22 January he had already made one appearance in the television series produced by Mike Mansfield. Kit is what I would describe as a writer and musical comedy performer with a strong personality and a unique worldview.

Where much of Jenny's comedy is personal and observational, Kit's humour derives from a more surreal outlook on life (he once claimed his first job was as apprentice to me when I was an 'artificial inseminator of pigs'!), which he expresses with a sharp brain and talent for writing music and lyrics. He also has a risqué streak which audiences find highly entertaining.

Take, for example, this poetic contribution from Kit when handed the subject of 'Rhyming Couplets' in a broadcast of 2 August 1999. Kit is joined here on the panel by Peter Jones, Jenny Eclair and comedian Stephen Frost.

Kit:
When I gaze at Stephen Frost,
He flex his pecs and I am lost!
Look again at Miss Eclair,
By Jove's, she's got a lovely ... pear ... crumble recipe!
Even Peter Jones,
There's still some flesh on them old bones.
But when I look at Nicholas Par ... sons,
All I see is a right royal ... are some examples of rhyming couplets.
[HUGE AUDIENCE LAUGH]

In the same show from the Oxford Union in which Jenny picked out the 'cute' man in the audience, just before that moment, and still on the subject of 'Thinking Out Loud', Kit cleverly took a famous novel partly set in the colleges of that world-renowned university, and twisted its title in an extraordinary and unexpected manner. I cannot imagine what Evelyn Waugh would have made of this. What I do know, however, is that the students in the audience reacted with a huge amount of laughter to Kit's outrageous manipulation.

Kit: Thinking out loud, I can see that Nicholas Parsons' buttocks are particularly tightly clenched tonight. [BIG LAUGH] Whether it is because he is at this ancient university and scared that his Brideshead might become Revisited, I do not know!

[EVEN BIGGER LAUGH]

Kit's bizarrely individual outlook is perhaps best illustrated by his remarkably energetic take on the seemingly innocuous subject of 'Nursery Rhymes'.

> **Kit:** Nursery rhymes are supposed to evoke the innocence of childhood and the purity of infancy. But just consider 'Wee Willie Winkie ran through the town'. Imagine calling somebody that!! They would be psychologically cauterised for life! [BIG LAUGH] The Grand Old Duke of York may have had 10,000 men; it's a little too much information for somebody that age to handle! As for Mary having a little lamb, my God! The King of Spain's daughter came to visit me, and all on account of my nuts! It's pornography! It's filth!!! We should give them *Lady Chatterley's Lover, Knave* and *Hustler* instead of all this! Ride a cock horse to Banbury Cross! What are we doing to the infants of this country? I can bear it no longer!
> [BUZZ FOLLOWED BY AUDIENCE APPLAUSE]

Paul successfully challenges, with Kit having clearly run out of steam. Paul then speaks to the end of the round, offering a very different view from Kit on the subject: 'On the other hand, they are charming little rhymes that enchant our children.'

Kit may also hold a *Just a Minute* record – for the longest stretch of seconds without speech not challenged for hesitation. In a show of 3 August 1998, recorded in Blenheim Palace, Kit wins the subject of 'The Experiment' from Derek Nimmo, with 23 seconds to go. He speaks for approximately 12 seconds. The remaining time on the clock is filled with laughter and applause from everybody present until the whistle blows.

> **Kit:** I like the experiments that turn up in jokes. To wit, how many feminists does it take to change a light bulb? Five. One to do so, and four to celebrate the passive role of the socket …

It is unsurprising that when Graham Norton made his *Just a Minute* radio debut, in a broadcast on 3 February 1996, he had already clearly identified the way in which he wanted to play the game. Having honed his skills in numerous appearances during the 1993 Edinburgh stage run, followed by three guest spots on television between 1994 and 1995, by the time he moved on to the radio he had most certainly found his voice.

Graham hit the ground running. With his now trademark wit, charm, apparent innocence and daring edge, he completed a full, uninterrupted minute on the very first subject he was given, 'Dreams'. (Thanks, it should be noted, to some sporting generosity afforded him by fellow panellists Derek Nimmo, Peter Jones and Tony Hawks who overlooked Graham elongating numerous words while talking very slowly.) The wonderful attributes that he displayed to such effect that evening have been entertaining audiences and listeners ever since.

> **Graham:** Freud is often associated with dreams. He placed great importance on them, though I feel myself, that he just *pretended* they were important. Because psychotherapy is so *boring* most of his clients would just nod off on his leather couchette and he felt a bit guilty charging them for nothing more than a kip! So when they woke up, he'd pretend that what they were saying had some sort of import or meaning. Now, a lot of adolescent boys (healthy, young, bursting souls that they are – though this never happened to me myself!) have what are known in psychotherapy parlance as wet dreams!! This is …
> [WHISTLE FOLLOWED BY LOUD APPLAUSE AND CHEERS]

Graham obviously thoroughly enjoys the show. He, like Paul Merton, does not need *Just a Minute* in order to enhance his lifestyle. Both those players are too successful for their appearances to make any real difference to how they live. Look at the breadth of Graham's professional life. He has his own prime-time television chat show, presents music programmes on Radio 2, writes a weekly newspaper advice column, and is now the BBC's voice of the extremely popular Eurovision Song Contest, an engagement he talked about during a *Just a Minute* broadcast of 20 May 2013. Not that Graham brought up his other work interests gratuitously. Not a bit of it. He did not really have much choice; the subject *was* 'History of Eurovision'.

Graham: Finally, a subject I know something about, *nay*, upon which I am an expert. Now I won't bog you down with too many facts or figures, so let me begin by saying the Eurovision Song Contest began *ages* ago, somewhere in this continent. Now, the Eurovision area has expanded vastly in that period of time. *I-I-I know* this because last year I was chasing a hard-boiled goat's eye around a plate in Baku, capital of Azerbaijan. Euro … *hello*?? I don't think so. However, this year we are back in Sweden. However, to take the shine off that, they couldn't host it in Stockholm. *Oh no!* We are in *Malmö*, home of the … who knows what? It is some sort of town, I suppose. It must have a venue, unless the whole thing …

[WHISTLE AND APPLAUSE]

One of the reasons, I suspect, that Graham is happy to appear on *Just a Minute* is that there is no rehearsal required. It is spontaneous. You turn up half an hour before the recordings begin and get on with it. This, no doubt, is in welcome contrast to his chat show, which must require considerable preparation.

Here he is coming in with a very sharp line during a December 1999 broadcast from Newcastle. Clement Freud is starting the round, talking on 'Out of Body Experiences'.

Clement: There is in my body a thin man [BIG AUDIENCE LAUGH] who's been trying to get out for many years now. He is about 11 stone, has lots of hair [MORE AUDIENCE LAUGHTER], more teeth than I, and ears which protrude unfortunately. But this chap who occupies …

BUZZ

Nicholas: Paul Merton challenged. What's your challenge?
Paul: Well, we're not expected to listen to this, are we? He's got a man inside him who's got protruding ears!
Graham: Is that why he can't get out? [HUGE AUDIENCE LAUGH FOLLOWED BY ENTHUSIASTIC APPLAUSE]

Graham was born in the 1960s, a decade which he once explained was known in his home country of Ireland as 'the end of the world'. In a similar way to many of the best players of the game, Graham calls on childhood experiences from time to time in order to talk on potentially tricky topics. In July 1999 it was 'The Final Twist', which, like the best subjects, is open to a variety of interpretations.

Graham: In my school we'd a special dance to celebrate the end of the potato harvest. [AUDIENCE LAUGH] Yes!! It was known as the Spud Hop! And we all remember the final twist at that! Miss Doody, the Irish teacher (I think she'd had a spritzer or a glass of sherry), decided to venture onto the floor. *Twist she did!* Fell over like a dead cow!! [AUDIENCE LAUGH] And she broke her leg! I know it sounds cruel … but we laughed! Forgive us, we were children. We were young! We didn't know!

Graham carries on for a few more seconds before tying himself in knots and losing the subject, at which point he receives a big round of applause, having left the audience with a very clear vision of one of his school discos and the unfortunate teacher.

A further tale of Graham as a young lad growing up in Ireland emerges during a recording in Chester, broadcast on 7 February 2000. I have asked Graham to talk on 'Raspberries' and his response is laced with double meaning, which the audience find hilarious.

Graham: Raspberries are small fruits with quite a lot of hair on them, and thus I feel a strange affinity to them! [BIG LAUGH FROM AUDIENCE WHICH THEN GROWS AND IS JOINED

WITH APPLAUSE AS WHAT GRAHAM IS SAYING SINKS
IN] As a schoolboy we went raspberry picking! [LOTS OF
APPLAUSE] You're too late to save me now, kind audience!

Graham cut his professional teeth in stand-up comedy, an
entertainment genre that was dominated by observational humour
as he was learning his trade. It is a brand of comedy Graham has
employed with great skill and timing on *Just a Minute*. In this example,
I have given Graham the subject of 'Security'.

> **Graham:** We must live in a crime-ridden society! I've noticed
> as I trawl my way around the land that come a certain hour
> even public toilets are locked! Why???? Are they afraid that
> somebody might break in and *clean* them? [BIG LAUGHTER
> FROM AUDIENCE AND PANEL FOLLOWED BY SUSTAINED
> AND ENTHUSIASTIC APPLAUSE]

There is no question that Graham brings a set of unique talents to
Just a Minute, but at times there is more than an echo of Kenneth
Williams in his delivery, specifically his slow, drawn-out manner of
speech. The subject here is 'Golden Oldies' from a 21 February 2005
show, with Graham stretching out his words to such an extent that
Paul feels obliged to challenge.

> **Graham:** *Gold-en* oldies are *tuunes* that we *ado-o-re* to listen to
> over and again. I find my *fav-ou-rites* are *uuusually* by the *Car-pen-
> ters* or sometimes by *the Osss-monnnds* or …
> BUZZ
> **Nicholas:** Paul challenged.
> **Paul:** Sorry, he's whipping me up into a light coma here! For a
> moment I didn't think I was going to live long enough to get to
> the end of the word 'Osmonds'! [HUGE AUDIENCE LAUGH]

The various chat shows that Graham has hosted over the years have
obviously brought him into contact with a great number of celebrities.

It is to this aspect of his working life that Graham most often returns in *Just a Minute*, much to the delight of his many devoted fans. On the surface, Graham could be seen as being very cutting in his remarks, but with his delightful delivery and comic timing it is clear everything he says is in jest. When Graham lets the audience in on some of his celebrity 'gossip', it often generates the biggest laugh of the show.

When Graham is given the subject 'In the Year 2525' in a February 2007 programme, it is a major star of stage, screen and television who becomes the focus of his attention.

> **Graham:** In the year 2525 there will be many mysteries. One of which will be how is Kim Cattrall still 40? [BIG LAUGH]

Listeners to the programme on 27 December 1999 found themselves being confronted with an extremely disturbing (and very funny) image when Graham was given the subject of 'Keeping the Wolf from the Door'. Surely this topic could have nothing to do with the world of celebrity?

> **Graham:** Keeping the wolf from the door is something I'm sure Ulrika Jonsson became very familiar with [AUDIENCE START LAUGHING AS THEY REALISE WHERE GRAHAM IS GOING] when working as a hostess on the sports slash entertainment show *Gladiators*. Late at night she'd be in her room eating smoked fish or whatever Swedish people *have* as a bedtime titbit and she would hear a familiar noise. 'Oh n-o-o,' she'd think, 'surely that is the sound of Lycra against cheap hotel carpet! [BIG AUDIENCE LAUGH] *The Wolf* is *craw-ling* down the corridor towards *my room*!!!

No one, it seems, is safe from Graham's scrutiny. Not even the most powerful couple on the planet – the President and First Lady of the United States of America. The Clintons are still White House residents in July 2000 when Graham is given the subject of 'Socks'. What could be more mundane?

Graham: Socks is famously the name of Bill Clinton's cat. And I'm reliably informed it's the only pussy in the White House that Hillary doesn't mind Bill Clinton stroking! [HUGE LAUGH]

The topic of 'Celebrity Weddings' is clearly a subject chosen specifically with Graham in mind, and he does not disappoint in this extract from 8 July 2002, with the audience in hysterics all the way through.

Graham: Celebrities, unlike normal people, don't get married in church or registry offices, but rather in the pages of *OK!* magazine. Now, I've only been to one celebrity wedding but it was quite a corker. It was Liza Minnelli marrying David – *oh my God, have you seen him?* – Gest! I was astonished because when I did see the photographs I thought, 'Oh, they used black-and-white film.' But no! They were in colour, just everyone *looked like that*! It was a wild old day. Strangely moving. After the ceremony – *oh, let's call it a freak show* – we moved on to the reception. I can't believe these people fed me and I'm now slagging them off like this!!! But never mind. I paid for my own flight! But … er … oh, that's hesitation! [HUGE LAUGH FROM AUDIENCE]

As accomplished as he is in the world of celebrity, even Graham Norton on occasion makes a mistake. Below he is speaking on 'New Year's Resolutions' from 3 January 1998, when he realises he has got himself mixed up. American comedian Greg Proops is on the panel and makes a correct challenge, but everyone wants to know who it is that Graham has in mind.

Graham: My New Year's resolution is to pay less attention to the wise words of Anne Diamond! Because I honestly believe that she has the ability to poison a mind! I *really* do!!! And at this point in the little chat, I've suddenly realised I'm not talking about that person at all. I meant another person … oh, I've said person …

BUZZ

Nicholas: Greg Proops challenged.

Greg: I believe there was a repetition of the word 'person'.

Nicholas: Yes! But which person was Graham thinking about?

Graham: *Anne Robinson* is actually who I meant!!! [HUGE LAUGH]

...on the subject of *Locations*

Since our first excursion outside central London in 1992, to celebrate our silver anniversary, *Just a Minute* has toured the country and gone much further afield on one occasion. Here is a full list of all the locations we have visited and the years in which the shows were broadcast, up to and including Series 68 (February–March 2014).

1992: Highgate, north London

1993: Bury St Edmunds and Llandudno

1994: Scarborough, Edinburgh and Norwich

1995: Cardiff, Norwich, Edinburgh and Lincoln

1996: Edinburgh, Ayr, Nottingham and Alnwick

1997: Edinburgh, Worcester, Jersey, St Andrews, Manchester, Glasgow and Loughborough

1998: Manchester, Belfast, Edinburgh, Bath, Loughborough, Blenheim Palace and Glasgow

1999: Sheffield, Brighton, Edinburgh, Guernsey, Birmingham (TV), Glasgow, Oxford and York

2000: Newcastle, Norwich, Chester, Dartmouth, Nottingham, Dorking, High Wycombe and Edinburgh

2001: Buxton, King's Lynn, Southampton, Brighton, Leeds, Cardiff and Edinburgh

2002: Winchester, Hastings, Harrogate, Southsea, Fowey, Bradford, Canterbury and Edinburgh

2003: Canterbury, Bristol, Beverley, Snape, Edinburgh,

Westcliff, Malvern and Southwold
2004: Leeds, Southwold, Dundee, Warwick, Cheltenham,
Swansea and Edinburgh
2005: Watford, Guildford, Oxford, Berkhamsted, Mold,
Henley and Edinburgh
2006: Redhill, Exeter, Greenwich, Newcastle, Bournemouth
and Edinburgh
2007: Winchester, Tunbridge Wells, Cheltenham, Brighton,
Hay-on-Wye, Hastings, Edinburgh and Stratford-upon-Avon
2008: Leicester, King's Lynn, Stratford-upon-Avon, Salisbury,
Bristol, Southwold, Hay-on-Wye, Manchester and Edinburgh
2009: Lincoln and Edinburgh
2010: Derby, Edinburgh and Salford
2011: Edinburgh and Lichfield
2012: Mumbai, Bridlington, Evesham, Edinburgh
2013: Derry and Edinburgh

Graham Norton is not alone in pushing boundaries in *Just a Minute*. In fact, he is probably not even the game's most frequent 'offender'. I would suggest that the debutant of 25 January 1997, Julian Clary, has snatched that accolade, although with his astute sense of comedy timing and his professionalism he never goes too far. Julian understands the audience and listeners he is playing to and respects the show too much to cross the boundary of good taste into territory that could offend. He does, however, step right up to that line and in so doing generates wonderful entertainment.

In a similar fashion to Graham, Julian enjoys casting his eye over the world of celebrity and popular culture. When asked to speak on the subject of 'Bergerac' on his debut (recorded on the island of Jersey where the TV series was filmed) Julian demonstrates immediately that he is someone who would never shy away from risking the ire of an audience in the search for a good joke. In the wrong hands, this can be a risky strategy, but Julian knows exactly what he is doing. Exuding charm, and with a twinkle in his eye, Julian delivers his line perfectly and his audiences fall about laughing.

> **Julian:** Oh Bergerac! It's a television detective series! Some would call it a *defective* series! [BIG LAUGH]

In February 2000 I hand Julian the unusual subject of 'Sexing a Tadpole'. This is clearly too good an opportunity to miss.

> **Julian:** As far as I understand it, sexing a tadpole is impossible because their genitals aren't yet fully formed, not unlike Dale Winton! [BIG LAUGH]

Ten years later, the subject is 'An Icy Stare', which provides Julian with the ideal introduction to a highly amusing celebrity anecdote.

> **Julian:** I was on the Royal Variety Show once. And during the line-up part at the after-show party, I found myself standing next to Cher, who fixed me with an icy stare. I thought, 'Miserable cow!' Turned out she'd just had a lot of work done and she was unable to kind of smile in the more natural … [BIG AUDIENCE LAUGH]

While it is Graham who remains the king of 'celebrity humour', Julian is without doubt the supreme ruler when it comes to 'innocent' innuendo, a position he secured when he spoke for the very first time on the show.

Julian correctly challenges on the subject of 'Jersey', with 26 seconds remaining, and uses that time to announce his arrival on *Just a Minute* to great effect. The audience in St Helier loves every moment.

> **Julian:** There are several things I like about Jersey. First of all, I should mention St Peter's Bunker. It's very, very snug indeed. And then I must move on to your mouth-watering cucumbers. And then of course there's plums, which are not only juicy but

full of flavour. Jersey is an ideal spot to attend if you like rich people …

[WHISTLE AND APPLAUSE]

Julian may not have been the first to introduce naughty plays on words into the show, but since his arrival their use has been reinvigorated. Here is Clement talking on the subject of 'The Craic' in January 1998.

Clement: The sort of thing you would hear at a craic would be a story about Prince Charles going to the north of England to make a speech wearing Davy Crockett headgear. And at the end of his address, someone went up to him and said, 'Brilliant, but what an extraordinary thing you have got on your head.' And he said, 'It was Mama's idea. I told her I was going to Scunthorpe, and she said, "Wear the fox hat?"'" [HUGE AUDIENCE LAUGH]

Six months later Paul Merton proves he too enjoys pushing boundaries with his take on the topic of 'Loose Ends'.

Paul: When I was coaching a rugby union team I wasn't very pleased with the speed of their rucking. I said, 'I suppose a quick ruck is out of the question?' [BIG LAUGH]

Fast forward to August 2005 and Gyles Brandreth is exploring a similar comic theme, once again to the great amusement of the audience. Clement's sharp line at the end of the exchange is also much enjoyed. Paul is speaking first, on the subject of 'Hypnotists'.

Paul: When I was walking through a park once, I met a hypnotist who looked me squarely in the eye and said, 'I am going to make you think you are a duck.' And he hypnotised me and within moments I was quacking all over the place. It was the most extraordinary exhibition I have ever seen in my life! One of the great …

BUZZ

Nicholas: Gyles challenged.

Gyles: Deviation, you would not be able to see your own exhibition unless you had a mirror at the time.

Paul: It was videoed! It was for a TV programme called *That's My Duck*. [BIG LAUGH] For celebrities that are hypnotised as ducks. Don't you remember? Do you remember, Nicholas? You were a mallard for six months, do you remember? [MORE LAUGHTER]

Nicholas: I know, and we had that amazing affair because you were the duck. Right ... [HUGD LAUGH]

Gyles: *P-lease!*

Paul: Well, it wasn't that amazing, to be honest!

Gyles: When you said, 'I suppose a quick duck's out of the question?'!!! [LAUGHTER CONTINUING THROUGHOUT]

Nicholas: Right, yes!

Clement: [DEADPAN] Did he put it on your bill? [MORE LAUGHTER]

While his fellow panellists are clearly adept at this brand of humour, there is no question that Julian remains king of the double entendre. Below he is talking on the subject of 'Rank Outsiders' during his third show, broadcast on 8 June 1998. Only Julian could think of this. And get away with it. As always, it is his innocent delivery that makes what he says so successful.

Julian: A rank outsider is an outsider with a personal hygiene problem. [BIG LAUGH] I think to be an outsider is bad enough but to be a *rank* outsider must be terrible. The good thing about being a rank outsider is it gives you the opportunity to come from behind! [AUDIENCE BEGIN LAUGHING, WHICH GROWS INCREASINGLY LOUD AS JULIAN CONTINUES] Which ... ah ... in my experience is not to be sniffed at. If you follow my drift!

A little later in the same recording, Julian wins the subject of 'Gratuities' with seven seconds remaining.

> **Julian:** I always like to give a large tip, especially if I'm in a Greek restaurant and there's a Greek waiter who looks like he might be hung …
> BUZZ
> **Nicholas:** Derek challenged.
> **Derek:** Two Greek waiters.
> **Nicholas:** Two Greeks, yes.
> **Julian:** Oh, what a lovely idea!!! [AUDIENCE BURST INTO LOUD AND SUSTAINED LAUGHTER AND APPLAUSE]

Recognising the popularity of Julian's comedy, by his fourth appearance on 27 July 1998, I am searching for opportunities to set him up for a funny line. Paul also joins in on this occasion.

> **Nicholas:** Right. Derek Nimmo was speaking as the whistle went then. He's moved forward, he's equal in second place with Clement Freud, one point behind our leader Paul Merton but coming up fast behind is Julian Clary …
> **Julian:** That's how I like it! [BIG LAUGH FROM AUDIENCE]
> **Paul:** There's a surprise!!

In a broadcast on Valentine's Day 2000, Julian enters into the spirit of romance when talking on 'Stretching My Legs'.

> **Julian:** The other day I was very busy stretching my legs and, do you know, I did in fact pull a muscle. His name was Mary.

The subject of 'Brighton Rock' proves irresistible to Julian in a show recorded in that city and broadcast on 9 July 2001.

> **Julian:** There's a lot to be said for having something long, pink and hard in your mouth! [HUGE AUDIENCE LAUGH WHICH

INCREASES IN VOLUME AS JULIAN CONTINUES SPEAKING]
The longer the better, I always say!! And particularly delicious
when that sugary coating slips down the back of your throat! I
never leave Brighton without a bag full of Brighton Rock! It's
what I come here for! It's delicious! I can't get enough of it!!! It's
particularly …
[BUZZ FOLLOWED BY LOUD APPLAUSE]

Paul has challenged for Julian's slight hesitation, 'Just in time!' as I
comment, receiving a big laugh from the audience.

Julian Clary continues to be one of *Just a Minute*'s most popular
players, not only because he is very funny and likeable, but also
because he is happy to set himself up for others to deliver the funny
line. Here it is the talented comedian Linda Smith, who has just been
challenged by Julian.

Julian: Are we not deviating?
Nicholas: What's wrong?
Julian: From the subject.
Linda: Oh, that's a bit rich! *Accused of deviation by Julian Clary!!!!*
[HUGE LAUGH]

With the arrival of this new wave of comedians such as Julian,
Linda, Graham and Jenny, *Just a Minute* had placed itself in a healthy
position to enter the new century. This proved to be critical, as some
very testing times lay just ahead.

Challenge!

Q: Who is the only person Clement Freud never challenged during a show on which he was a panellist?

A: His daughter Emma, who appeared on *Just a Minute* once in a broadcast of 14 April 1990.

Q: What role does David Haines play in *Just a Minute*?

A: He is the pianist on the show's theme music, the Minute Waltz.

Q: Which player has spoken at the fastest rate of words per second on *Just a Minute*?

A: Kenneth Williams, who has achieved an incredible 6.1 words per second.

Q: Which four *Just a Minute* recording locations have required the crossing of a significant body of water?

A: Northern Ireland, Guernsey, Jersey and India.

Q: In the history of *Just a Minute* there has been no subject beginning with the letter 'X', however there have been four beginning with the letter 'Z'. What are they? (Note: 'The' is not counted as beginning a subject.)

A: 'Zen Buddhism', 'Zero', 'Zeus' and 'The Zeeman Effect'.

Sue Perkins

There are some things in life I'll always remember. My first kiss (no. 466 bus stop, Croydon, 1982), my first heartbreak (no. 466 bus stop, Croydon, 1982) and my first *Just a Minute* (Dorking Halls, 2000).

I grew up with *Just a Minute*. It was as much a part of my family as casual hostility, underage drinking and a propensity for cake. As I started out on what I'm rather augustly deeming 'a career', the show seemed an unimaginable and unassailable peak; something too remote and classy to even contemplate being a part of.

But asked I was, fourteen years ago almost to the day. (I still believe it was an administrative error and they were trying to book Su Pollard.)

In 2000, the world was younger. I had two eyes rather than four, and we believed that all computers would self-destruct and bring about the end of the universe on the eve of the millennium. That summer, I was asked to appear in one of the *Just a Minute* touring shows, which that week found itself in the Surrey suburbs of Dorking. I know – it's *unimaginably* exotic. I arrived by train, wearing an itchy lambswool jumper, which I immediately regretted, as the more anxious I became, the more my temperature spiked. Why didn't I take it off? Well, in my nervous delirium I had forgotten to put a T-shirt on underneath, and as much as I wanted to make an impression, I didn't want to make *that* sort of impression.

On the panel were the late Sir Clement Freud, Tony Hawks and Jeremy Hardy. Sir Clement was embarking on his 414th game, I was the red-faced virgin in a cable-knit. I'd say he put me at my ease, but that wasn't Clement's style. There again, part of the joy of Clement was he was so unapologetically, terrifyingly and resolutely himself.

My first subject was 'My Worst Nightmare'. It couldn't have been more prescient. By that point my face was a deep puce and the small of my back molten with perspiration. My dry mouth attempted the odd sentence or two, but it's fair to say I didn't cover myself in glory – overwhelmed as I was by both the pedigree of the panel and the unbearable heat of that regrettable woollen.

The second recording that night was the more memorable of the two. For starters, it was first of many occasions where Nicholas got my name wrong. He called me Sue Perks, who, it transpires, was one of his early flames (the rogue). Since then I've been Porks, Perky, Spew and my own favourite, Poo Serkins. But the main reason that second show sticks deep in my memory is that it's the only time I can think of where three panellists spoke for a minute consecutively. And one of them happened to be me.

A minute. A MINUTE. It's such a tiny unit of time – it goes by relatively unmarked unless you're boiling an egg or counting down to a nuclear catastrophe. But on this show – it's everything. When you're in that minute, eyes bulging, neck straining, it feels like an hour. It feels like a lifetime. It feels like wading through treacle while the synapses of your brain desperately hunt for synonyms. It feels like panic and pain and then, suddenly, at around the 50-second mark, it feels like you're flying. It is, I believe, the closest thing we'll ever get to flying.

The real joy of the game, of course, has nothing whatsoever to do with winning (thank goodness). It's about the ping-pong of banter, the tangential back alleyways, the mercurial energy of a show entirely improvised. Sometimes it's all I can do just to sit back in my chair and marvel at my colleagues

– the soaring, imaginative flights of the game's ultimate genius, Paul Merton, the picture-postcard cheek of Gyles Brandreth, the stretched-to-breaking-point vowels and joyous generosity of Graham Norton. I am reminded each and every time how very lucky I am to be in the same room as the players who grace the Radio Theatre and place their fingers on those legendary buzzers.

But most of all, the show is lifted from being a damn fine parlour game into a worldwide and long-standing classic by the one and only Nicholas. Wonderful Nicholas. The showman. The ringmaster. A performer who moves from ditzy to canny, from sardonic to silly in a heartbeat. A man whom you underestimate at your peril. A man, in short, who does not need the benefit of the doubt.

Fourteen years ago, *Just a Minute* became, in a heartbeat, my favourite gig of all time, as well as my hottest. It remains so to this day. It is as global as it is timeless. It is forever refreshed and unpredictable. I love it. Where else but British radio could you have a show so fiendish you get penalised for annunciating the name of the broadcaster who airs it?

May its Minute Waltz never fade away.

The Twenty-first Century

The decade through Just a Minute

Global warming
Of course it's happening. Look at the polar bear, a shadow of its former self, wandering around the decimated ice caps looking for fish. As we all do on a bank holiday.

SUE PERKINS
26 JANUARY 2009

My expenses
I applied to Mark Thompson, the Director General, for a floating duck pond. I said I needed it for research in case this subject comes up on *Just a Minute*.

GYLES BRANDRETH
17 AUGUST 2009

Electronic books
Some say that electronic books signal the demise of the public library. It would be extremely sad for Nicholas Parsons, who would have nowhere to go in the daytime.

KIT HESKETH-HARVEY
12 MARCH 2012

In a chat room
A chat room depends on the language you are speaking. In English it would be a place on a computer where people could have a virtual conversation. In French it would be a place where you keep a cat.

DAVE GORMAN
10 SEPTEMBER 2007

Sushi
Sushi is a sort of anti-food. Yes, they killed it, but then felt so guilty they didn't want to cook it!

GRAHAM NORTON
13 SEPTEMBER 2004

Text messages

So this man I was seeing texted me on a frequent basis, and I would text back. Eventually we graduated to the use of a telecommunications system and I went off him entirely. Isn't it funny how life works out?

JULIAN CLARY
30 JULY 2001

Allergies

I'm actually allergic to mobile phones. This bloke on the train was making so many calls it was just like being in his office! I wouldn't have minded, but he had me doing photocopying and making coffee.

TONY HAWKS
24 JULY 2000

Answering machine messages

If you want to buy marijuana, press the hash key!

CLEMENT FREUD
3 SEPTEMBER 2001

If women ruled the world

If women ruled the world George W. Bush would be stacking supermarket shelves!

PAUL MERTON
23 AUGUST 2004

It-girls

Tara Palmer-Tomkinson, Tamara Beckwith, Lady Victoria Hervey, they are all It-girls. They have little funny stick limbs, hardly big enough to hold up a glass of champagne, and yet somehow they can! God, they're brave!

GRAHAM NORTON
11 AUGUST 2003

The dawn of the millennium should have been a cause of great joy for all those associated with *Just a Minute*. The game, the seeds of which had been planted in a schoolroom in the 1930s and bloomed onto the airwaves in the 1960s, had survived and flourished into a new century. That surely deserved a celebration. However, as the year 2000 approached, the fun we were generating was laced with great sadness.

In February 1999 we lost Derek Nimmo after a dreadful accident at his home three months previously. Derek critically injured himself in a fall down stairs in early December that left him in a coma. He did eventually regain consciousness but was never able to leave hospital. Derek was only 68 years old when he died. Far too young.

Nine months on from Derek's death, at the age of 79, Ian Messiter finally lost his ten-year fight against the illness that had forced him to step away from the *Just a Minute* stage. Within months of the loss of Ian, Peter Jones fell seriously ill and was soon gone, also aged 79.

Thankfully, the fourth member of the show's classic quartet, Clement Freud, continued to entertain us for a further nine years after Peter died. In strictly chronological terms, therefore, it may seem out of place at the beginning of this chapter on *Just a Minute* in the 21st century to address Clement's death alongside those of Derek and Peter. To me it is absolutely appropriate. With Kenneth Williams, whose sad loss I wrote about earlier, they formed a close-knit and wonderful team. That is how I think of them still, as a team, and that is how I would like to say goodbye. To Derek, Peter and Clement together.

I miss them deeply.

Derek remained the same wonderful performer, right up to his last appearance in a broadcast of 22 March 1999. On the subject of 'The Information Highway' Derek reminded us of his entrepreneurial skills in staging theatrical performances around the world.

Derek: I must say it has changed my life considerably because I put on plays in places like, say, Jakarta, and if I want to send a poster down the line, full of the design and colour, I use the information highway. And somehow or other, how it works I have no idea, sitting on a desk in Indonesia, out it pops and they can then print the artwork from it. It is an absolute miracle. [WHISTLE AND APPLAUSE]

Later in that final show, Derek entertains his many fans with a trademark play on words that sums up his enormous contribution to *Just a Minute* over his 307 radio broadcasts. The subject is 'Patois'.

Derek: When I'm in south-west France at the Dordogne, one of my favourite things to eat is *patois de foie gras*. [HUGE LAUGH FROM AUDIENCE AND PANEL FOLLOWED BY ENTHUSIASTIC APPLAUSE] It is absolutely delicious. On the other hand if you're travelling in the ... [WHISTLE AND MORE APPLAUSE]

Finally, in almost his last contribution to the game, on the topic of 'Buffer', Derek signs off in fine style, combining travel, ageing and his unfailing gentlemanly instincts, before being challenged for repetition.

Derek: Sometimes a buffer state can be very useful to the country which actually is the buffer. For instance Thailand. It was never colonised or occupied because it stood between British Burma, India and Malaya on one side, and Vietnam, Laos and Cambodia, which were French, on the other. And that was greatly to their benefit. I myself am rapidly becoming a silly old buffer. [AUDIENCE LAUGH] Now it's not something

that I contemplated some years ago when I started doing this programme. But I *find myself*, I still stand up and let ladies sit down …
BUZZ

Of the four classic regulars, it was Peter Jones (with 324 radio broadcasts) who slowed down most notably towards the end, preferring to sit out much of the cut and thrust of the show's banter in favour of stepping in at the last moment with an apt and witty comment.

Here he is in a broadcast from 13 July 1998. I have given Peter the subject 'Entrepreneurs', and he opens with the following statement. 'Richard Branson comes to mind immediately. And an entrepreneur is someone who has a wonderful idea, and is able to persuade other people to carry it out, and carry it through …' Peter is successfully challenged by comedian Stephen Frost for the repetition of 'carry' but manages to win the subject back briefly, before again falling, this time to Paul Merton who takes up the topic.

Paul: Well, I suppose, entrepreneurs, as Peter said, are people who have ideas and then get other people to carry them out …
BUZZ
Nicholas: Peter challenged. [LAUGHTER FROM THE PANEL AND MYSELF]
Peter: He's just done what I …
Stephen: [INCREDULOUSLY AND WHILE LAUGHING] He's just copying exactly what you said!!
Paul: Including repetition!!!
Nicholas: [THROUGH MY LAUGHTER] Yes! He copied it word for word, including repetition.
Peter: I've thought for years he's been using my material!
[HUGE LAUGHTER FROM PANEL AND AUDIENCE FOLLOWED BY LOUD APPLAUSE]

In July 1999 I am giving the final scores when again Peter steps in with a very entertaining line to finish off the show with a big laugh as he so often did. It is no wonder he was so popular.

> **Nicholas:** Jenny Eclair was leading for quite a long time, and she gave incredible value as she always does, but she did finish up only just in fourth place and Peter Jones came from nowhere and he finished up just ahead of Jenny …
> **Peter:** I came from London! [BIG LAUGH]

Clement Freud died on 15 April 2009, appropriately for someone whose professional life was so active, at his desk. He was 84 years old, and only the month before had appeared in his 541st *Just a Minute* radio show, an incredible achievement. He, like Derek, remained true to his unique and humorous approach to the game right up until the end. In his final recording Clement is joined by a newcomer, the comic performer and writer David Mitchell, plus Sheila Hancock and Paul Merton.

Clement is speaking here in the slightly slower manner he adopted in the later years, which helped him to keep going. The subject is 'After-Dinner Speaking', something in which he was expert, and naturally he manages to start a list.

> **Clement:** Let me begin by saying that I am still available [AUDIENCE LAUGH] and very recently, like last Tuesday, I made an after-dinner speech. I will repeat it now. 'Emperor,' I said, 'Your Majesty, Royal Highnesses, Dukes, Earls, Marquises …'
> BUZZ

David is challenging for hesitation, which I accept, much to Clement's annoyance. Clement's competitive streak clearly remains undiminished, which is just as it should be given how much that side of his character has contributed to the entertainment of *Just a Minute* over so many years.

Later in the show, Clement reveals just how infuriated he feels at having been interrupted earlier by David. He has just successfully challenged Sheila to win the highly appropriate subject of 'My Ego'.

Clement: The word 'ee-go' is often pronounced 'eg-oh', which I actually prefer. *The Ego and the Id*, a book for which I get royalties [BIG AUDIENCE LAUGH], written by my grandfather, is an *extremely* interesting volume which I would urge everyone to purchase …
   BUZZ
Nicholas: Sheila Hancock challenged.
Sheila: It's not extremely interesting. It's one of the most boring books I've ever read in my life! Deviation! [AUDIENCE LAUGH]
Nicholas: Well, it's a difficult one. I mean he *thinks* that everybody thinks it's interesting. I mean if you will write something, you like to think that. It's a very difficult one for me to make a decision.
Sheila: All right, let him 'ave it! [AUDIENCE LAUGH]
Nicholas: I'll give him the benefit of the doubt.
Clement: No, I want more than that. [BIG AUDIENCE LAUGH]
Nicholas: All right. So, Clement, we give you an incorrect challenge and 15 seconds, 'My Ego', starting now.
Clement: 'Egomania' is a word which flourishes in our …
   BUZZ
Nicholas: David challenged.
David: I thought a little hesitation.
Nicholas: Yes.
Clement: I, I, I have a pause between words! [AUDIENCE LAUGH] And I've been doing this for some 60 years. [EVEN BIGGER AUDIENCE LAUGHTER] And for someone who's only been here for ten minutes … [LAUGHTER COMBINED WITH GOOD-NATURED BOOS] Okay, *five* minutes! [HUGE LAUGH FROM AUDIENCE AND PANEL]

Alongside Kenneth Williams, the contributions made to *Just a Minute* by Derek, Peter and Clement cannot be overstated. They brought enormous fun and erudition to every show in which they appeared, a rare gift. In this farewell, I think it is most fitting to leave it to their fellow players to describe each of them, sometimes with heartfelt honesty and sometimes with tongues firmly in cheeks. That, after all, has always been the *Just a Minute* way. Starting now ...

Derek Nimmo
(19 September 1930 to 24 February 1999)

From 29 December 1967:

> **Nicholas:** Sheila Hancock, would you talk for just a minute, please, on the subject of 'Derek Nimmo', starting now.
> **Sheila:** This is a subject I know a great deal about it because I lived with Derek intimately for six weeks. Well, for the sake of his wife, I will add that I meant during the six weeks in which we did *The Bedsit Girl*. Derek is very kinky about yogurt! Instead of having a coffee break he used to have a yogurt break during *The Bedsit Girl*. He's also inclined to be hesitant, devious, very devious. He has a stutter, he's tall, handsome ...

From 2 March 1971, again on the subject of 'Derek Nimmo', with Clement and Kenneth contributing:

> **Clement:** Derek Nimmo lives rather humbly in a flat ...
> BUZZ
> **Nicholas:** Kenneth Williams, why have you challenged?
> **Kenneth:** Completely untrue! He's never been humble in his life!! He's the most arrogant man I know!!!

More than 40 years later, on 6 February 2012, 'Derek Nimmo' is again the topic, with Gyles Brandreth speaking:

> **Gyles:** Ah, Derek Robert Nimmo would indeed have been here

back in 1967. Born in … '30 was the year, and then lived on until the end of the century, died before his time. Began life in Liverpool, became an actor, and then found his nose to be too large and became a comedic player as a result of it. Famous, of course, for playing clergymen, especially in *All Gas and Gaiters*. A glorious fellow, a *bon viveur*, a raconteur, and a man who could twiddle his toes.

Peter Jones
(12 June 1920 to 10 April 2000)

On 29 January 1980, the subject of 'Peter Jones' is tackled first by Aimi MacDonald and then later in the round by Clement, and finally Kenneth:

Aimi: [WITH A STRING OF INTERRUPTIONS] Aw, I think Peter Jones is so divine. When I first started doing a show called *Just a Minute* I, to be very honest, was petrified. I didn't know what would be expected of me. I was scared stiff. What rescued me, of course, was the fact that Peter Jones was ever present. The others don't know that I have it in my contract that Peter does the show with me. So that when Kenneth Williams turns up and says, 'Why do we have these dumb blondes on the show?' Peter comes to my rescue.

Clement: Peter Jones is really one of the very best chaps I have ever met. I worship at the shrine of Mr Jones regardless of whether this be in Brighton or St John's Wood, where he has his town residence.

Kenneth: Well, he's due to have a store named after him as a matter of fact!!!

Clement Freud
(24 April 1924 to 15 April 2009)

From 23 February 1968. Derek is laughing his way through the subject of 'Things I Warn My Children About', with everyone thoroughly enjoying themselves, Clement perhaps most of all.

> **Derek:** The thing that I first warn my children about is Clement Freud. I manage to do this really by teaching them simple nursery rhymes like, 'Little Miss Muffet sat on a tuffet, eating her curds and whey. Then came a big Freud, and sat down beside and frightened Miss Muffet away.' A little later on I manage to continue the education of my children, warning them about Clement Freud by telling them about the teddy bears' picnic. I mean, 'Don't go down to the woods today, because today's the day Clement Freud has one of his dreadful picnics.'

From 2 March 1971. It is Derek who again does the describing, having been given the subject of 'Clement Freud', with Kenneth rounding the moment off in fine, disparaging style.

> **Derek:** Clement Freud is a *ra-ther ba-lding, bo-ring, el-derly* gastronome with five children, three houses within the British Isles and a flat on top of the Bunny Club. [BIG AUDIENCE LAUGH] What he does there has not been revealed to man nor beast! He writes for the *Financial Times*. He makes *vast sums of money* in things like the *Daily Mail*, raised by very devious means indeed, which I'd like to tell you about but he might sue me for all sorts of nasty things afterwards. He owns racehorses and restaurants and he's *far too successful*. I am very jealous of him in fact altogether. But sometimes on a moonlit night in Venice a different Clement Freud emerges.
> BUZZ
> **Nicholas:** Kenneth Williams, why have you challenged?
> **Kenneth:** Deviation! On a moonlit night, he's just the same!!!
> [BIG LAUGH]

During a 29 January 1980 broadcast, when given the subject 'Clement Freud', Kenneth takes the opportunity to praise his friend in what I am certain is a genuine show of affection and admiration expressed with real enthusiasm … before Peter Jones interrupts Kenneth's flow with a correct challenge for repetition. 'Disgraceful' and 'petty' is Kenneth's unsurprising reaction.

> **Kenneth:** What a formidable task to describe a man, a raconteur, orator, wit, a great charmer and handsome to boot!!! This is a difficult, onerous indeed, position, but I will endeavour to meet it. For not only in public life is this man enlightening as well as fun, but as a host immeasurable. We can't say in words that would really do justice to this man's culinary brilllance!

At the end of the opening show of the first series broadcast after Clement died, I made a short announcement in honour of my friend. Below I have paraphrased it, because it applies equally to Kenneth, Derek and Peter.

> We miss them very much. Thank you. Let's give them a final round of applause for all the years they were in the show and their major contributions: Kenneth Williams, Derek Nimmo, Peter Jones and Clement Freud!

Given how much each one of these three players of the game enjoyed talking and entertaining, I think they should provide their own final words too, starting with Derek Nimmo.

Twice during his time on *Just a Minute*, Derek informed us of his favourite epitaph, although he did admit that it was not personally terribly applicable. Even so, he thought it clever and funny, and accordingly it has its place here.

> **Derek:**
> *Here lives the grave of Elizabeth Charlotte,*
> *Born a virgin, died a harlot.*
> *She was a virgin, aye, at seventeen,*
> *A very rare thing, in Aberdeen.*

Just over a year before he died, Peter Jones offered the following poignant opinion on death when speaking on 'The Final Demand', generating laughter from the audience throughout.

> **Peter:** Well … the final demand is usually uttered by the Grim Reaper himself, who says, 'Follow me!' Now then, when he says this to myself, I shall probably decline the invitation because I don't want to go into the next world, as he would no doubt have me do, because I don't believe that it's going to be a great deal better than the one I'm living in now. So I shan't agree to the final demand and he may easily get the sack!

Peter also suggested what he felt would be an appropriate epitaph.

> **Peter:** Oh, it's one in America and the first line I've forgotten but after that it went,
> *And let your breezes blow free,*
> *I held on to mine and they killed me.*
> I thought that was very sweet … particularly for someone who suffered from dyspepsia or any kind of gastronomic trouble!!

Clement Freud twice offered his thoughts on how he would like his epitaph to read. On the first occasion, 29 January 2001, it was simple and brought that show to a tumultuous end, with roaring laughter and ringing applause.

> **Clement:** I think just my name, the date of my death and best before!

By August 2006, Clement had given the issue more thought, the results of which proved to be equally entertaining. Clement leaves his final message hanging here, presumably intending for whoever is reading it to add for themselves, '… when the final whistle went'. A perfect example of Clement's wonderfully dry sense of humour.

Clement: When you're my sort of age, you think less about immortality than mortality. And I have spent many hours of my time trying to find a legend to put on my tombstone, which originally was going to be, 'He never insulted anyone unintentionally.' I have now decided that the ideal message to put on this stone over my grave is, 'He was not speaking ...'

How did *Just a Minute* continue to prosper into the 21st century?

When people ask me if I can identify one aspect of the show that is responsible for it remaining successful and popular for so long, I always reply with the same answer: it is because we generate fun.

Noël Coward said that 'work is more fun than fun'. That is a very apt quote in relation to *Just a Minute*. The players who appear on the show do so primarily because they enjoy it, and the positive, uplifting energy which is produced is transmitted to the audience and listeners. Ensuring this continues to flourish, however, is an active exercise. It does not happen by chance. Instead it is an ongoing process of re-evaluation that began right from the early days, spearheaded then by Ian Messiter and David Hatch.

One of the first elements of those early shows they saw fit to let go, as I have previously mentioned, was the idea of penalty rounds where certain words such as 'and' or 'I' were banned. Appealing to the audience for their decision on certain challenges should probably also have been dropped at the same time. I was encouraged to make these appeals but they seem very amateurish now, interrupting the pace of those shows. Somehow they struggled through until the 1980s.

The unwritten 15-second rule is an interesting illustration of how the game has evolved.

In the first couple of shows there were a lot of challenges because nobody really understood what on earth was going on. We were learning as we went along and it resulted in very irritating programmes, full of interruptions. The balance of the shows was wrong. Then as the panellists began to grasp the rules and develop their individual styles, challenges became less frequent, more haphazard. Basically, the players talked for longer. This is how the game *should* be played, seemed to be the consensus. That was certainly Clement's opinion, and in order to facilitate this approach, the unwritten rule was introduced to allow whoever was speaking to find their flow.

I now think that is alien to the whole concept of the show.

We allowed the game to lurch too far in the direction of giving players the opportunity to show off their erudition, with challenges becoming secondary. We overlooked the fact that much of the laughter is generated by challenges. By the mid 1970s we had to find a way back, and the 15-second rule was dropped. Not that everyone seems to have been aware of the change. Or perhaps they just did not want to accept it.

The following is an extract from a broadcast on 22 May 1979, with a rather tetchy Kenneth Williams about to speak on the subject 'The Most Extraordinary Person I Have Ever Met'.

Kenneth: The most extraordinary person I ever met was actually covered in … [KENNETH BREAKS OFF TO SHOUT ACROSS AT PETER JONES] Don't do that! He's doing it deliberately!!

BUZZ

Nicholas: Peter Jones has challenged.

Peter: Hesitation!

Kenneth: No, I wasn't hesitating. I said, 'Don't do that!' [POINTING AT PETER] He's just sitting there, looking at me and making funny faces and trying to put me off.

Nicholas: I know! And *he* succeeded.

Kenneth: Ah, that's not in the rules. The rules of the game state that you should be allowed to proceed!

Clement: No, no, no!

Kenneth: It does!!!

Nicholas: There's nothing about being allowed to proceed!

Kenneth: It does! It says in the book, without hindrance! It's in the book!!

Nicholas: Now there's a book about it! You're making up new rules as you go along!

The balance today feels correct. We have a number of regular players who are very experienced and are unlikely to make mistakes right at the beginning. If they do, the others may overlook a small error, but they certainly will not let a major one go by. That is absolutely as it should be. It means that when there are early challenges, because it is such a rare event, it is much more interesting. People react very well when it happens.

The definition of a hesitation is another good example of how Ian and David tweaked the basics of the game early on. Initially, challenges on that basis were made as though the sin was for a *hesitating thought*, a break in the logical narrative of what was being said, rather than a *verbal pause*. That is far too woolly and the rule was quickly tightened to give the game a more robust structure.

A major shift in the rules introduced by around Series 4 was that the panellists were allowed to repeat any of the words in the title of the subject. This helped the pace of the games tremendously.

Strange as it may seem now, the repetition of words in the first few shows did not always result in a challenge, and if it did the challenger was not always successful. Think back to Derek Nimmo's attempt in the pilot to interrupt Clement as he talked on 'Knitting a Cable Stitch Jumper' with the words 'purl one, plain two, purl two, plain three, purl three, plain one'. Clement retained the subject. As I mentioned at the beginning of the book, had Derek challenged them on the repetition of an *idea* that had already been introduced he probably would have been successful. Once again, this was the more cerebral approach favoured by Clement – the repetition of a concept constituting the error rather than of an actual word.

Ian and David realised this was an untenable situation as the lack of precision meant no one could properly follow what was going on, and they made it clear that words were not allowed to be repeated.

That too caused problems, however, because initially players were still not permitted to repeat the words contained in the subject. This proved extremely inhibiting and resulted in the rules being changed.

Clever players learned to use this development to their advantage in order to help them find their way into a subject. Here is Derek Nimmo talking in September 1982 on the subject, 'Things of Mine Refused by the Garbage Collectors'. Ironically, it is Clement Freud who challenges for hesitation at the end here, while Derek is listing.

Derek: I rather like having subjects like the things of mine refused by garbage collectors, because you are allowed to repeat that line, the things of mine refused by garbage collectors. And if you get a long question like this, it occupies most of the minute you are trying to speak. Now some of the things of mine that have been refused by garbage collectors include an old crow's nest, garden refuse, cast wheels, rabbit hutches …

Derek stays just within acceptable boundaries here, but repeating the subject *ad infinitum* is not allowed, a refinement that, perhaps inevitably, can lead to friction. In this May 1990 broadcast Wendy Richard pushes the rule beyond its limits while talking on the subject of 'Coo'. She is not happy with my ruling.

Wendy: I'm not an expert on 'coo' but I do believe that pigeons coo. In fact some mornings I can hear them, they wake me up, just sitting on the window ledges going coo. They seem to spend all day just going coo coo coo coo. [AUDIENCE LAUGH]
BUZZ
Nicholas: Clement Freud challenged.
Clement: [LAUGHING] I think that was a repetition!
Nicholas: [I AM ALSO LAUGHING] I think that was …
Wendy: I'm allowed to say coo!
Nicholas: I know it is the subject on the card, Wendy, but you can't keep going forever. [BIG AUDIENCE LAUGH] You could go for a whole minute saying, 'coo coo coo coo coo coo

coo coo'.

Wendy: I wasn't going to do that! Neither was I going to do a list like some other members of the team! [AUDIENCE LAUGH AND APPLAUD]

This issue continues to cause a degree of controversy. In an incident reminiscent of Wendy's 'cooing', from a July 2003 programme, Paul Merton wins the subject 'Spam' from Clement Freud who has been listing various ways in which that foodstuff can be prepared. Charles Collingwood and Tony Hawks find themselves caught up in the ensuing debate, with Tony introducing some welcome humour.

Paul: There's a Monty Python sketch featuring Terry Jones at a transport café where the menu consisted of nothing but spam. So when the customer came in and said, 'What have you got?' She said, 'Spam, spam, spam, spam, spam, spam, spam, spam, spam, spam, spam, spam, spam, spam …' [AUDIENCE LAUGHING]

BUZZ

Paul: I'm quoting from the sketch!

Nicholas: I know. Clement has challenged you though.

Clement: I think that's too often.

Nicholas: I think that's too often.

Paul: That's rich! I didn't say I had spam in Greenwich, Norwich, Cambridge … [AUDIENCE LAUGH]

Nicholas: You know after all the years you've played the game, you can't say any word indefinitely, Paul. So 25 seconds, Clement, with you on 'Spam', starting now.

Clement: There are people who find spam unpalatable, even unappetising. And I suggest that pickles, chutney, macerated cucumber, gherkins, capers, all sorts of condiments and spices are extremely …

BUZZ

Nicholas: Paul has challenged you.

Paul: Well, we got a list of condiments and spices, we've moved away from the spam!

Clement: They're with spam.

Paul: We're talking about other foodstuffs.

Nicholas: He did establish that you can have all these condiments with spam.

Paul: Oh, but that's just ridiculous! You might as well say all the people who have eaten spam, Winston Churchill, Thomas … Where do you go with that? You've got to stick to the subject.

Tony: Charles and I have decided not to play in this round!

Charles: And having just said spam 46 times I don't think …

Paul: I stuck to the subject, didn't I!!

Charles: I don't think you speak from a position of strength, quite frankly, Paul.

Paul: I speak from a very strong position, I didn't deviate or hesitate …

Tony: Charles, I've got some cards here! Come on, let's have a game of cards!

The audience are enjoying this exchange and the banter continues in a similar vein until eventually Clement completes the round.

As *Just a Minute* deals in the world of sound, a further aspect of the rule that players are allowed to repeat the words of the subject required some clarification. It does not matter how a word is spelt, the key issue is how it is pronounced. For instance, if the subject is 'My Favourite Jeans' a clever player may decide to twist the meaning and speak on his or her favourite 'genes'. Such a tactic is perfectly permissible and has generated many inventive and amusing rounds over the years.

...on the subject of Jokes

Attempting to tell an actual joke on *Just a Minute* is really quite ambitious, for the simple reason that the essence of many jokes lies in the repeating of certain words. However, skilled players of the game have over the years demonstrated that it is possible (with just a touch of repetition). Here is a selection of my favourites.

Irish humour: My favourite example of Irish humour is the Irish gentleman who went to a foreman on a building site and said, 'I want a job.' And this supervisor replied, 'All you Irish are the same, you don't even know the difference between a joist and a girder.' To which the Irishman replies, 'Yes, I do. Joyce wrote *Ulysses* and Goethe wrote *Faust!*' (Clement Freud, 16 May 1981)

Creatures from the deep: Having been handed a long-tentacled, fishy thing by a friend, I said, 'What's this?' And he said 'It's the sick squid I owe you.' (Tim Rice, 25 April 1981)

Handyman: A man goes for a job on a building site and the bloke says, 'What do you do?' And he says, 'I'm a handyman.' He says, 'Can you build a brick wall?' And he said, 'No.' 'Can you mend plumbing? And he says, 'I can't do that.' And he says, 'In what sense are you a handyman?' And he says, 'I only live around the corner!' (Paul Merton, 22 June 1998)

Losing the plot: The Beckhams were staying at the Savoy Hotel and got a taxi to London airport. The driver said, 'Did you find anywhere good to eat?' To which the great Manchester United and Real Madrid footballer said, 'We did actually. Give me the name of a station.' The taxi driver said, 'Waterloo?' He said, 'No.' 'King's Cross?' He said, 'No.' 'Paddington?' He said 'No.' 'Victoria?' He said, 'Oh yes! Victoria, where did we have dinner?' (Clement Freud, 4 August 2008)

Making an impression: I went to the doctor and said, 'I broke my arm in three places.' He said, 'Don't go to those destinations!' (Charles Collingwood impersonating Tommy Cooper, 7 September 2009)

My favourite joke: Two flies are playing football in a saucer. One says to the other, 'Practice!' He says, 'Why?' 'Because next week we are in the cup!' (Paul Merton, 9 March 2009)

When Ian Messiter's health required him to take a step back from regular day-to-day involvement in *Just a Minute* at the end of the 1980s, the onus fell on others – primarily the producers and myself – to ensure that the rules and approach to the game were continually assessed, honed and tweaked in order for recordings to remain fresh and dynamic. It is a huge credit to the genius of Ian's creation, its deceptive simplicity as I have described it previously, that such reinterpretations and adjustments were possible while still remaining true to his original concept.

For instance, I reintroduced the business of awarding bonus points for clever, but incorrect, challenges. I say 'reintroduced' because the idea of bonus points did exist during the early shows but then drifted out of usage. This was during the period when the four regulars became so adept at the game, and the rules more precise, that frivolous challenges designed purely to generate laughs featured far less.

However, as the new generation of younger players began to emerge during the 1990s, I felt it was important to encourage witty and sharp contributions by the awarding of points based purely on entertainment value rather than a strict interpretation of the rules. This small innovation has, I believe, helped nurture the overriding sense of fun that prevails today.

The one actual rule change introduced during this period of the 1990s concerned the challenge of deviation. The rules of the game originally stated that players were not allowed to hesitate, repeat or deviate *from the subject*. I then broadened this strict interpretation to encompass deviation *generally*. The idea here was once again to develop the comic aspects of the game by giving panellists confidence and scope to interject with bizarre and clever challenges: deviation from the English language, for instance. These generate laughs in themselves, and also require an adjudication that often elicits strong audience reactions. All this contributes to the entertainment on offer.

Unsurprisingly, this development did not meet with universal approval, and the complaints did not come from Clement Freud on this occasion. The BBC received letters of protest from ardent fans, complaining that we had altered the rules. As a result I was asked to appear on the *Feedback* programme of Radio 4 to defend the decision. I was happy to do so as I felt strongly that the change was essential, and explained as clearly as I could that in my view for *Just a Minute* to achieve longevity it had to undergo a process of continuous assessment. Otherwise, shows risked becoming stale and uninteresting. I feel certain that this ongoing and vital process is the reason why *Just a Minute*, now in its sixth decade, remains one of Radio 4's flagship comedy programmes.

The introduction of bright new talent has been a significant feature of *Just a Minute* since the 1990s. In the new century that policy has been accelerated, with many skilled comics and performers joining the ranks of panellists.

Stephen Frost and Linda Smith are two of the talented comedians who made their first appearances during the 1990s and continued to entertain *Just a Minute* audiences into the new millennium.

Stephen, or Steve as he is also known professionally, brought an offbeat humour that he must have developed through his ability for improvisation. You never quite knew in which direction Stephen would take a subject. For a spontaneous show such as ours, that is a wonderful asset.

Here is Stephen in one of his early appearances, from February 1995, talking on 'Odd First Names'.

Stephen: When I was at school, there was a boy who was called Three. [AUDIENCE LAUGH] And that is what I call an odd first name. [MORE LAUGHTER] He also had a brother called Five and Seven. And I asked them, 'Why did their parents call you that, it just doesn't add up!' [BIG AUDIENCE LAUGH]

In July 1998, having just handed Stephen the subject of 'First Words', I certainly do not expect the introduction of a tale from classical Rome.

Stephen: I think most parents in the world can't wait to hear the first words of their offspring. Will it be 'Mama' or 'Dada'? Perhaps [HOWLING] 'Ah-ooooooooo!' in the case of Romulus and Remus. [AUDIENCE LAUGHTER]

Nor do I anticipate in the same broadcast, which we recorded in Loughborough, that the subject 'Shires' will produce a Terry-Thomas impersonation.

Stephen: We had a very well-spoken gym master at school who would say after the game, 'Get into the *shires*, will you?' [BIG AUDIENCE LAUGH AT STEPHEN'S POSH ACCENT SOUNDING AS THOUGH HE IS SAYING 'SHOWERS'] And of course we did. He reminded me a bit of Terry-Thomas, who used to say, 'You absolute shire!' as well. [EVEN BIGGER AUDIENCE LAUGH]

Stephen's focus tended to be on creating laughs above being competitive, but that did not prevent him from enjoying winning some points with smart challenges. In August 2001 Clement Freud is speaking on 'Health Food'.

Clement: Health food is one of the great growth industries of the moment. Go down any road or street or mews or crescent, and you will find health food emporia.

BUZZ

Nicholas: Steve, you challenged.

Steve: Deviation! You can't go down a crescent, you go round it! [AUDIENCE CHEER AND APPLAUD]

Linda Smith, who very sadly died far too young, at the age of 48 in 2006 after a four-year battle with cancer, was a natural comic broadcaster, with a quirky view on life. Linda won legions of fans for her appearances on *Just a Minute* and *The News Quiz*, and in 2002 was voted the 'Wittiest Living Person' by Radio 4 listeners. It is easy to see why from this small sample from her 34 radio appearances on the show.

On the subject of 'Feng Shui' from 7 August 2000:

Linda: Feng shui, which should be correctly pronounced 'a number 39', is the ancient oriental art of getting money off of simpletons! [BIG LAUGH] It involves someone coming to your house and saying, 'Oh, the sofa in front of the front door, that's *really* bad karma!' If I want furniture moved, I get Pickfords [BIGGER LAUGH] not some dopey hippy called Crispin in a kaftan. [HUGE LAUGH]

Here she is on 29 January 2001 enjoying a touch of celebrity comment while painting a vivid picture with her excellent command of language. The subject is 'The Shopping Channel'.

Linda: The Shopping Channel is a source of many delights, not least of which is the chance of catching a glimpse of Joan Rivers, who has had so much plastic surgery that this woman resembles a Siamese cat walking into a gale! [HUGE AUDIENCE LAUGHTER]

Eight months later, in August, Linda is talking on 'Hedgehogs' and it is a celebrity chef who finds himself in her sights.

Linda: Hedgehogs have lovely spiky haircuts, which look so cute on them and so tragic on Gary Rhodes! [BIG LAUGH]

Finally, here is an example of Linda's ability to focus on a simple aspect of modern life and to give it a unique spin with an entertaining observation. The subject is 'Junk Mail', in a show from 18 February 2002.

Linda: Junk mail, I don't think there's any such thing as junk mail. Only unlicensed cab firms you haven't met yet. [HUGE AUDIENCE LAUGH AND APPLAUSE]

The year 2000 saw the debuts of two very popular and talented comics, both of whom continue to make highly valued contributions on *Just a Minute* – comedian, writer and broadcaster Sue Perkins made her first appearance on 17 July, followed by actor and comic Ross Noble just over a month later.

With her brilliant, analytical mind, Sue has established herself as a much-loved regular on the show. She is an intelligent person and she uses her academic brain to great effect, talking at pace with wit, agility and precision.

Now that we know each other well, Sue is also very cheeky to me, sometimes with quite a naughty undertow ('You are very strict, Nicholas,' she might say, 'but I like it!), which produces a great deal of laughter. Like all the current regulars, Sue knows I will not be offended when she has fun at my expense.

During a television appearance in March 2012, Sue is handed a perfect opportunity for just such a gag. Quite rightly, she takes full advantage. The subject is, well, 'Nicholas Parsons'.

Sue: Nicholas Parsons was born before records began, but we do know he was friends with Methuselah. Aged 24, he struck a deal with Mephistopheles so that he would never age.

[BIG LAUGH]

The extent of Sue's imagination is daunting, and she is very capable of calling on it to paint a totally fictional, but very funny, picture of me. Here, the subject is 'Power Struggles' from February 2013.

> **Sue:** *Just a Minute* is one of the eternal power struggles. Us *mere* panellists vying for supremacy, but Nicholas overseeing it like the Lord of Misrule! [BIG AUDIENCE LAUGH] Ultimately he controls the show – it's Machiavellian but you'd never know because he dresses like very much the urban dandy!! [MORE LAUGHTER] He operates his own strings. There is no puppet master!! He rules supreme! And we know it. Afterwards when we are getting into the giant jacuzzi together [HUGE LAUGH] we often look upon him as a father figure. He's gentle then, less commandeering. [LAUGHTER CONTINUES]

Speed of delivery is one of Sue's trademark tactics, used to bamboozle her fellow panellists. Frankly, however, bamboozling is often not required. Sue possesses an ability to launch herself into complicated stories and descriptions without repeating or deviating, and yet still managing to retain a logical sense to what she is saying ('logical' in *Just a Minute* terms, that is). Sometimes, however, even Sue has to breathe.

In this example from a 21 February 2005 broadcast, Sue manages to talk quite wonderfully for 54 seconds before collapsing in need of air. She is granted a small element of leniency towards the end, as everyone wants to hear what is coming next, and for Sue to complete the minute if she can. Other than a slight repetition it is an extraordinary effort, one that the audience, panel and I adore all the way through. The subject is 'Smoothies'.

> **Sue:** The best way to make a smoothie is take Clive Owen, Pierce Brosnan and Alastair Stewart, pop them into a food processor, and blitz for nineteen seconds. At the end of which

there'll be a charming orange puree, which stinks somewhat
of cheese and has a redolent whiff of cologne. When drinking
it, you'll be transported magically to the casinos of Monaco,
where you'll want to put down chips and stare into the cleavages
of buxom ladies, all called Candy. 'More!' you shout, as this
breathless whirl of excitement carries you on through, up the
stairway where a man in a dinner jacket looks longingly and
says, 'Come this way.' He may be Russian, who knows? It's too
early to say. His Middle-East-European accent luring you into
a strange world, down again into the recesses, to an odd serial-
killer-like figure with a strange pistol in his pocket, who points it
at you and says …

At this point Sue grinds to a halt, virtually collapsing onto her desk
having run out of steam. Paul presses his buzzer just before Sue tries
desperately to retrieve the situation by claiming her momentary
pause was necessary, '… because he's mute!' It is a valiant effort, but
she did hesitate, leaving Paul with a correct challenge and six seconds
remaining to the end of the round.

The following is a brilliant précis of 'Chick Lit', the subject Sue
has 30 seconds to speak on during a broadcast of 21 September 2009.
It is a remarkably accurate description of this modern fiction genre,
although perhaps Sue would have altered her final remarks had *Fifty
Shades of Grey* been published at the time! It is perfectly possible that
Sue could face an early challenge for deviation here, as there is no
mention of anything related to literature until right at the end. Her
fellow panellists, however, are happy to overlook this in favour of
enjoying what Sue has to say.

Sue: Alex is a doctor, slack-jawed and ready to roll. *She* doesn't
have a job, but wants babies. Oh, my ovaries are drying. Must
find a man. Where can I go? The supermarket? I don't care.
I'll travel miles because a baby will take my mind off the lack
of personality that the writer has ascribed to me. He looks hot.
What does he do? Is that a stethoscope? Touch me but maybe

don't, because let's face it, I want to widen the audience that buys these books and pornography will simply detract from the overall theme.
[WHISTLE FOLLOWED BY WILDLY ENTHUSIASTIC APPLAUSE AND CHEERS]

Given how smart she is, and the fact she was President of Cambridge University Footlights, it is no surprise that Sue is not only a fast and clever talker, she is also a sharp comedian who delivers punchlines with perfect timing.
In August 2009 she is given the subject 'Shabby Chic'.

Sue: Shabby chic is the term used by the *Sunday Times Style* magazine to describe wealthy people who want to look like rough sleepers. There seems to be a bizarre trend amongst the aristocratic to wear clothes that look as if they have been sourced from a bin. And therefore wander about with a cravat smelling of wee! [BIG AUDIENCE LAUGH]

Sue's politics occasionally make an appearance in *Just a Minute*, never stridently and always with the goal of adding to the humour of the show. Here in May 2012 it is the Education Secretary who is on the receiving end of her gag, when the subject 'Sloth' comes up.

Sue: Sloth is one of the seven deadly sins along with envy, pride and thinking that Michael Gove is an acceptable human being.

It was thanks to Sue that I 'enjoyed' one of my most embarrassing moments on *Just a Minute*.
The scene is the BBC Radio Theatre in 2011. We are coming to the close of our second recording, which Sue has won. Alongside her on the panel is Paul Merton, Stephen Fry, and a newcomer, broadcaster and journalist Fi Glover. Sue has been on dynamite form, much to the delight of four ardent fans who are sitting in the front row of the audience. Just as I begin my wind-up they can hardly contain

themselves and begin shifting excitedly in their seats, keen to show appreciation of Sue's victory.

Here is what happens next.

Nicholas: Let me give you the final situation. Paul Merton, who has been known to excel and win on many occasions, finished in a slightly strong fourth place. Fi Glover, who has only played the game once before, filled in a magnificent third place. Stephen Fry, who won last time these four were together, is in second place. But out in the lead, and nearly five or six points ahead of Stephen, is Sue Perkins. So we say Pooh Serkins …
[THE AUDIENCE BURST OUT LAUGHING, AS DO ALL FOUR PANELLISTS]
Stephen: [LAUGHING LOUDLY] We say pooh?? We say pooh!!!
Pooh!!!! [AT THIS POINT STEPHEN, SUE AND PAUL, PLUS SOME AUDIENCE MEMBERS, STRIKE UP A LOUD CHORUS]
Stephen, Sue, Paul: Pooh! Pooh! Pooh! Pooh! Pooh!
Pooh! [THE AUDIENCE AND PANEL ARE NOW IN NEAR HYSTERICS. STRUGGLING WITH MY OWN LAUGHTER, I TRY TO EXPLAIN WHAT HAS HAPPENED]
Nicholas: I'll tell you what actually threw me. I was about to say …
Stephen, Sue, Paul: Pooh! Pooh! Pooh!
Nicholas: … there were four people in the front row there with their hands like that, ready to clap, and it just threw me for a moment!!!

The chanting and laughter continues until I eventually manage to close out the show, which ends in wild applause.

The second debutant in 2000 was, as I mentioned, Ross Noble. Ross is an exceptionally talented comedian, with a very sharp and unusual comic mind, at ease either improvising or delivering stand-up routines. He also has a delightful Northumbrian accent that comes across wonderfully on radio and which Ross drew on with hilarious results when speaking on the subject of 'My Accent' in a broadcast from 26 August 2002.

> **Ross:** Well, for those of you listening on the World Service who don't know England, my accent is the *poshest* in all of the land! This is how people who are really at the top of their professions sound, like the lords and ladies swanning around at garden parties. 'Whey-aye, your Majesty!' will be heard coming across from there. 'I'd very much like to enjoy one of your *champion* Ferrero Rochers!' You might even hear the beautiful refrain of, 'Oooh, Ambassador' with the …
> [WHISTLE, LAUGHTER AND HUGE APPLAUSE]

Since his first show in 2000, Ross has not made quite as many appearances as Sue, for the simple reason that for a number of years he lived in Queensland with his Australian wife, returning to the UK in 2010. Had he been more readily available there is no question Ross would have been invited on many more shows.

Ross and I made a strong connection when we first met. He agreed to be a guest on my Edinburgh Festival Fringe show, the *Nicholas Parsons Happy Hour* in 2001, even though he did not have a performance of his own to promote. We bonded immediately and created a lot of spontaneous laughter. The Pleasance management saw a potential in this unusual pairing and put together a special one-off event in their big venue at the Pleasance Courtyard, which proved to be a success. They called it *Sneakers and Cravat*, a delightful title that conveyed something of the disparity in our appearances.

Ross and I thoroughly enjoyed performing together. It was a delight to be on stage with him, experiencing his incredible improvisation skill at close quarters. A skill, I am delighted to say, that he has subsequently displayed to great effect on *Just a Minute*.

Ross has the ability to take any subject and fly off in a totally unexpected direction. In some respects, his approach is similar to that of Paul Merton, but where Paul tends to launch into the truly surreal, Ross takes his subjects down a more absurd path. Both styles are, without question, hilarious.

Here is Ross talking on the final subject ('How to Treat Pregnant Ladies') in a broadcast from February 2004. Ross not only manages the full minute uninterrupted, he also wins the game. The audience reaction at the end is one of sustained and very loud cheers and applause.

Ross: How to treat pregnant ladies? Well, you could always take them out and buy them some big pants. That's what they like, yes! There you go, love, dive in, help yourself to the largest elasticated wear that you could possibly muster!! But try not to look like a clown, that's very important. How many times have I made that mistake?! Bought a beautiful maternity dress, only to realise they are in fact hooped pantaloons that should be given to Coco and his hilarious mates from the circus! Oh, those poor pregnant ladies as they squirt their flowers at each other, their hats flying off their head as they try and wallpaper the baby's room, hitting each other with planks in the face, falling over as everyone rolls around, confetti everywhere!!! A tiny little car comes in, honking and exploding, as the wheels fly off, right, left and centre. Who would have thought it, that Mothercare would have to provide a special service that would be important ...
[WHISTLE CHEERS AND APPLAUSE]

During a show from July 2003, featuring Clement Freud, Jenny Eclair and Tony Hawks, Ross successfully challenges Clement who has been speaking on 'VAT' for seven seconds. Ross then 'mishears' the subject when I give it to him, and begins talking on the totally unrelated topic of a television show from the 1980s.

Ross: They were a crack commando unit sent to prison for a crime they didn't commit! They would drive around in a big black van with a red ...
BUZZ
Nicholas: Jenny challenged.
Jenny: I'm really sorry, but he did say 'they' three times. 'They'

did that, 'they' did that. But I'll tell you what, it's a dull challenge so I'll withdraw it and let him go on with the story, because it's a good story! But don't take a point off me! Fair dos!!!

Nicholas: No, all I'm going to say is it is a correct challenge, but if you feel you want to be fair to Ross and let him keep it …

Jenny: Yeah!

Nicholas: … I will give you a point because it was a correct challenge, a tough one but correct one. But we leave the subject with Ross who continues on 'VAT' with 46 seconds to go, starting now.

Ross [IN THE VOICE OF THE CHARACTER B.A. BARACUS] 'I ain't going on no plane, *fool!*' That's what he used to say whenever he was in trouble. They would often drug a cake and that's how they would get him on to the aeroplane. Sometimes when people would get in trouble, they would be hired, and it would be necessary for them to use their military skills that they used in Vietnam …

BUZZ

Nicholas: Tony challenged.

Tony: I hesitate to come in with this challenge. But has he wandered off the subject of 'VAT' ever so slightly?

Ross: Oh, you said 'VAT'?? I thought you said '*The A-Team*'!!!

[HUGE AUDIENCE LAUGH]

Ross's ploy of mishearing in this example received such a wonderful audience response that it spearheaded something of a *Just a Minute* sub-genre of 'mistaken subjects'. This has produced some very funny moments.

For example, in September 2004, Steve Frost 'mishears' the subject 'Annoying Habits', leading to a Paul Merton challenge.

Steve: Frodo, because what he did was came into the little building …

BUZZ

Nicholas: Paul challenged.

Paul: Habits, not *hobbits*!!! [BIG LAUGH]

Almost three years later it is Graham Norton who cannot resist going down this route, in what is a classic example from July 2007. The subject I have just given him is 'How to be a Thespian'. On this occasion comedian Chris Addison provides the necessary challenge.

> **Graham:** How to be a thespian is very simple. Throw away your lipstick and your high-heeled shoes, invest in some sensible slacks and a stout sweater. Begin listening to k.d. lang albums. [AUDIENCE START TO LAUGH] Take up an interest in golf and ladies' tennis …
> BUZZ
> **Nicholas:** Chris Addison, you've challenged, why?
> **Chris:** My challenge was deviation.
> **Nicholas:** From what?
> **Chris:** The subject. He was talking about *lesbians*, not thespians!!! [HUGE AUDIENCE LAUGH]
> **Graham:** [IN MOCK INNOCENCE] I do feel a *silly*! I must have misheard our chairman!

Ross is also extremely sharp when the opportunity arises to deliver fast, one- or two-line gags. In a superb show broadcast on 6 August 2001, Ross produces three absolutely wonderful examples of this comic art. Each one brings the house down. First he is talking on the subject 'Sloth'.

> **Ross:** I feel a bit sorry for the sloth because it's just a normal little animal … but he's also one of the deadly sins!!

Next came 'Yodelling'.

> **Ross:** Yodelling is what dyslexic people write down when they're trying to describe Kate Moss's profession!! The other important aspect of yodelling is what is often used to describe

the child of the Grand Jedi Master.

Then 'Nostrils'.

> **Ross:** Flared nostrils are often a sign of anger. It was also the most fashionable way to have your nose in the 1970s.

'A Busman's Holiday' is the subject from January 2004.

> **Ross:** Busman was the most rubbish of all the superheroes! [BIG AUDIENCE LAUGH] Unlike Superman, who was able to leap tall buildings in a single stride, fly across the metropolis, sadly Busman wasn't up to scratch. All that he could do was get loads of kids and take them to school! [HUGE LAUGH]

And finally, from the same show, Ross on 'Bingo'.

> **Ross:** I did a charity gig recently for the *Big Issue*. While playing bingo for people who live on the streets, it's always difficult to shout, 'House!'

Such witty gags are an integral part of *Just a Minute*, and Ross is without doubt a master. His other work commitments have meant he has not been able to appear on the show for a couple of years but I very much hope he will return soon to entertain us all.

On 23 July 2001 another panellist who continues to make appearances to this day joined the *Just a Minute* team – broadcaster and actress Liza Tarbuck. Liza is perhaps the least aggressive of all the semi-regular players, but what she lacks in competitive drive she more than makes up for in her warmth, dry humour and infectious laugh. She is hugely popular with audiences and listeners alike, partly because she brings a feel-good factor to every recording. She is enjoying herself and it shows. She would admit, I am sure, that she is not the most skilled player of the game, but in many ways that is one of her great assets. Winning points is secondary to sharing laughter with whoever is joining her on stage.

During only her second appearance, Liza was already displaying the lovely personality that has made her such a favourite. Here I am helping Liza out, which the audience responds to with great affection, as she attempts to challenge Steve Frost who has been talking on the subject 'Old Nick'.

Nicholas: Liza, you challenged.
Liza: Ah ... hesitation? [LIZA LOOKS CONFUSED SO I TRY TO HELP]
Nicholas: No, repetition!
Liza: [NODDING VIGOROUSLY] Repetition! [BIG AUDIENCE LAUGH AND APPLAUSE]
Nicholas: That's right, repetition of 'sound'.
Liza: Oh yes! [BURSTING INTO LAUGHTER] Hahahaha!

Later in the same recording, Liza twice demonstrates what a great sport she is. First she reveals an unusual fact from her childhood that very much endears her to everyone in the Broadcasting House theatre. She then gamely talks for a full minute on a potentially sensitive subject that receives a huge round of applause. Such positive audience reaction has been a hallmark of Liza's appearances ever since.

Nicholas: Liza, it's your turn to begin. The subject is 'Worms'. Tell us something about worms in just a minute, starting now.
Liza: My mother said when I was young, 'If you didn't have worms, you'd never lived!' [AUDIENCE LAUGH] Which was interesting coming from her ... hahahaha ... because she's actually terrified of them ... hahahaha [AUDIENCE START TO LAUGH LOUDLY AND CONTINUE THROUGHOUT]
     BUZZ
Nicholas: [LIZA'S LAUGHTER HAS SPARKED ME OFF AND I AM STRUGGLING TO SPEAK] Paul Merton ... you challenged.
Liza: [STILL LAUGHING] She did!!!

Paul: I think this is a philosophy I would like to distance myself from! [AUDIENCE AND LIZA CONTINUE TO LAUGH LOUDLY]

Nicholas: I know! Poor Mum! How will she recover from it?! How did you get your worms, by the way?

Liza: I don't know. If you'd listen to my grandmother, from eating dog's bones or something, which of course I hadn't done! I don't know, it was virulent! [STARTS TO GIGGLE]

Nicholas: I think I got them once from eating snails from the garden. Anyway, so what's your challenge, Paul, within the rules of *Just a Minute*?

Paul: Well, I think it's deviation to say unless you've had worms, you haven't lived. [AUDIENCE LAUGH]

Nicholas: Yeah, I think it probably is. In spite of what Liza's mother said. [AUDIENCE SHOW THEIR SUPPORT OF LIZA WITH A LOUD CHORUS OF 'AWWWWW']

Liza: Thank you *very* much!

Paul: [TO AUDIENCE] Just because you've had worms!!! [BIG LAUGH]

Nicholas: No, wait a minute. I've rethought that, because on the other hand, Liza's mother can *say* that. It doesn't mean to say … it may be a devious thought but she can still say it and Liza can repeat what her mother said, so she hasn't deviated in *Just a Minute*. [LOUD SHOUTS OF 'HURRAY!' FROM AUDIENCE FOLLOWED BY APPLAUSE]

Liza: Hurray!!!

A wonderful atmosphere has been building throughout this whole exchange and to boost it even further I deliberately make a mistake when asking Liza to continue with the subject, to which Liza responds with an excellent pay-off line.

Nicholas: So Liza, you still have worms … I'm … I'm sorry! [BIG AUDIENCE LAUGH]

Liza: That's why I'm fidgeting! [LAUGHTER CONTINUES AS

LIZA TAKES UP THE SUBJECT ONCE AGAIN]

Later Liza manages a full minute, with some sporting generosity from the other players because everyone is enjoying what she is saying.

Nicholas: And, Liza, it's your turn to begin, 'Cellulite'.
Liza: Ah, how kind!
Nicholas: That is the subject. I don't know why it's been chosen for you but talk on it if you can …
Liza: I'll show you later! [BIG AUDIENCE LAUGH]
Nicholas: … starting now.
Liza: Hahahaha!
Nicholas: Sixty seconds, Liza, starting now.
Liza: Cellulite is the ugly fat that lurks beneath the skin, *normally* to the rear of a person. Men and women can get cellulite. It *looks* sort of like a mountain range but from a distance if you see what I mean. Er … sort of a ranch-type style stuff that you can affix rather like a conservatory to the back of your thigh [AUDIENCE LAUGHTER] and jog round with it so that it dribbles over your knee. It's not attractive but I am sure, warmed up and jiggled with the right amount of alcohol down your throat, it could be something of a *spectacular* occurrence somewhere in the middle of Crewe. [BIG AUDIENCE LAUGH] I'm now waffling on about cellulite because I don't know that much about it. Obviously now I'm going to claim that I've never seen it before in my life. But in women's changing rooms, I have seen it, and I've eyed it *quite scarily*, quite ruefully. And it's something that just occurs to you, maybe in your late thirties. I don't know, maybe it comes earlier. Maybe people are blessed with orange skin peels …
[WHISTLE FOLLOWED BY CHEERS AND APPLAUSE]

Liza Tarbuck was a new arrival to the show in 2002, the year that also welcomed the return of a personality familiar to *Just a Minute* radio listeners during the mid 1980s and television viewers in the late

1990s: Gyles Brandreth.

Over the years Gyles and I have grown very close, and I think this helped him feel comfortable stepping into one of the thematic *Just a Minute* vacancies left by the loss of two other dear friends, Derek Nimmo and Peter Jones. The vacancy I am referring to is, of course, the job of being rude to the chairman! As was the case with both Derek and Peter, Gyles has proved to be a master at this, damning with faint praise, making facetious comments at my expense, or just plain fabricating stories but always delivered with a smile.

In September 2007 Gyles is successfully challenged by Graham Norton for deviation while speaking on 'A Feast for Your Eyes', after which I announce, 'I didn't enjoy it but the audience did! And that's what I'm here for, to have fun at my expense!' This is the tale from Gyles that the audience find so entertaining.

> **Gyles:** Many years ago, in younger and happier days, I saw Nicholas Parsons in his underpants! This was indeed a feast for the eyes!! I have never witnessed anything quite so extraordinary! Waxing on a mature man – it works!! As well as that, there was oil all over his extraordinary silky skin!

In a broadcast from February 2009, it seems initially that Gyles is praising me (how lovely and kind) … until he continues. Paul Merton is speaking first, on the subject 'Endorphins', which he cleverly reinterprets. I should also point out that Lord Reith left the BBC in 1938!

> **Paul:** Well, they are beautiful creatures. Flipper was my favourite. [BIG LAUGH] He would bounce around, swim around the sea, bottle-nosed variety. And people would say, where is he heading for? And then they would search across the ocean and he would lead them …
> BUZZ
> **Nicholas:** Gyles challenged.
> **Gyles:** This is very droll. But it's a slight on your diction! It's an

insult to you! You're famous for your diction. You're only here, I know, because you knew Lord Reith personally!!! When he appointed you a while ago, at the end of the last hostilities, he said, 'Nicholas, I like you because you seem to have your own teeth!' [BIG LAUGH]

Later in the same show, I ask Gyles to speak on one of those subjects that is designed to make me nervous, 'If Nicholas Was a Superhero'. Once again, he is all sweetness and light … to begin with.

Gyles: *If* Nicholas was a superhero is a misnomer. *He is a superhero!!* The personification of glory in our eyes! Look at the physique, the silver hair, the proud brow, that powerful nose, *teeth that fit*, the hearing aid so discreetly hidden!! Then a chin, in fact several, they are so beautiful. Shoulders that are powerful, underpants, you can actually see them rising above his trousers, the natural garb of the true superhero!! [HUGE AUDIENCE LAUGH]

Gyles is now a very popular regular on the show and I am glad to say he is still making outrageous (and wholly untrue!) comments and statements about my life and career. In a broadcast from 2012 the film *Mary Poppins* was mentioned in passing, which Gyles leapt on immediately to fabricate a professional disappointment I had supposedly suffered. 'I know you feel a bit difficult about this, Nicholas. Because Dick Van Dyke got the part Nicholas hoped for. But they preferred Dick's accent!'

As for my private life, well, in recent recordings I have been accused of attending 'bunga bunga' parties (favoured allegedly by a certain ex-Prime Minister of Italy) and of enjoying sadomasochistic Saga cruises! Complete with whips, leather outfits and goodness knows what else.

Gyles brings a great deal of energy and physicality to *Just a Minute*, more than any other player except perhaps Kenneth Williams. When Gyles is telling a story, rattling along, making things up, he puts himself under such enormous pressure not to repeat, hesitate or deviate that he forces his imagination to work overtime, producing a physical reaction. You can see it.

When he is about to talk on a subject, Gyles begins to wind himself up, drawing in deep breaths, sitting upright, his eyes sparkling with anticipation. Suddenly he launches himself into the narrative with great gusto, often clutching his waistband as he becomes more and more animated and enthused. Gyles' passionate approach to the game is a wonderful asset to the show.

On 28 September 2009, Gyles produces a virtuoso performance when handed the subject, 'Pretentious Vocabulary'. Gyles' speed of delivery increases throughout, eventually reaching a frenetic pace. The audience are enjoying this so much and laughing along, that I indicate to the other panellists not to challenge and stop the whistle being blown. Gyles hurtles past the minute mark, talking for a further 15 seconds before the whistle finally brings him to a close.

Gyles: I suspect this has come about, Nicholas, in a most amusing and delightful way because once I said to you a slight inclination of the cranium is as adequate as a spasmodic movement of one optic to an equine quadruped utterly devoid of visionary capacity, when I really meant a nod is as good as a wink to a blind horse! And you said, 'Pretentious vocabulary, *mon brave*, we don't need any of that on our show.' And I replied, 'In your presence, *monsieur*, we need to talk in the most remarkable way because language is power. It's what defines us and differentiates us from the animals, whose hands do trail upon the ground.' As the great philosopher Bertrand Russell said, 'No matter how eloquently a dog may bark, it cannot tell you that its parents were poor but honest.' A pretentious vocabulary allows this. William Shakespeare had a pretentious vocabulary of thirty thousand different words. James Joyce in just one work, *Ulysses*, used a comparable number, several of which I hope you have not yet come across, oh my gorgeous chairman! When we speak of the language or vocabulary, pretention, beauty, honestness and exotic power, they all come to bear. And tension is mounting and here we are as the Minute Waltz fades away and the second series begins, the autumn comes upon us, night falls, dusk rises and we think about our language and its beauty …

[WHISTLE FOLLOWED BY LOUD CHEERS AND APPLAUSE]

This ability to accelerate verbally from 0 to 60 in a split second has allowed Gyles to get away with *Just a Minute* murder on occasions. Here he is in a broadcast from 14 September 2009, talking on 'The Long Arm of the Law'. Graham Norton is also on the panel.

Gyles: Once upon a time, within the Metropolitan costabluary there were rules …
BUZZ
Nicholas: Paul challenged.
Paul: Sorry, that was deviation – 'costabluu-aaarry'? What sort of word is that? [BIG AUDIENCE LAUGH]
Gyles: Oh we now mock people with speech impediments, do we? [MORE LAUGHTER]
Graham: I never knew you had a speech impediment. Do you?
Gyles: No, I …
Graham: I just thought you were posh! I just thought he was rich and talked like that! [HUGE AUDIENCE LAUGH]
Nicholas: Though he was speaking fast, he did convey the fact that he was trying to say 'constabulary'.
Paul: Oh okay, I got that he was trying to say it, obviously. I think we just disagree on his amount of success! [ANOTHER HUGE AUDIENCE LAUGH BEFORE GYLES TAKES UP THE SUBJECT AGAIN AND CONTINUES TO THE END OF THE ROUND]

In the above extract, Graham refers to Gyles as being 'posh'. He isn't, he is merely well educated. However, he did once live in an upmarket area of London – Kensington – a fact he enjoyed bringing up in the show from time to time.

Back in April 1983, the rather unlikely subject of 'The Most Loveable Points of a Rhinoceros' came up. Here is what Gyles had to say as he started off the 60 seconds.

Gyles: I have a small zoo at my home. And I live in the heart of rhinoceros country, Kensington West Eight. It is the part of the world where sex is what we have our potatoes delivered in!

Many years later, in August 2009, his London borough comes up again, this time in relation to 'Mummies'.

Gyles: I wish to speak of yummy mummies. In Kensington, where I live, a 'crèche' is what happens when two cars collide!

One of the great skills of accomplished raconteurs such as Gyles is that they can repeatedly return to certain topics and make each visit funny. With Gyles, the period of his life between 1992 and 1997, during which he was the elected Conservative MP for Chester, has proved a rich source of entertainment for *Just a Minute* audiences and listeners. Here he is in July 2002 describing how his Westminster experience affected him personally. The subject is 'Loyalty Cards'.

Gyles: When I was a member of parliament the mighty Matthew Parris said of me that I was very loyal and something of a card. And consequently I feel that this is a good subject for me to speak upon. I was so, in fact, faithful to my leadership that when Mr Major became Prime Minister, I went grey overnight! Subsequently when William Hague topped my party, I began to go bald!! I was so grateful that Ann Widdecombe did not become leader!!! [HUGE AUDIENCE LAUGH]

In 1997 Gyles' life as an MP came to an end after the general election, when his constituents chose not to re-elect him. This is an event that Gyles is more than happy to revisit in *Just a Minute*.

Here he is during a broadcast of 25 January 2010, talking on

'Blowing the Whistle on Someone.'

Gyles: I was a member of parliament until the people blew the whistle on me! A hundred and eighty-two thousand, seven hundred and thirty-two individuals got up on the same day and began whistling this terrible sound. And I knew my time was up. They didn't like me, they weren't going to love me, they wanted me out!

On 26 September 2011, in the cathedral city of Lichfield, the subject is 'Middle England'.

Gyles: They wear red trousers and have ginger hair growing out of their cheeks. If they knew they were called 'buggers' grips', they'd shave them off!! These dubious people sit around expostulating on the benefit culture, immigration and every other issue that disturbs them. I despise and loathe these lowly scum of the earth. I …
[WHISTLE FOLLOWED BY LOUD APPLAUSE]
Nicholas: Listen, people of Lichfield and further afield, I don't know why you are applauding that!! Because some people would think that the Middle Englanders were the salt of the earth, not the scum that he refers to. Gyles, I am surprised at you. No wonder you lost that by-election!
Gyles: You're absolutely right. The one thing I could not stand about being an MP were my constituents! [HUGE LAUGH]

Being an MP has not been Gyles' only venture into public service. In 1971, having just come down from Oxford, he received a telephone call from a certain Lord Longford who enquired whether Gyles would be interested in becoming involved in a particular independent commission of inquiry. As Gyles simply stated in his diary of the time, 'I said yes.'

The composition and aims of this vital commission have found their way into *Just a Minute* on a couple of occasions and make for fascinating listening, although I feel it necessary to point out that not everything Gyles relates is accurate! Specifically, I was never involved in any of the commission's activities, despite what Gyles may suggest.

Here is an example from September 2007. The subject is 'Misdemeanours' which Gyles picks up with 48 seconds to go. During the recording, Gyles is challenged numerous times but perseveres. Here is what he says, excluding the interruptions, but including some malicious lies about me!

> **Gyles:** Thirty years ago I was on a committee set up to investigate the scourge of pornography in our society, and I still have the raincoat I bought at the time! We were a strange group: a bishop, an archbishop, a rabbi … and Cliff Richard!! We went over to Copenhagen to reap the alien porn, and there in the capital of Denmark we found misdemeanours … Miss Demeanours on that particular occasion adopted the costume of a milkmaid and said that she would do for us anything that we wished, and she got out this extraordinary bucket and produced these false udders. This was the moment at which Nicholas became quite nervous, indeed began to perspire, and the slight toupee that he was wearing slipped forward on his head and his neck began to flush in a most extraordinary way that I hadn't seen in a man of his years before!!!
>
> BUZZ

The audience are in hysterics by now, as Gyles is correctly challenged for repetition of 'extraordinary' and loses the subject.

Jenny Eclair, as I mentioned previously, is probably the game's *most* competitive current player, but Gyles Brandreth comes a very close second. In fact, he has in the past been known to be a touch over-keen to win points, sometimes fixating on events earlier in a game that had not gone his way. Gyles recognised this aspect of his performances himself and has adjusted his style in recent years.

Here he is in February 2010, adamant that he is correct (he is not) with a challenge on Paul, who had been speaking about 'Working from Home'.

> **Nicholas:** Gyles challenged.
> **Gyles:** Two offices.
> **Paul:** No! 'Office' … 'offices'.
> **Gyles:** No, no, no, no, no. I love your commanding presence but I was listening most carefully. There were two offices, both of them in the singular. Please replay the tape to yourself!
> **Nicholas:** I have replayed the tape in my mind. He definitely said 'office' the first time …
> **Gyles:** But your mind is playing tricks with you, Nicholas!!! 'Office' and then 'office'! I bow to your superior judgement of course!
> **Nicholas:** We love your presence, and we love your aggression and your enthusiasm …
> **Gyles:** But you don't like any of my challenges! You haven't allowed a challenge from me since 1963!!
> **Nicholas:** Well, that's because they weren't correct!!! [BIG AUDIENCE LAUGH]

Gyles can get away with almost anything on *Just a Minute*, scandalous behaviour and actions, because whatever he is up to, it always comes from the position of looking for laughs. He is not trying to create or project any particular image of himself, he is just hoping to entertain. For instance, whoever is sitting next to Gyles on the panel, male or female, runs the risk that Gyles will suddenly announce that he fancies them, or that they are his love child. (In the past, Gyles has even claimed to be *my* love child!)

Whatever routine he launches into, he is looking for opportunities to add something to the show, to create humour. No one ever takes offence, because there is none there to take. After all, Gyles is equally outrageous in what he says about himself.

For instance, in January 2007 Gyles speaks for 52 seconds on the topic of 'Infamy' before being challenged by Clement. During these seconds we learn about his parents, the derivation of his name, his ancestors and his own professional inadequacies! It is quite a feat, and the audience love it, giving Gyles a long round of appreciative applause at the end.

Gyles: I am Anglo-Welsh, my parents burnt down their own cottage! [BIG LAUGH] Therefore infamy has been part and parcel of my heritage since my birth. Indeed, my very name, Brandreth, has been the subject of infamy, because if you look it up in the *Oxford English Dictionary*, you will see that the definition is a substructure of piles. [LAUGHTER BUILDING] Indeed, one of my forebears was the notorious Jeremiah of the same ilk, who in fact was the last person to be beheaded for treason. Hence the infamy going back for several generations. In my own circumstance, my career began with an instant of infamy that was indeed most shaming. Because I was a young actor in a live radio programme playing a detective. My only line was to say, 'That was the chair Schmidt sat in when he was shot.' But unfortunately my diction at the time was poor. [HUGE OUTBURST OF LAUGHTER] And as a consequence of this, my infamy led to my not being employed, almost for a generation.
BUZZ

A few months later, in a broadcast from Stratford-upon-Avon, Gyles once again returns to his brief excursions into the world of acting. The subject is 'Brevity is the Soul of Wit'.

Gyles: 'Brevity is the soul of wit' is a line from Shakespeare's most famous play. I assayed the role on one occasion, but was so poor that the audience threw eggs at me. I went on as Hamlet and came off as Omelette!!! [BIG LAUGH]

The story Gyles tells during a December 2010 broadcast would have brought tears to the eye of the most hard-hearted audience member, had it not been so funny! The subject is 'Second-Hand Books'.

Gyles: I was visiting a second-hand bookshop on the Marylebone Road not far from where I had been brought up as a child when I saw a volume of my own work. I was excited, purchased it, only a penny. I must say that was a little bit insulting! Got out into the street and thought, 'This is thrilling.' Opened it up and there I read the words, 'Darling Mummy and Daddy, this is my first book. In joy, signed Gyles Brandreth.' [BIG AUDIENCE LAUGH] This was somewhat of a hurtful moment in my literary career!!

The contrast in panellists is an important element in *Just a Minute* to ensure the humour arrives from a number of different angles, unexpected and spontaneous. Gyles provides an energetic, high-impact, outrageous and loud presence; the person who made her radio debut on 20 January 2003, with her lilting West Country accent and gentle humour, could almost be described in exactly opposite terms. The juxtaposition when they appear together is wonderful. I am talking of course about the delightful and very funny poet, Pam Ayres.

Pam actually first made her acquaintance with *Just a Minute* during the 1999 television run. She was understandably very nervous at the beginning of that recording, and at one stage I even left my chair to help her out.

Pam has been speaking on the subject 'Hymn Singing' but is then successfully challenged by Peter Jones for repetition.

Nicholas: Peter, there are 31 seconds left, 'Hymn Singing' with you, and another point of course, starting now.
Peter: Your arithmetic is incredible! Twenty-nine from sixty is thirty-one! He got it straight away like that! Didn't you?
Nicholas: I know! Deviation … [I LOOK TOWARDS PAM] … Quickly, press your buzzer! Press your buzzer! [PAM IS UNSURE WHAT TO DO SO I JUMP OUT OF MY SEAT AND PRESS HER BUZZER]
   BUZZ

Nicholas: [SITTING BACK DOWN] Yes, Pam, what was your challenge?

Pam: Um … I don't know! What was it? [THE AUDIENCE BURST OUT LAUGHING]

Nicholas: He actually hesitated and he was deviating from 'Hymn Singing'.

Pam: Yes, he hesitated and deviated from the subject of hymn singing! Without a doubt, Peter.

Nicholas: Absolutely. He didn't mention it at all, did he? [THE AUDIENCE CONTINUE TO LAUGH THROUGHOUT THIS EXCHANGE]

Pam: No, he didn't!

Nicholas: How quick you are sometimes!

Pam: It's amazing really!!!

With Pam having retaken the subject, and perhaps gaining in confidence, we have a first glimpse of the lovely brand of humour she serves up in *Just a Minute*.

Nicholas: So, Pam, you got the subject of 'Hymn Singing' back, and you've got a point for a correct challenge and there are 20 seconds available, starting now.

Pam: One of the hymns that I particularly loved singing was the childhood one, 'There is a Green Hill Far Away'. However I was always troubled and deeply perplexed to the very core by the second line which is, 'Without a city wall'. Oh, I wondered to myself, what had happened to it? [BIG AUDIENCE LAUGH]

I do not know whether the experience of the two television shows she appeared on put Pam off for a while, but she did not reappear until the 35th anniversary programme on 1 January 2003, recorded in the Playhouse Theatre where the pilot took place. This special show ran for an hour, and as a one-off a number of well-known personalities had been invited to sit in the front row of the audience and set some of the subjects. Pam was one of the guests, and was clearly nervous about having agreed to take part in a regular edition later in that 42nd Series. Graham Norton and Paul Merton are on the panel.

Nicholas: In our audience we have the lovely Pam Ayres, who is shortly going to be in one of our shows, I'm delighted to say. And she's come here today and she's got a subject which we would like you to give to Paul Merton. Pam?

Pam: Oh well, I feel very nervous actually, as you can probably tell from my tremulous voice. Because having been asked to appear on the programme, and having now seen the cut-throat and murderous nature …

Nicholas: I'll protect you, Pam, don't worry!

Pam: Will you?

Nicholas: Yes!

Pam: Well, in that …

Graham: Run! Run! Don't walk, Pam!!

Paul: He'll protect you, but remember he's clinging to life!

Pam: It may only be protection in the short term then! Eh … but in view of my fears and apprehension, I would like to ask you, Paul, how to win points, even by underhand means, on *Just a Minute*.

Nicholas: Pam, can we condense that to 'How to Win Points on *Just a Minute*'? And cut out the 'underhand means'?

Pam: Oh, all right then.

Nicholas: You like that as well, do you?

Pam: Oh, I wouldn't mind a bit of underhand means!!

[AUDIENCE LAUGH]

Pam is an experienced professional, and after having made her radio debut on 20 January 2003 she soon identified the style in which she would be most comfortable playing the game. As with so many newcomers, she had to find her own, distinct voice, and having done so she relaxed, and has continued to provide delightful entertainment ever since.

One of the features of Pam's contributions to the show is that you never quite know which 'Pam' will be speaking – the Pam that offers sensible and witty homespun advice, or the Pam that is happy to divulge surprising personal revelations. Both versions generate a huge amount of laughter.

Down-to-earth Pam first.

On her third radio appearance, in February 2003, Pam provides a warning to our Bristol audience about the dangers that could develop if someone takes 'My Idea of Romance' too far, and she does so for a joyful, uninterrupted minute.

Pam: I have never gone in for the contrived idea of romance with intimate dinners for two, scented candles and sumptuous gowns. In my experience this takes a great deal of pulling off, and often goes pear-shaped! [BIG AUDIENCE LAUGH] I find that the food does not work out as you had wished. The most boring person on the face of the Earth comes banging on the door and you dislike the fragrance of the flames! I once heard an American woman in a ladies' toilet proclaim that the pinnacle of her romantic aspirations was to make love on a tigerskin rug in front of an open fire. Apart from the obvious conservation issue here ... [HUGE AUDIENCE LAUGH] I would be very afraid that a burning brand would roll from the fire and set fire to me camisole! And I would feel inspired to clutch a fire extinguisher ... to my chest!

[WHISTLE FOLLOWED BY LOUD, RAUCOUS CHEERS AND APPLAUSE]

In July 2006 Pam offers some advice to one of the country's leading modern artists when talking on 'Fame'.

Pam: Tracey Emin achieved fame by displaying her unmade bed, which looked very frosty to me, and as though it could have done with a jolly good boil-up in the washer! [BIG LAUGH]

Now Pam's other life.

During that show from February 2003, in which Pam highlights the fact that burning coals and camisoles do not mix, she also recalls a much-loved present she received during her days as a young girl growing up in Berkshire. The subject is 'My Favourite Cousin'.

> **Pam:** My favourite cousin Fred was a sailor on board the aircraft carrier HMS *Eagle* during the 1950s. He travelled to such thrilling places and would visit us laden with *exotic* gifts! [AUDIENCE LAUGH] Imagine my joy as a child from the council estate to be given a white silk kimono … [AUDIENCE LAUGH] … emblazoned with dragons stitched in gold thread all down the back and sleeves. My mother too received a sumptuous pink fluted shell … [AUDIENCE LAUGH THROUGHOUT AS PAM'S DESCRIPTIONS BECOME MORE OUTLANDISH] … fashioned into the shape of a lamp and a glorious rug bearing Eastern scenes of a caravan decamped in the desert and *exotic* dancers *cavorting* in the firelight!!! My cousin Fred …
>
> BUZZ

Tony Hawks' challenge here for the repetition of 'Fred' is met with boos from the audience who have been enraptured by Pam's description.

In March 2010 Pam's revelations about 'My Diary' left everyone in the Radio Theatre, Broadcasting House, wanting to know more … a lot more.

> **Pam:** My diary is so full of depraved and salacious information that I have to keep it under constant lock and key, swathed in chains, razor wire and high-voltage cable! [BIG LAUGH] If the gutter press and the paparazzi got hold of my diary, shock waves would reverberate throughout the civilised world!! People would be shocked and horrified if they expected to see humdrum entries like, 'Went and had a crown put on my teeth',

or, 'Walked the dog twice.' They would be sorely disappointed.
Ho ho ho, yes!
    BUZZ

Pam's revelations are cut short here with that repetition of 'Ho ho
ho', which is spotted by Jenny Eclair. We never did find out what was
in that diary.

Pam is, of course, a renowned and best-selling poet and it is her
unique ability in shaping words to paint the most vivid and captivating
pictures that places Pam up amongst the very best players of *Just
a Minute.* Earlier I discussed how important variety is to the game.
Well, Pam Ayres can start talking on a subject and carry everyone
listening to a place no other player could even dream of visiting. It
is a wonderful gift.

Here she is in July 2007 on 'A Wing and a Prayer'. Midway through
she is challenged on the basis that 'skipper' is not an expression used
in the RAF. After much entertaining discussion, I adjudicate in
Pam's favour and she picks up her story exactly where she left off.
This sends shivers up my spine. Needless to say, the audience love it.

> **Pam:** When I hear the expression, 'a wing and a prayer', I
> envisage a young pilot in his shattered craft, limping home,
> his fuselage in tatters, coming in over The Wash and calling out
> on his crackling radio, 'I can't hold her, skipper, my rudder's
> shot!' … Clad in his leather bomber jacket with cream sheepskin
> collar, goggles and close-fitting helmet, he descends through the
> cloud canopy and sees to his inestimable relief the flickering,
> blinking lights of the runway, stretched out across the Fens,
> guiding him home. Breathless with emotion, he calls down the
> intercom, 'We're coming home, by God! On a wing and
> a prayer …'

Pam hesitates at this moment in her tale, having brought the pilot
safely home, loses the subject and receives a huge round of applause
from a captivated audience.

In July 2009 'Mother Nature' is the focus of Pam's descriptive talents. On this occasion she is interrupted more than once, with entertaining but unsuccessful challenges. After one such challenge from Tony Hawks, Pam claims Tony has 'interrupted my flow! He's interrupted the flow of the silver river now, he has!' In truth, however, as Pam continues there is no indication that her flow has been the least bit interrupted. At the end of the round, I describe it as a 'classic'. It is.

Pam: It is easy to imagine Mother Nature as a benevolent figure, her fat arms laden with fruits, vegetables, flowers, nuts, seeds, straddling as she does the silver fish-filled rivers beside green pastures whereupon the cattle graze and multiply … But do not be deceived. Nature red in tooth and claw, look beyond the amiable countenance to the venom-filled fang of the snake, the bloody jaw of the wolf and the ink of the squid … The survival of the fittest, the predation of the weak by the strong, the abandonment of the runt.

…on the subject of *The World Service*

There was a definite sense of irony surrounding the BBC's decision in the autumn of 2004 to cease broadcasting *Just a Minute* on the World Service.

Just a Minute was not singled out specifically. The station's light entertainment slot – which also featured shows such as *Quote, Unquote* and *I'm Sorry I Haven't a Clue* – was abolished altogether by January 2005. This was part of a policy initiative that saw the World Service move away from performance-based programmes such as comedy and musical recitals to a more news and current affairs-focused schedule. The reason given for this shift in emphasis was the belief that most people who tuned into the network did so in order to hear comment and analysis, rather than broad entertainment. In addition, it was stated that as 90 per cent of the listeners had English as a second language, there was a belief that the comedy output did not travel well.

I thought at the time this was a great shame, and I still do. Comedy is an integral and positive part of the British way of life and the World Service offered a global window to this important element of our culture; a window that is now closed.

The reach was phenomenal. Paul Merton tells a lovely story of a conversation he had during the Edinburgh Festival a number of years ago. A stranger approached him and said, 'Oh, I was listening to you on *Just a Minute* in the summer.' 'Oh yes?' replied Paul, and the man continued. 'Yes, I was crossing the Gobi Desert in a jeep, listening to the World Service!'

Tony Hawks recites a similar tale, with a nice punchline, when given the subject 'The World Service' during a recording from February 2002.

Tony: A friend of mine, John Sweeney, a journalist for the *Observer*, was driving through northern Iraq when the radio came on and he heard the dulcet tones of Nicholas Parsons saying, 'Welcome to *Just a Minute*!' Is there nowhere in the world where you are safe from this man?! [AUDIENCE LAUGH] He was reporting on the Kurdish troubles and felt this could not happen to him, and yet he was plummeted into depression by the sound of our esteemed chairman's voice. Fortunately I was speaking next so he cheered up a bit! [BIG AUDIENCE LAUGH]

Fast forward to March 2012, during our extraordinary expedition to record *Just a Minute* in Mumbai, India, and Paul expresses a very different point of view when talking on 'The Voice of New India'.

Paul: The voice of new India sounds like the kind of

programme that should be on the World Service, like *Just a Minute* used to be until some idiot cancelled it years ago.

Paul was certainly not alone in his opinion. I received numerous letters from a wide selection of countries, expressing disappointment that *Just a Minute* was no longer available on their radios. One in particular stands out. It arrived from a gentleman named George McAdams, a listener from Alabama, who wrote as follows (deliberately using the English spelling of 'humour' to ensure there was no possibility of confusion!).

Dear Mr Parsons,

I cannot tell you how upsetting it has been for me, after almost 20 years of listening to the BBC, to have the World Service stop broadcasting programs such as Just a Minute. Do the powers-that-be not recognize that these programs do more than just take up broadcast time? These programs show the whole world what a great resource Britain has in its humour, and this resource should be mined and shared like precious gold. The last time Britain took such a drastic misstep it lost 'The Empire'. I fear the BBC's decision not to share its comedy will cause a downfall in the appreciation of British humour that may never be regained.

George then went on to explain that he felt so strongly about this that he was copying in Prime Minister Tony Blair and Her Majesty The Queen because 'they may be the only ones with clear heads that can reverse this decision'! I do not know if George ever received replies, but I do understand the sentiments he expressed.

What of the irony I mentioned? Well, when Kenneth Williams died and the possibility was mooted that this sad event might mark the end of the show altogether, it was the World Service who stepped in to help save the day. They made it known that if Radio 4 did indeed stop broadcasting, they would take over the recordings of *Just a Minute* as the show was one of their most popular programmes. There is a certain degree of rivalry along the corridors of the BBC, and when Radio 4 executives heard about the World Service's proposal *Just a Minute* was reprieved. Given what then happened in 2004, I think it is more than ironic.

Yes, it is true that *Just a Minute* is now available via the internet, which clearly offers extensive global exposure. That is wonderful, and I make reference to this fact during my introductions when I welcome listeners around the world. On the negative side, however, not everyone has online access and even those who do are generally confined to listening on their computers, as handheld devices are expensive and the quality of mobile coverage is very varied. Do cars today driving in the Gobi Desert or northern Iraq pick up the internet? Despite the incredible technological advances in the decade since the show was taken off the World Service, I still believe we do not reach as many listeners as we once did, which as I said, is a real shame.

The past couple of years have seen two exciting developments in the *Just a Minute* story, one of which – the trip to India that I have already made reference to – came about as a direct result of seeds sown during the long period of World Service broadcasts before the plug was pulled.

From the many effusive fan letters I received from India over those years it became clear that the people of that country had a very strong relationship with the language and humour that lie at the core of *Just a Minute*. In fact our show, and others, had struck such a deep chord that many Indian schools were beginning to use quizzing and games as an educational tool. I discussed this with a very clever producer called Jo Meek who worked for an independent company, All Out Productions. She put forward a synopsis to BBC Radio, which we called The Quiz Exchange. They liked the idea and a programme was commissioned.

We flew to Bangalore where we interviewed schoolchildren, parents and teachers about this relationship between general knowledge quizzes and learning. It was a fascinating experience and I came away with huge admiration for the enthusiasm and ambition of the pupils we met. I asked one little girl, I remember, what she wanted to do when she grew up and she replied quite firmly, 'I want to be Prime Minister.' I thought that was wonderful.

While we were there I also discovered something concerning *Just a Minute* of which I had not previously been aware – the existence of 'JAM' clubs, where fans gather to enjoy playing the game and at the same time improve their English. As this fitted in with the premise of the programme we were making, we decided to visit one such club. What an experience that proved to be. The overwhelming impression I had as I watched and then joined in for a while, was one of such fun and laughter. They had developed their own version of the game, with rapid and constant challenges, and quite simply they were having a ball.

On my return to the UK I described all this to our producer, Tilusha Ghelani, and suggested that it would be wonderful if we could take *Just a Minute* to India. Tilusha is very enterprising; she loved the idea and began to pursue it, eventually selling the idea to BBC radio on the basis of making a documentary about *Just a Minute* in India. This would involve me visiting JAM clubs and also incorporate a double recording of the show for the regular series, with Paul Merton and comedian Marcus Brigstocke playing alongside two local comedians.

Marcus, who made his first appearance in September 2004, is a sharp and incisive comedian with a quick mind, and was an ideal choice to accompany Paul, given the more hectic Indian approach to the game.

In order to justify the cost, the BBC commissioned a documentary about the whole enterprise. I flew initially with Tilusha and a film crew to Bangalore where we visited JAM clubs, interviewed individuals who had listened to *Just a Minute* and also film an international

JAM tournament, in which I was also asked to take part. We then flew to Mumbai where we met up with Paul Merton and Marcus Brigstocke. We were all staying at the Grand Hyatt Hotel in Mumbai who looked after us very well. As part of the documentary, I travelled to St Xavier's School where I was asked to make an impromptu speech about education and how much I admired the pupils' love of language. Afterwards one of the students asked me to sign the notes she had made. I was touched and also immensely impressed that she had taken time to write down and absorb my thoughts. It was another marvellous example of the passion for learning that I witnessed while visiting that fascinating country.

The recordings of the two shows, which were to be included in the next series of *Just a Minute* (the first ever outside the British Isles) took place in Mumbai's Comedy Store and were broadcast in March 2012.

Tilusha had found two excellent stand-up comedians to complete the panel: the flamboyant Cyrus Broacha, who could have been described as the Kenneth Williams of India given the energy he brought to the show, and the more laid-back Anuvab Pal, who entertained everyone with his witty comments. Both recordings proved to be highly successful and entertaining, performed in front of a warm, enthusiastic, loud and very engaged audience.

The choice of subjects was very well pitched, mixing quintessentially British topics with those of a particular relevance to India, together with some that had resonance in both countries. It all made for a unique experience and led me to think back on *Just a Minute*'s origins and to picture all those who had been involved over the years but were no longer with us – Ian Messiter in particular. With those people in my mind, it made me very proud on their behalf to announce, 'This show is actually coming not from Broadcasting House in London, not even from England or Scotland or Wales or Northern Ireland, it is coming from Mumbai in India!' That really was something.

The banter generated between the four panellists was one of the highlights of the shows, sparked into life almost from the very beginning because of the slightly different interpretation of the game in India, where challenges are far more frequent.

Here is Marcus talking on the very first subject, 'A Cultural Exchange', and he is about to be sharply challenged by Cyrus Broacha.

> **Marcus:** The rules of this particular cultural exchange, which of course is very special, are that if I succeed this evening, I'll be allowed to stay here in Mumbai for the rest of my life. [AUDIENCE LAUGHTER] However if I don't win the show, I will be forced to leave immediately …
>
> BUZZ
>
> **Nicholas:** Cyrus?
>
> **Cyrus:** He said 'I' about four times. [BIG AUDIENCE LAUGH AND APPLAUSE]
>
> **Nicholas:** Well done, Cyrus! We let one 'I' go, or two, but four, I quite agree. Anuvab, yes, you want to say something.
>
> **Anuvab:** I hate to interject, Nicholas, but I have a quick question. I'm not sure if he is talking about a cultural exchange, or he is seeking asylum?! [BIG AUDIENCE LAUGH]

Cyrus then takes up the subject, with Marcus ready to pounce.

> **Cyrus:** Cultural exchange is very important in the context of living in my particular building where we have 11 different people from different cultures …
>
> BUZZ
>
> **Nicholas:** And Marcus challenged.
>
> **Marcus:** Yeah, repetition of 'different'.
>
> **Nicholas:** Different people, different countries.
>
> **Cyrus:** You rascal! You mean, mean man!! You evil person!!! [AUDIENCE LAUGH]
>
> **Marcus:** You started it! [BIG AUDIENCE LAUGH]

The subject of 'The Beatles' brings out Paul's acting skills as he slips into a Liverpudlian accent, much to the delight of the audience who laugh throughout.

Paul: Well, when I first started in the Beatles round about 1959, I remember saying to George and Paul and John, saying, 'This is fantastic, being in the Beatles. Do you think we'll be able to make records and sell 'em all over the world?' And they said, 'Yeah, we think that's a great idea, why don't we do that?' I wish I hadn't started on this accent now cos I don't know how much longer I have got to speak … and I'm not going anywhere because the thing with the Beatles was they were …

    BUZZ

Nicholas: Anuvab, you've challenged.

Paul: Thank God somebody did!! [HUGE AUDIENCE LAUGH]

Nicholas: What is your challenge, Anuvab?

Anuvab: Nicholas, I feel it was a deviation.

Nicholas: Because his accent wasn't very genuine?!

[MORE LAUGHTER FROM AUDIENCE]

'Sherlock Holmes' offers another opportunity for Anuvab to come in with a funny comment. Paul is speaking first, cleverly avoiding repeating the number two.

Paul: Sherlock Holmes lived at 2 ditto 1B Baker Street and his homely fan … what am I talking about? 'Homely fan' doesn't mean anything but they haven't picked me up on it …

    BUZZ

Nicholas: Marcus challenged.

Marcus: Yeah, repetition of 'homely' and deviation from confidence, sadly. [HUGE AUDIENCE LAUGH AND APPLAUSE. ANUVAB THEN CATCHES MY ATTENTION]

Nicholas: Anuvab, yes?

Anuvab: I was just worried. In India we studied 221 Baker Street, but maybe it *is* 2 ditto 1 Baker Street. I have no idea! [BIG AUDIENCE LAUGH]

Cyrus then wins the subject and offers an unusual slant on 'Sherlock Holmes' (seemingly he came from an area of Mumbai, according to

Cyrus …), until his running 'battle' with Marcus rears its head again.

> **Cyrus:** People don't know this about Sherlock Holmes. He was born in a Parsi baug in India, Rustom Baug to be precise. His actual name was Kersi Meher-Homji [BIG LAUGH], he was six foot four inches tall, he had long deep pockets wherever he went to carry …
> BUZZ
> **Nicholas:** Marcus challenged.
> **Marcus:** Repetition of 'he'. He he he he. [HUGE AUDIENCE LAUGH AND APPLAUSE]
> **Nicholas:** Yes, I think that's what we call being hoisted on your own petard. [BIG LAUGH] You had him on the 'I's, he got you on the 'he's.

During the second recording, the subject of 'Mumbai Traffic' is tackled by Marcus and receives a very clever challenge from Anuvab.

> **Marcus:** [IN A WISTFUL VOICE] As you wander softly through the boulevards of old Mumbai, you may be fortunate enough to catch sight of a motor vehicle as it breezes past you exploring the old streets with the driver perhaps staring listlessly out of the window, wondering if he'll be lucky enough to see another motorist …
> BUZZ
> **Nicholas:** Anuvab, you've challenged.
> **Anuvab:** Deviation.
> **Nicholas:** Why?
> **Anuvab:** From reality. [LOUD CHEERS AND APPLAUSE FROM AUDIENCE]

There was one particularly interesting moment during the first recording that goes a long way to illustrate that British humour does indeed travel. Marcus Brigstocke has just taken over the subject of 'Colonial India' and says the following:

Marcus: The subject is colonial India, so now seems a perfectly reasonable time for me to say, 'Sorry'.

At the time I thought this was a touch risky, but I should not have been surprised. Marcus is unafraid of pushing boundaries with his comedy. He is comfortable taking his humour right up to the line, especially when least expected, but he never crosses it.

For instance, in a *Just a Minute* recording from January 2007 Marcus twists the subject 'Whippersnappers' by explaining that 'at fetish parties, it is considered extremely bad manners to turn up with a camera!' In August of the same year he then wants the audience to be absolutely clear on the meaning of 'Ging Gang Goolie', which, he reassures, 'isn't a nasty cycling accident where you fail to lift your leg high enough to get over the saddle. It is a song enjoyed by scouts, sitting round a campfire!' Finally, in March 2001 while talking on the subject of 'Hobnobbing', Marcus once again strives to clear up any possible misunderstanding. 'It is not to be confused with "hobbit knobbing", which is of course illegal in New Zealand!!'

Marcus delivered his line in Mumbai with perfect timing, having correctly gauged that the audience would know he was making the comment to raise a laugh and generate a big reaction. He certainly succeeded. They loved it, whistling, cheering and applauding with huge enthusiasm. It proved to be one of those moments that demonstrated how valuable the trip had been; an opportunity to enjoy and experience two comedy cultures coming together.

It was an unforgettable visit to a wonderful country. I felt privileged to have been involved.

The second of the two new developments in recent *Just a Minute* history occurred 18 months after the Indian recordings, when in November 2013 Radio 4 Extra broadcast five *Junior Just a Minute* shows over the course of a week.

The idea came from Elizabeth Clark, a senior content producer at the BBC, who realised that children enjoy playing the game in school playgrounds. As someone once said to me, 'Nicholas, you are so lucky, you are part of a show that has an audience from nine to ninety.' That is absolutely correct, and Elizabeth cleverly took that notion and produced an excellent series.

There were a few very sensible tweaks made to the rules, which contributed significantly to the success of the recordings. The first was the recognition that it may prove too daunting for four young contestants to play as individuals, and as a result the decision was taken to create two teams, with Jenny Eclair and Josie Lawrence partnering one junior player each.

Jenny and Josie were inspired choices. Jenny has many years' experience of the game, dating back to 1994 and approaching 50 radio shows, while Josie, who herself has made almost 20 appearances, in particular could empathise with how the youngsters would be feeling. She experienced considerable nerves when she first joined the *Just a Minute* team.

Josie is without doubt a brilliant actress and highly accomplished improv comic, but even with all her skills and ability there is something about *Just a Minute*, the fact that it is the only completely spontaneous game on radio, played for laughs with no script, that can seem overwhelming at the beginning.

Josie admitted as much before her first recordings, which also featured Paul Merton, Clement Freud and comedian (and ex-producer) Chris Neill. I think perhaps Josie contributed to her nerves by setting herself such high standards that then became inhibiting. She need not have worried. During that first double recording Josie did admit that, 'Oh, it's a tough game' and 'Gosh, it's complex,' and when asked to speak for the very first time, on 'Big Ben', said, 'As most of us know, Big Ben is actually the bell. And I actually went … Oh bugger!' but still proved to be an excellent addition to the show that day, and on every other appearance since.

Not that Paul gave her much slack on her debut. Here is Josie during that first show, broadcast on 7 January 2008, speaking after I set her first subject.

Nicholas: Oh, I don't know whether this is anything personal to you, but the subject we've been given is 'The Morning After'. [AUDIENCE LAUGH] You have 60 seconds as usual, your time starts now.

Josie: The morning after, now the morning after usually means something that happened the night before that was either momentous, historic …

BUZZ

Nicholas: Paul, why have you challenged?

Paul: Well, the morning after doesn't really mean something that happened the night before.

Josie: I was going on to explain …

Nicholas: I'm sorry, Paul, I was completely with her. [AUDIENCE APPLAUD] I realised the morning after usually occurs after something momentous the night before. Right, Josie, it was an incorrect challenge, you still have the subject, you have 51 seconds, the morning after, and your time starts now.

Josie: I remember …

BUZZ

Nicholas: Right, Paul?

Paul: I don't dare challenge Josie on anything! [JOSIE BURSTS OUT LAUGHING, AS DOES THE AUDIENCE]

Nicholas: Nothing's ever held you back!

Paul: Hesitation.

Nicholas: It wasn't!

Paul: It wasn't a hesitation? Sorry I've gone deaf then for a moment.

Nicholas: No, no. I was sitting beside her, there was a noise coming out of …

Paul: Was there?

Nicholas: … her very attractive mouth. [BIG AUDIENCE LAUGH]

Paul: [NODDING HIS HEAD IN MOCK UNDERSTANDING] She's very nervous. It's the first time she's played the game. *But it's about articulation, not noises!!* [AUDIENCE LAUGH]

Nicholas: It was the beginning of a word but she hadn't quite articulated it.

Paul: What! We've got to wait for it to evolve?? What do you mean? What are you talking about?! [BIG AUDIENCE LAUGH]

At this point I explain to Paul that although the two of them are friends, that does not change the fact that as this is Josie's first appearance I feel she should be encouraged and treated with leniency. Paul agrees and Josie continues with the subject.

During the second recording Josie is clearly already relaxing and gaining in confidence, as demonstrated by her sharp interjection in this short exchange.

Nicholas: Forty-five seconds, Clement, with you – 'What the Butler Saw', starting now.

Clement: The most tragic thing is a blind butler. Poor sod, he goes around life seeing absolutely nothing! People undress in front of him …

BUZZ

Nicholas: Paul challenged.

Paul: How did he get the job in the first place?! You can't have a blind butler, can you?

Josie: You can have a dumb waiter! [BIG AUDIENCE LAUGH]

By her third appearance, in February 2009, Josie has found her voice and knows exactly how she wants to play the game, with clever twists and surprising revelations.

Nicholas: You have the subject, you have 'My Secret Vice' – not mine, that's the subject – and you have 21 seconds, starting now.

Josie: I have many vices. I like smoking, drinking, parties, bathing in tubs of melted chocolate. But my secret vice I keep under my bed. I take it out, I put it on the table and I clamp my boyfriend's head with it. I love my vice but I have to keep it secret or else people would think it is strange ... [BIG LAUGH]

Josie now brings a great variety to her performances on *Just a Minute*, with impersonations and funny voices (we have had an evil witch and the Hunchback of Notre Dame to name only two), an infectious laugh and a surprising degree of naughtiness given the sweet and innocent persona she can project. Here she is in March 2010 inadvertently pressing her buzzer, which leads her into delivering a brilliantly funny line. Comedian and writer Justin Moorhouse is speaking on 'The Perfect Date'.

Justin: The perfect date is the first one you taste on Christmas Eve. Specially ...
BUZZ
Nicholas: Josie Lawrence.
Josie: I pressed my thumb against the thing by mistake! ... Which is part of my perfect date!!! Sorry, Nicholas. [HUGE BURST OF LAUGHTER FROM AUDIENCE]

Josie's innocent persona not only hides a high degree of mischief, it also masks a steely side to her character, especially when points are at stake. In this 2011 exchange with comedian, broadcaster and *Never Mind the Buzzcocks* team captain Phill Jupitus, Josie stands her ground magnificently and delivers a delightful gag at the end.

Nicholas: So anyway, Josie, you've got it, you've got 41 seconds on 'King Arthur', starting now.
Josie: If Arthur hadn't been a king, he would have been a brilliant dentist. Very good at extracting things from difficult places! [AUDIENCE LAUGH] He pulled the sword out of the stone, Escalibur and ...
BUZZ
Nicholas: Phill challenged.
Phill: I think you'll find it is *Ex*calibur.
Nicholas: I think she said 'Excalibur', didn't she?

Phill: *Es*calibur.

Josie: I said Excalibur!

Phill: You said Escalibur!!

Josie: I said Excalibur!!! [LAUGHTER BUILDS THROUGHOUT THIS EXCHANGE]

Nicholas: Well, it's got further to travel to you. I should explain to our listeners, Phill's one side of the room and Josie's the other. Josie's right beside me and I think she actually said *Ex*calibur.

Phill: If only someone had recorded this, Nicholas, and we could hear it again.

Nicholas: Well, the show *is* actually transmitted. If I am wrong I will send a nice little gift to you.

Phill: A point will suffice, Nicholas! [BIG LAUGH]

Nicholas: No, I think she said Excalibur, it came over to me as *Ex*calibur. And I'm sure that's what she meant to say if it didn't come out as Excalibur. Often people say 'ex', it sounds a bit like 'es'.

Josie: Yeah, my es-boyfriend was always telling me that!!! [HUGE LAUGH]

Another skill Josie regularly demonstrates on *Just a Minute* is that of storytelling. She is a natural. The following are two examples from 2012, both of which she insists are true.

In this first one, from February, the subject is 'Advice from My Hairdresser'. Josie does not quite finish her tale before being correctly challenged by Kit Hesketh-Harvey for hesitation with three seconds remaining. It does not matter. It is clear from what we have already learned what happens next.

> **Josie:** My hairdresser is actually my best friend. She is called Michelle, and the best advice she ever gave me was, 'I think we had better unlock the refrigerator now.' Let me go back in time to explain this. We went out one day, after she had cut and dried my hair in my flat, to a little bar in Soho, and then to another one. And then we started to drink a little more until

it was three o'clock in the morning! You have to remember we were very young, it was the 1980s and crazy times. We went past Spitalfields Market and saw all these blokes travelling about on their little trolleys. Thought it might be fun to join them. So we got on one of the said wheelery machinery thingies and said, 'Do you enjoy your work?' 'Yes,' they replied, 'but we don't like our boss.' So me and my hairdresser decided to lock said person …
BUZZ

Kit's challenge elicits a groan of sympathy from the audience who realise there can only be a couple of seconds left, followed by loud applause.

In March the subject of 'The Worst Put-Down I Ever Had' produced another very funny story from Josie.

Josie: No word of a lie! I was in a black cab once and the chap turned to me and said, 'Do you know you look just like Catherine Zeta Jones! Only uglier!' And I couldn't believe what I was hearing, so I laughed. He then said, 'Don't worry, I didn't mean it as an insult!' [BIG LAUGH]

With Josie and Jenny's help, *Junior Just a Minute* proved to be a great success. Both of them embraced the new team format enthusiastically. If either had already spoken in a round, and then won the subject back, I might make a suggestion that their younger partner take over, to which both Josie and Jenny would readily agree. This helped reduce any sense of pressure and kept the game flowing, with everyone involved.

In addition to being played in teams, there were other slight adjustments to the rules. In order to the help the contestants settle, the first rounds consisted of 40-second subjects, then 50, and up to the full minute for the final rounds. The subjects were also chosen with the age group of the players in mind (11–13), including such topics as 'If I Were Harry Potter', 'Flying a Kite', 'Dinosaurs', 'Writing a Thank You Letter', 'Baking a Cake' and 'Hide and Seek'.

These minor variations did not in any way detract from the fact that this was *Just a Minute* as regularly played, recorded in front of an audience at the RADA Studios. There were no concessions in my rulings or in the challenges because none were required. The reason for that is really rather simple – the youngsters themselves proved to be stars.

The number of children who applied was apparently incredible, much more than anticipated, and following a series of auditions, Elizabeth Clark produced a group of very able, intelligent players who were excellent at the game and highly entertaining. One of them even had the audacity to play a devious trick, by repeating exactly what the previous speaker had just said when he took over the subject.

Another series has been commissioned as *Junior Just a Minute* proved to be a highly successful experiment. It also left me with one overriding happy thought: a new generation already exists who love the game and are keen to become involved.

The future of *Just a Minute* seems bright – very bright.

So what of that future?

Well, before I look ahead, a glimpse into the past is in order. Or to be more accurate, a glimpse into the *present* past.

The opening line of L. P. Hartley's *The Go-Between* reads, 'The past is a foreign country: they do things differently there.' I know what he means, but I do not think the sentiment entirely applies to *Just a Minute*. Over the course of 47 years the show has built its own traditions, many of which continue to this day. That is important; the past matters in a show such as ours because the previous players *did not do everything differently there*.

The thread that connects Ian, Derek, Clement, Kenneth, Peter, Aimi, Wendy and so many others remains strong today. It is one of the key factors contributing to the show's longevity and success, but equally it does not inhibit us. Constant evolution continues, rule changes and innovations such as the broadcasts from India and *Junior Just a Minute* add to the freshness, and yet the laughter of the past continues to echo in the present.

A brief look at two of our recent recordings, from 24 February and 3 March 2014, illustrates what I mean.

In both shows, banter flies back and forth, sporting generosity is evident, innuendo is present, a newcomer contributes well, a classic tactic generates laughter, jokes are made at my expense, our longest standing player delivers a virtuoso minute, there are clever plays on words, sharp challenges and our old friend 'bugger' even makes a spontaneous appearance. In short, the traditions of *Just a Minute* are upheld magnificently, unobtrusively underpinning the fresh, modern approach of the players.

In the first of the shows, Paul Merton, Sheila Hancock, Josie Lawrence and comedian Richard Herring make up the panel. Paul takes the opening subject of 'Hot Cross Buns', and a favourite theme soon emerges from the surreal direction in which Paul has taken the topic.

> **Paul:** The hot cross bun was first invented by Florence Nightingale on a visit to Sweden in 1862. She was appearing as a support act for Nicholas Parsons' one-man show! [BIG LAUGH]

Sheila has the following subject, 'How to Win an Argument with a Teenager', and she delivers a measured and marvellous performance over 60 uninterrupted seconds.

> **Sheila:** It is a funny thing, but today I was with my daughter, eldest one, and she was having the most dreadful argument with her teenager and I *loved* every minute of it because it reminded me that that was *exactly* what I went through with her. And you are on a losing wicket, I'll tell you. You have to choose the arguments that you want to win and those you can afford to lose. Only the important things do you continue with, and that's part of the kid's training because they have to learn limits and to

live on their own conscience. However, sometimes you have to put your foot down or they might *die* [BIG AUDIENCE LAUGH] because there are so many horrible things going on in the world. I do remember my husband, when she arrived wearing a Goth look, with black hair and white face, lots of safety pins, saying, 'You're not going out looking like *that*, are you??' And she said … [WHISTLE AND HUGE APPLAUSE]

A little later, Sheila again has the subject, 'French Exchange', during which she describes a very personal moment from her youth, which generates considerable entertainment and reminds me of a youthful story of my own.

Sheila: I went on a French exchange when I was about 14 and I had the time of my life. I had my first passionate kiss there also. We were by the seaside and there was a band who used to play in the local café, and one day *Claude* [AUDIENCE LAUGH] walked me home and he gave me this embrace that I will never forget. It just …

BUZZ

[A CRY OF 'AAAWWW' FROM AUDIENCE AND MYSELF]
Nicholas: Richard?
Richard: There was hesitation, unfortunately. It nearly got into French kissing and French exchanging of fluids and it's a shame to break it up.
Nicholas: And you were so fluent, Sheila, you went for 48 seconds.
Sheila: Did I?!
Josie: It was a lovely story. I liked the sound of Claude.
[BIG AUDIENCE LAUGH]
Sheila: He was lovely. He was my yardstick for the rest of my life.
Josie: I wondered what you were going to say there!!
[BIG AUDIENCE LAUGH AND APPLAUSE]
Paul: I am surprised you got close enough to embrace him!

[HUGE LAUGH FROM AUDIENCE AND PANEL]

Nicholas: Sheila, Claude has brought you a bonus point there, and he brought you other things as well, I'm sure. [BIG AUDIENCE LAUGH] But we won't go into that.

Sheila: Listen, they were innocent days then. It was all different!

Nicholas: I had a French girlfriend and it wasn't as innocent as all that! [BIG AUDIENCE LAUGH] My French girlfriend was called *Nicole* and she was absolutely lovely. I loved the accent when she spoke [PUTTING ON MY FRENCH ACCENT], *like that to me.* And she said to me one day, '*Do you know, in London I get so worried about all these buggers!*' And I said, '*What?!*' '*You see them on the street, all these buggers, asking for money.*' [PANEL AND AUDIENCE BEGIN LAUGHING] '*Oh, beggars!*' '*Ah, so the buggers are beggars!*' [HUGE LAUGHTER ALL AROUND]

The final subject in the show is 'Camping in Wales', during which Josie displays her witty wordplay.

Josie: I don't think it would be possible camping in Wales. First of all you'd have to find one, then you would have to get into its mouth with your rucksack on! [AUDIENCE BEGIN LAUGHING AS THEY SEE JOSIE'S TWIST] Now the famous person who camped in a whale was *Jonah.* He was sucked …

BUZZ

Nicholas: Sheila challenged.

Sheila: I don't think you can say that Jonah was *camping in whale*!!! [HUGE AUDIENCE LAUGH]

The panel for the broadcast of 3 March consists of Paul Merton, Graham Norton, actor and comedian Miles Jupp, and stand-up comic Holly Walsh, who is making her debut. Holly's excellent contribution is such that she ends up winning the game. Her very first challenge, as Graham is talking on 'The Tempest', illustrates her confidence and also opens the door for a funny comment from Graham.

Graham: We all know the story of *The Tempest*, so I won't bore you …

BUZZ

Holly: I don't know it! [BIG AUDIENCE LAUGH AND APPLAUSE]

Nicholas: Holly, what I'm going to do immediately, because the audience applauded you for that, and it is your first time on the show, I am going to give you a bonus point. [AUDIENCE CHEER]

Holly: Aww, thank you.

Nicholas: And I think, on her challenge, I am going to give her the benefit of the doubt on this one. [AUDIENCE LAUGH]

Graham: You reward ignorance!! That's what's wrong with this country, Nicholas! [BIG AUDIENCE LAUGH]

It is Graham who is first to speak on the following subject, 'Inside the Glove Compartment of My Car'. In this round Holly again makes an amusing contribution.

Graham: Inside the glove compartment of my car you will find various old sandwiches, half-eaten apples, but the most space is taken up by a leather-bound manual telling me how to actually *drive my car!* [AUDIENCE LAUGH]

BUZZ

Nicholas: Holly challenged.

Holly: I just don't believe you don't have a chauffeur! [HUGE LAUGH FROM GRAHAM AND AUDIENCE]

Holly earns a bonus point and Graham continues until successfully challenged by Paul who, in his inimitable style, moves the subject in a bizarre direction.

Paul: Inside the glove compartment of my car is a blow-up doll, 'Buxom Betty', endorsed by Nicholas Parsons on YouTube!

[BIG LAUGH FROM AUDIENCE WHILE GRAHAM CACKLES LOUDLY]

Paul continues in this vein through to the whistle, gaining a point and receiving an enthusiastic round of applause.

Nicholas: What lovely deviation, Paul, for which you weren't challenged. I've been in your car but I didn't see the doll.
Holly: He didn't need it that time! [BIG LAUGH FROM AUDIENCE AND PANEL]

The next subject, 'Oliver Cromwell', which I hand to Paul, leads to him and Graham delivering a series of funny lines after I point out a slight error Paul makes.

Paul: I went to see the film *Oliver Cromwell* with Richard Harris (well, not the two of us together, he happened to be in it!) and it wasn't historically very accurate. There were MPs who appeared in 1536 that had been killed some ten years before. And it was rather ironic that an Irishman should be playing the title lead given Mr Cromwell's attitude towards the Irish during the seventeenth century. One thinks of …
BUZZ
Nicholas: Graham challenged.
Graham: Repetition of Irish?
Nicholas: Yes, yes, I think so. You could have had him for deviation, but it is too late now.
Paul: What was the deviation?
Nicholas: Well, it was in 1653, not 15 …
Graham: Nicholas remembers! [BIG AUDIENCE LAUGH]
Paul: To be fair, he was doing the warm-up act for Charles I's execution [HUGE AUDIENCE LAUGH].
Graham: He's still got the bladder on the stick!
Paul: Unfortunately for different reasons these days!!!

[HUGE LAUGHTER FROM AUDIENCE AND PANEL
FOLLOWED BY APPLAUSE]

Miles has the next subject, 'Cardigans', during which he attempts to
emulate Clement Freud. The result produces a funny challenge from
Paul and an unexpected artistic twist to the topic.

Miles: I have one of the largest and most extensive and exciting
selection of cardigans in the whole of south London. There is a
blue one, yellow, orange, grey, puce, vermeer, tartan ...
  BUZZ
Paul: [INCREDULOUS] Vermeer?! You've got a Vermeer
cardigan?!!!
Miles: It may not be an original. [HUGE AUDIENCE LAUGH]

Holly eventually completes that round, and in the following one
Miles again tries a touch of listing when speaking on '*Just a Minute*
in Different Languages'. Like so many others before him, Miles
discovers that the tactic really is not as easy as it first appears.
His valiant attempt, however, does allow Paul to take one more
entertaining pot shot in my direction.

Miles: *Just a Minute* has been recorded in French, Belgian,
Flemish, Walloon, Greek, Latin, Italian, Spanish ...
  BUZZ
Nicholas: Graham challenged.
Graham: It has not been done in Latin. [AUDIENCE LAUGH]
Paul: Well, when Nicholas first did it, it was! [HUGE AUDIENCE
LAUGH]

One could continue enjoying incidents from over the decades of *Just
a Minute* ad infinitum. However, as with the show itself, there comes
a moment when you have to wind up and bring the fun to a close.

It has given me enormous pleasure contributing to a programme that has increased in popularity as the years have passed. *Just a Minute* is a show that combines the past and present, tradition and innovation, new voices and old friends. To be a part of that has always been entertaining. Ian Messiter created a game fit for the 20th and the 21st centuries. It is a remarkable achievement. If Ian were still with us he would be justifiably proud.

As I wrote earlier, I did not want the job of chairman. I did not think I was suited to it. I had never been a presenter or hosted a game show. I was thrust into the role by circumstance. I do not think I was even very good at it when I began. On hearing the early recordings again I certainly did not enjoy my performance. I developed my own style, however, and found a way to make the role of chairman work for me and for the show. I think I must have done something right. I am still filling that role after 47 years. It is now my favourite job.

Will I eventually retire? It does not work like that in this business. Ours is a profession that retires you. Once you can no longer do the job – make the audience laugh – that is it. You are finished. You are on the entertainment scrapheap. With a diary full of professional commitments stretching into the future, at present I feel very far away from that situation.

I have a theory that has helped me through life. It is really quite simple: the more you use your brain the younger you remain. I am very fortunate in having plenty of work that exercises my mind and keeps me active, and one job in particular that I both love and enjoy immensely. It is the very nature of that job that keeps me younger than my years. In *Just a Minute* I have to remain sharp, keep some sense of control, maintain the fun, occasionally generate humour, listen intently and concentrate throughout every second of every recording in order to make instant decisions on whether challenges are correct. The show has become a part of me.

I have not missed a second of *Just a Minute* in any format. Not a single one. That cannot last forever of course. Some day, still away in the future, someone else will sit in my seat and stamp his or her own mark on the show. That is as it should be, and is one of the joys of *Just a Minute*. The basic format, as I hope I have successfully demonstrated in these pages, allows adaptation and evolution. It is truly amazing in that respect.

The story of *Just a Minute* is filled with amazing characters and memorable moments. They have lit up my life and brought pleasure to so many people. I laughed at the time, and in recalling these people and incidents for the writing of this book, I laughed all over again.

As you have been reading these reminiscences, I hope you have enjoyed some of that same precious ingredient: laughter.

Challenge!

Q: Who has been the only topless player of the game?

A: Paul Merton, removing his shirt to reveal his chest while talking on the subject of 'Strip Poker' in a show broadcast on 9 August 2004. (Tony Hawks was very disappointed when the whistle blew at that moment – he wanted to challenge Paul on repetition of nipples!)

Q: Up to and including Series 68 (which was broadcast in February and March 2014), and counting television editions and *Junior Just a Minute*, how many original *Just a Minute* shows have I appeared in? (Note: special compilation shows and *Classic Just a Minute* do not count.)

A: 887.

Q: Up to and including Series 68, and counting television editions, name the 22 panellists who have won on their first appearance?

A: Derek Nimmo, Lucy Bartlett, Nicholas Parsons, Tim Brooke-Taylor, Tim Rice, Brian Johnston, Libby Purves, Gyles Brandreth, Victoria Wood, Jeremy Beadle, Jan Ravens, Richard Morton, Mariella Frostrup, Ann Bryson, Dale Winton, Neil Mullarkey, Jo Brand, Ted Robbins, Linda Smith, John Sergeant, Russell Kane and Holly Walsh.

Q: Who, in terms of percentage wins, is the most successful player of the game?

A: Paul Merton, who has won more than 60 per cent of his games.

Q: Which edition of *Just a Minute* featured the following subjects: 'Different Fertilisers', 'The Art of Pruning', 'The Curse of Slugs and Snails' and 'Jack Frost'?

A: *Just a Garden Minute* in 2012, a *Children in Need* Special with a panel consisting of *Gardeners' Question Time* chairman Eric Robson, and experts Pippa Greenwood, Chris Beardshaw and Matthew Wilson. The winner was Chris Beardshaw and the whistleblower was the *GQT* producer Howard Shannon.

Q: Which panellist has appeared most often without winning a game?

A: Chris Neill.

Q: Up to and including Series 68 and counting television editions and the ten *Junior Just a Minute* contestants, how many panellists have appeared on *Just a Minute*?

A: 218.

Q: Which panellist has appeared in the most shows, radio and television combined?

A: Clement Freud, with a remarkable 545 appearances. Up to and including Series 68, Kenneth Williams remains second on the list with 344. However, Paul Merton is fast closing in on that total.

Just a Minute Top 20! *

1=	magic
1=	tongue twisters
3=	chips
3=	making up
3=	power
3=	punch
3=	red tape
3=	sharks
3=	slang
10=	bugs
10=	censorship
10=	fishing
10=	marbles
10=	my giddy aunt
10=	my hobby
10=	pop
10=	porridge
10=	press
10=	records
10=	superstitions
10=	wine

* Applies up to the end of Series 68 in March 2014. Radio, TV and
Junior Just a Minute shows are all included. Researched and compiled
by Dean Bedford who runs the website www.just-a-minute.info.

Top 20 panellists by number of appearances

1	Clement Freud
2	Kenneth Williams
3	Peter Jones
4	Paul Merton
5	Derek Nimmo
6	Tony Hawks
7	Sheila Hancock
8	Graham Norton
9	Gyles Brandreth
10	Jenny Eclair
11	Sue Perkins
12	Andree Melly
13	Julian Clary
14	Tim Rice
15	Kit Hesketh-Harvey
16	Linda Smith
17	Wendy Richard
18	Ross Noble
19	Aimi MacDonald
20=	Tony Slattery
20=	Liza Tarbuck

Top 20 most frequent winners

1	Clement Freud
2	Paul Merton
3	Derek Nimmo
4	Kenneth Williams
5	Peter Jones
6	Tony Hawks
7	Gyles Brandreth
8	Sheila Hancock
9=	Graham Norton
9=	Sue Perkins
11=	Tim Rice
11=	Tony Slattery
13=	Julian Clary
13=	Stephen Fry
15=	Kit Hesketh-Harvey
15=	Josie Lawrence
15=	Wendy Richard
18=	Marcus Brigstocke
18=	Jenny Eclair
18=	Andree Melly
18=	Ross Noble

Top 20 players who have completed uninterrupted minutes

1	Kenneth Williams
2	Clement Freud
3	Derek Nimmo
4	Paul Merton
5	Peter Jones
6	Sue Perkins
7	Gyles Brandreth
8=	Sheila Hancock
8=	Graham Norton
10	Pam Ayres
11=	Janet Brown
11=	Julian Clary
13=	Jenny Eclair
13=	Ross Noble
13=	Linda Smith
13=	Liza Tarbuck
17=	Ray Alan
17=	Charles Collingwood
17=	Kevin Eldon
17=	Stephen Fry
17=	Graeme Garden
17=	Tony Hawks
17=	Aimi MacDonald
17=	Andree Melly

Top 20 famous names who appeared on Just a Minute only once or twice

1 Elisabeth Beresford
2 Prunella Scales
3 Marjorie Proops
4 Teddie Beverley
5 Barbara Castle
6 Warren Mitchell
7 Michael Palin
8 Thora Hird
9 June Whitfield
10 Kenny Everett
11 Bob Monkhouse
12 Elaine Stritch
13 Jeremy Beadle
14 Ian Hislop
15 Craig Ferguson
16 Eddie Izzard
17 Tony Blackburn
18 Clare Balding
19 Terry Wogan
20 Hugh Bonneville

Picture Credits

Every effort has been made to trace copyright holders and obtain their permission for the use of copyright material. The publisher apologies for any errors or omissions and would be grateful if notified of any corrections that should be incorporated in future reprints or editions of this book. Page numbers refer to the plate section in this book.

p.1 Top: © BBC Photo Library; Bottom left: © BBC Photo Library; Bottom Right: © BBC Photo Library; p.2 Top left: © ITV/REX; Top right: © BBC Photo Library; 3 cartoon strips: © Radio Times; p.3 Top left: © BBC Photo Library; Top right: © BBC Photo Library; Centre right: © REX/Sten Rosenlund; Bottom left: © BBC Photo Library; p.4 Top left: ©PA Images; Top centre: © Getty Images; Top right: © Joseph King/Corbis; Bottom left: © Neil Spence/ Alamy; Bottom centre: © Rex/ITV; Bottom right: © Allan Ollay/ TV Times/IPC+ Syndication; p.5 Top: © ITV/REX; Bottom: © ITV/REX; p.6 Top: © BBC Photo Library; Bottom: © BBC Photo Library; p.7 Top: © BBC Photo Library; Bottom left: © BBC 2012; Bottom right: © BBC 2012; Top: © BBC 2012; Bottom left: © BBC 2012; Bottom right: © BBC Photo Library

Index